Theories for Radical Change

Studies in Critical Social Sciences

VOLUME 323

The titles published in this series are listed at *brill.com/scss*

Theories for Radical Change

Key Texts from the Political Economy of Marx and Lenin

By

Raju J Das

BRILL

LEIDEN | BOSTON

Cover illustration: © wal_172619 via Pixabay.

The Library of Congress Cataloging-in-Publication Data is available online at https://catalog.loc.gov

Typeface for the Latin, Greek, and Cyrillic scripts: "Brill". See and download: brill.com/brill-typeface.

ISSN 1573-4234
ISBN 978-90-04-73039-7 (hardback)
ISBN 978-90-04-73047-2 (e-book)
DOI 10.1163/9789004730472

This book is printed on acid-free paper and produced in a sustainable manner.

Contents

Acknowledgements

This book is in defense of the idea that production and production relations absolutely matter. I have benefitted from my (email or in-person) communication with many scholars of Marxist political economy on this and related topics, directly or otherwise. They include Greg Albo, Tom Brass, Joseph Choonara, Kevin Cox, Jamie Gough, Robert Latham, Stavros Mavroudeas, Michael Roberts, Alfredo Saad-Filho, Murray Smith as well as my colleagues on the manuscript collective of *Science & Society*, including David Laibman, Julio Huato, Nana Liu, Barbara Foley, and others. Current and former graduate supervisees, and students in my graduate course on Marxist political economy have been a source of my learning in ways they might not recognize. Educating others gives the educators an opportunity to be (re)educated. Members of the Marxist reading group in Toronto, under the auspices of 'the Marx center' at York University (https://marxiststudies.blog.yorku.ca/), have provided a stimulating milieu. One of its meetings was on *Grundrisse*, and the long commentary I wrote for the meeting became chapters 3–4 of this book. As Marx says in his 'Introduction' to *Grundrisse*, there is a constant connection between the producing individual and the wider society. This applies to individuals in academia. Even if we produce ideas as individuals, that production can only happen as a part of a wider structure of relations which include a large number of thinkers, not just in academia but also outside.

A grant from the office of York University's Vice President for Research has made it possible for me to get some assistance needed to complete the book. Ankit Singh, a PhD student of mine, has kindly collated several lists of references into one consolidated list. The book contains many diagrams. I made rough sketches of these. Aishwarya Bhattacharyya, another PhD student of mine, was able to convert one such sketch into a more suitable form. A former graduate student, Ashley Chen, did the same for a number of diagrams used in chapter 7–8 and 10. Their assistance is gratefully acknowledged.

I would not write this book, and if I did, I would not complete this book in 2024, if it was not for the constant encouragement from Professor David Fasenfest, the editor of Brill's Studies in Critical Social Sciences book series.

Figures and Tables

Figures

Tables

CHAPTER 1

Introduction

1 The Political Context

A spectre is haunting the world. This is the spectre of anti-capitalist and socialist sentiments in many parts of the world. The spectre of Marxism has returned.

Interests in anti-capitalism and in socialism are growing in many parts of the world. According to a poll conducted in 28 countries, including the United States, France, China and Russia, 56% agree that 'capitalism as it exists today does more harm than good in the world' (John, 2020). A June 2021 poll indicates that: 36% of Americans have a negative view of capitalism; this number is much higher among the youth: 46% of 18–34-year-olds and 54% of those aged 18–24 view capitalism negatively (Gustavo, 2021). Conversely, and interestingly, 41% of respondents from all ages have a positive view of socialism. This number is higher for the younger people: 52% of 18–24 year-olds, and 50% of young adults aged 25–34 have a positive view of socialism (ibid.). An October 2021 poll shows that: 53% of Americans have a negative view of the big business. According to this poll, among Democrats/Democratic-leaners, those with a positive view of socialism has been rising: from about 55% in 2010 to a massive 65% in 2021 (Jones, 2021).

The situation outside of the US within the advanced capitalist world is similar. According to an August 2021 poll in Canada: the majority of Canadians (53%) believe that 'we need to radically transform our economy', and 35% favour 'moving away from capitalism', while only 25% oppose or strongly oppose such an idea (Thompson, 2021). The poll reveals that opposition to capitalism is higher among the youth than among the general public in Canada too: 49% of women and 43% of men aged 18–34. Interestingly, opposing capitalism (35%) is more popular than voting for one of the main parties: Liberal (20%), Conservative (21%) and the mildly social-democratic, NDP (11%). The European situation is not dissimilar to the North American one. In 2016, 47% of Britons and 39% Germans held an unfavourable view of capitalism, while 36% of Britons and 45% of Germans had a favourable view of socialism (the corresponding numbers for the US were 27% and 29% respectively in 2016) (Dahlgreen, 2016).

 | DOI:10.1163/9789004730472_002

These survey results are reflected in online commentaries. One blog suggests:

> The term "Marxist" is trending, and it's not just academics and historians buzzing about Karl Marx's theories. From mainstream media debates to online discussions, the specter of Marxism seems to be haunting the political landscape, a curious development in a year marked by economic anxiety, geopolitical tensions, and a growing sense of societal unease. (Capitalist Money, 2024)

This blog concludes: 'The current interest in Marxism is not simply a nostalgic revival of a bygone era. It reflects the realities of our times, a world grappling with economic inequality, social injustice, and the challenges of a rapidly changing global landscape'. Indeed, the interests in Marxism *are* rising because of decades of neoliberal austerity, growing threats to democracy from demagogic bourgeois populists, mass impoverishment, rising inequality, endless predatory wars, climate crisis, and many other similar processes. It would be safe to say that in advanced capitalist countries, those who are anti-capitalists and those who support some form of socialism are relatively substantial segments of the population, and their numbers seem to be generally rising.

Two caveats need to be made. Firstly, the numbers of people who are critical of capitalism are not enough to end capitalism, but they form the basis for a movement to win over more people to the cause of socialism. Secondly, many of those who have a favourable view of socialism may not have an adequate conception of it – they may not exactly know how/why capitalism is the reason for their suffering, what the limits to the reforms within capitalism are, and what a genuinely socialist society in the Marxist sense can look like. People are radicalizing based on their experience of misery that capitalism has been inflicting. They may not be class conscious yet: that is, they may not be conscious of the incompatibility between their interests and those of capital. Theirs may be a spontaneous anti-capitalist consciousness more than a conscious awareness of capitalism with the help of scientific ideas. Experience can certainly teach a great deal. But there are limits to this. So, people who are experiencing difficult lives under capitalism require, and some of them may be in search of, knowledge about why capitalism must end and why socialism would be a much better society. A genuine socialist movement requires ideas that appropriately appreciate the progressiveness of capitalism, that are ruthlessly and consistently critical of capitalism's dark sides and limits, and that passionately and scientifically defend socialism.

2 The Theoretical Context

While there is a need for good theoretical ideas for radical change, much of the contemporary political economy discourse has serious problems. This was true about Marx's and Lenin's time as it is true about ours. It offers a range of problematic and revision*ist* claims (Lenin, 1908; Das, 2023a). These include denial of, or underemphasis on, a series of facts/processes in the capitalist society. There is a shift happening *from* materialist political economy towards considerations of cultural and emotional aspects of society, including working people's lives. Often it is the case that when one talks about the economic processes, one quickly shifts to culture and cultural politics so one just *appears* to be talking about economic processes and their attendant power relations while in fact one does not. So, if one speaks about political economic conditions without mentioning culture and cultural identity, one is bound to draw skepticism.

Or, in talking about economic processes, one avoids production and production relations and remains focussed on the unequal distribution of income, on consumption, and on exchange. Also, the focus becomes one on not-normal processes. Much of the political economy discourse is skeptical of – and in some cases, oppose – the primacy of production, and its relations over other elements of the economic realm, and the primacy of the economic realm over the non-economic realm. Some emphasize cheating and fraud in economic transactions, rather than take an approach that emphasizes the exchange of equivalents for the equivalents, without ignoring cheating and fraud. Some scholars say that it is not expanded reproduction but the modern incarnation of primitive accumulation, or accumulation by dispossession (redistribution of assets) that is capitalism's main form today. Others say that the entire global capitalist system is based on not normal exploitation of wage-labour on the basis of the appropriation of surplus value in absolute and relative forms, but *super*- or above-average exploitation of labour in the global periphery or super- or over-exploitation of the socially oppressed groups such as women and the racialized people (where wages are inevitably below the value of labour power). Some say that the system is based on petty producers being made to sell their products at a very low price. In other words, the emphasis in political economy is what Marx and Lenin would call the not-normal or conjunctural phenomena, howsoever important they may be today. While production and its relations involving wage labour are under-emphasized, all serious discussion of production, and its social relations, is accused of being production*ist*.

Everywhere there is talk of social justice and inequality but there is no serious attention to class exploitation, for to talk about class is considered class-ism. Inequality becomes inequality between groups defined on the basis of cultural identities. Social justice becomes the social justice for oppressed groups – usually, a demand for redistributions of resources among the relatively affluent people within the specially oppressed groups (Das, 2023b). In consideration of economy, there is a nostalgic for pre-capitalism or small-scale production, so the economic world and what is the to be done are often considered from the standpoint of small-scale producers, the very existence of whom is seen as being necessarily indicative of their power and resilience. Similarly, the local and the sub-national spatial scales are emphasized at the expense of a multi-scalar treatment, including the global. In discussions on even economic development, a lot more stress is given to space relations than to class relations (Das, 2017a). There is an inadequate appreciation of the dialectical relation between productive forces and production relations in capitalist society. The imperialist character of advanced capitalism is under-emphasized or incorrectly understood. There is an under-emphasis on the consideration of the social economy – and especially, capitalism – *as a totality*.

In the discussions on economic processes and their political implications, several ideas long-held within Marxist political economy inspired by Marx and Lenin are rejected or glossed over. These include the idea that the main contradictions in today's society are between capital and labour and not between groups defined on the basis of cultural identity while the cultural divisions and oppressions absolutely compound the effects of class exploitation on the oppressed groups and weaken working class unity; the proletariat, objectively speaking, is the chief agent of anti-capitalist and socialist revolution; and while the fight for reforms is necessary, only revolutionary overthrow of capitalism and the state can solve the problems of humanity.

In the political economy discourse, the relation of the economic to the political is crucial. Yet the discourse on the political economy of the state makes many problematic claims too. It is said that the state acts in the interests of capitalists because it is directly influenced by capitalists, but the question of what is it about the state that allows capitalists to control the state is not properly addressed. And why does the state not allow socialists – or workers interested in a cooperative society – to control it and indeed use its power to make sure that '[t]he expropriators are expropriated' (Marx, 1887: 540)? Or, what is it about the state that does not allow workers to use it to improve their conditions so there would be no need to expropriate the capitalists? The major problem is the fact that, and this might be hard to believe, the inherently class character of the capitalist state – the internal relation between class relations and the state – is under-emphasized in much existing theory, so the relation between the state and capitalist class relation is treated as an external relation, rather than an internal one. That means that the limits to the extent to which state can provide concessions are under-conceptualized.

It is often said that the capitalist state cannot do this or that because the capitalist class constrains state's actions because the state depends on taxes. The constraints on the state do exist; it is true that the state is indebted or the state depends on taxes. But these constraints have a derivative existence – they do not define the essential nature of the state. The separation of the state from capitalist economy is more a matter of the surface reality of capitalism.

Ideas in political economy are presented without any, or without much, consideration of their practical implications for the fight against capitalism or the ideas are simply reform-oriented. The political economy that is present in the key texts of Marx and Lenin responds to these problems and advances an alternative view on many of these themes.

There are different kinds of knowledge claim, says the philosopher of science, Andrew Sayer (Sayer, 1992). One type of knowledge claim makes 'propositions about the world' and is referential (p. 15). Another kind of knowledge claim produces critique of the world. As Sayer says, 'much of our knowledge and our uses of language ... have a directly social function providing the means by which we question, command, argue, confer respect or distribute contempt, establish relationships' and so on (Sayer, 1992: 21). Critique is necessary because the world fails to meet common people's needs owing to its exploitative structures and because ideas about the world and how to radically change it are so inadequate that they help reproduce such a world rather than radically transform such a world (Das, 2014).

It is the contention of this book that both types of knowledge claims that common people (workers and petty producers) and indeed, the newly radicalizing people, including students in colleges and universities, would benefit from enormously are present in key classical Marxist texts when read them with a scientific commitment, revolutionary passion and a critical attitude. These texts make propositional claims (as stylized or general empirical generalizations across times and places), which take the form of: X is generally Y. Many claims in these texts take the form, or should be seen as taking the form, of causal claims. These claims about causal tendencies do not mean that a given process (e.g. globalization of capitalist production) is complete, nor that a given process is uniform in time and space, nor that a theorized process is empirically manifested exactly as per theory. Causal claims mean that unless specified counter-acting conditions/processes operate, the *mechanism* M (which exists by virtue of certain social *relations*) will cause E as an *outcome*/effect, which is then *experienced* by people (albeit differently in different times and places).[1] In addition, there are claims in these texts that present critiques of the existing world and of the ideas about how it works and how to change it radically.

Marxism has four main inter-connected components. One is its materialist-dialectical philosophy, which emphasizes the idea that things have to be seen as *relations* and *processes* which create social *totality* that shapes the parts that constitute it, and that the totality *changes* because of *contradictions* in it. This philosophy shapes the second component of Marxism: historical materialism (Marxism's social theory). Historical materialism, as a field of knowledge, comprises a set of scientific generalizations across human society as such and across class societies. These generalizations concern, among other things, the dialectical (i.e. reciprocal and contradictory) relation between: 'productive forces' and 'production relations'; the producing individual and society; the economic and the extra-economic; class agency and class structures, and so on. Marxist philosophy and social theory shape Marxist political economy which is the scientific field of study of the economic conditions, in relation to political power, within capitalist and other forms of society. Finally, all these three fields of study shape the conception of socialist society and of the struggle for socialism.[2] Knowledge claims – propositional and critical – made in the key texts of Marxism that this book focusses on cover all these four fields even if some texts cover given areas more than other areas. My focus in this book will be political economy (in relation to other fields of Marxism).

Once human society is developed enough to produce a surplus, class society emerges in which economic processes (and well as non-economic processes) bear the stamp of the structure of class relations, and of class struggle. This is why theoretical ideas about the relation between economy and the state, and those about the relation between class relations and the state, tend to overlap. In Marxism, class relations (unequal social relations of production) are seen from the standpoint of political economy, and political economy (the matter of production and exchange, etc.) is dealt with from the standpoint of the antagonistically related classes.

1 The claim that capitalist relations have caused globalization does not mean that the world is completely globalized (that globalization is a completely finished process) or that all countries are equally globalized. The claim about the tendency to economic crisis does not mean that every single year and everywhere there is a crisis. The claim about class differentiation does not mean that all commodity producers have either become a proletarian or a member of the capitalist class or that class differentiation happens at a given pace everywhere and at all times.

2 I use 'socialism' and 'communism' interchangeably to refer to the post-capitalist forms of society where means of production are not in the private hands for use for making profits.

Fundamental to the field of political economy is the conceptualization of the economic realm itself which has four components (production, distribution, consumption and exchange) on its own and in relation to the extra-economic. A proper conceptualization of the economic realm in relation to the extra-economic and a class approach to political economy enable us to understand basic traits and effects of capitalist society. Capitalism is a progressive force (relative to pre-capitalist societies). It is also a regressive force. In terms of its regressive aspects, a crucial process is the capitalist social relations fettering the development of productive forces, in various ways that are not always systematically studied.

Marx introduces the concept of fettering in the *Communist Manifesto* written in 1848 and returns to it famously in his 1959 *Preface to A Contribution to the Critique of Political Economy*. Fettering is also discussed in *Capital*. To make 'optimal' use of Marx's concept of fettering would require further development of the concept beyond his schematic remarks as well as beyond some of its modern-day interpretations.[3] We need to better understand a) what might fettering exactly mean and b) what is it about social relations of production and productive forces which makes fettering of the latter by the former possible, and with what consequences for labour and nature?

In terms of the relation between the economic and the extra-economic, the state is taken as the most important part of the latter. The state is a fundamental category in political economy. Without the state, capitalism cannot exist for a day or a week. The capitalist state is an economically powerful agent.[4] Using its economic power (including the power to create money), the state produces those conditions for capitalism which the profit-driven individual capitalists will not generally produce and may indeed destroy. Yet following some theoretical discussions between 1950s and 1980s, there has been a decline in general theorizing of the state.[5] Luckily, in the last 15 years or so, there are signs of a slowly rising theoretical interest in the state.[6] The renewed intellectual interest in the political economy of the state reflects a new, or a newish, conjuncture, which includes, as Alami (2021: 163) notes in an article in the *Science*

3 I do not wish to provide an extensive review of these interpretations.

4 In fact, the part of total social capital that is spent by the state keeps rising, including under 'neoliberalism'. State spending as a percentage of GDP has increased from about 20% in 1975 to 27% in 2018 for the entire world economy. The European figures are about 25% and 35% (World Bank, n.d.).

5 This decline is partly due to the influence of post-modernism which rejects 'metanarratives'.

6 This is partly indicated by a symposium titled 'Marxist state theory today', published in the Marxist journal, *Science & Society* (2021). There are also many other recent interventions (Ellner, 2017; Lasslett, 2015; McNally, 2019).

& Society symposium on state theory: 'a "return" to various forms of state-led development across the less developed world since the early 2000s' as well as 'extensive state intervention following the 2008 global financial crisis in the developed world (including the massive bailouts of systemic financial institutions and quantitative easing)'.[7] The theoretical interest in the state is likely to increase, with a rising interest in Marxism and growing radicalization among sections of the population, as mentioned earlier (Jeffries, 2012; Niemuth, 2017). Vast sections of the population are being critical of the big business and pro-corporate state policies and demanding anti-corporate actions from the state (Das, 2022a).

Given the importance of the state, much has been written about the general features of the state. The existing Marxist work has examined the state from different vantage points: capitalist class agency; capitalist class structure; state's internal structure; state actors' agency; working-class agency. The ideas in the existing literature do reveal important aspects of the state. Some of these ideas are also more or less shared by Marx in *Capital* Volume 1. Yet, much of the existing theorization is at odds with some of the fundamental ideas about capitalism and/or the state that are present in that foundational text and with Marx's overall social theory informed by his political economy. This is why I devote three chapters to the political economy of the state, i.e. to the relation between capital and the state.

The relation between the state and class struggle has remained under-examined too because class struggle itself has remained under-examined: class struggle is viewed simply and automatically as the struggle for some concessions from the state. While there are many criticisms of the capitalist state, many scholars have an unreasoning belief in the ability of the state to significantly and durably alleviate humanity's social-ecological problems. Much of existing state theory is therefore reform-oriented. In fact, ideas about the state have become ideological justification for a theoretical and political escape from revolutionary action that Marx calls for in *Capital* Volume 1 and the *Communist Manifesto*.

Some of the existing writings *have* explored the insights from *Capital* volume 1 into the state.[8] The full potential of that foundational text of Marx for the development of state theory has not been realized, however. The discussion on the political economy of the state therefore is yet another attempt at the exploration of Marx's views on the state as they are present in that text.

---

7 In fact, some commentators (e.g. Elliott, 2021; Plender, 2008; Saad-Filho, 2020) are already debating the end of neoliberalism and beginning of progressive (i.e. welfare-oriented) state policies. The titles such as *The return of the state* have begun appearing (Allen et al., 2015).

8 See O'Kane, 2014. See also the discussion on state derivationism in Holloway and Picciotto (1978).

State theorizing inspired by *Capital* Volume 1 can help us avoid some of the problems with existing theorizing mentioned above.

Much of the existing Marxist theorization of the state has been excessively concerned with the so-called autonomy of the state, and has under-stated the similarity between the state in pre-capitalist class society and that in capitalism. A corollary of the autonomy fetishism is the surprisingly insufficient attention to the political economy – materiality – of the state.[9] The class character of the state and how exactly it functions (e.g. how autonomous it is) belong to different levels of analysis. They do not have the same causal importance in explaining what the state does. The first has primacy. And the degree of autonomy that the state possesses is much less than assumed. The fact that, as Marx argues in *Capital* volume 1, commodities, including labour power, are exchanged freely and that no one can force a worker to work for a certain capitalist explains some of the ways in which the state works, but it cannot explain the fact that in capitalism there is, and there will be, a state. That there is a state in capitalism is explained by the same fact that there is a state in pre-capitalism. Both types of the state bear the unmistakable stamp of class relations as Marx defines them in *Capital* Volume 1 as well as the *Communist Manifesto*. In both cases, the state, as a sphere of the political, is unmistakably shaped by economic conditions and relations as Marx points out *Capital* Volume 1. Lenin emphasized this too.

In the preface to the first German edition of *Capital* volume 1, Karl Marx says: 'It is the ultimate aim of this work, to lay bare the economic law of motion of modern society' (Marx, 1887: 7). There are economic laws that explain the 'spontaneous expansion of capital' (ibid.: 163) or 'the successive phases of its normal development' (ibid.: 7), and then there is state power, including 'legal enactments' and legislations or acts (ibid.). Marx prompts us to ask: how is the economic power of the capitalist class mediated by state power, or, how are the economic laws of capitalism modified by the state, and what *can* the capitalist state, the sphere of the extra-economic, *reveal* about commodity exchange and commodity production in capitalism?[10]

Marx says that the capitalist society is one where the wealth produced by the direct producers takes the form of commodity, so our 'investigation must therefore begin with the analysis of a commodity' (Marx, 1887: 27). If this is the case, then what sort of theoretical analysis of the state does this necessarily point to? This is especially important to ask because under the neoliberal form

9 Indeed, much theoretical discussion on the state explains the state and the political in terms of the political, thus resorting to politicism (Das, 1999 politicism).

10 Like the world itself, the concepts about the world possess varying levels of concreteness or abstractness. Some concepts are more concrete or more abstract than other concepts.

of capitalism, which began in the 1970s in many advanced countries and in the late 1980s and early 1990s in many parts of the global periphery, there has been a tendency towards commodification of everything. If capitalism is a society where, as Marx says, production and exchange are ruled by the law of value, where workers are without any control over capitalist property and over capitalist production, and are exploited by capitalists, and where laws of capitalist accumulation limit the extent to which the conditions of the majority can be improved, then what sort of state theory is presupposed by Marx's analysis in *Capital* Volume 1?

Marx says that political processes are, more or less, based in economic processes. If this is the case, then what could possibly show better the character of the capitalist state than the nature of capitalist commodity relations and relations of exploitation and accumulation (which he focused on in *Capital 1*)? If the 'spontaneous' development of capitalism and the competitive logic act as an economic force, and if capitalism develops and exploits and dispossesses people '*not merely by the force of economic relations, but by the help of the State*' (Marx, 1887: 181; italics in original), then what can we say about the state at a *theoretical* level? If Marx begins *Capital* Volume 1 with the concept of associated producers (and the idea that there is commodity fetishism because workers do not have *control* over production) and ends *Capital* Volume 1 with a clarion call for expropriating capitalists,[11] then what general implications for our understanding of the capitalist state and its limits do such claims by Marx indicate?

Further, if the state represents itself as an entity for everyone in society, why does it fail to meet the needs of the majority and why does it prioritize meeting the needs of the ruling class? Or why is it that people can only obtain what Marx calls in *Capital* Volume 1 'meagre concession wrung from capital'? Why does the state fail to meet the needs of the masses (e.g. provision of high-quality education and healthcare, and a living wage) even while doing so might serve some long-term interests of capital? And while the state fails to meet the needs of the masses, why do the masses – and their 'ideologues' (e.g. progressive academics) continue to hope that the state – or this or that institution of the state – will meet their needs? What *is* the relation between the state on the one hand, and capitalist production and production relations, on the other? This question is a part of a larger question: what is the relation between the state and society, including not only its different classes but also class struggle? What obstacles are produced by the state towards anti-capitalist and socialist revolution? More precisely, if the conquest of state power by the masses is in order as classical Marxists have

11 Harvey (2010a: 301) wrongly thinks that this call is only 'the *rhetoric* of the *Communist Manifesto*'.

correctly emphasized, then what kind of state theory is implied? The answers to these sorts of questions *prompted by* Marx's thinking in *Capital 1* should form an important part of state theory.

With its focus on the political economy of production, the book concentrates on: social relations of production which can be broadly seen as class relations; class differentiation among those engaged in commodity production; dual origins and different forms of capitalist production (e.g. agrarian and industrial forms) and its fundamental traits, including spatially uneven nature of production and exchange; progressive and regressive nature of capitalist production, including the fact that capitalist social relations of production promote and fetter the forces of production with adverse consequences for nature and labour; imperialism as the most globally developed form of capitalist production and exchange; the relation between the economic and extra-economic processes in society, including the society based on capitalist production and exchange; capitalist production and exchange shaping, and being shaped by, the nature and interventions of the most important component of the extra-economic sphere, i.e. the state; and economic conditions of common people and their struggle against the capitalist mode of production. Thus, the central focus of this book is on production – production seen as a process and as a set of relations. The book argues for the primacy of production and production relations relative to other moments of the economic realm. It explores the ways in which production relations of capitalism, including its 'highest' stage, i.e. imperialism, not only impede the development of the productive forces of nature and labour but also produce obstacles to the state being able to solve the problems created by capitalism, thus increasingly pushing people to fight against capitalism even if at this moment not much success is apparent.

3 Overview

Keeping in view the newly radicalizing elements of the public, including the youth, chapter 2 presents the ideas of *The Communist Manifesto* in the form of precise and systematically organized knowledge claims that cover the political economy of capitalism as advanced by Marx and Engels which is informed by their social theory (historical materialism) of class society and which sheds light on the ideas of class struggle and vision of a socialist society.[12] *The Communist Manifesto* advances an exemplary unified class approach to

12 An earlier version of this chapter has appeared in Das (2022a).

economy, politics and culture and to the question of what is to be done about capitalism. The claims of this text as discussed in chapter 2 are present in all the succeeding chapters of the book.

The political economic scope of Marx's *Grundrisse* is widely recognized to be broader than that of his magnificent multi-volume magnum opus, *Capital*. Marx begins the *Grundrisse* with his famous 'Introduction'. Chapters 3–4 systematically present Marx's ideas about political economy (including its relation to historical materialism) in the 'Introduction' to the *Grundrisse* in a slightly more systematic way than he himself does and in a more detailed manner than many of the recent commentators do.[13] Two questions are posed and briefly addressed: what implications does the 'Introduction' have for the contemporary Marxist discussions on economic crisis and primitive ('original') accumulation. Underlying these two topics is the question of the importance of production relative to distribution, exchange and consumption that Marx deals with. Marx sometimes appears to be ambivalent in his discussion on production's relation to other moments of the economy, and this is partly a reason why some Marxists can: a) suggest that the production of commodities under capitalism is not the main aspect of late capitalism but re-distribution of wealth is, and b) find the main reason for economic crisis outside of production. Read carefully, however, the 'Introduction' does provide enough ground to productively critique these views.

Chapter 3 presents Marx's ideas about the economic realm, including its various moments and their inter-relations. It also discusses the implications of Marx's ideas for the contemporary Marxist debates on the two above-mentioned topics. Chapter 4 discusses Marx's ideas about how his view of the economic realm shapes his overall social theory. It focusses on Marx's historical materialism that shapes his political economy around two themes: the relation between the producing individual and society (including its production relations), and the relation between the economic sphere and the extra-economic sphere (e.g. the state, and culture, including mythology). Chapter 4 also shows how it is that Marx's discussion of the relation between the economic and the extra-economic interestingly anticipates, among other things, Leon Trotsky's concept of uneven and combined development.

The Communist Manifesto heaps praise on capitalism because of its role in furthering the development of productive forces. It also points to how capitalist social relations fetter the productive forces. The idea of fettering is the main theme of Marx's 1859 famous 'Preface' where he presents a

13 Chapters 3–4 draw on Das (2024a).

summary of his political economic thinking. The concept of fettering is a relatively neglected component of Marx's social theory. A proper reformulation of the theory of fettering can help us raise, and answer, questions that concern numerous problems of the contemporary world of capitalist production and exchange such as periodic economic crisis, environmental damage, impoverishment of common people, imperialism and endless wars, the problems that exist partly because of the contradictions between productive forces of production and relations of production in capitalism.

Chapter 5 begins by discussing Marx's schematic remarks on fettering and then some interpretations of Marx's remarks.[14] The chapter presents a brief critique of these interpretations and offers an alternative reformulation of the perspective on fettering. Such a reformulation requires that the concept of productive forces must systematically include nature *and* human beings, apart from the produced means of production such as technology. As a productive force, nature needs constant improvement, but this does not happen *because* of capitalist relations. Human beings have certain needs which must be met for them to possess their productive abilities as direct producers, but capitalist relations fail to guarantee this. There are specific mechanisms by which capitalist social relations of production further and fetter the development of the forces of production, as a part of one single process. These mechanisms are carefully laid out. To go beyond the implicit nationalism in the existing conceptualization of fettering, the mechanisms, as Chapter 5 shows, one must include imperialist exploitation that fetters productive forces in the South.[15] The balance between capitalism's tendency to promote productive forces and its tendency to fetter them has tilted in favour of the latter today, so class struggle must replace antagonistic capitalist relations with socialist relations to ensure harmonious sustainable just development, nationally and globally.

One reason why the study of economic process (especially, production and exchange), including the dialectical relation between forces of production and relations of production, is *political* economic is that the state, as an 'extra-economic' realm, shapes, and is shaped by, capitalist economy, within a totality in which the economic has primacy. Another reason is that capitalist production and exchange, because they are exploitative, prompt people's struggle against it, which the state in turn seeks to suppress. Elements of state theory do exist to a *much larger extent* in Marx's *Capital* than often realized. That text strongly suggests how 'the state appears as government, as

---

14 Chapter 5 draws on Das (2024a).

15 The idea that imperialism fetters the development of productive forces in the developed world too is taken up in Chapter 10.

legislation ..., as police and armies' as well as the parliament (Cleaver, 2019: 51). Indeed, as Marx himself emphasizes, the state appears as factory inspectors and medical doctors who act on behalf of workers when it comes to the regulation of the working day and the protection of children and women in the workplace. *Capital* Volume 1 also suggests how it is that the economic laws of capitalism are modified by the state and how the political force (power of the state), is itself economic in character. Chapters 6–8 analyse the capitalist state based on the insights into capitalism as presented in *Capital* Volume 1.[16]

Based on Marx's *class theory* in *Capital* volume 1, chapter 6 deals with the state in relation to property relations: it examines the state at the level of class society as a whole and it deals with the state in relation to the capitalist form of class society. It then examines the state's relation to capitalist commodity and value relations. Chapter 7 turns to how the state is connected to the successive phases of the capital circuit, M–C–M′, which is further expanded to M–C(MP + LP)–P–C′–M′. It sheds light on the state's role in relation to accumulation and in relation to tendencies *and* counter-tendencies towards economic crisis. Chapter 8 is focussed on how the state functions to 'help' the working class in part as a response to the working-class politics. Partly by building on the arguments about the state's role concerning commodity and property relations in chapters 6–7, Chapter 8 theoretically examines the state's pro-worker interventions in relation to what I call the 'labour circuit'. Chapter 8 shows the driving forces behind the state's pro-worker measures. There *is* an objective pressure on the state (e.g. general and long-term interests of capital) to intervene on behalf of workers but this pressure is mediated by working-class struggle as well as inter-capitalist competition. There are, however, limits to what the state can do for workers under capitalism, the limits that exist because of the capitalist control over property and production, nature of capitalist accumulation and its crisis-proneness, and the capitalist state's bureaucratic functioning and its anti-worker politics.

The three chapters (i.e. chapters 6–8) show that the state is affected by numerous processes in a class society, and therefore an analysis of the state becomes a window to the 'secrets' of capitalist economy itself.[17] The state is affected by a variety of processes such as the changing balance of power of the basic classes (that is, class struggle from above and from below); the need to sustain capitalist accumulation and mitigate the contradiction between productive forces and relations leading to the crisis of production, all within the

16 Chapters 6–8 draw on Das (2022b: 22–172; 195–238).

17 Marx uses the term 'secret' in analysing the state-enabled bloody origin of capitalism as well as the mechanisms of capitalist profit-making.

limits of the class logic of the state, that is, the need to suppress the direct producers and reproduce exploitative private property rights.[18]

Marx's (Engels') political economy is continued by many. One of the most prominent of them is Vladimir Lenin, the greatest disciple of Marx and Engels. He has made many valuable contributions to political economy, although he is mistakenly treated as a political theorist and an activist only. Lenin says that Marx's theory has only laid the foundation stone of the science of political economy which *must* be developed in all directions. The scope of Lenin's political economy is broader than Marx's in many ways.

Lenin's (1899a) *Development of capitalism in Russia* is a model of Marx's (1887) *Capital* Volume 1, for the 20th century and beyond, and an exemplar of the class approach to political economy. Lenin's writings on imperialism, including his short book *Imperialism: the highest stage of capitalism*, innovatively develop some of the themes from Marx's general law of accumulation presented in Chapter 25 of *Capital* volume 1, and demonstrate the power of Marxist political economy when conducted at the global scale. Chapter 9 is focussed on Lenin's political economy. It begins with general (epistemological) comments on Lenin's view of political economy as a field of knowledge. It then presents a series of substantive claims on the political economy of capitalism along with its 'highest stage', called imperialism. It ends with a comradely critique of Lenin's political economy.[19]

Every single chapter of the book from Chapter 2 to Chapter 9 not only presents the ideas of the selected Marxist texts. Every single chapter also presents further theoretical implications of these ideas and situates them in relation to some of the contemporary discussions in political economy.

The final chapter, Chapter 10, brings together some of these implications in a relatively condensed form. More importantly, however, this chapter elaborates the implications of the theoretical ideas discussed in Chapters 2–9 for the global socialist struggle against capitalism, particularly by workers and small-scale producers, and for the broader conception of socialism. After all, Marxist political economy is defined by the unity of theory and practice.

---

18 The state is also shaped by: the need to intervene on behalf of society as a whole (clearing forests, making roads, providing for people during a pandemic or natural calamity, or checking excessive environmental damage) and the external threats to a society as well as the interests of state officials/ politicians with the autonomy they have partly because of the fact that they have the responsibility to manage the affairs of the state (Das, 2022b). These themes are not discussed here.

19 A much shorter version of this chapter is Das (2025).

CHAPTER 2

Marx and Engels' *The Communist Manifesto*: Class Relations, Global Capitalism, Workers' Conditions and Revolutionary Politics

The Communist Manifesto (hereafter, *Manifesto*) is one of the foundational texts in Marxism. Interestingly, while the popularity of Marxism as a whole appears to have fallen since the early 1980s,[1] the popularity of this text itself appears to have risen.

There have been many discussions on it in the last 25 years or so (Amin, 2018; Burawoy, 2000; Carver and Farr, 2015; Harvey, 2008; Panitch and Leys, 1998; Wood, 1998). But these discussions generally aim to pick out one or another element of the text to expand on and/or critique it. This is a defensible approach. But this is a partial approach, especially, given that *Manifesto* is an overarching short text that covers several areas of Marxism, including political economy. Given the theoretical and political importance of the text, I argue, there is a need to see the text *as a totality* as it is, and to articulate its central ideas, from the standpoint of its potential educational value for the newly-radicalizing elements in the public and especially, among the youth.

It may not be out of place to provide a piece of anecdotal evidence about its importance: the Indian state has been repressing the various revolutionary groups influenced by Maoism.[2] When asked how a Maoist is identified, a senior police official told reporters: 'Anyone caught with a copy of the *Manifesto* or Mao's *Little Red Book* becomes a suspicious character. We then watch him and often find clinching evidence' (Human Rights Watch Briefing Paper for the 59th Session of the United Nations Commission on Human Rights March 25, 2003).

1 This time coincides with the rise of post-modernism, identity politics, etc., the kind of projects that are antithetical to Marxism. Note that since the 2008-crisis, Marxism seems to be attracting an enhanced attention, as mentioned in the last chapter.

2 As a variant of Marxism, Maoism has made some theoretical contributions, including the class analysis of the countryside, and which has inspired hundreds of thousands of people to fight against injustice experienced by the most vulnerable groups of rural people, including the indigenous peoples, as in India. Yet, Maoism has serious theoretical and political problems, including: its adherence to a two-stage theory of revolution; class-collaborationist attitude to revolutionary agency; and class analysis of the South (i.e. the idea that less developed countries are not yet dominantly capitalist) (see Das, 2020a: 282–347).

 | DOI:10.1163/9789004730472_003

In *Manifesto*, as in other key texts of Marxism, there are propositional claims, including causal claims about tendencies in political economy of class society and of capitalism. In addition, there are claims that present critiques of the existing world and of the ideas about it, its future and how to get there. It is interesting that *Manifesto*'s view of capitalism and what needs to be done is shaped by its critique of certain socialistic ideas.

Of the four main inter-connected components of Marxism (materialist-dialectical philosophy, historical materialism, political economy, and ideas that directly inform communist practice/programme, including vision of communist society),[3] *Manifesto*'s knowledge claims cover the last three. It does not specifically talk about the first component – philosophy, although it is informed by it.[4]

In terms of historical materialism (discussed in section 1), *Manifesto* of Marx and Engels (henceforward, Marx) makes a series of claims about the key concepts in Marxist social theory: class; relation between social relations of production and productive forces;[5] class struggle; and class nature of public (or state) power.[6] In terms of political economy, *Manifesto* makes claims about the functioning of capitalism, and globalization of capitalism and its crisis-proneness (dealt with in section 2); and the miserable experience of workers and its economic struggle that capitalism both prompts and impedes (explained in section 3). In terms of the communist practice, *Manifesto* makes wide-ranging claims (covered in section 4). These claims are about: the reasons for the need to go beyond capitalism; the vision of post-capitalist society (socialism/communism); the necessity for revolutionary overthrow of capitalism; the rejection of reformism but not the pursuit of reforms; the measures to be taken by the proletariat following its conquest of power, and the distinctiveness of the proletariat as the key and leading anti-capitalist revolutionary agent.

1 Class Relations and the State across Class Societies

People should be seen in terms of classes, and not merely as people or as human beings as such. One must not talk about human beings 'in general',

3 I am not distinguishing between 'communist' and 'socialist'.

4 *Manifesto* was written after Marx and Engels had developed their materialist philosophy in *German Ideology*, so ideas in *Manifesto* could not but have been informed by that philosophy.

5 This is the focus of Chapter 5 below.

6 The state power is the focus on Chapters 6–8.

who belong 'to no class' and who exist 'only in the misty realm of philosophical fantasy' (p. 30).[7] So, one must be critical of all those who talk about 'not the interests of the proletariat, but the interests of Human Nature' (p. 30). So one cannot 'appeal to society at large, without the distinction of class' (p. 32). In the context of *national* oppression, however, people may be seen in terms of cultural-geographical aggregate, i.e. nation, which, in turn, are to be seen in terms of the classes (and class-fractions) that constitute the nation. (Such a view of class and nation has implications for the *Manifesto*'s view of communism.)

Classes as (large) *groups* of men and women presuppose *relationships* between classes: what one class is it is because of its relation to another class. These relations are objective and antagonistic. The relations between classes are antagonistic because one class controls property,[8] and another class has very limited, or non-existent, control over property. So the question of property – who owns/controls it and who does not – is a central aspect of the existence of classes. Private property can be based in one's labour or in the appropriation of other people's labour. Private property based in one's labour is, for example, 'the property of petty artisan and of the small peasant, a form of property that preceded the bourgeois form [of private property]'. Private property 'is alleged to be the groundwork of all personal freedom, activity and independence' (Marx and Engels, 1848).

However, property relations are only one criterion for class relations. The other criterion is exploitation – appropriation of surplus product/labour – of the property-less class by the propertied class. The class antagonisms that characterize all of written history have 'assumed different forms at different epochs' (and places).[9] However, 'whatever form they may have taken, one fact is common to' them all: i.e. 'the exploitation of one part of society by the other.' (p. 26). For exploitation to happen, a certain objective (i.e. economic/material) condition must be present: productive forces are developed to such an extent that a surplus is produced, without which 'the lavish existence' of the exploiting class cannot be guaranteed (p. 20).[10]

---

7 All page references to *The Communist Manifesto* are from Marx and Engels (1848).

8 Property is understood as property in the means of production, the things that are used to produce other things, including means of production and subsistence.

9 'Hitherto, every form of society [with a written record] has been based … on the antagonism of oppressing and oppressed classes' (p. 20).

10 The *Manifesto* does not distinguish between exploitation and oppression. However, there *is* an important distinction, as Wright (2015; 1995) has rightly argued. The latter is a process of exclusion of the marginalized groups by the powerful groups from what is valued

Classes do not exist merely objectively. They are subjective forces too. Antagonistic class relations and the objective conditions of existence of classes have a tendency to give rise to class struggles. That is why, *Manifesto* memorably says: 'The history of all hitherto existing society (with a written history) is the history of class struggles' (p. 14).

Class struggle is in two forms: class struggle is from the top and from the bottom. This means that: both the oppressor class and oppressed class – slave owners and slaves, the nobility/aristocrats and commoners, lords and serfs, independent medieval producers and their subordinate workers/apprentices, and capitalists and workers, or 'in a word, oppressor and oppressed' – have been engaged in class struggle (p. 14). In this sense, what the ruling class (and its state) do to counter/pre-empt the class struggle of the oppressed (i.e. class struggle from the bottom) is class struggle too. It is the class struggle from the top. So, the scope of the term class struggle is not exhausted by the struggle of the oppressed.

As long as there are classes, class struggle goes on, even if it may not be always observable: classes always have 'stood in constant opposition to one another, carried on in an uninterrupted, now hidden, now open fight' (p. 14).[11] However, the outcome of class struggle is not pre-determined or fixed. That is, it is not necessary that the ruling class, or the exploited class, will win in a given situation. Indeed, the fight between classes can end 'either in a revolutionary reconstitution of society at large, or in the common ruin of the contending classes' (p. 14). (Those who say Marxism is teleological are mistaken), therefore.

Implicit in *Manifesto* is the idea that every form of society can be seen in terms of a *mode of production in a broad sense*. The latter refers to the combination of two elements: social relations among people under which production and exchange occur, and the actual techniques of production and the associated development of productive forces.[12] In *class*-society, social relations of production and exchange become the relations between classes (and intra-class relations). Or, broadly speaking, they become unequal and exploitative relations of production and exchange.

---

in society, while exploitation is a process where the exploiter needs the exploited because the labour of the latter benefits the former.

11 The question never is: why is there no class struggle? Class struggle happens always. The question is, why it is that class struggle is overt now and covert at another time, and why does its intensity and forms vary across times and places?

12 The development of productive forces is indicative of humanity's control over nature and of the ease with which human society is able to produce its conditions of existence (both means of subsistence, and means of production, including tools used, and raw materials extracted from nature).

The development of productive forces, and antagonistic relations between classes are inter-connected. A given level of the development of productive forces allows society to produce a surplus above its minimum means of subsistence, the surplus that allows classes to exist. In turn a given set of social relations of production (inter-class relations combined with intra-class relations) can promote, or fetter, the development of productive forces.

Changes occur in society partly because of the changes in the mode of production in 'the narrow sense', i.e. the ways in which, and the efficiency with which, means of subsistence and production are produced. Society has been going through 'a long course of development', or 'a series of revolutions in the modes of production and of exchange' (p. 15).

For a period of time, there is more or less a smooth and harmonious development of productive forces. But a time comes when the development of productive forces beyond a limit becomes incompatible with the existing relations of production (existing inter-class and intra-class relations), which fetter the further development of productive forces. The fettering occurs when productive forces, instead of developing, stagnate, or go backward, or when the rate of growth in the development of productive forces slows down. Fettering can be (approximately) expressed as stagnant rate of economic growth in the production and exchange, negative economic growth, and deceleration in the rate of growth (we return to this topic in Chapter 5).

The incompatibility (or contradiction) that fettering signifies takes different forms in different class societies, and results in a crisis of production and subsistence. This crisis contributes to one mode of production giving way to another. For example, the feudal system of production was superior to, and superseded, the slavery-based mode of production (where the ruling class had to constantly monitor the slaves who were a part of the means of production as such), but feudalism, within which bourgeois relations were developing, went into crisis because: 'the conditions under which feudal society produced and exchanged, the feudal organisation of agriculture and manufacturing industry, in one word, the feudal relations of property became no longer compatible with the already developed productive forces; they became so many fetters' (p. 17). So, 'They had to be burst asunder; they were burst asunder' (p. 17).[13]

---

13 'The feudal system of industry, in which industrial production was monopolised by closed guilds, now no longer sufficed for the growing wants of the new markets. The manufacturing system took its place. The guild-masters were pushed on one side by the manufacturing middle class; division of labour between the different corporate guilds vanished in the face of division of labour in each single workshop' (p. 15).

'Meantime the markets kept ever growing, the demand ever rising. Even manufacturer no longer sufficed. Thereupon, steam and machinery revolutionised industrial

When the development of productive forces is fettered, this adversely affects the economic interest of contending classes, and fuels class struggle. Class struggle, of course, always goes on because of exploitation, as we have seen. But when class struggle happens in a context of society-wide crisis of production and exchange, then the importance of class struggle is valorized. On the one hand, the exploited class wants to be free from the crisis through emancipation from the ruling class. On the other hand, the ruling class, whose economic interest in the appropriation of wealth from the labour and income of the exploited class is negatively affected by the crisis of production and exchange, wishes to shift the burden of the crisis to the exploited class and to hold on to its control over the means of production. Apart from the economic crisis of feudal production, class struggle against feudal forms of production and exchange contributed to the emergence of capitalism. 'The French Revolution ... abolished feudal property in favour of bourgeois property' (p. 20). Every class struggle against existing economic structure (or, mode of production) is ultimately 'a political struggle' (p. 19).

No class society can exist without the public power, the state, whose main role is to keep the exploited in check. 'Political power, properly so called', i.e. the state, 'is merely the organised power of one class for oppressing another' (p. 27). The class that controls the means of production, more or less, controls public political power. The degree of separation of the state from the ruling class, at the level of agency or personnel, is a contingent matter. In other words, economic processes underlie political and cultural processes. *Manifesto's* social theory represents an application of Marx and Engels' materialist dialectics. This is indicated by Engels who says in his 1883 Preface to the German edition of *Manifesto*:

> The basic thought running through the Manifesto – that economic production, and the structure of society of every historical epoch necessarily arising therefrom, constitute the foundation for the political and intellectual history of that epoch; that consequently (ever since the dissolution of the primaeval communal ownership of land) all history has been a history of class struggles, of struggles between exploited and exploiting, between dominated and dominating classes at various stages of social evolution. (p. 6)

---

production. The place of manufacture was taken by the giant, Modern Industry; the place of the industrial middle class by industrial millionaires, the leaders of the whole industrial armies, the modern bourgeois' (p. 15).

2 Capitalist Economic System and World Market

As mentioned earlier, 'the development of class antagonisms' has historically 'assumed different forms at different epochs' or in different historically-existing class societies (p. 26). Capitalism is one of the many different forms of class society. Like any other form of (class) society, this society should be seen in terms of distinctive 'relations of production, of exchange and of property' (p. 17).

The capitalist society is a society under the rule of capital (money invested in production and exchange to make more money). The capitalist owns property (means of production) as personal property but this property is actually social property, one that has been created by numerous members of a society, and taken control over by the capitalist. 'Capital is a collective product' because 'only by the united action of all members of society, can it be set in motion' (p. 23). 'Capital is therefore not only personal; it is a social power' (ibid.).

Capitalism, the modern society under the rule of the bourgeoisie, is a progressive mode of production in that it promotes an immense development of the productive forces and the consequent potential for the flourishing of human abilities. *Manifesto* makes the following stunning claim about a causal tendency of capitalist relations: 'The bourgeoisie cannot exist without constantly revolutionising the instruments of production' (p. 16). There is proof for this. It has created wealth on a scale unimagined of in previous societies: 'The bourgeoisie has created more massive and more colossal productive forces than have all preceding generations together' (p. 17). It has thus 'been the first [among all ruling classes] to show what [human] activity can bring about' (p. 16). It has awakened humanity's 'productive forces slumbered in the lap of social labour' (p. 17).[14] Its admirable achievements include: 'Subjection of Nature's forces to [human beings], machinery, application of chemistry to industry and agriculture, steam-navigation, railways, electric telegraphs, clearing of whole continents for cultivation, canalisation of rivers' (p. 17).[15]

---

14 'It has accomplished wonders far surpassing Egyptian pyramids, Roman aqueducts, and Gothic cathedrals; it has conducted expeditions that put in the shade all former Exoduses of nations and crusades' (p. 16).

15 One can, of course, add to the list, all the more powerful achievements in the last 200 years or so (e.g. computers, biotechnology, AI, space science, neuroscience, Messenger RNA, or, mRNA, vaccines that teach human body cells how to make a protein that triggers an immune response, etc.).

The bourgeoisie (of advanced countries) has achieved all these wonderful things in two major ways.[16] One is that capitalist *relations* of production and exchange, once they start developing, have a tendency to unsettle, and then remove, pre-capitalist relations of production that had hitherto fettered the development of productive forces. The capitalist social relations of production 'put an end to all feudal, patriarchal, idyllic relations' and to 'pitilessly' tear asunder 'the motley feudal ties that bound man to his "natural superiors"' (p. 15). Secondly, driven by competitive relations, the bourgeoisie has resorted to a systematic (not sporadic or one-time) application of knowledge/science and the consequent transformation of nature-society relations. And, as the bourgeoisie causes the development of the productive forces,[17] this development contributes to its class power: 'in proportion as industry, commerce, navigation, railways extended, in the same proportion the bourgeoisie developed, increased its capital, and pushed into the background every class handed down from the Middle Ages' (p. 15).

The fact that the bourgeois society is able to revolutionize the means of production in a systematic and unprecedented way is what distinguishes it from pre-capitalist societies. There is another major difference. 'In the earlier epochs of history, we find almost everywhere a complicated arrangement of society into various orders, a manifold gradation of social rank' (p. 14).[18] However, the class structure – or, the class map – of capitalist society is a little clearer: 'the epoch of the bourgeoisie ... has simplified class antagonisms' (p. 15). This is in the sense that 'Society as a whole is more and more splitting up into two great hostile camps, into two great classes directly facing each other – Bourgeoisie and Proletariat' (ibid.).[19] Associated with the claim about the simplified class

16 Of course, a major factor is the capitalist-imperialist plunder which *Manifesto* does not talk about.

17 Marx here unfortunately abstracts from the environmental damage caused to nature by capital.

18 'In ancient Rome we have patricians, knights, plebeians, slaves; in the Middle Ages, feudal lords, vassals, guild-masters, journeymen, apprentices, serfs; in almost all of these classes, again, subordinate gradations' (p. 14).

19 The phrase 'more and more' speaks to a causal tendency (explained below), the outcome of which is uneven in time and space. It implies that there *are* classes other than these two major classes. Marx discusses various classes other than capital and labour, in his own political studies of, for example France, England, etc. Lenin (1899a) and Mao (1933) after him did the same in their own studies of class relations in Russia and China respectively. In recent Marxist literature, scholars (e.g. Wright) have drawn attention to non-proletarian and non-capitalist classes (managers, those who 'own' monopolizable skill/expertise, etc.). For a discussion and a critique of this literature, see Das (2017b: chapters 2 and 4).

structure of the capitalist society is the important claim that the bourgeoisie has produced its own grave-digger in the form of the proletariat (more on this later).

The development of productive forces under the rule of the capitalist class, like everything else, has taken a specific geographical form. Side by side with the concentration of property in a few hands, there has been geographical agglomeration of production and exchange, at multiple scales (in a few localities in specific countries, a few countries, etc.) in place of pre-capitalist localized system of production and exchange. In terms of capitalism's origin in urban areas, *Manifesto* says: 'From the serfs of the Middle Ages sprang the chartered burghers of the earliest towns. From these burgesses the first elements of the [urban] bourgeoisie were developed' (p. 15; parenthesis added). With the tendency towards the urbanization of productive forces and of capitalists and workers emerges the town-country inequality: 'The bourgeoisie has subjected the country [rural areas] to the rule of the towns. It has created enormous cities, has greatly increased the urban population as compared with the rural ... [It] has made the country dependent on the towns' (p. 17). The urbanization of capitalism is a part of an overall (spatial) agglomerative tendency within capitalism. 'The bourgeoisie keeps more and more doing away with the scattered state of the population, of the means of production, and of property. It has agglomerated population, centralised the means of production, and has concentrated property in a few hands' (p. 17). Indeed, the scale of capitalist production and exchange has increased from the local to the national and the global.

At the global scale, capitalism, in fact, originated in a few countries, and then spread. In its very origin, capitalism has been a global phenomenon.[20] There is a reason for this. Driven by competition which promotes productivity-enhancing technological change, a massive amount of product is produced in a country but the effective demand for it may not exist in that country (at a given level of investment), so the bourgeoisie is forced to sell things abroad. But what if other countries (which may or may not be capitalist or capitalist enough), do not need products from another country? One answer is competitive price (abstracting from colonial coercion): if a country can produce things at a lower price, it can break open the markets of foreign countries. And production for

20 The increasing scale of capitalism has had potential implications for the environmental damage, in particular, the decline in soil fertility: when forests and farm land are forced to meet the demands of capitalist export markets, they tend to be subjected to more intense exploitation, so improvements in nature become difficult (we will return to this topic in chapter 5).

the world market leads to demand for foreign sources of raw materials (and energy), and contributes to capitalist development in the exporting countries. 'Modern industry has established the world market ... [which] has given an immense development to commerce, to navigation, to communication by land. This development has, in its turn, reacted on the extension of industry' (p. 15). The concomitant impulse to the development of transportation and communication technologies, under the impact of mercantile and later industrial capitalist relations, contributes to international trade and thus to capitalism's globalness.[21]

There is probably no better account of globalization by an author living in a time when the tendencies towards globalization -- and indeed towards advanced global capitalism -- were not yet fully manifested than Marx's. 'The need of a constantly expanding market for its products chases the bourgeoisie over the entire surface of the globe. It must nestle everywhere, settle everywhere, establish connexions everywhere' (p. 16). 'The bourgeoisie has through its exploitation of the world market given a cosmopolitan character to production and consumption in every country' (ibid.).[22] This means that 'In place of the old local and national seclusion and self-sufficiency, we have intercourse in every direction, universal inter-dependence of nations' (ibid.) in the material sphere (production, exchange and consumption). 'The cheap prices of commodities are the heavy artillery with which it [the bourgeoisie of an advanced country] batters down all Chinese walls, with which it forces the [nations of the South] intensely obstinate hatred of foreigners to capitulate' (p. 16). This is partly how 'It compels all nations, on pain of extinction, to adopt the bourgeois mode of production; it compels them to introduce what it calls civilisation

21 'The discovery of America, the rounding of the Cape, opened up fresh ground for the rising bourgeoisie. The East-Indian and Chinese markets, the colonisation of America, trade with the colonies, the increase in the means of exchange and in commodities generally, gave to commerce, to navigation, to industry, an impulse never before known, and thereby, to the revolutionary element in the tottering feudal society, a rapid development' (p. 15).

22 '[It] has drawn from under the feet of industry the national ground on which it stood. All old-established national industries have been destroyed or are daily being destroyed. They are dislodged by new industries, whose introduction becomes a life and death question for all civilised nations, by industries that no longer work up indigenous raw material, but raw material drawn from the remotest zones; industries whose products are consumed, not only at home, but in every quarter of the globe. In place of the old wants, satisfied by the production of the country, we find new wants, requiring for their satisfaction the products of distant lands and climes. In place of the old local and national seclusion and self-sufficiency, we have intercourse in every direction, universal inter-dependence of nations' (p. 16).

into their midst, i.e., to become bourgeois themselves. In one word, it creates a world after its own image' (p. 16). By promoting 'the rapid improvement of all instruments of production, by the immensely facilitated means of communication' the capitalist class draws all, even the most under-developed nations into the orbit of its rule (p. 16). There is more: a major effect of the globalization is that capitalism has made the less developed countries dependent on more developed ones, 'nations of peasants on nations of bourgeois, the East on the West' (p. 17).[23]

While capitalism has promoted the development of productive forces within countries and at the global scale, such a process cannot be a linear affair. Capitalism experiences crisis of production, which is expressed as what Marx calls at the time (decades before he wrote about the tendency toward the rate of profit to fall in *Capital* volume 3) 'the epidemic of over-production' or 'commercial crises' (p. 17). Marx's explanation for capitalist crisis is the one that applies to all *class* societies, albeit in different forms: contradiction between productive forces and production relations. Under bourgeois property relations, wealth is produced only when profit will be made, but if profit cannot be made, wealth production is fettered. The colossal productive forces developed under 'the conditions of bourgeois property ... have become too powerful for these conditions, by which they are fettered' (p. 17). In other words, 'The conditions of bourgeois society are too narrow to comprise the wealth created by them' (p. 17).

Everything comes to a standstill when crises occur. Not just that. 'In these crises, a great part not only of the existing products, but also of the previously created productive forces, are periodically destroyed' (p. 17). The periodic crises which are unheard of in pre-capitalist societies 'put the existence of the entire bourgeois society on its trial, each time more threateningly' (p. 17). 'Society suddenly finds itself put back into a state of momentary barbarism; it appears as if a famine, a universal war of devastation, had cut off the supply of every means of subsistence; industry and commerce seem to be destroyed ... [because] there is ... too much means of subsistence, too much industry, too much commerce' (p. 17).[24] This is how the crisis is temporarily resolved.

---

23 This dependence would be theorized as a part of imperialism by Lenin, as discussed in chapter 9.

24 'A young girl asks her father, "Why is it so cold in the house?"
"We don't have any coal", he says.
"But why is there no coal?", she wants to know.
"Because I lost my job", he replies.
Still unsatisfied, she asks one more time – "And why did you lose your job?"
To which he answers, "Because there is too much coal"'
(as told by: Professor Bertell Ollman).

'The weapons', i.e. the efficient production techniques, 'with which the bourgeoisie felled feudalism to the ground are now turned against the bourgeoisie itself' (p. 18). So, 'the history of industry and commerce is but the history of the revolt of modern productive forces against modern conditions of production, against the property relations that are the conditions for the existence of the bourgeois and of its rule' (p. 17). The situation is one where the capitalist class has succeeded in creating something (i.e. massive development of productive forces) which it fails to control: 'Modern bourgeois society … [which] has conjured up such gigantic means of production and of exchange, is like the sorcerer who is no longer able to control the powers of the nether world whom he has called up by his spells' (p. 17).

> The productive forces at the disposal of society no longer tend to further the development of the conditions of bourgeois property; on the contrary, they have become too powerful for these conditions, by which they are fettered, and so soon as they overcome these fetters, they bring disorder into the whole of bourgeois society, endanger the existence of bourgeois property. The conditions of bourgeois society are too narrow to comprise the wealth created by them. (ibid.)

There are two ways in which the capitalist system responds to the crisis. One is the 'enforced destruction of a mass of productive forces' (p. 17) and of products, just referred to above. The other is globalization. Thus, the global-scale of production/exchange and crisis-proneness are inter-connected. A major reason for globalization is the crisis-proneness of capitalism, while globalization makes the crises more difficult to deal with: capitalism seeks to resolve its crisis by 'the conquest of new markets, and by the more thorough exploitation of the old ones' (p. 17). This in turn paves 'the way for more extensive and more destructive crises' and diminishes 'the means whereby crises are prevented' (ibid.). Crises become global. Originating in one country, they spread to other countries, because capitalism has linked together all the countries.

3 Capitalism, Culture and the State

Capitalism's impacts are not confined to the economic realm (production relations and productive forces, etc.). It produces enormous cultural impacts too.[25] 'The bourgeoisie … has left remaining no other nexus between [people] than

25 Marx pursues this theme in *Grundrisse* too, as we will see in chapter 4.

naked self-interest, than callous "cash payment" … It has resolved personal worth into exchange value' (pp. 15–16). Traditionally, people in certain occupations enjoyed a degree of prestige. No longer. 'The bourgeoisie has stripped of its halo every occupation hitherto honoured and looked up to with reverent awe. It has converted the physician, the lawyer, the priest, the poet, the man of science, into its paid wage labourers' (p. 16). Even 'Law, morality, religion, are … so many bourgeois prejudices, behind which lurk in ambush just as many bourgeois interests' (ibid.).

By fetishizing the cash nexus, the capitalist system has produced an impoverished view of human beings: 'From the moment when labour can no longer be converted into capital, money, or rent into a [monopolizable] social power', that is, 'from the moment when individual property can no longer be transformed into bourgeois property, into capital, from that moment', according to the bourgeoisie, 'individuality vanishes' (p. 23). In other words, one's individuality is one that is bourgeois (or bourgeois-like), or else, one has no individuality. If one fails to make money by investing money, one is not (much of) an individual. The capitalist relations have impacted the family too, which used to be a realm of extra-economic realm, one that is beyond the considerations of cash nexus. However, that has changed: 'The bourgeoisie has torn away from the family its sentimental veil, and has reduced the family relation to a mere money relation' (p. 16).

The capitalist system has not only increased the geographical/spatial scope of life and increased the scale of human interaction from the more local to the more global. It has quickened *the pace of life*. Time appears to pass quickly. Unlike the pre-capitalist times, the bourgeois epoch is characterized by 'Constant revolutionising of production, uninterrupted disturbance of all social conditions, everlasting uncertainty and agitation', so much so that 'ancient and venerable prejudices and opinions … are swept away, all new-formed ones become antiquated before they can ossify' (p. 16). In one word: 'All that is solid melts into air, all that is holy is profaned' (p. 16). Of course, these are tendencies emanating from relations of capitalism, the actual outcomes of which are not characterized by the finality that is suggested. There are residues or remnants from the past that are combined with modern capitalist development. Capitalist culture dominates pre-capitalist (type) culture.

Capitalism has brought enormous changes in the culture of consumption and consumption of culture. First of all, people in one country consume things from other countries: 'In place of the old wants, satisfied by the production of the country, we find new wants, requiring for their satisfaction the products of distant lands and climes' (p. 16). There is a general universalization of human interaction, socially and culturally, and not just materially: 'The intellectual creations of individual nations become common property' of [multi-national] humanity (p. 16). 'National one-sidedness and narrow-mindedness become more and more impossible, and from the numerous national and local literatures, there arises a world literature' (ibid.). In fact, *Manifesto* itself is an exemplar of world literature.[26] There is thus a tendency towards cultural globalization creating a world literature, coexisting with economic globalization, which produces a world-economy.

The bourgeois is not just in control of the economic and cultural conditions of society. It also controls politics and the state. It is the economic and cultural master. It is also the political master. 'Each step in the development of the bourgeoisie was accompanied by a corresponding political advance of that class' (p. 15). It was an oppressed class under 'the sway of the feudal nobility', but 'since the establishment of Modern Industry and of the world market, [it] conquered for itself, in the modern representative State, exclusive political sway' (p. 15). In fact: as *Manifesto* famously claims: 'The executive of the modern state is but a committee for managing the common affairs of the whole bourgeoisie' (p. 15). Implicit in the above claim is the idea that the state, over the long run, looks after the common affairs of the class of capitalists (at the expense of those of the masses). Also implicit is the idea that to meet the common affairs, the state may need a degree of independence vis a vis individual competing capitalists, including capitalists of different regions and sectors.

Just as the spatial scale of the system of production and exchange has got larger, so has the scale of public power (i.e. of the political regulation society's common affairs). The scalar character of economy and that of politics have got connected. We have seen that the capitalist class has geographically 'agglomerated population, centralised the means of production, and has concentrated property in a few hands' (p. 17). The necessary consequence of this economic process of centralization is 'political centralisation': 'Independent, or but loosely connected provinces, with separate interests, laws, governments, and systems of taxation, became lumped together into one nation, with one government, one code of laws, one national class-interest, one frontier, and one customs-tariff' (p. 17).[27]

---

26 In recent times, online socialist literature, including the massive www.wsws.org, is an example of world literature, which reflects, and shapes, the growing recent trend towards radicalization of the masses. Wikipedia is another example of world literature.

27 Of course, this process is geographically uneven and an on-going process (especially, in the South). In some countries, the ways in which cities are administered (including how they earn taxes and how they spend) are fairly uniform, while in the US, there is a lot of variation in this across cities.

4 Workers' Experience of Exploitation and Its Effects

The approach of the *Manifesto* to labour is dialectical as it explores its economic and political life *in relation to* the capitalist class and the capitalist system.[28] Labour is also seen in the *Manifesto* as both a suffering class and a fighting class.

The working class comprises men and women 'who must sell themselves piecemeal' (p. 18), as they have little to no property. The political economy of the capitalist class (in terms of what it does and what can happen to it), is internally connected to the political economy of the working class. 'The essential conditions for the existence and for the sway of the bourgeois class is the formation and augmentation of capital', and 'the condition for capital is wage-labour' (p. 21), which is the source of surplus value or profit converted to capital. So, 'In proportion as the bourgeoisie, i.e., capital, is developed, in the same proportion is the proletariat, the modern working class, developed' (p. 18). There cannot be capital without wage-labour.

The proletariat as a class has multiple class origins, like the bourgeoisie itself.[29] The proletariat 'is recruited from all classes of the population' (p. 18). Small-scale property owners become proletarianized as they cannot compete with capitalist production and as their specialized skills are no longer needed.[30] Even a capitalist proper can be proletarianized because they cannot successfully compete with their brothers and sisters.[31]

The early proletarians were men. Gradually, the class got feminized partly because of the progress of mechanization which lessens the demand for muscular energy.[32] 'The less the skill and exertion of strength implied in manual

28 This is in contrast to the approach to labour in the academic subdisciplines such as Labour geography, Labour sociology, Labour history, etc. which generally take a more voluntarist approach to labour (for a critique, see Das, 2017b: chapter 4).

29 It comes from various strata/classes: landlords; serfs; petty-bourgeoisie; merchants, etc. One can also add another layer: middle class professionals (doctors and engineers, accountants, etc.) and government officers and politicians.

30 'The lower strata of the middle class – the small tradespeople, shopkeepers, and retired tradesmen generally, the handicraftsmen and peasants – all these sink gradually into the proletariat, partly because their diminutive capital does not suffice for the scale on which Modern Industry is carried on, and is swamped in the competition with the large capitalists, partly because their specialised skill is rendered worthless by new methods of production' (p. 18). This theme of class differentiation is developed by Lenin (see chapter 9).

31 '[E]ntire sections of the ruling class are, by the advance of industry, precipitated into the proletariat, or are at least threatened in their conditions of existence. These also supply the proletariat with fresh elements of enlightenment and progress' (p. 19).

32 Of course, this is not the only reason for the feminization of the working class. Women's struggle for their right work outside of the home is one of the reasons too.

labour, in other words, the more modern industry becomes developed, the more is the labour of men superseded by that of women' (p. 18). Among other things, this indicates that capitalism is, more or less, gender neutral at an abstract (general level) level: 'Differences of age and sex have no longer any distinctive social validity for the working class. All are instruments of labour, more or less, expensive to use, according to their age and sex' (p. 18).[33] All men, women and children are tendentially reduced to one objective identity: tall of them must sell their ability to work or starve.[34]

The proletariat experiences a life of misery because they are subjected to exploitation. The working class is subject to primary exploitation in the workplace ('exploitation proper'), and secondary exploitation. Exploitation, or, primary exploitation, fundamentally refers to the appropriation of surplus labour from workers by capitalists, which means that capitalists materially benefit at the expense of workers. '[T]he cost of production' of workers 'is restricted, almost entirely, to the means of subsistence' that they require for their maintenance (p. 18), and for their generational reproduction, so workers' wage at best covers the cost of their reproduction. But the net product that they produce is more than what they receive in the form of wages. On the one hand, the price of labour power, like that of any commodity, 'is equal to its cost of production', and on the other hand, the nature of work is such that workers require 'only the most simple, most monotonous, and most easily acquired knack' (p. 18). Therefore, for the working class as a whole, 'In proportion … as the repulsiveness of the work increases, the wage decreases' (ibid.).

For most people, individual skills and intellectual ability are meaningless. The work life of the common people is charmless, it is not a source of enjoyment. Workers become an appendage of the machine, the purpose of which is to increase profit for capitalists, and not necessarily to decrease the burden of toil of workers. Thus workers' experience emotional suffering.

Workers' life is one of insecurity, or precarity, in terms of employment and wages. Workers 'live only so long as they find work', and they 'find work only so long as their labour increases capital' (p. 18). 'The increasing improvement of machinery, ever more rapidly developing, makes their livelihood more and

33 This claim anticipates Lenin (1914) who says: 'it makes no difference to the hired hand' whether he (or she) is exploited chiefly by the white male capitalists rather than the black female bourgeoisie.

As Eagleton (2011: 213), a contemporary British Marxist, says: capitalism is characterized by 'relative indifference to gender, ethnicity, social pedigree and so on when it comes to who it can exploit or to whom it can peddle its wares'.

34 Of course, this does not mean that there is no need for the capitalist class to subject women to discrimination. On the capitalist logic of oppression of women (and racialized minorities), in part based on the work of Marx and Lenin, see Das (2022c).

more precarious' as people lose their employment and as employment becomes increasingly irregular (p. 19). This implies that sometimes, being exploited may be better than not being exploited. The identity of the working class is that of a class which exists for the sake of, and in the interest of, the capitalist class. As the owner of commodity labour power, workers are 'exposed to all the vicissitudes of competition, to all the fluctuations of the market' (p. 18). It is not just that wages are low and are driven downward. Wages fluctuate enormously: 'The growing competition among the bourgeois, and the resulting commercial crises, make the wages of the workers ever more fluctuating' (p. 19).

Capitalists resort to various mechanisms to extract more labour from the working class every hour and every day. These include: 'prolongation of the working hours', and 'the increase of the work exacted in a given time or by increased speed of machinery, etc.' (p. 18). Apart from being economically exploited, workers at work are subjected to the despotic power of the capitalists. This power is directly exercised – i.e. bureaucratically – by capitalists or by those whom capitalists appoint. Crowded into the workplaces, workers 'are organised like soldiers' (p. 18). 'As privates of the industrial army they are placed under the command of a perfect hierarchy of officers and sergeants' (ibid.). Capitalists also use machines to control labour.[35] As 'slaves of the bourgeois class', workers 'are daily and hourly enslaved by the machine' (ibid.). Such control over men and women in the workplace is necessary to increase exploitation and reduce resistance to exploitation. And '[t]he more openly this despotism [in the workplace] proclaims gain to be its end and aim, the more petty, the more hateful and the more embittering it is' (ibid.). Such despotism is bound to cause workers' emotional suffering.

Workers are also subjected to secondary exploitation which happens outside of the workplace: 'No sooner is the exploitation of the labourer by the [capitalist in the workplace], so far, at an end, that he receives his wages in cash, than he is set upon by the other portions of the bourgeoisie, the landlord, the shopkeeper, the pawnbroker, etc.' (p. 18).[36] And, apart from being exploited in the sphere of economy, workers are subjected to subjugation in the political sphere. Workers are slaves not only of the bourgeois class but also 'of the bourgeois State' (ibid.). When workers go on a strike, the full force of the state in the form of the police, courts, etc. faces them.

35 In our times, various surveillance mechanisms and Artificial Intelligence are weapons in the hands of capitalists to control labour in the workplace.

36 One can add: real estate agents, and financial institutions (including payday loan institutions) lending money to buy houses, etc.

5 Workers' Struggle within and against Capitalism

5.1 *Economic Struggle*

The proletariat is not just a suffering class. It is also a fighting class: Marx rejects the reformers' idea that the working class people suffer from the lack 'any historical initiative or any independent political movement' (p. 32) to change their own conditions.[37] In fact, 'With its birth begins its struggle with the bourgeoisie.' (p. 18).

The anti-capitalist struggle does not appear at once. It is a protracted process. It is a temporally and geographically uneven process. And the struggle takes different forms at different stages of its political development: 'The proletariat goes through various stages of development' (p. 18). Initially, 'the contest is carried on by individual labourers, then by the workpeople of a factory, then by the operative of one trade, in one locality, against the individual bourgeois who directly exploits them' (p. 18).[38] This is still the pre-trade union state of proletarian struggle. With the progress of capitalist development, 'the workers begin to form combinations (Trades' Unions) against the bourgeois; they club together in order to keep up the rate of wages' (p. 19). They also establish 'permanent associations in order to make provision beforehand for these occasional revolts' (p. 19). And, 'Here and there, the contest breaks out into riots' (p. 19). Gradually, 'the collisions between individual workmen and individual bourgeois take more and more the character of collisions *between two classes*' (p. 19; italics added). A scalar transformation of workers' politics happens: as proletarian struggles are transformed from more localized struggle to struggles at the national scale, what are merely economic struggles between a group of workers and their employers (within a factory or within a trade or sector) become class struggle 'proper'. After all, at the national scale is concentrated state power that defends the basic interests of the bourgeois class against the masses.

Workers exist as a class objectively – after all, capitalism cannot exist without them, but they may not always exist in a form in which they can fight in their own interests vis a vis the capitalist class. There are factors that undermine their organization and action. One is the geography of workers' life:

37 Some reformers 'are conscious of caring chiefly for the interests of the working class, as being the most suffering class. Only from the point of view of being the most suffering class does the proletariat exist for them' (p. 32).

38 'They direct their attacks not against the bourgeois conditions of production, but against the instruments of production themselves; they destroy imported wares that compete with their labour, they smash to pieces machinery, they set factories ablaze, they seek to restore by force the vanished status of the workman of the Middle Ages.' (p. 18).

the fact that labourers are 'scattered over the whole country' (p. 19). Another is 'the isolation of the labourers, due to competition' among them (p. 21).[39] '[T]he organisation of the proletarians into a class, and, consequently into a political party, is continually being upset ... by the competition between the workers themselves' (p. 19). Besides, there are sections of the proletariat – the lumpen elements which are hardly employed and who are part of the lowest layers of society – who may serve as 'a bribed tool of reactionary intrigue' (p. 20), even if they 'may, here and there, be swept into the movement by a proletarian revolution' (p. 20). They can indeed be agents of capitalist politics.[40]

However, there are many processes that promote unity among workers too. The bourgeoisie needs workers. '[T]he condition for capital is wage-labour' (p. 21), so capitalist accumulation increases the number of workers who are concentrated in cities and city-regions. This increases its fighting power: 'with the development of industry, the proletariat not only increases in number; it becomes concentrated in greater masses, its strength grows, and it feels that strength more' (p. 19). Workers' unity is 'helped on by the improved means of communication that are created by' capitalism in its own interest, which 'place the workers of different localities in contact with one another' (p. 19). This process helps to 'centralise the numerous local struggles, all of the same character, into one national struggle between classes' (p. 19).[41]

Besides, capitalist competition that drives mechanization, and expansion of capitalist production and exchange, has a tendency to create similar working class conditions in different places and countries. This homogenization process can promote unity among workers. 'The various interests and conditions of life within the ranks of the proletariat are more and more equalised, in proportion as machinery obliterates all distinctions of labour, and nearly everywhere reduces wages to the same low level' (p. 19). In *all* nations, workers have no property or very little of it; and *all* nations are the same as regards 'modern subjection to capital', which tends to strip the working class 'of every trace of national character' (p. 20). In addition, intra-propertied class conflicts can politicize the working class. In some contexts, the bourgeoise unites and politicizes the working class by mobilizing it in its own fight against non-proletarian

39 'Wage-labour rests exclusively on competition between the labourers.' (p. 21).

40 Consider how these elements can be hired by the capitalist class and/or agents of its state to kill leaders off trade unions and working class leaders.

41 '[T]hat union, to attain which the burghers of the Middle Ages, with their miserable highways, required centuries, the modern proletarian, thanks to railways, achieve in a few years.' (p. 19).

classes (and this is especially true in the Global South). In many ways, 'collisions between the classes of the old society further ... the course of development of the proletariat' (p. 19).[42]

The bourgeoise itself is split into many factions. One faction fights another and in the process politicizes the working class. One faction fights 'with those portions of the bourgeoisie itself, whose interests have become antagonistic to the progress of industry' (p. 19). The bourgeoisie of one country fights 'at all time with the bourgeoisie of foreign countries' (p. 19). And, in all these battles with non-proletarian classes, including with foreign capitalists, the bourgeoisie of a country is 'compelled to appeal to the proletariat, to ask for help, and thus, to drag it into the political arena' (p. 19). This is how the bourgeoisie itself unwittingly 'supplies the proletariat with its own elements of political and general education, in other words, it furnishes the proletariat with weapons for fighting the bourgeoisie' (ibid.).

The bourgeoisie is a very small minority, so it is forced to rule in the name of the proletariat even if most of the things it does in its own interests hurt the proletarians: 'Free trade: for the benefit of the working class. Protective duties: for the benefit of the working class. Prison Reform: for the benefit of the working class' (p. 32). In other words, 'the bourgeois is a bourgeois – for the benefit of the working class.' (ibid.). In its own interests, the bourgeoisie appeals to the proletariat, and in the process contributes to the proletariat's politicization. This politicization is also helped partly by the fact that sometimes, sections of the capitalist class – in particular, some bourgeois ideologists – get de-classed and go over to the proletariat and contribute to the working class politics, at least intellectually.[43]

---

42 '[T]he bourgeoisie ... in order to attain its own political ends, is compelled to set the whole proletariat in motion ... At this stage, therefore, the proletarians do not fight their enemies, but the enemies of their enemies, the remnants of absolute monarchy, the landowners, the non-industrial bourgeois, the petty bourgeois. Thus, the whole historical movement is concentrated in the hands of the bourgeoisie; every victory so obtained is a victory for the bourgeoisie.' (p. 19).

43 '[I]n times when the class struggle nears the decisive hour, the progress of dissolution going on within the ruling class, in fact within the whole range of old society, assumes such a violent, glaring character, that a small section of the ruling class cuts itself adrift, and joins the revolutionary class, the class that holds the future in its hands. Just as, therefore, at an earlier period, a section of the nobility went over to the bourgeoisie, so now a portion of the bourgeoisie goes over to the proletariat, and in particular, a portion of the bourgeois ideologists, who have raised themselves to the level of comprehending theoretically the historical movement as a whole' (pp. 19–20).

The working class struggle produces some concessions (e.g. pro-worker legislations).[44] 'It compels legislative recognition of particular interests of the workers, by taking advantage of the divisions among the bourgeoisie itself. Thus, the ten-hours' bill in England was carried' (p. 19). In their struggle against capitalism, 'Now and then the workers are victorious, but only for a time' (p. 19). However, 'The real fruit of their battles lies, not in the immediate result, but in the ever expanding union of the workers' (p. 19), because ultimately the aim of the struggle is revolution against capitalism, against wage-slavery.

5.2 *From Economic Class Struggle to Revolution*

Capitalism is based on the creation and expansion of the proletariat. The proletariat in turn can become capitalism's grave diggers. By subjecting workers to abject exploitation, the bourgeois drives them to fight against capitalism: 'What the bourgeoisie therefore produces, above all, are its own grave-diggers' (p. 21). In fact, 'not only has the bourgeoisie forged the weapons that bring death to itself; it has also called into existence the [people] who are to wield those weapons – the modern working class – the proletarians' (p. 18). Why? Why can workers not fight for only small reforms?

In previous societies, 'All the preceding classes' (e.g. slaves, serfs, petty bourgeoisie, etc.) 'that got the upper hand sought to fortify their already acquired status by subjecting society at large to their conditions of appropriation' (p. 20). For example, 'The serf, in the period of serfdom, raised himself to membership in the commune, just as the petty bourgeois, under the yoke of the feudal absolutism, managed to develop into a bourgeois' (ibid.). The proletariat as the rising class of the capitalist class is different. The proletarians have no property. 'They have nothing of their own to secure and to fortify; their mission is to destroy all previous securities for, and insurances of, individual property' (p. 20). Their ability to work is the only thing they have but this cannot be put to work unless it is combined the means of production which they lack. 'The proletarians cannot become masters of the productive forces' in a future society, 'except by abolishing their own previous mode of appropriation, and thereby also every other previous mode of appropriation' (p. 20). Their conditions cannot be improved durably and significantly under capitalist property relations by their economic struggle only:

> The modern labourer ... instead of rising with the process of industry, sinks deeper and deeper below the conditions of existence of his own

---

44 This is explored in chapter 8.

> class. He becomes a pauper, and pauperism develops more rapidly than population and wealth. (p. 20)

This means that the bourgeoisie is unfit to rule:

> it becomes evident, that the bourgeoisie is unfit any longer to be the ruling class in society, … because it is incompetent to assure an existence to its slave within his slavery, because it cannot help letting him sink into such a state, that it has to feed him, instead of being fed by him. Society can no longer live under this bourgeoisie, in other words, its existence is no longer compatible with society.[45]

In class societies, there is class struggle. All oppressed classes have engaged in class struggle. The proletarian class struggle within and against capitalism is different in that its aim is to remove class from the map of human history. In self-emancipating, the proletariat emancipates the whole society.[46] The current society cannot meet its needs durably and significantly.

5.3 *Proletarian Vision of Communism*

A new society has to be a communist/socialist society. 'The distinguishing feature of Communism is not the abolition of property generally, but the abolition of bourgeois property' (p. 22). In capitalism, 'private property is already done away' or almost done away, 'for nine-tenths of the population; its existence for the few is solely due to its non-existence in the hands of those nine-tenths' (p. 23). Communism wishes 'to do away with a form of property, the necessary condition for whose existence is the non-existence of any property for the immense majority of society' (ibid.). So communism is the abolition of private property in its capitalist form, which 'is the final and most complete expression of the system of producing and appropriating products, that is based on class antagonisms, on the exploitation of the many by the few' (ibid.).

---

45 Revolutionaries are opposed to 'social quacks who, by all manner of tinkering, professed to redress, without any danger to capital and profit, all sorts of social grievances, in both cases men outside the working-class movement, and looking rather to the "educated" classes for support' (p. 8).

46 The struggle of the workers against the capitalists 'has now reached a stage where the exploited and oppressed class (the proletariat) can no longer emancipate itself from the class which exploits and oppresses it (the bourgeoisie), without at the same time forever freeing the whole of society from exploitation, oppression, class struggles – this basic thought belongs solely and exclusively to Marx', says Engels in his Preface to the 1883 German edition of *The Communist Manifesto*.

In capitalism, 'What … the wage-labourer appropriates by means of his labour, merely suffices to prolong and reproduce a bare existence' (p. 23). This 'personal appropriation of the products of labour' will not be abolished but what *will be* abolished is 'the miserable character of this appropriation, under which the labourer lives merely to increase capital, and is allowed to live only in so far as the interest of the ruling class requires it' (p. 23). In contrast to bourgeois society where 'living labour is but a means to increase accumulated labour', under communism, accumulated labour will be 'but a means to widen, to enrich, to promote the existence of the labourer.' (p. 23). Communism will not deprive people 'of the power to appropriate the products of society' (p. 24). But communism *will* deprive people 'of the power to subjugate the labour of others by means of such appropriations' (p. 24).

Communism will vanish that view of individuality where an individual is seen as 'no other person than the bourgeois, than the middle-class owner of property' (p. 24), one who monopolizes the social power of wealth produced by the whole society and who transforms individual private property to capitalist private property. Under communism, '*This* person must, indeed, be swept out of the way, and made impossible' (ibid.; italics added). Communism will replace 'the old bourgeois society, with its classes and class antagonisms' with 'an association, in which the free development of each is the condition for the free development of all' (p. 27).

Communism is a society where there is no class exploitation nor is there national or racial oppression:

> In proportion as the exploitation of one individual by another will also be put an end to, the exploitation of one nation by another will also be put an end to. In proportion as the antagonism between classes within the nation vanishes, the hostility of one nation to another will come to an end. (p. 25)

5.4 *Need for Communist Revolution*

Communism can be only achieved by revolution, which is the ultimate point of proletarian class struggle:

> The Communists disdain to conceal their views and aims. They openly declare that their ends can be attained only by the forcible overthrow of all existing social conditions. Let the ruling classes tremble at a Communistic revolution. The proletarians have nothing to lose but their chains. They have a world to win.

Because of the comprehensive vision of change in existing society that drives it, 'The Communist revolution is the most radical rupture with traditional property relations; no wonder that its development involved the most radical rupture with traditional ideas' (p. 26).

Communist revolution – preparation for it – is a process. It does involve fighting for reforms within capitalism. 'The Communists fight for the attainment of the immediate aims, for the enforcement of the momentary interests of the working class' (p. 34). As revolutionists, communists, however, reject the pursuit of reforms as the only and final goal of class struggle. Communists reject those who wish to merely pursue reforms in the economic conditions, the reforms 'that in no respect affect the relations between capital and labour, but, at the best, lessen the cost, and simplify the administrative work, of bourgeois government' (p. 31). They therefore reject reform*ist* approaches according to which communist class struggle is 'destructive' (p. 31). These approaches, called socialist, include the idea that: capitalism can be regulated to redress social grievances;[47] material conditions of existence can be changed by administrative reforms, without the revolutionary abolition of the bourgeois relations of production; small-scale (commercial) production can be promoted to solve society's problems; one should try to 'improve the condition of every member of society, even that of the most favoured' and therefore 'all political, and especially all revolutionary action' should be rejected; and conditions can be improved 'by peaceful means' (p. 32).

The communist approach to the fight for reforms is not reform*ist* because: 'in the movement of the present, they also represent and take care of the future of that movement' (p. 34). In their struggle for reforms within capitalism, 'they bring to the front, as the leading question in each, the property question, no matter what its degree of development at the time.' (p. 34). The aim of the communist class struggle is not merely to get some concessions within capitalism but the 'overthrow of the bourgeois supremacy, conquest of political power by the proletariat' (p. 22) and the establishment of a proletarian state. '[T]he first step in the revolution by the working class is to raise the proletariat to the position of ruling class' (p. 26). This is because, as Marx and Engels write in the Preface to the 1872 German edition after their careful reflection on the experience of the Paris commune, 'the working class cannot simply lay hold of the ready-made state machinery, and wield it for its own purposes'.

47 'A part of the bourgeoisie is desirous of redressing social grievances in order to secure the continued existence of bourgeois society' (p. 31).

The *capitalist* state cannot wither away. It – at least all of its anti-workers or anti-people apparatuses – has to be smashed.[48]

Communist struggle is multi-scalar. But ultimately, it is international or global. The working people have no country, because in all countries they are more or less subjected to capitalist subjugation and misery. 'Since the proletariat must first of all acquire political supremacy, must rise to be the leading class of the nation, must constitute itself *the* nation, it is so far, itself national, though not in the bourgeois sense of the word' (p. 25). So, its struggle initially takes a national form: 'Though not in substance, yet in form, the struggle of the proletariat with the bourgeoisie is at first a national struggle. The proletariat of each country must, of course, first of all settle matters with its own bourgeoisie' (p. 20). And, such a struggle, given Marx's internationalist approach to economy and politics, would have to be *a part of* the multi-scalar, and indeed, international, struggle for communism, because even if successful, a struggle against the capitalist class in one country cannot produce communism in that country isolated from the rest of the world. Communism cannot be established in a single country, poor or rich, given the global character of capitalist production and exchange (and finance).[49]

In some cases, the communists have to fight along with less revolutionary forces, and enter into an alliance with social-democratic forces.[50] But if they do, 'they never cease, for a single instant, to instill into the working class the clearest possible recognition of the hostile antagonism between bourgeoisie and proletariat' (p. 34). So, while communists are the most radical, they oppose

48 This is the point Lenin (1949) developed in his *State and revolution*.

49 We will return to this topic in chapter 6.

50 Marx provides many examples. 'In France, the Communists ally with the Social-Democrats against the conservative and radical bourgeoisie, reserving, however, the right to take up a critical position in regard to phases and illusions traditionally handed down from the great Revolution' (p. 34).

'In Switzerland, they support the Radicals, without losing sight of the fact that this party consists of antagonistic elements, partly of Democratic Socialists, in the French sense, partly of radical bourgeois' (ibid.). 'In Poland, they support the party that insists on an agrarian revolution as the prime condition for national emancipation' (ibid.). 'In Germany, they fight with the bourgeoisie whenever it acts in a revolutionary way, against the absolute monarchy, the feudal squirearchy, and the petty bourgeoisie' (ibid.).

Of course, the idea that the proletariat can fight along with, or support, progressive bourgeois factions against, say, feudal type forces, is a contentious issue. This not only goes against Marx's own principle that the proletarians must maintain their political independence. This also betrays the fact that the bourgeoisie turns to reaction when mass struggle against feudal type forces intensify. On the other hand, when fascism is knocking on the door, the communist forces fighting along with social-democratic workers *within* a united front, this remains a useful tactic.

sectarianism, an advice that is prescient given the extreme disunity among Marxists/communists in the world.[51] Communists, Marx says, 'have no interests separate and apart from those of the proletariat as a whole', nor do they 'set up any sectarian principles of their own, by which to shape and mould the proletarian movement' (p. 22). 'In the national struggles of the proletarians of the different countries', communists 'bring to the front the *common interests* of the entire proletariat, independently of all nationality' (ibid.; italics added). And, 'In the various stages of development which the struggle of the working class against the bourgeoisie has to pass through, they always and everywhere represent the interests of the movement as a whole' (ibid.). 'In short, the Communists everywhere support every revolutionary movement against the existing social and political order of things' (ibid.).

The communist revolution is a sharp break with the existing society, but the construction of communist society will happen in inter-connected 'stages'[52] on the basis of specific measures that the proletariat, the new ruling class, will take.

> The proletariat will use its political supremacy to wrest, by degree, all capital from the bourgeoisie, to centralise all instruments of production in the hands of the State, *i.e.*, of the proletariat organised as the ruling class; and to increase the total productive forces as rapidly as possible. (p. 26)

On taking power the proletariat will make 'despotic inroads on the rights of property, and on the conditions of bourgeois production' and it will do this 'by means of [certain] measures' (p. 26).[53] These measures will, of course, be different in different countries. In the context of most advanced countries, these measures would include: abolition of property in land and application of all rents of land to public purposes; a heavy progressive or graduated income tax; abolition of rights of inheritance; confiscation of the property of all emigrants and rebels; centralisation of credit in the hands of the state, by means

51 On Marx's politics as basically non-sectarian class politics, see Das (2019).

52 These stages are not to be conflated with the democratic revolution stage now and socialist revolution stage in future, where the pre-socialist state presiding over what would effectively be an 'egalitarian' capitalist society is run by the proletarian party for an indefinite period of time.

53 They 'appear economically insufficient and untenable', but 'in the course of the movement', they will 'outstrip themselves, necessitate further inroads upon the old social order, and are unavoidable as a means of entirely revolutionising the mode of production' (p. 26).

of a national bank with State capital and an exclusive monopoly; centralisation of the means of communication and transport in the hands of the State; extension of factories and instruments of production owned by the State; the bringing into cultivation of waste-lands, and the improvement of the soil generally in accordance with a common plan; equal liability of all to work; combination of agriculture with manufacturing industries, and gradual abolition of all the distinction between town and country by a more equable distribution of the populace over the country; free education for all children in public schools, and abolition of children's factory labour in its present form, and so on (pp. 26–27).[54]

5.5 *Who Will Bell the Capitalist Cat?: the Question of Key Revolutionary Agent*[55]

While the proletariat's *interest* is in the communist revolution, who will bring about such a revolution? Many other classes and groups other than the proletariat suffer. Could another class or strata bring about such a revolution? No. Non-proletarian suffering masses cannot be truly revolutionary: 'The lower middle class, the small manufacturer, the shopkeeper, the artisan, the peasant, all these fight against the bourgeoisie, to save from extinction their existence as fractions of the middle class. They are therefore not revolutionary …'.

Sometimes the non-proletarian classes/strata *can be* revolutionary but their revolutionary purpose and action are limited to reproducing capitalism in a modified form, i.e. a capitalism without landlords, usurers, greedy merchants, authoritarian officers/politicians, etc.: 'If by chance, they are revolutionary, they are only so in view of their impending transfer into the proletariat; they thus defend not their present, but their future interests, they desert their own standpoint to place themselves at that of the proletariat' (p. 20).

The proletariat is the only potentially revolutionary class. 'Of all the classes that stand face to face with the bourgeoisie today, the proletariat alone is a really revolutionary class … [T]he proletariat is its special and essential product' (p. 20). Besides, the proletarians have the numbers to their advantage: tendentially, men and women who dominantly depend on wages to

54 Many of these measures apply to the less developed world. Many of these measures have been adopted in, for example, China, where the current state owes its origin to the communist revolution in 1949.

55 This is an important question given that many Marxists (David Harvey, Leo Panitch, Erik Wright, Stephen Resnick and Richard Wolff, among others) do not accept the leading role of the proletariat in the fight against capitalism (for a critique, see Das, 2017b: chapter 4).

live – proletarians – are the majority in most of the large countries. This lends a unique character to the proletarian movement against capitalism:

> All previous historical movements were movements of minorities, or in the interest of minorities. The proletarian movement is the self-conscious, independent movement of the immense majority, in the interest of the immense majority.

The proletariat can meet its needs only under communism. And it is the main agent to fight for that society. There can be no substitute for the proletariat even if the proletariat may have to be allied with independent, non-exploiting small-scale producers of goods and services in rural areas (as Lenin was to emphasize later).

6 Conclusion

The two kinds of knowledge claim in *Manifesto* – propositional/referential and critical-political – remarkably anticipate two things: 1) Marx's and Engels' thinking in their 'mature' work, including in *Capital* Volume 1, 2) many claims of 20th century revolutionary Marxism of Lenin and his legacy. Besides, many claims of *Manifesto* speak to the actuality of the capitalist world as observed in the 20th century and now, to a much larger extent than during the time when it was written. Thus it anticipates the capitalist world of the 20th and 21st centuries rather well. Its claims speak to the processes that had just begun in mid-19th century and are on-going. These claims are schematically presented in the Appendix in extremely brief and empirically corroborable or conceptually defensible forms, reflecting a summary of the foregoing discussion.

Manifesto takes a class approach to society: society should be seen in terms of the exploiting and exploited classes that constitute it. The relations between classes are antagonistic as they involve a) differential control over property (a minority controls property and the majority do not) and b) exploitation of the property-less (or property-poor) by the propertied. Capitalism is a transient form of class society. It is a better society relative to pre-capitalism: it promotes the development of productive forces, it simplifies class structure, and it brings into being a special class (the proletariat) which is the truly revolutionary class: by leading oppressed masses and non-proletarian producers, the proletariat can emancipate itself from capitalism and in the process emancipate all other oppressed classes/strata. The proletarian revolutionary struggle as a process does not exclude the fight for reforms. Yet, the fight for socialism requires more than the fight for reforms. Socialism/communism, which is the aim of proletariat's political struggle, is more than egalitarianism or a few pro-worker policies. Socialism/ communism stands for the abolition of capitalist private property and the overthrow of the capitalist state. The fight for socialism/communism requires working class unity that avoids sectarianism and that is based on principles that are informed by a revolutionary class theory and political economy of society.

Appendix

Selected Theses from The Communist Manifesto

1. People should be seen in terms of classes and not just as people or humans as such.
2. In the context of national oppression, people may be seen in terms of a nation which in turn is seen in terms of the classes that constitute the nation.
3. Classes have antagonistic relations which exist because the class that has control over property (means of production) appropriates surplus product from the class that does not.
4. The class that owns property, more or less, controls political power (i.e. the state) which is the organised power of one class for oppressing another.
5. Antagonistic class relations cause class struggle, but its outcome is not fixed, as it can cause a revolutionary reconstitution of society or the common ruin of classes.
6. One class society changes into another when production relations fetter the development of productive forces, and when the ensuing crisis is accompanied by struggle from below.
7. A form of class society, capitalism is more and more splitting into two hostile classes, i.e. the bourgeoisie, which controls means of production, and the proletariat which does not.
8. Driven by competitive relations, capitalism promotes an immense development of productive forces and potential flourishing of human abilities.
9. Capitalism has caused an agglomeration of production and exchange in a few areas/ countries. The urbanization of capitalism is a part of this agglomerative tendency.
10. It produces uneven development between villages and cities, and between nations.

11. The need to expand markets and the consequent development of transportation and communication technologies contribute to capitalism's globalness.
12. Driven by competition, capitalism experiences crisis of production, which is expressed as the epidemic of 'over-production'.
13. Capitalism seeks to resolve its crisis partly by conquering foreign markets, which advanced countries break open by the artillery of their lower prices (and coercion).
14. Global capitalism has made less developed countries dependent on more developed ones.
15. Capitalism has produced immense cultural impact as it reduces human social relations, including in the family, to the relations based on naked self-interest and cash nexus.
16. By its tendency to constantly revolutionise economic production and ideas, capitalism has quickened the pace of life.
17. There is a general universalization of human interaction, socially and culturally, and not just materially. There is universal inter-dependence among nations.
18. Capitalism has changed consumption of culture and culture of consumption, as people in one country consume material and cultural products from other countries. It is also producing a world literature, of which *Manifesto* itself is an example.
19. By controlling the economy, the capitalist class controls the state. The capitalist state is but a committee for the purpose of managing the common affairs of the bourgeois class.
20. The working class comprises men and women who must sell their ability to work. The bourgeois class depends on the augmentation of capital, which depends on wage labour.
21. The proletariat is recruited from small-scale property owners who cannot compete with capitalist production and whose skills are no longer in demand because of mechanization.
22. The working class has got progressively feminized, partly thanks to mechanization. But at a general level, capital is relatively indifferent to the gender of the workers it exploits.
23. Working men and women are subjected to primary exploitation in the workplace and secondary exploitation outside it (by landlord, the shopkeeper, the pawnbroker, etc.).
24. Capitalists increase extraction of labour by prolonging the working day, by increasing of the work exacted in a given time and by using productivity-enhancing machinery.

25. The work life is not a source of enjoyment because of the extensive use of machinery, which enslaves the worker, and the division of labour causing extreme specialization.
26. Placed under the command of a hired hierarchy of officers in the workplace, workers are subjected to despotic control to increase the amount of work and reduce their resistance.
27. The proletariat is not just a suffering class. The conditions created by capitalism compel it to be a fighting class too.
28. Capitalism impedes working class struggle. Competition for work disunites it. Lumpen elements are hired as capitalist agents.
29. Capitalism also promotes working class struggle by increasing number of workers and concentrating them a few areas/cities and by improved means of communication.
30. Expansion of capitalist production and exchange tend to create similar working class conditions in different places/countries, and this can promote workers' unity.
31. The working-class struggle goes through many stages, pre-trade union struggle, trade union struggle and political struggle against wage-slavery itself.
32. The working-class struggle produces some concessions (e.g. pro-worker laws). But ultimately the aim of the struggle is revolution against capitalist production and exchange.
33. There are non-proletarian classes who also suffer but they cannot be revolutionary against capitalism: these other classes only try to save from extinction and want a better capitalism.
34. The proletariat is the only potentially revolutionary class. Its conditions cannot be durably and significantly improved without the abolition of wage slavery.
35. The fight for reforms is important but it has to be a part of the fight to abolish capitalism, i.e. a part of the fight for communism, a society without class and national exploitation.
36. The construction of communist society can begin only when the proletariat by replacing the capitalist state in a revolutionary process becomes the new ruling class and takes a series of measures, which involve making inroads on capitalist private property.

CHAPTER 3

Marx's *Introduction to Grundrisse*: Primacy of Production over Distribution, Exchange and Consumption

The scope of Marx's *Grundrisse* ('Outlines'), written almost 10 years after *Manifesto*, is widely known to be broader than that of his multi-volume magnum opus, *Capital*. If the explicit focus of *Capital* is on capital (i.e. the logic of capitalist commodity circulation and production, including the crisis-ridden and exploitative accumulation of capital), the *Grundrisse*'s scope can be said to be capital*ism* (i.e. the society – the social totality – dominated by the logic of capital). The *Grundrisse* contains 'the only outline of Marx's full political-economic project', even if presented in a fragmented manner (Nicolaus, 1973b: 7). 'It remains in many ways the most central of Marx's works' (McLellan, 2003: 379).

Marx begins the *Grundrisse* with his famous 'Introduction'[1] which presents three broad themes: fundamental categories in political economy; the role of the producing individual and the relation between economy and extra-economic processes in historical materialism; a map of political economy as a field; and epistemology of political economy. This chapter and its sequel (i.e. chapter 4) deal with the first three themes, respectively. In terms of the first theme (i.e. political economy), on the basis of his dialogue with classical economists (e.g. Ricardo), Marx discusses the economic realm as comprising production, distribution, exchange and also consumption, and their reciprocal interrelations, where the latter include especially the ways in which production relates to other moments of the economic realm.[2]

Chapters 3–4 discuss Marx' ideas about political economy and historical materialism in the 'Introduction' in a slightly more systematic way than he himself does and in a more detailed manner than many of the recent

1 Marx's 'Introduction' to the *Grundrisse* (Marx, 1973) parallels his famous Preface to *Critique of Political economy* (Marx, 1859) in theoretical importance. The 'Introduction' – about 28 pages long in the print edition of the text translated by Nicolaus – is an introduction to Marx's proposed six-volume work on economics (McLellan, 2003: 375).

2 The relation of production to other moments of the economic realm has been a controversial topic.

 | DOI:10.1163/9789004730472_004

commentaries (e.g. David Harvey and Stuart Hall) on the 'Introduction' do.[3] In doing this, the two chapters keep in the background Marx's overall theory of society and of capitalism, recent commentaries on the *Grundrisse*, and certain themes in contemporary Marxism. Also discussed in these two chapters are the implications of Marx's views which he does not adequately develop as his aim was to produce what are merely notebooks for his writings that have ultimately been different volumes of *Capital*. These two chapters also make an attempt to fill the gaps in Marx's own thinking in the 'Introduction' *on the basis* of his own overall approach to society as a totality and to capitalism.

This chapter presents Marx's ideas about the economic realm, including its various moments[4] and their inter-relations. Section 1 discusses production as a moment of the economic realm while sections 2–3 discuss, respectively the elements of the economic realm other than production, and their relation to production. Section 4 discusses the implications of Marx's ideas for the contemporary Marxist debates on the two above-mentioned topics. The final section draws some theoretical implications.

1 Production as a Moment of the Economic Realm

Production is a part of society's economic realm which also includes distribution and exchange. All of these are related to consumption.

> [I]n production the members of society appropriate (create, shape) the products of nature in accord with human needs; distribution determines the proportion in which the individual shares in the product; exchange delivers the particular products into which the individual desires to convert the portion which distribution has assigned to him. (Marx, 1973: 22)

And, 'finally, in consumption, the products become objects of [individual] gratification, of individual appropriation' (ibid.). How are each of these moments of the totality of the economic realm and their interconnectedness to be conceptualized?

---

3 The *Grundrisse*, like another important text, *German Ideology*, was left in a draft form (Marx, 1968). It was not meant for publication.

4 To Marx, the historical materialist, movement, or change, 'is the only constant', so he, like Hegel, uses the term 'moment' to refer to what in a system at rest would be called 'element' or 'factor'. In Marx the term carries the senses both of 'period of time' and of 'force of a moving mass' (Nicolaus, 1973: 29). For Marx, 'moment' is, however, more historical than for Hegel (ibid.).

Production refers to the fact that human beings interacting with one another and working on/with products that are directly or indirectly derived from nature produce use-values to meet their needs. Their needs are subsistence needs or productive needs (e.g. need for a machine to help produce food).[5]

'[T]o talk about production at all we must either pursue the process of historic development through its different phases', or we deal with 'a specific historic epoch such as e.g. modern bourgeois production' (ibid.: 19). To the extent that in the history of humanity, production develops through various epochs, 'all epochs of production have certain common traits, common characteristics' (ibid.). These common traits are those that the more developed forms of production share with the less developed forms, just as 'the most developed languages have laws and characteristics in common with the least developed' (ibid.). '*Production in general* is an abstraction' but it is a fruitful abstraction – 'a rational abstraction in so far as it really brings out and fixes the common element and thus saves us repetition' (ibid.).

One common trait of production across all forms of human society (classless and class societies and different forms of class society) is that production, seen as a labour process, is a universal need: all societies must perform productive work because of the nature-imposed necessity to produce the conditions of life, no matter what sorts of social relations of production they live under. And, productive work or production is not possible without instruments of work or instruments of production. 'No production [is] possible without an instrument of production, even if this instrument is only the hand' (ibid.). In other words, 'No production [is possible] without stored-up, past labour, even if it is only the facility gathered together and concentrated in the hand of the savage by repeated practice' (ibid.).[6] In the *capitalist* form of production, which is only a historically specific form of production, the following principle applies: 'Capital is, among other things, also an instrument of production, also objectified, past labour. Therefore capital is a general, eternal relation of nature [only] … if I leave out just the specific quality which alone makes "instrument of production" and "stored-up labour" into capital' (Marx, 1973: 19).

Another common trait, related to the previous two traits is that production is a material act: it involves metabolic (reciprocal) relation with nature, and therefore appropriation of use-values from nature aimed at meeting human

5 Subsistence needs are material (e.g. need for food) and non-material or cultural.

6 Production seen as universal labour process is the production of use-values, and has three components in all forms of society: 'work itself', 'the subject of that work' (e.g. raw materials and energy, etc.), and 'its instruments' (Marx, 1887: 127). These 'simple elements remain common to all social forms of development' (Marx, 1894: 631).

needs. Indeed 'All production is appropriation of nature on the part of an individual within and through a specific form of society' (Marx, 1973: 21). '[T]he labour-process is solely a process between [people] and Nature', Marx (1894: 631). Human body is a part of nature, and what are considered the subject and instruments of work are derived from nature directly or otherwise.

The fourth element of production across epochs is the fact that the material act of production is also a social act: it is based on [objective] social relations. Indeed, production is always 'production by social individuals' (ibid.: 18). Because production is social, it is historical, as human beings progressive alter social relations as well as productive forces including natural conditions to be able to better meet their needs. Like society as such, its specific moment, i.e. production, develops historically. It goes through stages of development. Production always means 'production at a definite stage of social development' (ibid.).

The fact that production is a historical process demands that it be analyzed historically: the common element that characterizes production must be 'sifted out by comparison' (p. 19), a process that will show that 'Some determinations [of production] belong to all epochs, others only to a few. [Some] determinations will be shared by the most modern epoch and the most ancient' (ibid.). In other words: those things which determine the changes in production over time, 'i.e. the elements which are not general and common, must be separated out from the determinations valid for production as such', i.e. production in general (p. 19). In this way we can analyze the *different* aspects of production, 'in their unity' (i.e. the unity of general and historically-specific aspects – determinations – of production) which does not ignore 'their essential difference' (ibid.).

Such a procedure will also ensure that the existence of a present-day society be not projected 'into the past' (p. 17), even if elements of the present-day society were present in past societies. However, non-Marxist scholars deviate from this principle: 'The whole profundity of those modern economists who demonstrate the eternity and harmoniousness of the existing social relations lies in this forgetting' (p. 19). Indeed, in the analysis of economic traits of society, including production, property, etc., '*bourgeois* relations are ... quietly smuggled in as the inviolable natural laws on which society in the abstract is founded' (p. 19).

'Production is always a *particular* branch of production – e.g. agriculture, cattle-raising, manufactures etc. – or it is a *totality*', i.e. the sum total of productive activities in all the branches (p. 19). Production means production of means of production and production of means of subsistence. Economic development depends on, and economic development means, the former, and shapes the latter. And economic development is the development of productive forces and associated rise in labour productivity per hour.

Production – or economic development in general – is an uneven process. The unevenness of the economic realm, including productive forces and production relations, is relative to the development of culture. The unevenness in the economic realm is also geographical. For example, different areas specialize in the production of different things, and different areas development their productive forces differently.[7] Geographical unevenness is also at the global scale (e.g. unevenness between the US and Europe). This is mediated by, for example, the 'Influence of means of communication' (p. 42). In all forms of society, means of communication are important. This is especially so in societies dominated by capitalist commodity exchange. Marx has more to say about this later in *Grundrisse*, i.e. after his 'Introduction' (p. 449):

> The more production comes to rest on exchange value, hence on exchange, the more important do the physical conditions of exchange – the means of communication and transport – become for the costs of circulation. Capital by its nature drives beyond every spatial barrier. Thus the creation of the physical conditions of exchange – of the means of communication and transport – the annihilation of space by time – becomes an extraordinary necessity for it.

Means of communication help realization (sale of things produced), and means of communication themselves become a direct medium of realization (when road construction becomes an outlet for the sale of cement). Marx thus goes on to add:

> Only in so far as the direct product can be realized in distant markets in mass quantities in proportion to reductions in the transport costs, and only in so far as at the same time the means of communication and transport themselves can yield spheres of realization for labour, driven by capital; only in so far as commercial traffic takes place in massive volume … *only to that extent is the production of cheap means of communication and transport a condition for production based on capital, and promoted by it for that reason.* (ibid.; italics added)

7 We will return to the question of geographical unevenness, including in chapter 9.

And because all the countries exchanging their products within the world market are increasingly integrated, in part thanks to the means of communication across countries, humanity's history is increasingly world history but 'World history has not always existed; history as world history a result' (p. 42).

There is not just unevenness in the sense that not all places experience the same or similar level of the development of capitalist production. Development is also combined – the past relations coexist, and interact with, present relations within a social formation that is dominantly capitalist: in 'bourgeois society ..., relations derived from earlier forms will often be found within it only in an entirely stunted form, or even travestied. For example, communal property' (Marx, 1973: 38). Or, one can add feudal relations, as another example.

There are '*general preconditions* of all production', i.e. 'the conditions without which production is not possible' (p. 20). Then there are 'the conditions which promote production to a greater or lesser degree' (p. 20). These conditions could include, as mainstream thinkers recognize, 'locations, climates, natural conditions such as harbours, soil fertility etc.' (ibid.).[8] But emphasizing these general conditions is not enough. One 'would require investigations into the periodization of *degrees of productivity* in the development of individual peoples' in relation to such social processes as 'competition, accumulation etc.' (p. 20).[9] Society produces things, and society produces relations of production too under which production can only occur as a social activity.[10]

When the idea that all production requires instruments of production and producing human beings is combined with the idea that production can only happen under certain social relations (including specific distribution of means

8 'This too amounts to the tautology that wealth is more easily created where its elements [such as natural conditions] are subjectively and objectively present to a greater degree.' (Marx, 1973: 20).

9 'Production for value and surplus-value implies, as has been shown in the course of our analysis, the constantly operating tendency to reduce the labour-time necessary for the production of a commodity, i.e., its value, below the actually prevailing social average. The pressure to reduce cost-price to its minimum becomes the strongest lever for raising the social productiveness of labour, which, however, appears here only as a continual increase in the productiveness of capital' (Marx, 1894: 630).

10 Marx makes this point in *Capital* Volume 3 and *Capital* volume 1, respectively: 'if the capitalist mode of production presupposes [a] definite social form of the conditions of production, so does it reproduce it continually. It produces not merely the material products, but reproduces continually the production relations in which the former are produced, and thereby also the corresponding distribution relations' (Marx, 1894: 629).

'Capitalist production ... produces not only commodities, not only surplus-value, but it also produces and reproduces the capitalist relation; on the one side the capitalist, on the other the wage labourer' (Marx, 1887: 405).

of production), an important conclusion follows: this is the '*Dialectic of the concepts productive force* (*means of production*) *and relation of production*', a dialectic 'which does not suspend the real difference' between the two concepts (productive forces and productive relations) (ibid.: 42).[11] And this is a dialectic 'whose boundaries are to be determined' (ibid.).

This is an important point which Marx however does not explain in the 'Introduction'. It is possible to say that these above-mentioned boundaries are conceptual and geographical. Conceptual in the sense that while given production relations promote further development of productive forces, those relations can also act as barriers to such development, when the level of development goes beyond a certain level. And geographical in the sense that the dialectic is a multi-scalar dialectic and ultimately global: the relations between productive forces and relations must be ultimately examined at the global level. This means that whether economic development has created conditions for a particular set of social relations (e.g. socialist relations) cannot be judged on a nation-by-nation basis, but globally. This is why Marx could say in a different context that, for example, a given country (e.g. Russia of his time) as a part of a world-system of countries does not have to go through capitalism (separation of direct producers from the means of production) if productive forces are developed to a sufficient level elsewhere to support the socialist transition in that country. 'It is only thanks to the contemporaneity of capitalist production that it [that given country] can appropriate from it all its positive acquisitions without passing through its hideous vicissitudes' (Marx, 1881).

Production is often related to property relations, which are related to social relations of production. As we have seen, 'All production is appropriation of nature on the part of an individual' within given social relations (Marx, 1973: 21). Production involves appropriation which implies property (relations of control): there cannot be 'An appropriation which does not make something into property' (p. 21). So, 'it is a tautology to say that property (appropriation) is a precondition of production' or that 'there can be no production and hence no society where some form of property does not exist' (ibid.). As well, one cannot also assume private property is always necessary for production to exist and flourish. It is correct to say that all production involves property. But it is wrong to leap from this idea to the idea that all property is private property. 'History rather shows common property (e.g. in India, among the Slavs, the early Celts, etc.) to be the more original form, a form which long continues to play a significant role' (ibid.). It is also wrong to assume that private property is

---

11 On this dialectic, see chapter 5.

necessarily capitalist or bourgeois private property. Indeed, it is not acceptable that '*bourgeois* relations are … quietly smuggled in as the inviolable natural laws on which society in the abstract is founded' (p. 20). And, then there is the 'question whether wealth develops better in this or another form of property' (p. 21). This implies that certain property relations may promote development and other relations do not do so, at a given point in time and in a given place.

Production, along with the relations of production, exists at multiple levels (this idea is only implicit in the 'Introduction'). These levels are: all societies; all class societies (appropriation of the surplus product from direct producers thus causing their exploitation); and capitalist class society, where exploitation takes the form of the appropriation of surplus *value*.[12] At the level of all societies (society as such), production involves metabolic interaction with nature and social interaction among people to produce the things society needs. At the level of class societies, production involves the distinction between necessary and surplus labour. This is the fact that on the one hand the direct producers receive a quantity of food and other means of subsistence 'which makes it possible for them to exist' as direct producers, and on the other hand, the direct producers also produce surplus product (a product of surplus labour) that goes into the hands of the ruling class which continuously appropriates the surplus product (Marx, 1973: 21). At the level of capitalist class society based on market relations, which is the most developed form of society based on class antagonisms, surplus labour takes the form of surplus value.

Capitalism is preceded by different social forms of production (different forms of class society). Concepts that apply to, and reflect, bourgeois society including production, exchange, etc. shed light on pre-capitalist economies:

> Bourgeois society is the most developed and the most complex historic organization of production. The categories which express its relations, the comprehension of its structure, thereby also allows insights into the structure and the relations of production of all the vanished social formations out of whose ruins and elements it built itself up, whose partly still unconquered remnants are carried along within it, whose mere nuances have developed explicit significance within it. (Marx, 1973: 38)[13]

12 On the details about the levels of generality in class analysis and historical materialism, see Das (2017b: 212–248).

13 There is a general lesson here: 'Human anatomy contains a key to the anatomy of the ape. The intimations of higher development among the subordinate animal species, however, can be understood only after the higher development is already known. The bourgeois economy thus supplies the key to the ancient, etc. But not at all in the manner of those

2 Distribution, Exchange and Consumption as Moments of the Economic Realm

Just as production is the production of means of production and of means of subsistence, similarly, distribution is the distribution of means of production and of means of subsistence. Distribution in the first sense – the distribution of means of production – is a part of production itself. Distribution in the second sense – distribution of means of subsistence – is a process that divides the total social product produced in the society according to social laws. Distribution determines the proportion in which the individual shares in the product.

The process of distribution in the first sense conditions which social groups get what and how (and where – town and country, etc.). Like production, the process of distribution undergoes changes over time. These changes have some underlying common traits.[14] The common characteristics of distribution across epochs lie in the fact that, for example, and as already mentioned, the direct producers, 'the slave, the serf and the wage labourer' receive a quantity of food and other means of subsistence 'which makes it possible for them to exist as slaves, as serfs, as wage labourers' (Marx, 1973: 21). Similarly, 'The conqueror who lives from tribute, or the official who lives from taxes, or the landed proprietor and his rent, or the monk and his alms, or the Levite and his tithe, all receive a quota of social production, which is determined by other laws than that of the slave's, etc.' (ibid.).

Exchange is another moment of the economic realm. Exchange is a process that 'delivers the particular products into which the individual desires to convert the portion which distribution has assigned to [them]', so exchange parcels out the already divided shares of the social product in accord with individual needs (p. 22). What is called circulation itself is 'exchange regarded in its totality' (p. 32).

Consumption has two forms: subjective and objective. Consumption is the consumption of the means of subsistence (e.g. food) to reproduce people.[15] '[T]he individual not only develops his abilities in production, but also expends

economists who smudge over all historical differences and see bourgeois relations in all forms of society.' (Marx, 1973: 38).

14 With respect to distribution, Marx says: 'it must be possible here also, just as with production, to single out common characteristics, and just as possible to confound or to extinguish all historic differences under *general human* laws.' (Marx, 1973: 21).

15 Strictly speaking, consumption is 'extra-economic' to a certain extent: '[C]onsumption, which is conceived not only as a terminal point but also as an end-in-itself, actually belongs outside economics except in so far as it reacts in turn upon the point of departure and initiates the whole process anew' (Marx, 1973: 23).

them, uses them up in the act of production, just as natural procreation is a consumption of life forces' (p. 23). Consumption is also the 'consumption of the means of production, which become worn out through use, and are partly (e.g. in combustion) dissolved into their elements again' (p. 24). Productive consumption refers to the 'consumption of the raw material, which loses its natural form and composition by being used up. The act of production is therefore in all its moments also an act of consumption' (ibid.). And a given item of final consumption can of course be an item of productive consumption.[16]

3 Production's Primacy over Other Moments of the Economic Realm

All the different moments of the economic realm influence one another. However, production and its relations influence distribution, exchange and consumption more than the latter influence the former.

3.1 *Production and Consumption*

'Production ... is also immediately consumption, consumption is also immediately production. Each is immediately its opposite' (Marx, 1973: 24). As we have seen, consumption is productive (e.g. consumption of raw materials in a factory) and final or private (e.g. eating food), or 'consumption proper' (ibid.). '[A] mediating movement takes place between the two': 'Production ... creates the latter's material; without it, consumption would lack an object' (if no food is produced, there is no food to consume), and consumption 'alone creates for the products the subject for whom they are products' (p. 24). 'Without production, no consumption; but also, without consumption, no production; since production would then be purposeless' (Marx, 1973: 25).

Marx appears to elevate the importance of consumption to the status of production in at least two ways.[17] First, 'A product becomes a real product only by being consumed. For example, a garment becomes a real garment only in the act of being worn; a house where no one lives is in fact not a real house' (p. 25). 'A railway on which no trains run, hence which is not used up, not consumed, is a railway only [as a] potential and not in reality' (p. 24). Thus 'the product, unlike a mere natural object, proves itself to be, *becomes*, a product only through consumption' (p. 25). '[T]he product is production not as objectified activity, but rather only as object for the active subject'; 'consumption

16 'A product, though ready for immediate consumption, may yet serve as raw material for a further product, as grapes when they become the raw material for wine' (Marx, 1887: 129).

17 'Consumption produces production in a double way' (Marx, 1973: 25).

creates the need for *new* production' (p. 25). 'Consumption creates the motive for production; it also creates the object which is active in production as its determinant aim' (ibid.). Marx *seems* to under-emphasize the fact that while final consumption is not an un-important moment, it is the case that in capitalism, the driving force behind production is *not* final consumption, but profit-making.

Second, 'Consumption is ... immediately production' in the sense that every kind of consumption ... in one way or another produces human beings in some particular aspect' (p. 24).[18] For example, 'in taking in food, ... which is a form of consumption, the human being produces [their] own body' (ibid.). In the sphere of private consumption, society produces the bodies – reproduce the existing body of workers – through processes that material production does not control in all its details.[19]

While appearing to over-emphasize consumption, Marx hastens to add that: '[T]his consumptive production – even though it is an immediate unity of production and consumption – is essentially different from production proper' (p. 24). He also brings to attention two aspects of the relation between production and consumption that suggest that production has primacy over consumption seen as final consumption. Firstly, transhistorically, one cannot consume anything if it has not been produced: it is production that 'furnishes the material and the object for consumption' (p. 25). 'Consumption without an object is not consumption; therefore, in this respect, production creates, produces consumption' (p. 25). Secondly, 'the object is not the only thing [e.g. food] which production creates for consumption' (ibid.). 'Production also gives consumption its specificity, its character' (p. 25). 'The object [that is consumed] is not an object in general, but a specific object which must be consumed in a specific manner, to be mediated in its turn by production itself' (p. 25). 'Hunger

18 This is similar to a process in nature where 'the consumption of the elements and chemical substances is the production of the plant.' (ibid.).

19 The body that is reproduced is only partly material. There are all sorts of ideological-material aspects of the body and its reproduction, including the 'domestic' labour needed to reproduce the body, the associated division of labour and exhaustions of reproductive work, the conception of the reproductive work and of women on the shoulders of whom much of this work has traditionally fallen, and so on. And all these aspects cannot be *reduced to* the logic of capitalist production even though they cannot be un-impacted by that logic.

It can also be said that the significance of private or subjective consumption (consumption of food) itself changes from one mode of production to another: in a slave society reproduction of people working as direct producers (e.g. slaves) is an act of production because slaves are a part of the constant capital like coal is. This is generally not the case in capitalism: reproduction of labour power is more or less outside the direct control of production and its relations (Fine, 1980).

is hunger, but the hunger gratified by cooked meat eaten with a knife and fork is a different hunger from that which bolts down raw meat with the aid of hand, nail and tooth', and whether hunger is met this or that way depends on production and on the distribution of products which is ultimately determined by production. Indeed, 'Production thus produces not only the object but also the manner of consumption, not only objectively but also subjectively' (p. 25). 'Production thus creates the consumer', the subject of consumption (ibid.).

Implicit in Marx's discussion in 'Introduction' is the labour aspect of consumption which he develops in *Capital* volume 3. For the reproduction of the body and production of things, society consumes different kinds of product which are produced by different kinds of labour (see Table 3.1). One part of subjective or reproductive consumption is at the *individual level*: this is the consumption of means of subsistence such as food by both direct producers and the ruling classes. Another part of subjective or reproductive consumption is at a *collective level* (e.g. driving on city roads, and such roads have to be produced too by labour). Different from subjective consumption is the productive consumption (using machines in a factory which need to be produced by labour). All these types of consumption correspond to three types of labour.[20]

TABLE 3.1 Types of consumption and labour

Types of consumption	Types of labour involved in production
Workers' individual consumption (e.g. food at home)	Necessary labour
Workers' collective consumption (e.g. roads and parks)	Surplus labour
Private consumption by the ruling class	Surplus labour
Productive consumption by the ruling class (e.g. use of machines or labour power in a factory)	Necessary & surplus labour

20 As Marx (1894: 628) says in *Capital* volume 3: if we assume 'some form of social production to exist', we can make 'a distinction ... between that portion of labour whose product is directly consumed individually by the producers and their families and ... that portion of labour which is invariably surplus-labour, whose product serves constantly to satisfy the general social needs no matter how this surplus product may be divided, and no matter who may function as representative of these social needs'; apart from these two types, there is 'the part [of the socially produced product] which is productively consumed', i.e. consumed inside the realm of production as instruments and raw materials, etc.

3.2 *Production and Distribution*

The process of distribution refers to the distribution of means of production and distribution of means of subsistence. 'A change in distribution changes production' (Marx, 1973: 33). Changes in production include social and spatial: for example, 'concentration of capital' and 'different distribution of the population between town and country, etc.', respectively (ibid.).

The distribution of the means of production is a part of production. Distribution of the means of production in this sense is a process that divides the total social product produced in the realm of production according to social laws. Distribution, which is a precondition for production, changes. 'The application of machinery, for example, changed the distribution of instruments of production as well as of products. Modern large-scale landed property is itself the product of modern commerce and of modern industry, as well as of the application of the latter to agriculture' (p. 30).

'As regards whole societies, distribution [of means of production] seems to precede production and to determine it in yet another respect, almost as if it were a pre-economic fact' (p. 29). Often this production-determining distribution of means of production that exists in a particular epoch is an extra-economic fact. For example, 'A conquering people divides the land among the conquerors, thus imposes a certain distribution and form of property in land, and thus determines production. Or it enslaves the conquered and so makes slave labour the foundation of production' (ibid.).[21] To give another example: 'a people rises in revolution and smashes the great landed estates into small parcels, and hence, by this new distribution, gives production a new character' (p. 29). Or 'a system of laws assigns property in land to certain families in perpetuity, or distributes labour [as] a hereditary privilege and thus confines it within certain castes' (ibid.). 'In all these cases, ... *it seems that* distribution is not structured and determined by production, but rather the opposite, production by distribution' (ibid.; italics added). This appearance is deceptive. This is because: 'before distribution can be the distribution of products' to be consumed by people, distribution is: '(1) the distribution of the instruments of production, and (2), which is a further specification of the same relation,

---

21 'In all cases of conquest, three things are possible. The conquering people subjugates the conquered under its own mode of production (e.g. the English in Ireland in this century, and partly in India); or it leaves the old mode intact and contents itself with a tribute (e.g. Turks and Romans); or a reciprocal interaction takes place whereby something new, a synthesis, arises (the Germanic conquests, in part). In all cases, the mode of production, whether that of the conquering people, that of the conquered, or that emerging from the fusion of both, is decisive for the new distribution which arises' (Marx, 1973: 30–31).

the distribution of the members of the society among the different kinds of production' (p. 29).[22]

Distribution determines the proportion in which the individual shares in the product. 'The structure of distribution is completely determined by the structure of production. Distribution is itself a product of production, not only in its object, in that only the results of production can be distributed, but also in its form, in that the specific kind of participation in production determines the specific forms of distribution, i.e. the pattern of participation in distribution' (p. 28). For example, 'An individual who participates in production in the form of wage labour shares in the products, in the results of production, in the form of wages' (28).

Marx further develops the idea about the relation between production and distribution in *Capital* volume 3. Distribution of products is determined by the distribution of means of production and by overall dynamics of production proper in capitalist society:

> The new value added by the annual newly added labour ... is ... split into three parts, which assume three different forms of revenue, into forms which express one portion of this value as belonging or falling to the share of the owner of labour-power, another portion to the owner of capital, and a third portion to the owner of landed property. These, then, are relations, or forms of distribution, for they express the relations under which the newly produced total value is distributed among the owners of the various production factors. (Marx, 1894: 628)

Scientific analysis of the capitalist mode of production demonstrates not only that the production relations of capitalism correspond to 'historically

22 This is the 'Subsumption of the individuals under specific relations of production' (Marx, 1973: 29).

'The distribution of products is evidently only a result of this distribution, which is comprised within the process of production itself and determines the structure of production. To examine production while disregarding this internal distribution within it is obviously an empty abstraction; while conversely, the distribution of products follows by itself from this distribution which forms an original moment of production' (Marx, 1973: 29–30).

'[T]he relation between this production-determining distribution, and production, belongs evidently within production itself. If it is said that, since production must begin with a certain distribution of the instruments of production, it follows that distribution', which is historically created 'at least in this sense precedes and forms the presupposition of production' (Marx, 1973: 30).

determined mode of production', but also that 'the distribution relations essentially coincident with these production relations are their opposite side, so that both share the same historically transitory character.' (ibid.).

'In the study of distribution relations, the initial point of departure is the *alleged* fact that the annual product is apportioned among wages, profit and rent. But if so expressed, it is a misstatement' (Marx, 1894: 628; italics added). The reason is that: 'The product is apportioned on one side to capital, on the other to revenue. One of these revenues, wages, never itself assumes the form of revenue, revenue of the labourer, until it has first confronted this labourer in the form of capital [variable capital]' (pp. 628–629). As mentioned earlier, distribution is the distribution of 'produced conditions of labour and of the products of labour' but the latter are forms of capital (p. 629). 'The confrontation of produced conditions of labour and of the products of labour generally, as capital, with the direct producers implies from the outset a definite social character of the material conditions of labour in relation to the labourers, and thereby a definite relationship into which they enter with the owners of the means of production and among themselves during production itself' (p. 629). Simply put, 'If one portion of the product were not transformed into capital, the other would not assume the forms of wages, profit and rent' (ibid.: 629).

Just as wage is not merely a distribution category, 'profit is [also] not a mere distribution category of the individually consumable product' (Marx, 1894: 631). 'The entire process of capitalist production is ... regulated by the prices of the products. But the regulating prices of production are themselves in turn regulated by the equalisation of the rate of profit and its corresponding distribution of capital among the various social spheres of production' (ibid.). Therefore, '*Profit ... appears here as the main factor*, not of the distribution of products, but of their production itself, as a factor in the distribution of capitals and labour itself among the various spheres of production'. (Marx, 1894: 631; italics added).[23]

In considering 'the so-called distribution relations themselves' one can say that: 'The wage presupposes wage-labour, and profit – capital. These definite forms of distribution thus presuppose definite social characteristics of production conditions, and definite social relations of production agents. The specific

23 As well, 'The division of profit into profit of enterprise and interest appears as the distribution of the same revenue. But it arises, to begin with, from the development of capital as a self-expanding value, a creator of surplus-value, i.e., from this specific social form of the prevailing process of production. It evolves credit and credit institutions out of itself, and thereby the form of production. As interest, etc., the ostensible distribution forms enter into the price as determining production factors' (Marx, 1894: 631).

distribution relations are thus merely the expression of the specific historical *production* relations' (Marx, 1894: 631; italics added). Distribution relations are not independent of production relations. Much rather, 'The so-called distribution relations correspond to and arise from historically determined specific social forms of the process of production and mutual relations entered into by [people] in the reproduction process of human life'. (p. 631).[24]

Similarly, 'Ground-rent might *seem to be* a mere form of distribution, because landed property as such does not perform any, or at least any normal, function in the process of production itself'. Such an appearance is deceptive, for it is because of the capitalist mode of production that 'rent is limited to the excess above the average profit, and that 2) the landlord is reduced from the manager and master of the process of production and of the entire process of social life to the position of mere lessor of land, usurer in land and mere collector of rent' (Marx, 1894: 631; italics added).[25]

What is merely a distributional approach to society views society as a terrain of conflict over what/who gets what part of the social product, i.e. conflict over exploitation as expressed in an inverse relationship between what the exploiting class received and what the direct producers receive (e.g. profits vs wages) But profits are derived from production itself. So distribution between profits and wages is ultimately derived from production and its relations. Wages are advanced as a precondition for production, and profits, as the form of surplus value in exchange, are the result of production, itself a conflict between capital and labour over the labour process. So distributional relations are not primarily a conflict over the shares of the social product. Distribution relations are the result of a conflict between classes over *production.*

There are two meanings of distribution, as mentioned earlier: distribution proper, and distribution as a part of production. Distribution of means of production 'differs altogether' from the distribution of 'the product which goes into individual consumption' (Marx, 1894: 629). 'The latter – distribution of means of consumption (and of exchange value – money – needed to access the means of consumption) – is distribution proper' (ibid.).

---

24 'The historical character of these distribution relations is the historical character of production relations, of which they express merely one aspect. Capitalist distribution differs from those forms of distribution which arise from other modes of production, and every form of distribution disappears with the specific form of production from which it is descended and to which it corresponds' (p. 631).

25 'The fact that landed property assumes forms which permit the capitalist mode of operation in agriculture is a product of the specific character of this mode of production' (Marx, 1894: 631).

The relations of distribution of means of production,

> on the contrary, are the basis of special social functions performed within the production relations by certain of their agents, as opposed to the direct producers. They imbue the conditions of production themselves and their representatives with a specific social quality. They determine the entire character and the entire movement of production. (ibid.)

3.3 *Production and Exchange*

Exchange is the process that 'parcels out the already divided shares of the social product in accord with individual needs' (Marx, 1973: 22). 'Exchange appears as independent of and indifferent to production only in the final phase where the product is exchanged directly for consumption.' (Marx, 1973: 32). But this appearance is also deceptive.

First of all, 'there is no exchange without division of labour, whether the latter is spontaneous, natural, or already a product of historic development'; second, 'private exchange presupposes private production', and third; 'the intensity of exchange, as well as its extension and its manner, are determined by the development and structure of production' (p. 32). Whether exchange is the exchange between areas (e.g. 'Exchange between town and country') or between individuals and between groups of individuals, exchange in all its moments is determined by production (ibid.).

Certain aspects of exchange itself are a part of production. As we have seen, '*exchange* is merely a moment mediating between production with its production-determined distribution on one side and consumption on the other', and in so far as this is the case, exchange itself 'appears as a moment of production', i.e. it is 'a moment within the latter' (p. 32). So exchange has a productive moment (when one buys fertilizers to produce food for sale) and a consumptive moment (when one buys a painting for one's living room), with the latter ultimately being determined by production.

Exchange relates to, and is determined by, production in three ways. First, 'the exchange of activities and abilities which takes place within production': exchange involving raw materials, for example, 'itself belongs directly to production and essentially constitutes it'. Second, the same holds ... for the exchange of products, in so far as that exchange is the means of finishing the product, (for example, buying fertilizers to produce food), 'and making it fit for direct consumption. To that extent, exchange is an act comprised within production itself'. Third, 'the so-called exchange between dealers and dealers is by its very organization entirely determined by production, as well as being itself a producing activity' (p. 32).

Exchange is a process in which all individuals participate unlike in production. In the exchange between capital and labour, labour gives more than it gets, and this extra value that capital gets is produced within the production process, and without the possibility of that extra value, there will be no capitalist exchange with labour. Contrary to the ideology of freedom of exchange, exchange is coerced (people are forced to produce more than what they get in the form of wages in the process of exchange). Whether the subjects know it or not is a different matter.

3.4 *Primacy of Production*

The economic realm comprises four moments: 'Production creates the objects which correspond to the given needs; distribution divides them up according to social laws; exchange further parcels out the already divided shares (e.g. the total wage of the wage laborer) in accord with individual needs' (ibid.: 22). And, 'in consumption, the product steps outside this social movement and becomes a direct object and servant of individual need, and satisfies it in being consumed' (ibid.). All in all, production, distribution, exchange and consumption are not identical, but 'they all form the members of a totality, distinctions within a unity' (p. 32). As in any organic whole, 'Mutual interaction takes place between the different moments' (33). This inter-connection can be seen from the standpoint of labour:

> Every child knows ... that the masses of products [that are produced] corresponding to the different needs [of consumption] required different and quantitatively determined masses of the total labor of society. That this *necessity* of the *distribution* of social labor in definite proportions cannot possibly be done away with by a *particular form* of social production but can only change the *mode* of its *appearance*, is self-evident. ... And the form in which this proportional distribution of labor asserts itself, in the state of society where the interconnection of social labor is manifested in the *private exchange* of the individual products of labor, is precisely the *exchange value* of these products. (Marx, 1868)

It is true that '*in its one-sided form*, production is itself determined by the other moments. For example if the market, i.e. the sphere of exchange, expands, then production grows in quantity and the divisions between its different branches become deeper. A change in distribution changes production, e.g. concentration of capital, different distribution of the population between town and country, etc. Finally, the needs of consumption determine production' (p. 33).

Yet, the fact of the matter is that: 'Production *predominates* ... over the other moments' (p. 32; italics added). 'That exchange and consumption cannot be predominant is self-evident. Likewise, distribution as distribution of products; while as distribution of the agents of production it is itself a moment of production. A definite production thus determines a definite consumption, distribution and exchange as well as *definite relations between these different moments*' (pp. 32–33). The dominance of distribution, consumption and exchange over production is only an appearance.

This appearance is deceptive, including in relation to the relation between production and exchange. Exchange is the most immediate aspect of economy, so to many, exchange is the site of market failure causing crisis – for example crisis happens when trade unions push wages above the level at which there is an equilibrium between supply and demand in the labour market. Similarly, less developed countries are considered to be exploited mainly in the realm of exchange: through unequal trade (Brenner, 1977). As we have seen, such exchange-based views are mistaken.

Not only does production determine other moments of the economic realm. It is also the case that in a given society, one type or form production (including in terms of the nature of means of production used and the purpose of production, etc.) dominates over other form.

> In all forms of society there is one specific kind of production which predominates over the rest, whose relations thus assign rank and influence to the others. It is a general illumination which bathes all the other colours and modifies their particularity. It is a particular ether which determines the specific gravity of every being which has materialized within it. (pp. 39–40)

Consider the following examples (pp. 39–40). 'Certain forms of tillage occur among [pastoralists].... Landed property is determined by this. It is held in common, and retains this form to a greater or lesser degree according to the greater or lesser degree of attachment displayed by these peoples to their tradition, e.g. the communal property of the Slavs'. Consider now settled agriculture which is a 'great step' forward from pastoral production: 'Among peoples with a settled agriculture ... where this predominates, as in antiquity and in the feudal order, even industry, together with its organization and the forms of property corresponding to it, has a more or less landed-proprietary character; is either completely dependent on it, as among the earlier Romans, or, as in the Middle Ages, imitates, within the city and its relations, the organization of the land'. Consider the Middle Ages where capital exists to a degree. Even then, 'In the Middle Ages, capital itself – apart from pure money-capital – in the form of the traditional artisans' tools etc., has this landed-proprietary character'. However, in contrast, 'In bourgeois society ... [land-based production such as farming] more and more becomes merely a branch of industry, and is entirely dominated by capital. Ground rent likewise. In all forms where landed property rules, the natural relation [is] still predominant. In those where capital rules, the social, historically created element' (pp. 39–40). If in a society, different social relations or social forms of production coexist, one type generally dominates:

> Capital is the all-dominating economic power of bourgeois society. It must form the starting-point as well as the finishing-point, and must be dealt with before landed property. After both have been examined in particular, their interrelation must be examined. (p. 40)

This implies that, for example, 'Ground rent cannot be understood without capital. But capital can certainly be understood without ground rent' (p. 40).

Marx draws attention to production's unevenness. There is not just unevenness in the sense that not all places experience the same or similar level of the development of capitalist production. It is also the case that: in 'bourgeois society', says Marx, 'relations derived from earlier forms will often be found within it only in an entirely stunted form, or even travestied. For example, communal property' (Marx, 1973: 38). Or, one can add feudal relations, as another example.

The dialectical Marx sees production in terms of a dialectical relation between productive forces and relations (Marx, 1973: 42), relates production to moments of economy other than production (private consumption; distribution of product, exchange of in terms for personal consumption, etc.). This allows him to provide conceptual maps of society, which should be understood in the light of his points about culture (including art) discussed earlier.

According to one such conceptual map presented in his 'Introduction' (Marx, 1973: 41), one must begin with 'the general, abstract determinants which obtain in more or less all forms of society'. This applies to production, distribution, etc. Then, second, one must examine: 'The categories which make up the inner structure of' a given society (e.g. the 'bourgeois society) and on which the fundamental classes rest' such as 'Capital, wage labour, landed property', as processes and 'Their interrelation' and exchange between them. One must also study 'The three great social classes. Exchange between them. Circulation. Credit system'. Also to be analyzed are the geographical forms of society, including: 'Town and country'.

Third, one must examine a) 'The international relation of production. International division of labour. International exchange. Export and import. Rate of exchange' and b) 'The world market and crises [which may begin nationally but which becomes a global process]'.

Finally, since economic processes are deeply linked to political power, one must examine 'Concentration of bourgeois society in the form of the state'. Then there are processes shaped by or connected to the state such as: 'The "unproductive" classes [e.g. civil servants]. Taxes. State debt. Public credit. The population [held together by the state on the basis of an ideology such as nationalism]. The colonies [that colonizing states create and possess, and with this process, the redivisions of the world market that come with it]. Emigration [which the state controls in the interests of its business class]'. This conceptual map of political economy displays Marx's dialectical imagination that prioritizes a relational and processual view of society in which things are seen as processes and processes.

In thinking about the economic realm, one must examine production, distribution, exchange and consumption separately and in terms of their mutual inter-connection. However, production influences other moments more than it is influenced by these moments, at least at the level of society as a whole and over a long time period.

4 Implications of the Primacy of Production for Contemporary Debates in Political Economy

4.1 *Economic Crisis*

Given that capitalism has more or less constantly been in a crisis-mode (Roberts, 2016a), what are the implications of Marx thinking about the totality of production, distribution, exchange and consumption for the analysis of crisis? In theoretical discussions on economic crisis, either production is under-emphasized relative to distribution, exchange and consumption, or where production is given some importance, its capitalist character driven by value relations is under-emphasized: production is reduced to production of things, while production of value and surplus value is neglected.

According to some (e.g. Adam Smith), if more and more capital accumulates, and if the volume of production increases, the price of commodities produced relative to the cost of production will fall. With this the profit-margin per unit of output will fall, and since the output per unit of capital stock is given, this will mean a fall in the rate of profit per unit of capital stock (Patnaik,

2023).[26] Then there is David Ricardo's argument, which asserts that as accumulation proceeds, the demand for the wage-good, corn, keeps increasing; since the available land of any given quality is limited, raising the *production* of corn involves moving cultivation to increasingly inferior land which therefore increases the difficulty of producing corn, causing a fall in the rate of profit (Patnaik, 2023). This, however, would happen only if the fall in price is greater than the fall in the average unit of labour cost, that is, if the fall in price at any given money wage rate, owing to technological progress, is such that the share of wages rises, so that for any given output per unit of capital stock, the rate of profit falls. But why the fall in prices should be greater than the fall in average unit labour cost? To say that the wage-share in the sphere of *distribution* rises with technological progress is just an assertion, with little theoretical or empirical support (ibid.).

There is a group of Marxists who think that the main reason for periodic crisis lies *outside of production*. Some of these Marxists attribute the crisis to conflicts in distribution of the social product: profit squeeze. When real wages rise, the rate of profit drops over time. Other Marxists in this group think that crisis is ultimately because of under-consumption: workers get paid less than the total net value produced, so their consumption is not sufficient to buy back what they produce, producing a demand gap, the magnitude of which rises as the share of profits in the total net product rises. The bulk of the capitalist income is not consumed, and this also dampens demand.[27] This theory implies that the shortfall in consumption (effective demand in the realm of exchange)

---

26 A version of Smith's argument in recent times is that: capital accumulation, purely because of the fact of competition, creates a tendency towards a falling rate of profit. This states that technological progress accompanying capital accumulation causes a rise in labour productivity, and hence, for any given level of money wages, a fall in prices that is large enough to cause a lowering of the rate of profit (Patnaik, 2023).

Smith's argument is valid for a single sphere of production, but the analogy between the single sphere and the economy as a whole, breaks down. The demand in the economy as a whole is obviously for the totality of the output produced in that economy (abstracting from trade). If accumulation occurs in the economy, then more outputs of all goods are produced, just as more outputs of all goods are demanded. There could, of course, be excess demand for some goods and excess supply of others at the base prices, but that *per se* is entirely irrelevant to the issue of the rate of profit in the economy as a whole (ibid.).

27 An insufficient growth in aggregate demand (*consumption*) translates itself, other things constant, to a decline over time in the degree of capacity utilisation (consider Marx's example of trains being there but no travellers) and hence to the rate of profit. And if profit-margins are deliberately raised, that is, if the *distribution* between wages and profits is altered in favour of profits, then that accentuates the tendency towards falling profitability (Patnaik, 2023).

must come from outside of capitalist production and or from government spending.

Some scholars (e.g. David Harvey) explain the crisis in terms of neither overproduction nor under-consumption as such but what they call overaccumulation. Given capitalism's tendency towards constant technical change and dynamics, it will produce more than can be profitably sold. Such crises are typically registered as surpluses of capital (in commodity, money, or productive capacity forms) and surpluses of labour power side by side, without there apparently being any means to bring them together profitably to accomplish socially useful tasks (Harvey, 2003). 'Since it is the lack of profitable opportunities that lies at the heart of the difficulty, the key economic (as opposed to social and political) problem lies with capital. If devaluation is to be avoided, then profitable ways must be found to absorb the capital surpluses.[28] Geographical expansion and spatial reorganization provide one such option. But this option cannot be divorced from temporal shifts in which surplus capital gets displaced into long-term projects 'that take many years to return their value to circulation through the productive activity they support' (p. 88). 'Flows of capital are drawn off from the realm of immediate production and consumption (the primary circuit) [because of lack of effective demand] and redirected into either a secondary circuit of fixed capital and consumption fund formation or into a tertiary circuit of social expenditures and research and development. [Investments in the] secondary and tertiary circuits absorb excess capital into investments of long duration' (109). 'Investments of this sort offer relief, at least for a time, for the overaccumulation problem' (p. 112). 'But overinvestment in the secondary and tertiary circuits of capital can also occur, in which case there will be surpluses of housing, office space, and factory and port facilities, as well as excess capacity in, say, the educational system' (p. 112).

In short, capitalism is technologically dynamic, so it producers more commodities than can be sold for a profit or it produces more capital than can be invested for an expected rate of profit, the latter being called over-accumulation. However, what Harvey calls 'overaccumulation ... might be best understood as a generalisation of Luxemburg's theory of underconsumption' (Fine, 2006: 142–143). The focus of the latter theory 'was on the need for more capitalist markets and how these might be provided, indeed were required in her view, by incorporation of non-capitalist formations with inevitably limited scope'

28 Geographical expansion and spatial reorganization provide one such option. But this option cannot be divorced from temporal shifts in which surplus capital gets displaced into long-term projects that take many years to return their value to circulation through the productive activity they support' (p. 88; see Harvey, 1978).

(p. 143). Fine concludes, 'Harvey … seems to displace and widen the scope of the underconsumptionist argument. He does so by appeal to the notion of overaccumulation and/or surplus capital (as opposed to relying exclusively on a surplus of commodities to be sold).' (Fine, 2006: 144).

There are a minority of Marxists who correctly deny the fundamental role of consumption (or the distribution of items of final consumption) and who think crisis is ultimately because of contradictions inherent in the process of *production* and attendant capital accumulation of value produced, although the crisis can be aggravated by, say, rising wages relative to profit. The best representative of this theory is Marx himself. His argument is at two levels. Firstly, as Marx (1894) says, in *Capital* volume 3, it is in production that one finds the key to why and how one mode of production changes into another, through a crisis

> Whenever a certain stage of maturity has been reached, the specific historical form is discarded and makes way for a higher one. (p. 631)
>
> The moment of arrival of such a crisis is disclosed by the depth and breadth attained by the contradictions and antagonisms between … production relations, on the one hand, and the productive forces, the production powers and the development of their agencies, on the other hand. A conflict then ensues between the material development of production and its social form. (p. 632)

Secondly: the dialectic between productive forces and relations of production that Marx talks about the 'Introduction' to the *Grundrisse* is expressed in the form of the crisis of profitability in capitalism: 'The progressive tendency of the general rate of profit to fall is, therefore, just an expression peculiar to the capitalist mode of production of the progressive development of the social productivity of labour' (Marx, 1894: 154). Of course, the rate of profit may fall 'temporarily for other reasons'. But 'proceeding from the nature of the capitalist mode of production, it is thereby proved logical necessity that in its development the general average rate of surplus-value must express itself in a falling general rate of profit'. (Marx, 1894: 154). This logical necessity is as follows. '[T]he mass of the employed living labour is continually on the decline as compared to the mass of materialised labour set in motion by it, i.e., to the productively consumed means of production' (ibid.). Therefore, 'the portion of living labour, unpaid and congealed in surplus-value, must also be continually on the decrease compared to the amount of value represented by the invested total capital'. 'Since the ratio of the mass of surplus-value to the value of the invested total capital forms the rate of profit, this rate must constantly fall' (ibid.). And the rate of profit has been shown to have been falling in the US and in many advanced countries and at the level of the world market (Roberts, 2016b).

There are of course countertendencies to the tendency (Marx, 1894; Grossman, 1929). But many of them are also connected to production: increasing exploitation of labour at the site of *production*; increasing efficiency in *production* leading to the cheapening of constant capital; wage rate falling below the value of labour power, in part due to the relative surplus population caused by technical change in *production*; and cheapening of consumption goods and capital goods through imports from countries where the cost of *production* is lower, and so on.

Although Marx sometimes explains crisis in terms of underconsumption, his overall view against this, as he makes clear in a few lines in *Capital* volume 2:

> That commodities are unsaleable means only that no effective purchasers have been found for them, i.e., consumers. ... But if one were to attempt to give this tautology the semblance of a profounder justification by saying that the working-class receives too small a portion of its own product and the evil would be remedied as soon as it receives a larger share of it and its wages increase in consequence, one could only remark that crises are always prepared by precisely a period in which wages rise generally and the working-class actually gets a larger share of that part of the annual product which is intended for consumption. (Marx, 1956: 251)

Therefore: 'It is sheer tautology to say that crises are caused by the scarcity of effective consumption, or of effective consumers' (ibid.: 250).[29]

What about overproduction then? What is called overproduction is really a symptom of overproduction of capital (c + v), which the surplus value already *produced*, relative to the surplus value (s) produced by and extracted from labour:

> The so-called plethora [over-production] of capital always applies essentially to a plethora of the capital for which the fall in the rate of profit is not compensated through the mass of profit ... Over-production of

29 Empirically, 'personal consumption as a share of GDP rose in advanced economies throughout the postwar period and stayed high even during the start of the Great depression, while profits dropped before the great depressions and investment plunged. Consumption only fell afterward and was clearly a consequence of the slump' (Roberts, 2016a: 19).

> capital, not of individual commodities – although over-production of capital always includes over-production of commodities – is … simply over-accumulation of capital. (Marx, 1894: 176–177)

4.2 *Primitive Accumulation*

Some contemporary Marxists say that a response to the on-going capitalist crisis is a redistribution of means of production: capitalists are buying up at a cheap (below-market) price, or obtaining through coercive mechanisms, means of production from non-capitalist owners or from the state, or from weaker capitalists. This process is seen as the modern form of primitive accumulation. Harvey (2007) includes this process under what he calls accumulation by dispossession. What implication does Marx's 'Introduction' have for this idea, and especially, the idea that production and its relations are no longer the dominant aspect of capitalism?

While distribution – or redistribution – of means of production can be an extra-economic fact, it is ultimately determined by economic processes (production). 'It is a received opinion that in certain periods people lived from pillage alone. But, for pillage to be possible, there must be some thing to be pillaged, hence production' (Marx, 1973: 31). Not just that: 'the mode of pillage is itself in turn determined by the mode of production' (ibid.). Consider the following examples (p. 31). 'A stock-jobbing nation … cannot be pillaged in the same manner as a nation of cow-herds'. Or, 'To steal a slave is to steal the instrument of production directly. But then the production of the country for which the slave is stolen must be structured to allow of slave labour, or (as in the southern part of America etc.) a mode of production corresponding to the slave must be created' (ibid.).

The coercive character of 'production-determining distribution' *is* a fact. For example, 'a system of laws assigns property in land to certain families in perpetuity, or distributes labour [as] a hereditary privilege and thus confines it within certain castes' (p. 29).[30] Or, in Marx's (1887) original formulation of original accumulation, or what is usually called primitive accumulation in *Capital* volume 1, the to-be-capitalists dispossess peasants and take away their private property, or divorce the peasants from access to public property (e.g. common grazing land), or convert state property into capitalist property, thus creating conditions for capitalist relations of production or further assisting existing capitalist production by cheapening constant capital.

30 From a different vantagepoint, common people may smash in a revolutionary way 'the great landed estates into small parcels' so the resultant 'new distribution' of means of production 'gives production a new character' (Marx, 1973: 29).

In all these cases of distribution or redistribution of means of production, 'it *seems* that distribution is not structured and determined by production, but rather the opposite, production by distribution' (Marx, 1973: 29; italics added). But that is just the appearance as mentioned earlier. At the dawn of capitalism and in the present times, primitive accumulation must be seen as distribution, or rather *re*distribution, of the *means of production*, and the latter is a part of production as such.

If distribution of means of production is a part of production (and it is) and if such a process is an on-going process just as production proper is (and it is), then modern-day primitive accumulation (the process in which direct producers are divorced from means of production) is an on-going process of distribution/redistribution of means of production.

> Capital itself (and landed property which it includes as its antithesis) already presupposes a distribution: the expropriation of the labourer from the conditions of labour, the concentration of these conditions in the hands of a minority of individuals, the exclusive ownership of land by other individuals, in short, all the relations which have been described in the part dealing with primitive accumulation. (Marx, 1894: 629)

Therefore, one would be mistaken to separate the on-going redistribution of means of production (primitive accumulation in its present forms) from capitalist production proper and to argue, as Harvey does, that the former (i.e. redistribution of means of production) is the dominant form of capitalism. And, modern day re-distribution of means of production in favour of capitalist owners, i.e. modern-day primitive or original accumulation, whether domestically or globally[31] could serve, just like trade does, as a countervailing tendency towards the tendency towards the rate of profit to fall caused by a tendency towards the rising organic composition of capital (c/v). This counter-tendency is the cheapening of constant capital, which modern-day original or primitive accumulation enables.

5 Conclusion

The economic realm comprises four moments: 'Production creates the objects which correspond to the given needs; distribution divides them up according

31 Consider how MNCs from advanced countries – as well as big capital of the South – obtain land at a cheap price in the South, including by using coercive mechanisms.

to social laws; exchange further parcels out the already divided shares (e.g. the total wage of the wage laborer) in accord with individual needs' (ibid.: 22). And, 'in consumption, the product steps outside this social movement and becomes a direct object and servant of individual need, and satisfies it in being consumed' (ibid.). All in all, production, distribution, exchange and consumption are not identical, but 'they all form the members of a totality, distinctions within a unity' (p. 32). As in any organic whole, 'Mutual interaction takes place between the different moments' (33). This inter-connection can be seen from the standpoint of labour. To recall Marx's point, 'the masses of products' that are *produced* 'corresponding to the different needs' for things that are *consumed* require 'different and quantitatively determined masses of the total *labor* of society' (Marx, 1869; italics added).[32]

In thinking about the economic realm, one must examine production, distribution, exchange and consumption separately and in terms of their mutual inter-connection. However, production influences other moments more than it is influenced by these moments, at least at the level of society as a whole and over a long time period. All non-production moments of the economic realm (e.g. distribution of items of direct consumption; exchange of things that are directly consumed) can and must be looked at from the vantagepoint of production: distribution, exchange and consumption of things already produced. These things – means of production and means of subsistence – have to be produced in the first place for them to be (re)distributed, exchanged and consumed.

The ways in which Marx thinks about the different moments of the economic realm point to his dialectical philosophy of internal relations. Production as a concept includes relations between productive forces and social relations of production. Production includes the process of distribution/redistribution of means of production. Production is also itself a Relation in so far as it is a product of, and reflects its relations to, the moments other than production as well as to culture and the state. And this relation is internally contradictory.

There are relations and processes that promote and/or impede production and productivity over time are crucial processes that also affect distribution, exchange and consumption. Similarly, production and relations of production

32 That this *necessity* of the *distribution* of social labor in definite proportions cannot possibly be done away with by a *particular form* of social production but can only change the *mode* of its *appearance*, is self-evident. ... And the form in which this proportional distribution of labor asserts itself, in the state of society where the interconnection of social labor is manifested in the *private exchange* of the individual products of labor, is precisely the *exchange value* of these products.

(class relations) along with exchange and its relations, govern political and cultural processes.

It is important to insist on terminological clarification, and not engage in a mere play of words. To say that consumption – or under-consumption – or more equal or less equal distribution has effects such as E_1 and E_2 means little unless one says exactly what one means by consumption and distribution. There is a world of difference between a) distribution, exchange and consumption of food and b) distribution, exchange and consumption of machines required to produce food. There is a difference between, to provide an example Marx gives, grapes for eating as a fruit, and grapes as the raw material for wine-making.

It is true that '*in its one-sided form*, production is itself determined by the other moments. For example if the market, i.e. the sphere of exchange, expands, then production grows in quantity and the divisions between its different branches become deeper. A change in distribution changes production, e.g. concentration of capital, different distribution of the population between town and country, etc. Finally, the needs of consumption determine production' (p. 33).

Yet, the fact of the matter is that: 'Production *predominates* ... over the other moments' (p. 32; italics added):

> That exchange and consumption cannot be predominant is self-evident. Likewise, distribution as distribution of products; while as distribution of the agents of production it is itself a moment of production. A definite production thus determines a definite consumption, distribution and exchange as well as *definite relations between these different moments.* (pp. 32–33)

The dominance of distribution, consumption and exchange over production is only an appearance.

This appearance is deceptive, including in relation to the relation between production and exchange. Exchange is the most immediate aspect of economy, so to many, exchange is the site of market failure causing crisis – for example crisis is said to happen when workers' organizations push wages above the level at which there is an equilibrium between supply and demand in the labour market. Similarly, less developed countries are considered to be exploited mainly in the realm of exchange: i.e. through unequal trade (Brenner, 1977). As we have seen, such exchange-based views are mistaken.

Production has a dominant and determinant influence on other moments of economy and on non-economic processes.

> Production specifies "the different relations between different moments" (our italics). It determines the form of those combinations out of which complex unities are formed ... In the Althusserian sense, production not only "determines" in the last instance but determines the form of the combination of forces and relations which make a mode of production a complex structure. Formally, production specifies the system of similarities and differences, the points of conjuncture, between all the instances of the mode, including which level is, at any moment of a conjuncture, "in dominance". This is the modal determinancy which production exercises in Marx's overall sense. (Hall, 2021: 36)

The process of production and its effects (including crisis-formation) ultimately are more important than other moments of the economic realm. So, one has to take with a grain of salt Harvey's (2023: 17) claim that: 'The question of whether production is more important in this flow [within the realm of value circulation] than consumption or distribution is not, in Marx's view, a valid question'. To support his claim, Harvey resorts to an unacceptable biologism: 'It would be like asking, are your liver or your lungs or your brain more important to your life than your heat?' According to Harvey, the primacy that Marx accords to production presents a concession to classical political economists: 'Marx concedes, in line with classical political economy, that "production is the real point of departure and hence also the predominant moment"' (Harvey, 223: 21). To him, 'Marx does not know exactly what the totality looks like' (ibid.). As I have said, Marx undoubtedly defends the primacy of the totality of production – seen as the combination of the process of production and relations of production – over other elements of the economic realm, and the primacy of the economic realm over the extra-economic realm.

Marx's view on the dominance of production can be used to correct all those who trace economic crisis to distribution or consumption rather than to the dynamics of production. Marx's discussion on the two meanings of distribution and his idea about the relation between production and distribution can be conceptually put to good use against all those (e.g. David Harvey) who mistakenly over-emphasize modern-day forms of primitive accumulation at the expense of the dynamics of actual production and who indeed appear to analytically *divorce* primitive accumulation from the ways in which production is affected by it. If 'pillage' of means of production is a fact, it is also the case that, as mentioned earlier, 'for pillage to be possible, there must be some thing [already produced] to be pillaged, hence production', and 'the mode of pillage is itself in turn determined by the mode of production' (Marx, 1973: 31).

Not only does production determine other moments of the economic realm. It is also the case that in a given society, one type or form production (including in terms of the nature of means of production used and the purpose of production, etc.) dominates over other form.

> In all forms of society there is one specific kind of production which predominates over the rest, whose relations thus assign rank and influence to the others. It is a general illumination which bathes all the other colours and modifies their particularity. It is a particular ether which determines the specific gravity of every being which has materialized within it. (pp. 39–40)

Consider the following examples (pp. 39–40). 'Certain forms of tillage occur among [pastoralists].... Landed property is determined by this. It is held in common, and retains this form to a greater or lesser degree according to the greater or lesser degree of attachment displayed by these peoples to their tradition, e.g. the communal property of the Slavs'. Consider now settled agriculture which is a 'great step' forward from pastoral production: 'Among peoples with a settled agriculture ... where this predominates, as in antiquity and in the feudal order, even industry, together with its organization and the forms of property corresponding to it, has a more or less landed-proprietary character; is either completely dependent on it, as among the earlier Romans, or, as in the Middle Ages, imitates, within the city and its relations, the organization of the land'. Consider the Middle Ages where capital exists to a degree. Even then, 'In the Middle Ages, capital itself – apart from pure money-capital – in the form of the traditional artisans' tools etc., has this landed-proprietary character'.

However, in contrast, 'In bourgeois society ... [land-based production such as farming] more and more becomes merely a branch of industry, and is entirely dominated by capital. Ground rent likewise. In all forms where landed property rules, the natural relation [is] still predominant. In those where capital rules, the social, historically created element' attains dominance (pp. 39–40). If in a society, different social relations or social forms of production coexist, one type generally dominates:

> Capital is the all-dominating economic power of bourgeois society. It must form the starting-point as well as the finishing-point, and must be dealt with before landed property. After both have been examined in particular, their interrelation must be examined. (p. 40)

This implies that, for example, 'Ground rent cannot be understood without capital. But capital can certainly be understood without ground rent' (p. 40).

Marx not only emphasizes the primacy of production over other elements of the economic realm. He also draws attention to production's unevenness. Unevenness is spatial: not all places experience the same or similar level of the development of capitalist production. Production is uneven temporally too. In 'bourgeois society', says Marx (1973: 38), 'relations derived from earlier forms' such as communal property relations or feudal relations, 'will often be found within it only in an entirely stunted form, or even travestied'. Marx here anticipates Trotsky's (1930) idea that development is both uneven and combined: the past archaic relations coexist and interact with present relations within a social formation that is dominantly capitalist.

According to Trotsky, modern technology and ideas borrowed from an advanced country by a less developed country are well adapted and developed in the latter, or are stunted or caricatured.

> A [technologically] backward country assimilates the material and intellectual conquests of the advanced countries. ... Although compelled to follow after the advanced countries, a backward country does not take things *in the same order*. The privilege of historic backwardness – and such a privilege exists – permits, or rather compels, the adoption of whatever is ready in advance of any specified date, *skipping a whole series of intermediate stages*. (italics added)[33]

As a result:

> The development of historically backward nations leads necessarily to a peculiar *combination of different stages* in the historic process. Their development as a whole acquires a planless, complex, *combined character*. (italics added)

In the dialectical approach to political economy, no process is absolute or contradiction-free:

> The possibility of skipping over intermediate steps is of course by no means absolute. Its degree is determined in the long run by the economic

33 Trotsky explains the idea by giving this example: 'Savages throw away their bows and arrows for rifles all at once, without travelling the road which lay between those two weapons in the past.' (ibid.).

> and cultural capacities of the country. The backward nation, moreover, not infrequently debases the achievements borrowed from outside in the process of adapting them to its own more primitive culture. In this the very process of assimilation acquires a self-contradictory character.[34]

When less developed countries with their less developed or archaic social relations of production – i.e. the social relations that correspond to a lower level of economic development relative to advanced countries – interact with the latter countries, the archaic social relations of production coexist and combine with more developed social relations *within* the less developed countries:

> The laws of history have nothing in common with a pedantic schematism. Unevenness, the most general law of the historic process, reveals itself most sharply and complexly in the destiny of the backward countries. Under the whip of external necessity their backward culture is compelled to make leaps. From the universal law of unevenness thus derives another law which, for the lack of a better name, we may call the law of *combined development* – by which we mean a drawing together of the different stages of the journey, a combining of the separate steps, an amalgam of archaic with more contemporary forms. (Trotsky, 1930)

Marx's dialectical political sees production as a process – i.e. in terms of a dialectical relation between productive forces and production relations (Marx, 1973: 42). He also relates production to moments of economy other than production (private consumption; distribution of product, exchange of in terms for personal consumption, etc.). This allows him to provide conceptual maps of society, which should be understood in the light of his points about culture (including art) discussed in the next chapter.

According to one such conceptual map presented in his 'Introduction' (Marx, 1973: 41), one must begin with 'the general, abstract determinants which obtain in more or less all forms of society'. This applies to production, distribution, etc. Then, second, one must examine: 'The categories which make up the inner structure of' a given society (e.g. the 'bourgeois society) and on which the fundamental classes rest' such as 'Capital, wage labour, landed property',

34 'Thus the introduction of certain elements of Western technique and training, above all military and industrial, under Peter I, led to a strengthening of serfdom as the fundamental form of labour organisation. European armament and European loans – both indubitable products of a higher culture – led to a strengthening of tzarism, which delayed in its turn the development of the country' (ibid.).

as processes and 'Their interrelation' and exchange between them. One must also study 'The three great social classes. Exchange between them. Circulation. Credit system'. Also to be analyzed are the geographical forms of society, including: 'Town and country'.

Third, one must examine a) 'The international relation of production. International division of labour. International exchange. Export and import. Rate of exchange' and b) 'The world market and crises [which may begin nationally but which becomes a global process]'.

Finally, since economic processes are deeply linked to political power, one must examine 'Concentration of bourgeois society in the form of the state'. Then there are processes shaped by or connected to the state such as: 'The "unproductive" classes [e.g. civil servants]. Taxes. State debt. Public credit. The population [held together by the state on the basis of an ideology such as nationalism]. The colonies [that colonizing states create and possess, and with this process, the redivisions of the world market that come with it]. Emigration [which the state controls in the interests of its business class]'. This conceptual map of political economy displays Marx's dialectical imagination that prioritizes a relational and processual view of society in which things are seen as processes and processes.

CHAPTER 4

Marx's *Introduction to Grundrisse*: the Relation of the Economic Realm to the Political and the Cultural Realms

Marx's 'Introduction' to *Grundrisse* not only makes useful claims about production as a moment of the economic sphere in relation to its other moments. His ideas about the economic realm shape his overall social theory or historical materialism. A scientific analysis of society, historical materialism points to traits of all society (classless or class society) and all forms of class society.[1] Two important common traits are emphasized in Marx's 'Introduction': the relation of the individual to society in the context of production, and the relation between the economic sphere and the extra-economic sphere (i.e. the political and cultural processes, including art/mythology).[2]

Section 1 of this chapter discusses Marx's conception of the producing individual in relation to society. Sections 2–3 discuss, respectively, the relation of the economic to the political and the cultural. Section 4 draws theoretical implications of Marx's conceptualizations, including for understanding right-wing cultural politics.

1 Conception of the Producing Individual in Relation to Society

'Individuals producing in society – hence socially determined individual production – is … the point of departure' for the analysis of society (Marx, 1973: 17). This is how Marx actually begins his 'Introduction' to the *Grundrisse*. 'Production by an isolated individual outside society … is as much of an absurdity as is the development of language without individuals living *together* and talking to each other' (p. 18).

'The human being is in the most literal sense … not merely a gregarious animal, but an animal which can individuate itself only in the midst of society'

1 A large number of books have appeared on historical materialism (Blackledge, 2006; Callinicos, 1988; Cohen, 2001; Holt, 20; Therborn, 1980; Wood, 1995). Marx's (1968) own *German Ideology* itself is an important text.

2 Society has four main spheres: economic, political, cultural, and environmental. Marx covers the first three in his 'Introduction' and touches on the last.

 | DOI:10.1163/9789004730472_005

(p. 18). An individual is a product of the past and the present. An individual in modern society is a product of a) the dissolution of past social forms (e.g. feudalism) and of b) present social conditions, including the new forces of production developed under capitalism.

Society has a history, so does the individual living in it. 'The more deeply we go back into history, the more does the individual, and hence also the *producing* individual, appear as dependent, as belonging to a greater whole' (p. 18; italics added). The 'whole' or the totality refers to the various structured aggregates of social relation or social connectedness: the family; the family expanded into the clan; 'various forms of communal society arising out of the antitheses and fusions of the clan' and so on (p. 18). In capitalist society, as in other types of society, individuals depend on social groups and relations, but only in capitalism 'do the various forms of social connectedness confront the individual as a *mere* means towards his private purposes. ...'[3] (p. 18; italics added), so this characteristic of capitalism with its private property, private exchange, etc., produces 'isolated individual' (p. 18).

But the epoch, i.e. capitalism, 'which produces this standpoint [ideology] ... of the isolated individual, is also precisely that of the hitherto most developed social ... relations' (p. 18), for this is an epoch where the different parts of the social totality are interconnected to a much larger extent than in the previous forms of society.[4]

The individualism that is prevalent in capitalist society is an all-sided dependence which appears as mutual indifference, as Marx (1973: 87) says a later part of the *Grundrisse*:

> The reciprocal and all-sided dependence of individuals who are indifferent to one another forms their social connection. This social bond is expressed in exchange value, by means of which alone each individual's own activity or his product becomes an activity and a product for him; he must produce a general product – exchange value, or, the latter isolated for itself and individualized, money. On the other side, the power which each individual exercises over the activity of others or over social wealth exists in him as the owner of exchange values, of money.

---

3 The academic literature on social capital emphasizes the idea that social relations of reciprocity among people have an economic significance and can meet the needs of individuals (Das et al., 2023).

4 Marx (1868: 6) says in *German Ideology*:
'If in all ideology [people] and their circumstances appear upside-down as in a camera obscura, this phenomenon arises just as much from their historical life-process as the inversion of objects on the retina does from their physical life-process.'

Marx continues:

> The individual carries his social power, as well as his bond with society, in his pocket. Activity, regardless of its individual manifestation, and the product of activity, regardless of its particular make-up, are always exchange value, and exchange value is a generality, in which all individuality and peculiarity are negated and extinguished. This indeed is a condition very different from that in which the individual or the individual member of a family or clan (later, community) directly and naturally reproduces himself, or in which his productive activity and his share in production are bound to a specific form of labour and of product, which determine his relation to others in just that specific way.

2 The Relation of the Economic to the Political

As already discussed, the economic realm comprises production, distribution and exchange, which then shape, and are shaped by, consumption. The extra-economic realm comprises the state and its laws and its actions. An important part of the extra-economic realm is also the cultural, which includes the artistic and the mythological. The relation of the economic to the state and to culture as Marx conceptualizes it in his 'Introduction' to *Grundrisse* is discussed in this and the next section, respectively.

Production relations are not a product of state action. It is indeed wrong to see the 'history of production relations' as 'a malicious forgery perpetrated by governments' (Marx, 1973: 19). The chain of causation points in the opposite direction.[5] But production and its relations are also very much affected by the state, including government actions and legal relations. 'Relations of production develop unevenly as legal relations'. This is indicated by 'the relation of Roman private law … to modern production' (Marx, 1973: 42).[6]

The laws of the state can shape distribution of means of production, which is a moment of production: 'Laws may perpetuate an instrument of production, e.g. land, in certain families. These laws achieve economic significance only when large-scale landed property is in harmony with the society's production, as e.g. in England. In France, small-scale agriculture survived despite the

5 Some people (e.g. anarchists such as Bakunin) have a politicist – statist – understanding of society's problems which are seen as chiefly caused by the state rather than by capital (Engels, 1872). For further discussion, see chapter 10.

6 A more detailed discussion of the economic processes to the state is presented in chapters 6–8.

great landed estates, hence the latter were smashed by the revolution' (Marx, 1973: 31). There are limits to the extent to which laws can shape the distribution of means of production. Marx asks: 'can laws perpetuate the small-scale allotment?' (p. 31). His answer is no: 'Despite these laws, ownership is again becoming concentrated' (ibid.). Also the ways in which and the extent to which laws shape distribution of means of production (and the economy more generally) vary geographically. This is why: 'The influence of laws in stabilizing relations of distribution, and hence their effect on production, requires to be determined in each specific instance' (ibid.).

Production involves property or acquisition, and the latter must be defended. Indeed, 'every form of production creates its own legal relations, form of government, etc.' (Marx, 1973: 21). It is true, and all the bourgeois economists are aware of this, that 'production can be carried on better under the modern police than e.g. on the principle of might makes right' (p. 22). However, one should not forget 'that this principle is also a legal relation, and that the right of the stronger prevails in [the] "constitutional republics" as well, only in another form' (ibid.). This view of Marx anticipates his overall approach to the state which is that the state is fundamentally the state that functions for and on behalf of the basic interests of the ruling class of an epoch.

The right of the stronger over the weaker prevails domestically. It also prevails externally as indicated by (endless) war-making, which is connected to the economic realm. '*War* developed earlier than peace ... [C]ertain economic relations such as wage labour, machinery etc. develop earlier, owing to war and in the armies etc., than in the interior of bourgeois society' (Marx, 1973: 42). As well, 'The relation of productive force and relations of exchange [are] also especially vivid in the army' (ibid.). War-making presupposes the fact that the state exists in the forms of multiple states, and multiple *nation* states (this is just like capital existing in the form of multiple capitals). This means that the economic realm and a given society is shaped by what Marx calls 'international relations', a theme on which he had planned to write a book.[7]

7 This theme of the relation between the economy and the army is also developed elsewhere by Marx. For example in a letter to Engels, Marx (1857) writes: 'the history of the army demonstrates the rightness of our views as to the connection between the productive forces and social relations. Altogether, the army is of importance in economic development'. For example, 'it was in the army of Antiquity that the *salaire* [wages] was first fully developed'. 'Likewise the *peculium castrense* in Rome, the first legal form according recognition to the movable property of others than fathers of families'. The army has been a site for 'the first use of machinery on a large scale' as well as the division of labour: 'Even the special value of metals and their use as money would seem to have been based originally ... on their significance in war'. (ibid.).

3 The Relation of the Economic to the Cultural

Production is not merely material production, although that is the primary focus in the 'Introduction' as it is in *Capital* volume 1. Non-material things are also produced when we see production as the transformation of existing things and practices into new things and practices. Society produces political and ideological things, processes and relationships, including means of legitimation of the relations of production that involve injustice and exploitation, broadly within the limits of material production and its relations.[8]

The same principle 'applies to mental production as expressed in the language of politics, laws, morality, religion, metaphysics, etc. of a people' (ibid.). In other words, 'conditioned by a definite development of their productive forces and of the intercourse [social relations of production] corresponding to these' human beings produce 'their conceptions, ideas, etc.' (ibid.).

Economic development – including, especially, material production – broadly shapes cultural processes, including artistic work and mythology. However, sometimes the level of cultural development in a country can be greater than what one would expect from a given level of economic development. This points to: 'The uneven development of material production relative to e.g. artistic development' and vice versa (Marx, 1973: 42). 'In the case of the arts', indeed, 'certain periods of their flowering are out of all proportion to the general development of society, hence also to the material foundation, the skeletal structure as it were, of its organization' (pp. 42–43). For example, 'the Greeks compared to the moderns or also Shakespeare' (ibid.). And this could be said about Indian and Chinese civilizations too.

Mythology is a raw material for the production of art. 'Greek art presupposes Greek mythology, i.e. nature and the social forms already reworked in an unconsciously artistic way by the popular imagination' (p. 43). So, 'Greek mythology is not only the arsenal of Greek art but also its foundation' (p. 43). One can ask:

> Is the view of nature and of social relations on which the Greek imagination and hence Greek [mythology] is based possible with self-acting mule spindles and railways and locomotives and electrical telegraphs?

This point resonates with our times when many modern technologies including the internet, AI, etc. have bene developed (generally with assistance from the state) within the defense sector.

8 'The production of ideas, of conceptions, of consciousness, is at first directly interwoven with the material activity and the material intercourse of [people], the language of real life. Conceiving, thinking, the mental intercourse of [people], appear at this stage as the direct efflux of their material behaviour', as Marx (1968: 6) says in *German Ideology*.

> Or the *Iliad* [possible] with the printing press, not to mention the printing machine? Do not the song and the saga and the muse necessarily come to an end with the printer's bar, hence do not the necessary conditions of epic poetry vanish? (p. 43)

The answer is that mythology as the foundation of art presupposes a low level of economic development, and as the latter vanishes (as society makes economic progress), the material condition for mythology vanishes. 'All mythology overcomes and dominates and shapes the forces of nature in the imagination and by the imagination; it therefore vanishes with the advent of real mastery over them', a mastery that comes with economic progress. (p. 43). Indeed, 'certain forms of art, e.g. the epic, can no longer be produced in their world epoch-making, classical stature' (p. 43). This is because 'certain significant forms within the realm of the arts are possible only at an undeveloped stage of artistic development' (p. 43). In a sense, there can be cultural advantages of economic backwardness. On the other hand, a more developed society has little need for all 'mythologizing relations to nature', as that society will demand 'of the artist an imagination not dependent on mythology' (ibid.).

It is not just that the relation between economy and art/mythology is uneven – that is, that the progress – temporality – of one may be out of sync with that of another. The relation between art and mythology – or more broadly, the relation within the cultural sphere among different aspects or moments of culture – is also uneven. While art presupposes mythology, 'Not any mythology', 'i.e. not an arbitrarily chosen unconsciously artistic reworking of nature [and society]' would work (p. 43). The relation between art and mythology within the cultural sphere is mediated by uneven geographical development. This is in the sense that mythology of one country cannot necessarily be the basis for art in another. For example, 'Egyptian mythology could never have been the foundation or the womb of Greek art' (p. 43).

While culture – e.g. Greek arts and epic – is 'bound up with certain forms of social development' (p. 44), it is also the case that such arts and mythology, developed long ago (representing the stage of a child in the life of a human being) '*still* afford us artistic pleasure and that in a certain respect they count as a norm and as an unattainable model' (p. 43; italics added). 'A man cannot become a child again, or he becomes childish. But does he not find joy in the child's naïvité ...?'. (p. 43).

Marx's discussion on the relation between economic processes and art/mythology points to important lessons. One is that: art and mythology produced a long time ago *imagine* a future time where human beings have greater mastery over nature and over society[9] (its oppressive relations). Such imagination is necessary and possible because human beings have limited control over nature and society. This may be a reason why 'the historic childhood of humanity, its most beautiful unfolding, as a stage never to return, exercise[s] an eternal charm ...'.[10] The charm of Greek art does not lie in the contradiction between art and the 'undeveloped stage of society on which it grew'. Much rather the charm of such art 'is inextricably bound up ... with the fact that the unripe [under-developed] social conditions under which it arose, and could alone arise, can never return'. (ibid.). Artistic imagination about the future is not just charmful. It inspires human beings to 'strive to reproduce its truth [e.g. imagined ability to fly] at a higher stage ...' (p. 44). In some of this imaginative labour lies the mental labour that produces utopian socialism too, a theme Marx does not explore here. Another lesson is that while mythology, which results in art presupposes a low level of economic development, in order to enjoy art and mythology, one generally needs a higher degree of economic development, a theme developed in Marx's earlier work.[11]

4 Conclusion

Marx's 'Introduction' to *Grundrisse*, read carefully and in conjunction with his other texts, suggests that: the economic realm shapes the extra-economic which has a reciprocal influence on the economic, but within a totality within which the economic realm has ultimate primacy.

In thinking about society, one has to keep in mind relations among the different moments of the economic realm, relations between economic and

9 In mythology, 'nature *and* the social forms already reworked in an unconsciously artistic way by the popular imagination' (p. 43).

10 'There are unruly children and precocious children. Many of the old peoples [who have created marvelous art form] belong in this category'. 'The Greeks were normal children' who produced charming art (p. 44).

11 'The care-burdened, poverty-stricken man has no sense for the finest play', just as 'the dealer in minerals sees only the commercial value but not the beauty and the specific character of the mineral' (Marx, 1844: 46).

non-economic realms, and relations among the different moments of the non-economic.

> In the same way that Marx works through his theory of capital in terms of inner relations between production, consumption, realization, distribution, and reinvestment, so a theory of capitalism [as a totality of internal relations among its moments] … might usefully be deployed to describe the interrelationalities of culture, nature, economy and politics in a far broader conception of how society works. (Harvey, 2023: 13)

Art and mythology, among other components of culture including conceptions of society, reflect objective material conditions. More generally, as Marx says in his famous 1859 'Preface', which is the topic of the next chapter, 'The mode of production of material life conditions the general process of social, political and intellectual life. It is not the consciousness of men that determines their existence, but their social existence that determines their consciousness.' (Marx, 1859).

Marx's concept of the isolated individual is an interesting one. 'This concept – that the capitalist mode of production depends on social connection assuming the "ideological" form of an individual disconnection – is one of the great, substantive themes of the *Grundrisse* as a whole', says Stuart Hall commenting on Marx's 'Introduction' (Hall, 2021: 22). Marx begins with the idea that production outside of society – social relations – is an empty category. It is an impossibility. 'It takes a gigantic social development to produce "the isolated individual" producer as a concept: only a highly elaborated form of developed social connectedness can appear as … [people] pursuing their egoistic interests as "indifferent", isolated, individuals in a "free" market organized by an "invisible hand"' (Hall, 2021: 22). Hall continues: even this individualism is an 'all sided dependence' which appears as mutual indifference: 'The reciprocal and all-sided dependence of individuals who are indifferent to one another forms their social connection. The social bond is expressed in exchange value'.

Right-wing thinking is obsessed with the sanctity of the individual – mainly the individual right to buy and sell for profit. It does not care about the fact that such buying and selling, which is a deeply social act, kills millions of individuals in wars or due lack of food or healthcare. Right-wing individualism is extended to members of the ruling class. Capitalists are seen as hardworking *individuals* whose wealth is because of who *they as individuals* are and because of their *work*. They are also seen as individuals who are benefactors to the whole society – as job providers, wealth-creators, etc.

Mythology is an important aspect of culture. Mythology, like all ideas, reflect a given level of economic development. Mythology reflects a relative absence of the advanced development of productive forces. So to make mythology fit the facts of a relatively more developed society is a mistake, a mistake committed by the right-wing as a part of its reactionary cultural politics of (late) capitalism. The treatment of mythological stories about deities and their followers as true produces a cultural (and majoritarian) politics of eternity that glorifies the past, a past that is said to have been ruined by outsiders or minorities. Such a politics is devoid of any real concern with facts, historical or contemporary. The right-wing political use of mythology is preoccupied with a longing for past moments that are extremely unlikely to have happened during the epochs that might have been actually disastrous for, say, the majority of Hindus (and not just Hindus) in India. Consider the thousands of years of oppression of lower castes by the upper castes, or of exploitation of Hindu masses by Hindu propertied strata with their monopoly over political power. A proper critical political-economic appreciation of mythology is necessary for the fight against fascistic cultural politics.

When social relations of production are not developed enough to promote a level of development of productive forces that allow human beings to understand nature and have a degree of control over it,[12] then human beings seek to meet their needs partly through imaginations expressed through mythologies. We now turn to the question concerning the relation between social relations of production and productive forces, a central issue in Marxist political economy.

---

12 Since body is a part of nature, the statement about understanding/controlling nature applies to the body, including its illnesses and longevity, etc. (see Timpanaro, 1985).

CHAPTER 5

Marx's 1859 *Preface to A Contribution to the Critique of Political Economy*

Fettering of Productive Forces by Social Relations, and Questions of Labour and Nature

Social relations of production promote the development of productive forces. But they can and do fetter (impede) that development too. The concept of 'fettering' is a central but neglected component of Marx's historical materialism and his theory of social change (Bowring, 2011: 137).[1] Indeed, a proper theory of fettering can help us raise, and answer, questions that concern numerous problems of the contemporary world such as periodic economic crisis, environmental damage, impoverishment of common people, imperialism, endless wars, etc. that exist partly because of the contradictions between productive forces and production relations of capitalism.

Marx introduces the concept of fettering in the *Communist Manifesto* and returns to it famously in his 1959 *Preface to A Contribution to the Critique of Political Economy*. To make 'optimal' use of Marx's concept of fettering would require further development of the concept beyond his schematic remarks as well as beyond some of its modern-day interpretations.[2] We need to better understand a) what might fettering exactly mean and b) what is it about the social relations of production and productive forces which makes fettering of the latter by the former possible? I begin by discussing Marx's 1859 remarks on fettering, in section one of the chapter. Section 2 focusses on some of the existing interpretations of Marx's remarks. Section 3 presents a brief critique. Section 4 offers an alternative perspective on fettering. The final section concludes the chapter and draws some of theoretical implications.

1 This concept can help us 'make sense of the role which contradictions play in the process of social and political change' (ibid.). See Harvey (2014) on contradictions.

2 I do not wish to provide an extensive review of these interpretations.

 | DOI:10.1163/9789004730472_006

1 Marx (and Engels) on Fettering of Productive Forces by Production Relations

Productive forces include means of production and direct producers' productive abilities. Development of productive forces, at the minimum, means improvement in the quality and quantity of productive forces. A basic theme in historical materialism is that objectively-existing production relations shape – enable and constrain – the development of productive forces.

The concept of fettering is central to Marx's political economy, even before he began a systematic study of political economy. Scholars generally associate the concept of fettering with the 1859 Preface and as a result have not paid much attention to it discussed in the *Manifesto*, where, as we have seen in chapter 2, Marx discusses how productive forces are fettered by production relations. Of course, the concept appears in his 1859 Preface as a part of his overall approach to political economy.

In the form of a 'sketch of the course of my studies in the domain of political economy', Marx (1859) says in his famous 'Preface' that: 'In the social production' of their means of existence, individuals 'inevitably enter into definite relations, which are independent of their will'. These relations are 'relations of production appropriate to a given stage in the development of their material forces of production'.[3] However, in the process of more or less continuous development of productive forces orchestrated by human beings in search for an improvement of their conditions, 'the material productive forces of society come into conflict with the existing relations of production':

> At a certain stage of development, the material productive forces of society come into conflict with the existing relations of production or – this merely expresses the same thing in legal terms – with the property relations within the framework of which they have operated hitherto.

As a result, 'From forms of development of the productive forces these relations turn into their *fetters*' following which 'begins an era of social revolution'

3 These relations could include: the relations between those who control productive resources and those who do not; and relations of competition, etc.

Marx's claim is also that: 'The totality of these relations of production constitutes the economic structure of society, the real foundation, on which arises *a legal and political superstructure* [including political-bureaucratic institutions – especially, the state] and to which correspond definite forms of social consciousness' [italics and parenthesis added].

(italics added).[4] 'In broad outline', Marx adds, 'the Asiatic, ancient, feudal and modern bourgeois modes of production may be designated as epochs marking *progress in the economic development* of society' (italics added).

Epistemologically, there is a difference between the study of economic change (i.e. progress in the economic development of society) and that of changes in the non-economic sphere (e.g. politics and culture):

> In studying [social] transformations it is always necessary to distinguish between the material transformation of the economic conditions of production, which can be determined with the precision of natural science, and the legal, political, religious, artistic or philosophic – in short, ideological forms in which men become conscious of this conflict and fight it out.

Changes in the economic sphere do not occur primarily because of changes in, say, consciousness. It is the other way around:

> Just as one does not judge an individual by what he thinks about himself, so one cannot judge such a period of transformation by its consciousness, but, on the contrary, this consciousness must be explained from the contradictions of material life, from the conflict existing between the social forces of production and the relations of production.

Marx appears to underestimate consciousness and politics in these remarks but as widely known, elsewhere he and Engels emphasize how consciousness and politics react back on economics.

A given set of social relations of production, i.e. a given economic structure (or, 'social order'), does not go away as long as it is able to enable and promote the development of productive forces. It is also that the case material conditions for new social relations of production mature within the womb of existing social relations:

4 Further: 'The changes in the economic foundation lead sooner or later to the transformation of the whole immense superstructure'. Note that: Marx ignores the role of class struggle in social transformation here. Marx also adds that: 'No social order is ever destroyed before all the productive forces for which it is sufficient have been developed, and new superior relations of production never replace older ones before the material conditions for their existence have matured within the framework of the old society'.

> No social order is ever destroyed before all the productive forces for which it is sufficient have been developed, and new superior relations of production never replace older ones before the material conditions for their existence have matured within the framework of the old society.[5]

It therefore implies that:

> Mankind thus inevitably sets itself only such tasks as it is able to solve, since closer examination will always show that the problem itself arises only when the material conditions for its solution are already present or at least in the course of formation.

As productive forces have been fettered by social relations of production, out of such conflict between the forces and relations of production, revolutionary changes in social relations of production and attendant productive forces, have occurred resulting in a transition from one type of class society to another.

'The bourgeois mode of production is the last antagonistic form of the social process of production', in the sense of 'an antagonism that emanates from the individuals' social conditions of existence'. However, 'the productive forces developing within bourgeois society create also the material conditions for a solution of this [social] antagonism. The prehistory of human society accordingly closes with this social formation'. The new, superior, social relations of production involving associated producers in a post-capitalist society are expected to un-fetter the development of productive forces. The new society will be more economically developed than the currently advanced capitalist society but it will be without class antagonism (and it will be without antagonism between society and nature).

Almost 30 years after Marx's famous 1859 'Preface', Marx's collaborator, Engels (1878), writes that historical materialism which is 'the materialist conception of history starts from the proposition that the production and, next to production, the exchange of things produced, is the basis of all social structure' and that 'the manner in which wealth is distributed and society divided into classes or estates', that is, the structure of social relations of production (and exchange), 'is dependent upon what is produced, how it is produced, and

5 For this reason scientific ideas about socialism can only begin to appear within capitalism. In pre-capitalist societies, conceptions of a better form of society can only appear in non-scientific forms, including in mythological forms. The relation between mythology and economic development is discussed in the last chapter.

how the products are exchanged'. If there is a 'growing perception that existing social institutions are unreasonable and unjust' that fact 'is only proof that in the modes of production and exchange changes have silently taken place with which the social order, adapted to earlier economic conditions, *is no longer in keeping*' (italics added).[6]

In their sketch on the fettering of productive forces by production relations, Marx and Engels do not adequately clarify the meaning of the development of productive forces. And to the extent that by development they mean increase in productive capacity, they, more or less, appear to abstract from the fact that while production relations can promote the *development* – growth – of productive forces, they may fetter their *use*. Also they do not seem to distinguish between fettering in its absolute form and that in its relative form.

2 Existing Interpretations of Marx's Concept of Fettering

If the development of productive forces means 'growth in their productive power, or increase in how much *can be* … produced', then the fettering of the development of productive forces means restricting the growth of a capacity: either the rate of growth of productive capacity is zero (absolute stagnation) or the rate of its growth is lower than it could be (Cohen, 2000: 329). What Cohen calls development fettering occurs when: 'the production relation can fetter or restrict, the *development* of the productive forces (Cohen, 2000: 41; italics added), where development means improvement or to actualize, or to bring a potential to fruition.

The fettering idea as articulated by Cohen out of Marx's 1859 remarks is presented by Wright et al. (1992: 19) in the form of following six theses:

> A given level of development of productive forces is compatible with only a limited range of relations of production (Thesis 1). Since the forces of production tend to develop over time[7] (Thesis 2), the forces eventually reach a level at which they are no longer compatible with existing relations of production (Thesis 3). When such incompatibilities arise,

6 'From this it also follows that the means of getting rid of the incongruities', i.e. the contradictions between productive forces and relations, 'that have been brought to light must also be present, in a more or less developed condition, within the changed modes of production themselves' (ibid.).

7 This is because of a transhistorical need on the part of human beings to develop the productive forces.

> the relations are said to "fetter" the forces of production. Because human beings are somewhat rational ..., when the forces are fettered by the relations, human beings have an interest in transforming the relations. If they also have the necessary capacities (Thesis 5), they will be able to do so (Thesis 5), and to substitute new relations of production that are optimal for the further development of productive forces (Thesis 6).

Production relations can fetter productive forces in an absolute or a relative sense.[8] Absolute fettering occurs when 'fettering relations prevent all further improvement in productivity' (Cohen, 2000: 326). Production relations fetter productive forces in a relative sense. This is in the sense that even when given relations of production, say, of capitalism, 'are stimulating faster productive development than has ever before occurred' in pre-capitalist societies, 'different feasible relations of production' such as socialist relations 'would develop the productive forces [still] faster. ... over a considerable period of time' than capitalist relations can (ibid.).

But development fettering in absolute or relative sense – i.e. the growth in productive capacity or development of productive forces – is a different matter from the *use* of the already produced and already-existing productive capacity, says Cohen.[9] So he offers an alternative view of fettering: use-fettering. The latter occurs when: production relations fetter the improvement *in the use*, rather than, the mere development of, productive forces (Cohen, 2000: 329). Use-fettering means that rational *use* of existing productive resources is blocked by the current set of class and intra-class relations. For example, capitalism may generate a new generation of computers more quickly than socialism but it does not make optimal use of any generation of computers: this is seen in the fact that each generation of computers creates unemployment, deskilling, and degradation of work, etc. (Cohen, 2000: 330). This is use-fettering.

Use-fettering can be in absolute and relative, just like development fettering is. In fact, as a general rule, all class societies are sooner or later unable to make optimal *use* of the developments in productive capacity which they induce or allow (ibid.: 331). For example, a capitalist depression might prevent the application – i.e. use – of a now known technique, says Cohen. This is fettering

8 Cohen takes seriously Miller's distinction between the absolute and relative fettering of the productive forces.

9 Marx might have included use fettering under development fettering saying that development-fettering relations are inherently use-fettering relations and that use fettering often accompanies development fettering (Cohen, 2000: 332).

not in the sense that capitalism fails to *create* a new technique or improve an existing one but in the sense that it fails to make *optimal use* of an existing technique: 'This form of non-development is a form of non-use of the productive force in question' (Cohen, 2000: 332).[10] In an absolute sense, use fettering means: 'a complete unemployment of all factors of production' (ibid.: 330). The discrepancy between capacity and use is not to be seen only in an absolute sense, however. As Cohen says, the question is not *under*-deployment (or under-use) of resources in an absolute sense, but 'grotesque *over*-deployment in some directions and injurious under-deployment in others' (italics added), indicating an irrational deployment of resources.

Apart from development fettering and use fettering (in absolute and relative senses), there is what Cohen calls net fettering, which is 'a multiple of level of development and degree of use' (p. 334). Given both the rate at which a system of social relations of production *develops* the forces of production and how well it *uses* them, that system produces net fettering if 'the amount of productive power it harnesses at given future times is less than what some alternative feasible system would harness' (p. 334). If a social system A develops productive powers very quickly but uses it less optimally than another system B, the former system may have a net positive impact on productive powers and in that sense B has a net fettering impact (ibid.: 334). The net effect of greater use of productive power would characterize A. So, a social system, A may be use fettering relative to B but B may be net fettering relative to A. People should bring B by overthrowing A. History is not the history of growth of productive power (increase in the creation of fastest computers) as such but it is the growth of used productive power (increase in the use of fastest computers created), where the latter is a function of two things: development of new productive powers and the use of existing productive powers.

If productive power means 'capacity to produce output' (Cohen, 2000: 336), and if we consider only relative fettering, Cohen's interpretation of Marx leads to the following conclusions: relative development fettering occurs when 'productive power ... grows more slowly than it could'; relative use fettering occurs when 'output from available productive forces is less than it could be'; and relative net fettering is when: 'the trajectory [i.e. rate of growth] of output levels is less high than it could be' (Cohen, 2000: 336). So: fettering now means that both development and optimal use as well as their interaction are impeded (ibid.: 56). Overall, use fettering is preferable to development fettering as a

10 And (ir-)rationality of deployment must be judged in turn from the standpoint of human preferences/needs, which, as Sutton (1996: 14) states, determine what objective capacities are being fettered.

concept, and net fettering is to be preferred to development fettering and use fettering (Cohen, 2000).

Irrespective of the concept of fettering that is used, it is important to think about the concept of social output. If we define output as gross national product (GNP), it is the case that: a social system A is superior from the use point of view if it produces more GNP with the given forces of production than B does. But then output does not have to be narrowly seen in terms of GNP. It can be seen in terms of how much leisure time people have, whether they have access to things such as education, housing, food, etc. Output can be seen in terms of 'realignment of labour, leisure and education', for example.[11] It is also the case that not only do production relation *fetter* productive forces but also can they *cause a decline* in them as seen in various forms of environmental gradation, a decline which constitutes the forfeiture of productive resources, as proposed by McMurty (Cohen, 2000: 338). I return to this idea below.

3 A Partial Critique of Existing Interpretations of Marx's Concept of Fettering

The existing thinking about fettering of productive forces by social relations is mistakenly split into various separate ideas leading to a litany of fetterings (see Table 5.1). Fettering *is* rightly seen as relative: a given set of relations may develop productive forces more slowly than the production relations of the future. But what is often ignored is the fact that the fettering is also relative in a spatial and sectoral sense: forces are fettered more here than there, and more in this sector than in that.

TABLE 5.1 Multiple concepts of fettering in Marxism

Development fettering	≠	Use fettering
Absolute	≠	Relative fettering
Development and use fettering	≠	Net fettering
Absolute development fettering	≠	Relative development fettering
Absolute use fettering	≠	Relative use fettering
Fettering	≠	Forfeiting

11 When capitalist fettering prevents such realignment, then one can say that the contradiction between forces and relations overlaps with spiritual alienation, according to Elster (Cohen, 2000: 336).

While knowledge about nature is correctly considered a productive force (by Cohen)[12] whose development or use is seen as being fettered, that knowledge is considered in isolation from the pre-conditions for that knowledge, where the pre-conditions are all the things that people need in order to acquire that knowledge and use it. There is in fact no need to see *development of productive forces* as separate from the increase in *the quality of life of common people* (as explained below). More specifically, the theory of fettering of productive forces does not give the attention to the most important productive force: direct producers. The discussion on development of productive forces and their fettering has mainly concerned physical (non-human) means of production at the expense of labour as a productive force, which is a co-producer of wealth, with nature. Implicitly emphasized is a physicalist notion of productive forces. Marx says that under capitalism 'the labourer co-operates systematically with others', so 'he strips off the fetters of his individuality, and develops the capabilities of his species' (Marx, 1887: 230). But can the capabilities of his/her species be developed if there are no food, housing, etc.? And the emphasis in much of the discussion is on the *produced* means of production (e.g. machines, software, etc.) at the cost of nature as a productive force.

The development of a new technique *is* to be analytically distinguished from the optimal use. One can accept that 'While development fettering refers to the holding back of the productive forces, use fettering implies the destructive use, and indeed overuse, of society's productive forces, an idea that certainly offers better leverage for unpicking the current irrationalities of capitalism' (Bowring, 2011: 150). But this distinction between development fettering and use fettering is exaggerated.

I would argue that there is no *development* of productive forces without the productive *use* of the forces (an existing computer is to be used to *develop* a newer type). Therefore, there is no fettering of the *development* of productive forces which is also not the fettering of the *use* of these forces. Similarly, forfeiture – loss of physical wealth due to environmental degradation – does not have to be separate from the fettering of productive forces. Forfeiture is an *extreme* form of fettering.

Lurking behind attempts to reinterpret Marx's original 1859 thesis is an anti-production tendency. For example, Bowring (2011: 149–150) says: 'the theory of fettering is seriously impaired by a nineteenth-century productivist paradigm, which does not accurately register the issues and concerns that have provoked the anti-capitalist movements of the last few decades'. In turn such a tendency leads to a chaotic concept of fettering, or what is called use fettering,

12 Cohen says that the application of knowledge to resource endowment is a determinant of productive power.

so the concept becomes a shopping basket of all the ills created by capitalism. Consider the following:

> Numerous examples of use fettering then spring easily to mind: the wasting of professional autonomy and goodwill by the imperatives of competition and performance-related pay; the failure to moderate the exploitation of natural resources so that they can renew themselves over time; the destruction of non-economic forms of mutual aid and self-provisioning by the aggressive marketing of commercial substitutes; the declining nutritional content of mass produced food; the rise in obesity and related diseases of overconsumption; the health costs of inequality in an affluent society; the crimes that increase with poverty and the reduction in public revenue caused by the tax-avoiding anti-social behaviour of the rich; the proliferation of 'positional goods' whose value declines the more people gain access to them; the psychological stresses of excessive consumer choice; and the endless creation of new needs, new deficiencies, new wants and dependencies at constantly growing levels of abundance. (Bowring, 2011: 150)

One wonders what common causal mechanism is behind all these examples.

To say that social relations fetter productive forces is too general: specific mechanisms of fettering must be provided. The theory of fettering indeed doesn't explain how exactly the fettering happens in advanced capitalism (Callinicos, 2006: 264). Cohen's analysis of 'fettering' in capitalism explicitly rejects the theory that the average rate of profit falls because of the rising organic composition of capital (Wright et al., 1992). Instead, he says fettering happens because capitalism is production for exchange rather than use, and capitalist relations of production have a built-in bias for using progress in productive forces to expand output rather than to expand leisure time. Still the mechanism of fettering is relatively unclear. And, the contradiction between use value and exchange value is only the tip of the ice-berg of capitalist fettering of productive forces, as we will see below. Given all these problems, what is needed is an integrative perspective.

4 Towards an Integrative Perspective on Fettering for Today's World

4.1 *Class Society, Capitalism, and Fettering*

Clarifying the concept of fettering of productive forces requires that we understand its opposite, i.e. development of productive forces. Often, the opposite of development is seen as under-development or non-development. But this is a descriptive approach. In an explanatory view, fettering is a better opposite of development as it *explains* under- or non-development.

To understand fettering, one must clarify the meaning of *productive forces* too. To do so, one must begin with the notion of *production itself.* Trans-historically, production means the combination of labour and means of production with the aim of producing use values, as Marx (1887) explains in Chapter 7 of *Capital* volume 1. For Marx, production as well as distribution, exchange and consumption are separate but are also interconnected, within a totality of economic processes in which production and *its relations* have primacy, as discussed in chapter 3. For Marx, distribution means the distribution of the social product in the form of wages, rent, profit, etc., and points to the problem of economic inequality. But distribution of means of production is also included in production. Similarly, consumption (i.e. use of use-values created in production) has two forms. One is subjective or final consumption, i.e. consumption of food. Another is *productive consumption*, i.e. the consumption of means of production (e.g. tractors) in the sphere of production. Its purpose is to produce use-values which can be means of production or means of *subjective* or final consumption. And exchange means exchange of means of final consumption or of productive consumption.

Production (including the distribution of means of production) is to be understood in relation to *forces of production* and *relations of production.* Forces of production refer to a) (non-human) objects (means of production) – i.e. raw materials, energy and tools/machines, science, AI, nature as a source of physical resources and a sink for emissions/waste, and geographical built environment and b) productive abilities of direct producers.[13] Development means, above all, the development, i.e. qualitative and quantitative increase, of the forces of *production*, as manifested in the rise of labour productivity per hour worked. Relations of production refer to the relations of ownership/control over the means of production, including the ways in which they are productively used, and over the production of the surplus.[14] Production relations in a class society refer to not only inter-class relations of exploitation (relations

13 In slave society, the separation between the two is blurred: labour is made to be a part of the means of production. In capitalism, it is separate.

14 The extent to which labour, as a productive force, is free is important here: in some cases, the direct producer may not have control over their own labour power, and in other cases they do (nominally free labour). *Relations* of production therefore include whether or not direct producers can freely relate to their labour, i.e. whether they control their own labour power. In capitalism, workers who do not have the freedom to commodify their labour power and workers who do, are not the same from the standpoint of relations of production; capitalists may de-proletarianize labour, in order to discipline them and extract more surplus value (Brass, 2011). See chapter 6 for more on labour unfreedom.

between slaves and slave owners or between capitalists and workers) but also intra-class relations of competition (e.g. competition among the members of a given propertied class such as capitalists).[15] Intra-class relations of competition exist in relation to inter-class relations, within a system in which inter-class relations have primacy. With the above notion of production as a part of the totality of the economic sphere as a set of processes, the alternative integrated perspective broadens the concept of forces of production and their development to include: a) nature and its development (improvement in natural conditions) and b) direct producers and their development (improvement in their social-economic conditions that are conducive to productive powers).[16]

Nature is a productive force, like the built environment including transportation networks, and it requires improvement (= development) (e.g. planting of trees; reducing the proportion of green house gases; reducing the imbalance between what use-values come from nature and what negative use-values goes into it). Social relations of capitalism fetter the improvement in the quality of nature as we will see in the next section. If development of productive forces means their improvement and if nature is a productive force, then development of productive forces must mean *improvement in nature*. Not to improve nature is to live in an ecologically unsustainable world, a world where the physical environment is not in a state of good health. Capitalist relations of production fetter not development of productive forces *per se*, but *sustainable* development of productive forces (Das, 2018a).

Under capitalist social relations, given certain level of technological development, a certain amount of damage to nature and certain amount of waste (or a certain amount of net damage to nature) is 'normal and inevitable' as the value of the waste is transferred to the value of the final product just like the value of the non-waste (i.e. the value of the means of production that are not wasted) because a certain level of waste or destruction of nature is a necessary condition for the production of the final output, but *the excess amount* of waste or damage to nature is not (Marx, 1887: 145).[17] 'Apart from the degree of

15 Production relations in a non-class society are the communitarian relations rather than inter- or intra-class relations (post-modernist Marxists consider such relations to be class relations, as discussed in chapter 6).

16 While both nature and labour are seen as productive forces, there is a difference between the two: it is only labour that is the source of value and surplus value, even if both co-produce use-values.

17 In capitalism, 'all wasteful consumption of raw material or instruments of labour is strictly forbidden, because what is so wasted, represents labour superfluously expended, labour that does not count in the product or enter into its value' (Marx, 1887: 137).

Marx adds: 'a means of production may take part as a whole in the formation of value, while into the labour-process it enters only bit by bit. Suppose that in spinning cotton, the

development, greater or less, in the form of social production, the productiveness of labour (total production divided by time spent) is fettered by physical conditions' (Marx, 1887: 359). If workers have harvested paddy but before it could be taken to the barn it is washed away by a sudden extreme weather event the likes of which are caused by climate change under capitalism, then the productivity of labour suffers. By causing environmental damage and unsustainable development, capitalism is therefore fettering the rise in the productive powers of labour as such.

Let us turn to direct producers as a productive force. The development of productive forces is separate from the impacts of development on the quality of life (or living standards) of the common people (wage workers and petty producers) or from the issue of who consumes what. That the two are analytically separate is clear: we can have new bullet trains but people may not have the money to ride them and therefore suffer from spatial isolation. Importantly, they are causally *connected*.

As mentioned earlier, forces of production refer to not only means of production but also the ability of human beings (as direct producers) to work on, and with, the means of production, in order to produce use-values (which under capitalism are exchange values). Productive abilities of direct producers' (or, wage-workers' under capitalism) are mental abilities. These include knowledge about nature and its relation to society, and their ability – a distinctly *human* ability – whereby a human being 'raises his structure in imagination before he erects it in reality' (Marx, 1887: 127).[18] Direct producers' abilities are also physical

---

waste for every 115 lbs. used amounts to 15 lbs., which is converted, not into yarn, but into "devil's dust." Now, although this 15 lbs. of cotton never becomes a constituent element of the yarn, yet assuming this amount of waste to be normal and inevitable under average conditions of spinning, its value is just as surely transferred to the value of the yarn, as is the value of the 100 lbs. that form the substance of the yarn. The use-value of 15 lbs. of cotton must vanish into dust, before 100 lbs. of yarn can be made. The destruction of this cotton is therefore a necessary condition in the production of the yarn. And because it is a necessary condition, and for no other reason, the value of that cotton is transferred to the product. The same holds good for every kind of refuse [or wastage] resulting from a labour-process, so far at least as such refuse cannot be further employed as a means in the production of new and independent use-values' (Marx, 1887: 145).

18 'We pre-suppose labour in a form that stamps it as exclusively human. A spider conducts operations that resemble those of a weaver, and a bee puts to shame many an architect in the construction of her cells. But what distinguishes the worst architect from the best of bees [or spiders] is this, that the architect raises his structure in imagination before he erects it in reality. At the end of every labour-process, we get a result that already existed in the imagination of the labourer at its commencement. He not only effects a change of form in the material on which he works, but he also realises a purpose of his own' (Marx, 1887: 127). I would argue that this sort of mental construction of the reality is not an exercise in [postmodernist type] idealism because it is a part of a totality which includes

abilities involved in the material transformation (planting trees; creating a pot out of clay; repairing a broken laptop). While means of production (e.g. machine or trees) as a productive force can be separated from human beings, there can be no separation between the ability of human beings (labour power) as a productive force and human beings themselves. Now, to remain as a human being and as a producing human being, which means engaging in 'labour in a form that [is] exclusively human' (ibid.), certain material and cultural needs must be met. Our ability to work, and to work more efficiently, and the increase in our ability, indeed depend on us being properly fed and housed and on our access to healthcare, education, a physically comfortable working and living environment (as opposed to scorching sites),[19] and so on, and on the fulfillment of the need to live in a society without fear of physical and emotional harm.

Thus if the development of productive forces is the development/improvement of the productive power of human beings, expressed as an increase in 'output' per hour worked, then such development/improvement depends on the fulfillment of their basic needs. So to say that capitalist social relations fetter the development of productive forces must be to say that these relations impede the development/improvement of not only nature and produced means of production but also of productive abilities of direct producers, the abilities which require the fulfilment of certain needs.[20] It follows that direct producers' impoverishment is an expression of capitalism fettering the productive forces. One might see the fettering of the power of workers as what Cohen calls 'net fettering': an increase in output in society between T_1 and T_2 is a function of the level of productive forces (in this case, abilities of direct producers) at T_1 and the use of these productive forces at T_1 and the multiple of the two at T_1.

Imputed costs of environmental degradation (cost of harvests or factories damaged due to extreme weather events caused by climate change such as flood) and costs of the loss of output due to avoidable deaths and illness of workers caused by capitalist fettering (i.e. neglect of their working and living conditions) must be deducted from gross output of labour. Doing so would

mental imagination and the objective construction of the reality as two necessary and inter-connected components.

19 On how climate change is creating heat-stressed unhealthy working and living environment, see Das (2024c). I owe the term 'scorching sites' to one of my PhD students, Aishwarya Bhattacharyya, who is researching climate change in relation to big capital and the state.

20 This suggests that relations among people – both relations of exploitation and subjugation between classes and relations of competition and cooperation within each – involved in production shape the relations between them and productive forces, including nature and things produced from nature to serve as means of production.

truly reveal the severity with which capitalist production relations fetter the development of productive forces.

Increase in output can be seen in value terms: increase in c, v and s. Output (c + v + s) can increase while, for example, v (labour's consumption fund) can decrease because of an increase in c and/or s. This shows capitalist fettering of the increase in output from the standpoint of labour. And of course, output can increase in the form of an increase in GNP but a large part of this increase in output can be an increase in the volume of things (e.g. pollutants; weapons; etc.) which do not improve quality of life which therefore adversely the development of productive power of labour.[21]

Fettering is the fettering of the development of productive forces. It includes so-called 'use fettering' in the sense of what Marx calls in *Grundrisse* subjective consumption: if workers do not consume what they need for a healthy life, their productive power is fettered. It also includes 'use fettering' in the sense of what Marx calls *productive consumption*: people have to use means of production (computers designed in T_1) to develop superior means of production (computers designed in T_2) but if such productive consumption does not happen now, new productive power will not occur in future. And fettering includes the fettering of the improvement in nature and is indicated by absence of sustainable development. Fettering of forces of production in all these forms produces a necessary condition for the replacement existing relations or systems of economy with new ones (see Figure 5.1 below). As Trotsky (1939) notes:

> 'The history of the development of human society is the history of the succession of various systems of economy, each operating in accordance with its own laws. … The primitive commune was either superseded or supplemented by slavery; slavery was succeeded by serfdom with its feudal superstructure; the commercial development of cities brought Europe in the sixteenth century to the capitalist order, which thereupon passed through several stages.' (Trotsky, 1939)
>
> The transition from one [economic] system [one set of production relations] to another was always determined by the growth of the productive forces, i.e., of technique and the organisation of labour. Up to a

21 '[GNP or] GDP does not discriminate between productive market transactions on the one hand, and those which are destructive, defensive, or productivist perspective: for unhappiness, ill-health, weak social bonds, tasteless food, long working hours and stressful work practices, the maldistribution of wealth, ubiquitous ugliness, cruelty and war these not just "costs" that that we will have to make good by foregoing future benefits. They are, rather, something less than what a human life should be. They fall below the threshold of a good life; they fetter human well-being' (Bowring, 2011: 150–151).

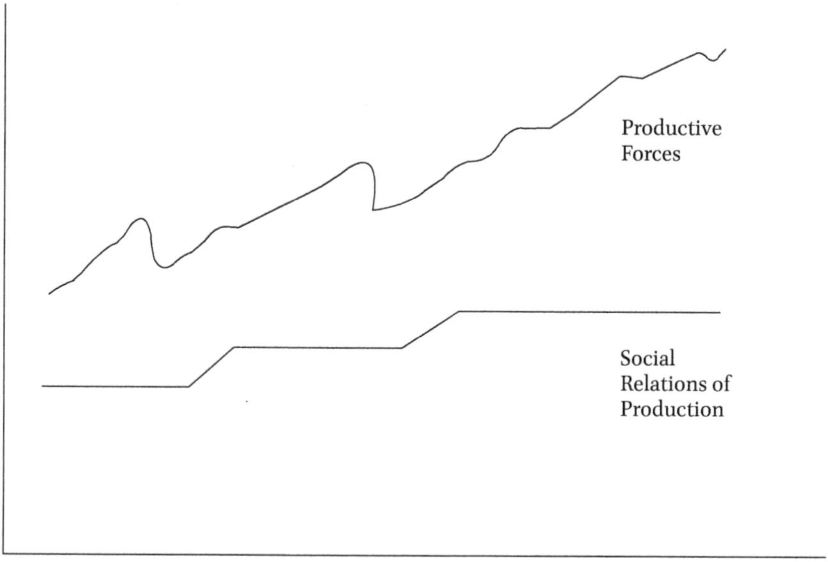

FIGURE 5.1 Productive forces and social relations of relations

> certain point, social changes [e.g. changes in techniques, etc.] are quantitative in character and do not alter the foundations of society, i.e., the prevalent forms of property. But a point is reached when the matured productive forces can no longer contain themselves within the old forms of property; then follows a radical change in the social order, accompanied by shocks. (ibid.)

4.2 *Mechanisms of Development of Productive Forces and Their Fettering*

Fettering of productive forces occurs in all class societies because of their antagonistic social relations of production. There are several examples of fettering.

Pre-capitalist society: In slave society, 'the productive force of slave labour was fettered by the slaves' awareness that no more and no less than bare existence was their fate, no matter how hard or feebly they worked' (Bowring, 2011: 140–141). The slave's motivation for labouring – and therefore their survival – thus appeared, in the words of Marx, 'as something predestined, as something independent of his own labour and determined by the mere needs of his physical existence' (ibid.: 141).

The theory of fettering is applicable to feudal society too. Such a society is characterized by small-scale production which impedes development of productive forces. It is also characterized by extra-economic coercion which fetters economic development:

> the labour-service system of economy and the patriarchal peasant economy inseparably connected with it are by their very nature based on routine technique, on the preservation of antiquated methods of production. There is nothing in the internal structure of that economic regime to stimulate the transformation of technique; on the contrary, the secluded and isolated character of that system of economy, and the poverty and downtrodden condition of the dependent peasant preclude the possibility of improvements. In particular, ... the payment of labour under the labour-service system is much lower ... than where hired labour is employed; and ... low wages are one of the most important obstacles to the introduction of machines. (Lenin, 1899a: 229)

In feudal society,

> the money capital formed by means of usury and commerce was prevented from turning into industrial capital, in the country by the feudal constitution, in the towns by the guild organisation. These fetters vanished with the dissolution of feudal society, with the expropriation and partial eviction of the country population. (Marx, 1887: 531)

The mode of production in feudalism,

> presupposes parcelling of the soil and scattering of the other means of production. As it excludes the concentration of these means of production, so also it excludes cooperation, division of labour within each separate process of production, the control over, and the productive application of the forces of Nature by society, and the free development of the social productive powers. It is compatible only with a system of production, and a society, moving within narrow and more or less primitive bounds. (Marx, 1887: 539)

So,

> At a certain stage of development, it brings forth the material agencies for its own dissolution. From that moment new forces and new passions spring up in the bosom of society; but the old social organisation fetters them and keeps them down. It must be annihilated; it is annihilated. Its annihilation, the transformation of the individualised and scattered means of production into socially concentrated ones, of the pigmy property of the many into the huge property of the few, the expropriation of

> the great mass of the people from the soil, from the means of subsistence, and from the means of labour, this fearful and painful expropriation of the mass of the people forms the prelude to the history of capital. (Marx, 1887: 539)

Fettering – or repression of development – of productive forces and their un-fettering (or development) happen as parts of the same process, and this is especially the case in the most developed form of class society, i.e. capitalism:

> the [bourgeois] production relations in which the bourgeoisie moves have ... a dual character; that in the selfsame relations in which wealth is produced, poverty is also produced; that in the selfsame relations in which there is a *development* of the productive forces, there is also a force producing *repression* that these relations produce bourgeois wealth – i.e., the wealth of the bourgeois class – only by continually annihilating the wealth of the individual members of this class and by producing an ever-growing proletariat. (Marx, 1847: 55; italics added)

Then the question is how exactly does capitalism fetter the development of productive forces including both nature and the power of the common people as it also promotes their development?

It is the case that over the long run, capitalism has delivered impressive rates of productive growth that have raised the consumption levels of most of the world's inhabitants well beyond the expectations of Marx. Commodity production, specialization, competition, etc. have together promoted the development of productive power of means of production:

> The transition from the manufactory to the factory signifies a complete technical revolution, which does away with the craftsman's manual skill that has taken centuries to acquire, and this technical revolution is inevitably followed by the most thoroughgoing destruction of social production relations, ... by a complete break with tradition, ... and at the same time by a mass socialisation of labour by capitalism [leading to a rise in productivity]. (Lenin, 1899a: 454)

Another important aspect of capitalist production relation has also contributed to the development of productive forces: this is the separation of workers from means of production. Doubly free worker must work harder if not to face unemployment and starvation (Brenner, 1986). Capital brings together a large number of workers who cooperate among themselves. This brings into being – develops – 'the social productive power of labour, or the productive power of social labour. This power is due to co-operation itself' (Marx, 1887: 230).

An immanent law of capitalist production is centralization of capital. 'One capitalist always kills many' (p. 540), so capital is increasingly concentrated in the hands of a few leading to monopolies. Now, relative to pre-capitalist societies where means of production are scattered and are under-developed, monopoly, which represents an attribute of capitalist production relation,[22] promotes the development of productive forces:

> Hand in hand with this centralisation, or this expropriation of many capitalists by few, develop, on an ever-extending scale, the cooperative form of the labour process, the conscious technical application of science, the methodical cultivation of the soil, the transformation of the instruments of labour into instruments of labour only usable in common, the economising of all means of production by their use as means of production of combined, socialised labour, the entanglement of all peoples in the net of the world market, and with this, the international character of the capitalistic regime. (ibid.)

While capitalism promotes productive forces, it also fetters them: mechanisms of development are also the mechanisms of fettering. We can discuss some of these fettering mechanisms.[23]

Nature's improvement is fettered by capitalist relations of production in a variety of ways. The fundamental fact is that nature has become a private property: 'From the standpoint of a higher economic form of society, private ownership of the globe by single individuals will appear quite as absurd as private ownership of one man by another. Even a whole society, a nation, or even all simultaneously existing societies taken together, are not [to be] the owners of the globe [or the earth]' but under capitalism, nature *has* come under capitalist relations of ownership and control, which lead to the fact that society fails to 'hand it down to succeeding generations in an *improved condition*' (Marx, 1894: 567; parentheses and italics added). Once nature becomes private property, the social relation of production of nature is a barrier to its improvement.

---

22 As mentioned above, the distribution of means of production is an aspect of production.

23 '[T]he most plausible application of Marx's theory of fettering is actually to the one mode of production that has yet to undergo a fundamental transformation', i.e. capitalism, the most advanced form of class society where antagonisms are the clearest (Bowring, 2011: 143).

A commodity that is bought and sold for profit, nature has become a means of profit-making. When the rate of profit falls due to rising organic composition of capital (explained further below), there is a tendency on the part of capital to cheapen means of production and this means that damage to nature becomes a way of cutting costs. Those who own nature as private property can do anything to/with it to increase their profit, while common people (workers) have no control over production and therefore over the interaction with nature which is a resource of the means of production and a site for storing waste. If people had control over production and therefore nature, they would collectively take steps to improve the natural conditions while utilizing those in a sustainable manner. But under capitalist social relations of production, people do not have such control.

Social relations of capitalism fetter the improvement in the quality of nature when society, driven by the pursuit of private profit, takes a lot more useful material out of nature than it returns to it – that is, when the metabolic relation between society and nature is adversely affected causing a rift in the relation (Burkett and Foster, 2017). 'Capitalist production [including in agriculture] ... develops technology, and the combining together of various processes into a social whole, only by *sapping* the original sources of all wealth', one of which is the environment/nature (Marx, 1887: 329; italics added). Given certain social relations, productive forces not only not grow in power but can also decline, leading to the forfeiture of the already-produced wealth. The forfeiture can take the form of pollution, depletion of resources including reckless deforestation, exhaustion of water supplies, desertification, perforation of the ozone layer, dissemination of nuclear waste, all these being 'induced by capitalist production', as Cohen correctly says acknowledging McMurty's proposal (Cohen, 2000: 339).[24]

Many of the mechanisms whereby capitalist social relations of production fetter the improvement in natural conditions also fetter the productive powers

24 'Planetary environmental degradation is ... consistent with continued progress in technical knowledge' (Cohen, 2000). Marx had a theory of forfeiture, notes Miller, relying on the following lines:

'Man never renounces what he has gained, but this does not mean that he never renounces the form of society in which he has acquired certain productive forces. On the contrary. If he is not to be deprived of the results obtained or to forfeit the fruits of civilisation, man is compelled to change all his traditional social forms as soon as the mode of commerce [in the wider sense] ceases to correspond to the productive forces acquired. ... With the acquisition of new productive faculties man changes his mode of production and with the mode of production he changes all the economic relations which were but the necessary relations of that particular mode of production' (Marx, 1846).

of labour. Workers do not control means of production, how they are used and for what purpose and they do not control means of subsistence either. When workers are un- or under-employed, their productive powers remain un- or under-used. When workers lack adequate access to means of subsistence, their abilities – their labour power – can only exist in 'a crippled state' (Marx, 1887: 122).[25] When workers' limbs are mutilated because safety rules are deliberately neglected or when they experience high level of mental stress due to the pressure of work, their productive powers diminish. Workers when they are ill-clad, ill-housed, ill-fed and under- or un-educated and lack access to healthcare, etc. because they are unemployed and/or wages are too low and the state fails them, then they exist as a productive force whose development has been fettered.[26] And to the extent that there *is* a sufficiently well-fed, well-clad, well-housed, well-educated and healthy working class in a place, *not using* that productive force optimally, this is also an example of fettering of the wage workers as a productive force (this happens when a large part of the class is forced to join the reserve army of labour and thus experience forced idleness). As well, 'in its blind unrestrainable passion, its were-wolf hunger for surplus labour', by subjecting workers to prolonged working days and fast pace of work, capital 'usurps the time for *growth, development*, and healthy maintenance of the body'[27] (Marx, 187: 179; italics added). Once again, 'Capitalist production … develops technology, and the combining together of various processes into a social whole, only by sapping the original sources of all wealth', one of which is 'the laborer' (Marx, 1887: 329). This sapping is fettering.[28]

New technologies develop productive powers to a much lesser extent than often thought. Many of the techniques developed and used hardly develop

25 'The minimum limit of the value of labour-power is determined by the value of the commodities, without the daily supply of which the labourer cannot renew his vital energy, consequently by the value of those means of subsistence that are physically indispensable. If the price of labour-power fall to this minimum, it falls below its value, since under such circumstances it can be maintained and developed only in a crippled state' (ibid.).

26 The fact that the working class does not have access to what are luxury items of consumption in a specific social context is not an example of an under-developed productive force.

27 Marx writes that '[capital] steals the time required for the consumption of fresh air and sunlight. It higgles over a meal-time, incorporating it where possible with the process of production itself, so that food is given to the labourer as to a mere means of production, as coal is supplied to the boiler, grease and oil to the machinery' (ibid.).

28 Capitalism not only fetters the development of the productive force in the form of wage workers. It also fetters the productive power of petty producers. Small-scale producers can continue to engage *as* small-scale producers by starvation and by under-feeding their cattle and working long hours thus depriving themselves of leisure time needed for a healthy body.

productive powers of labour: these include technologies used in polluting industries, technologies of surveillance and coercion over labour and common people as such; and technologies in arms industry and various unproductive activities such as insurance, advertisement, financial activities, etc. Besides, a society where modern technologies (e.g. faster computers; machine learning) are developed but workers' body-mind condition is reproduced in a crippled state is a society where productive forces are developing less than imagined if the fact of crippled reproduction of workers is neglected. Or as Marx (1887: 449) eloquently expresses:

> within the capitalist system all methods for raising the social productiveness of labour are brought about *at the cost of the individual labourer*; all means for the development of production transform themselves into means of domination over, and exploitation of, the producers; they *mutilate* the labourer into a fragment of a man, degrade him to the level of an *appendage* of a machine, *destroy every remnant of charm in his work* and turn it into a hated toil; they *estrange from him the intellectual potentialities* of the labour process in the same proportion as science is incorporated in it as an independent power; *they distort the conditions under which he works*, subject him during the labour process to a despotism the more hateful for its meanness; they transform his life-time into working-time, and drag his wife and child beneath the wheels of the Juggernaut of capital. But all methods for the production of surplus-value are at the same time methods of accumulation [and exploitation]; and every extension of accumulation becomes again a means for the development of those methods. It follows therefore that in proportion as capital accumulates, *the lot of the labourer, be his payment high or low, must grow worse.*

Capitalist relations fetter productive powers of society in other ways. The development of monopolies and large-scale industry promotes productive forces as we have seen above, but at some point in time, 'The monopoly of capital becomes a fetter upon the mode of production, which has sprung up and flourished along with, and under it' (Marx, 1887: 540). This fettering takes the form of relative technological stagnation. It is the case that 'capitalist monopoly, i.e., monopoly which has grown out of capitalism and which exists in the general environment of capitalism, commodity production and competition, in permanent and insoluble contradiction to this general environment ... inevitably engenders a tendency of stagnation and decay' (Lenin, 1916a). Why? 'Since monopoly prices are established, even temporarily, the motive cause of technical and, consequently, of all other progress disappears to a certain extent and, further, the economic possibility arises of deliberately retarding technical progress' (ibid.).[29]

Marx (1887: 541) says: 'Centralisation of the means of production and socialisation of labour at last reach a point where they become incompatible with their capitalist integument'. Thus capitalist property relations of monopoly become a barrier to further development of the power of physical means of production. Centralization of capital involves more efficient and larger-scale capitalists outcompeting and taking over less efficient ones as well as small-scale independent producers but this process adversely impacts direct producers:

> Along with the constantly diminishing number of the magnates of capital, who usurp and monopolise all advantages of this process of transformation, grows the mass of misery, oppression, slavery, degradation, exploitation. (p. 540)

The relations of monopoly along with aspects of capitalist production relations (e.g. competition among monopolies) fetter the development of the power of the living productive force (i.e. workers) because they do not live a good life as they lack access to means of subsistence for the development of their productive abilities. They lack access to means of subsistence not only because wages are low but also because they are un- or under-employed. Indeed, the reserve army of labour, produced by technologies change that raise productive powers of labour, allows capitalism to accumulate wealth while workers suffer:[30]

> Accumulation of wealth at one pole is … at the same time accumulation of misery, agony of toil slavery, ignorance, brutality, mental degradation, at the opposite pole, i.e., on the side of the class that produces its own product in the form of capital. (Marx, 1887: 449)

---

29 'For instance, in America, a certain Owens invented a machine which revolutionised the manufacture of bottles. The German bottle-manufacturing cartel purchased Owens's patent, but pigeonholed it, refrained from utilising it. Certainly, monopoly under capitalism can never completely, and for a very long period of time, eliminate competition in the world market (and this, by the by, is one of the reasons why the theory of ultra-imperialism is so absurd).' (Lenin, 1916).

30 'The industrial reserve army makes up an indispensable component part of the social mechanics of capitalism, as much as a supply of machines and raw materials in factory warehouses or of finished products in stores. Neither the general expansion of production nor the adaptation of capital to the periodic ebb and flow of the industrial cycle would be possible without a reserve of labour-power' (Trotsky, 1939).

This antagonism between capitalist production relations and the development of productive forces is expressed in political antagonism between capital and labour.

The fact that what is and how much produced and how (e.g. just or not, sustainable or not, healthy or not), depends on capitalist relations of ownership/ control has implications for the fettering of productive forces:

> despite grandiose productive possibilities, secured by experience and science, agrarian economy does not emerge from a putrescent crisis, while the number of the hungry, the preponderant majority of mankind, continues to increase faster than the population of our planet. (Trotsky, 1939)

It fails to 'raise the living standards of the masses, who, in spite of the amazing technical progress, are everywhere still half-starved and poverty-stricken'.[31]

The fact that property relations of capitalism associated with monopolies fetter the development of productive forces is not to be understood in an absolute sense though. 'Certainly, the possibility of reducing the cost of production and increasing profits by introducing technical improvements operates in the direction of change' (Lenin, 1916a). Indeed,

> It would be a mistake to believe that this tendency to decay precludes the rapid growth of capitalism. It does not. … [C]ertain branches of industry, certain strata of the bourgeoisie and certain countries betray, to a greater or lesser degree, now one and now another of these tendencies. On the whole, capitalism is growing far more rapidly than before;[32] but this growth is not only becoming more and more uneven in general, its unevenness also manifests itself, in particular, in the decay of the [most developed] countries. (ibid.)

Overall, the general tendency is 'the tendency to stagnation and decay, which is characteristic of monopoly [which] continues to operate, and in some branches of industry, in some countries, for certain periods of time, it gains the upper hand' (ibid.).

31 Indeed, 'both uneven development and a semistarvation level of existence of the masses are fundamental and inevitable conditions and constitute premises of this mode of production' (Lenin, 1916a).

32 '[T]he big banks' enterprises, worth many millions, can accelerate technical progress with means that cannot possibly be compared with those of the past. The banks, for example, set up special technical research societies' (Lenin, 1916a).

Spatial or temporal unevenness of a tendency does not negate its existence. Unevenness of fettering is expressed in the fact that capitalism fails to develop productive forces in agriculture as much as in industry.

> The marasmus [severe malnutrition] has acquired a particularly malignant and degrading character in the most ancient sphere of human activity, the one most closely connected with the basic vital needs of man – in agriculture. No longer satisfied with the obstacles which private ownership in its most reactionary form, that of small land holdings, places before the development of agriculture, capitalist governments [of advanced nations] see themselves not infrequently called upon to limit production artificially with the aid of statutory and administrative measures which would have frightened artisans in the guilds at the time of their decline. (Trotsky, 1939)

'By its very nature, capitalism in agriculture (as in industry) cannot develop evenly: in one place (in one country, in one area, on one farm) it pushes forward one aspect of agriculture, in another place another aspect, etc. In one case it transforms the technique of some, and in other cases of other agricultural operations, divorcing them from patriarchal peasant economy or from the patriarchal labour-service' (Lenin, 1899a: 314).

'[T]here is a limit, not inherent to production generally, but to production founded on capital. This limit is double, or rather the same regarded from two directions. It is enough here to demonstrate that capital contains a particular restriction of production – which contradicts its general tendency to drive beyond every barrier to production – in order to have uncovered the foundation of overproduction, the fundamental contradiction of developed capital' (Marx, 1973: 341). This 'overproduction' needs to be explained in relation to Marx's LTRPF. Capitalism is neither just about production of things as use-values or as exchange values (things with a price), but value and surplus value on the basis of rising investment in constant capital relative to variable capital. Given the tendency towards the rate of technical change rising faster than the rate of exploitation thus causing a tendency towards the rate of average profit to fall (Carchedi and Roberts, 2018; Smith, 2019; Roberts, 2016a), the capitalist system experiences a crisis of profitability, which may sectorally or geographically, or otherwise, *appear* as the crisis of over-production and over-accumulation. The chain of causal links is like this: rise in c/v faster than s/v à fall in average rate of profit à capitalists respond by over-accumulating ('over' relative to profitability)àmass of profit fails to rise over time (if not immediately) à capitalists

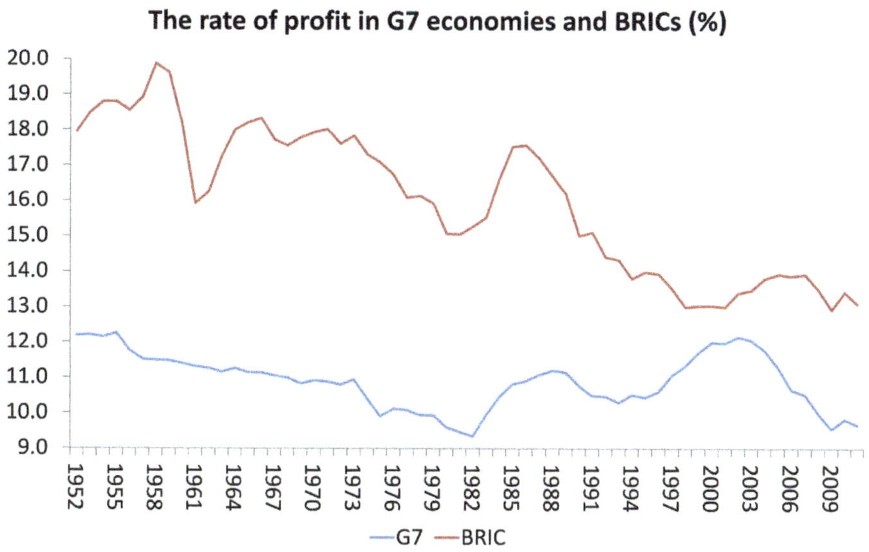

FIGURE 5.2 Falling profitability in less and more developed countries
SOURCE: ROBERTS (2016B)

stop investing and stop producing à overproduction.[33] Introduction of technical changes that enhance labour productivity faster than the rate of exploitation leads to a decline in the rate of profit, and this is what is happening in both relatively advanced and relatively less developed countries (Fig. 5.2) (Roberts, 2016b). This in turn dampens the incentive for investing in technical changes for some time. This process can cause relative stagnation in labour productivity: the rate of increase in labour productivity (output per hour worked) can

33 As Roberts (2010) says: 'the profitability of capitalist production does not stay stable, but is subject to an inexorable downward pressure (or tendency) [in some years the rate of profit may rise, but the general tendency is towards the fall in the profit rate]. That eventually leads to capitalists overinvesting (overaccumulating) relative to the profits they get out of [the exploitation of] the workers. At a certain point, overaccumulation relative to profit (ie. a falling rate of profit) leads to the total or *mass of profit* no longer rising. Then capitalists stop investing and producing and we have overproduction, or a capitalist crisis. So the falling rate of profit (and falling profits) causes overproduction, not vice versa. But a falling rate of profit does not directly lead to a crisis as long as the mass of profit can rise' (see also Roberts, 2016; Smith, 2018). 'In Marx, overproduction of commodities is the result of over-accumulation of capital, but over-accumulation of capital is the result of falling profitability and profit (absolute over-accumulation).' (Roberts, 2016).

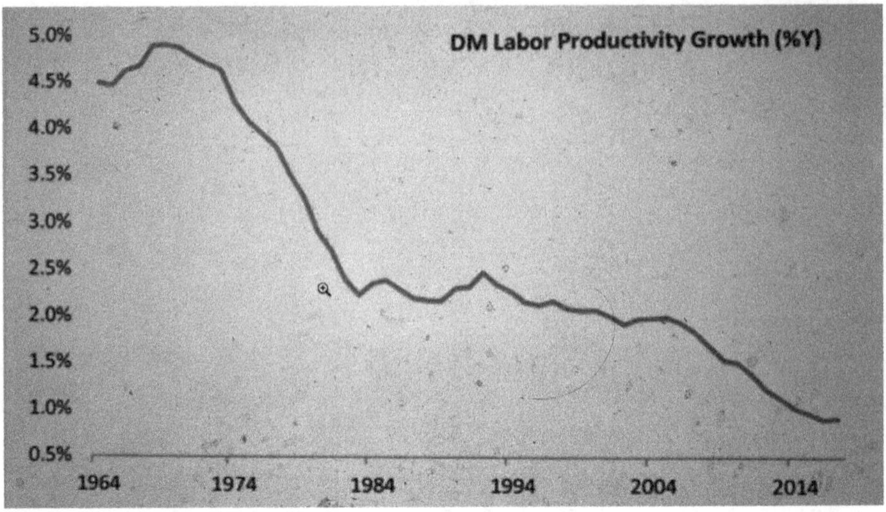

FIGURE 5.3 Labour productivity (output per hour worked) in Developed Market (DM) economies
SOURCE: ROBERTS (2019)

decrease (Fig. 5.3). This is exactly what appears to be happening in advanced capitalist countries.

There has been a slowdown in labour productivity across major economies. For the top G11 economies (which excludes China), annual labour productivity growth rate is less than 1% (it is about 0.7%) (Roberts, 2019). Because the rate of profit falls, this is seen in the fall in the rate of change in GDP.[34] Such a fall in GDP is stark especially in advanced capitalist nations (Figure 5.4).

Thanks to the capitalist law of value and competition, 'mankind up to a certain stage, approximately until the World War, grew, developed and enriched itself through partial and general crises. The private ownership of the means of production continued to be in that epoch a comparatively progressive factor. But now the blind control by the law of value refuses to render further service.

34 '[I]f total assets grow, due to the labour-shedding nature of new technologies, employment grows less (or even falls) than the growth in total assets. Since only labour produces value and surplus value, less surplus value is generated relative to total investments. The rate of profit falls and less capital is invested. Thus, the rate of change of the GDP falls. This is not a linear movement, it is the tendency' (Carchedi and Roberts, 2021). There are many counter-tendencies. One is the rising rate of surplus value appropriated from workers. As well, 'the imperialist appropriation of surplus value through unequal exchange in trade is an important counter-tendency to the decreasing growth of surplus value in the imperialist countries'. However, the counter tendencies cannot hold back the decrease in profitability for ever (Carchedi and Roberts, 2021).

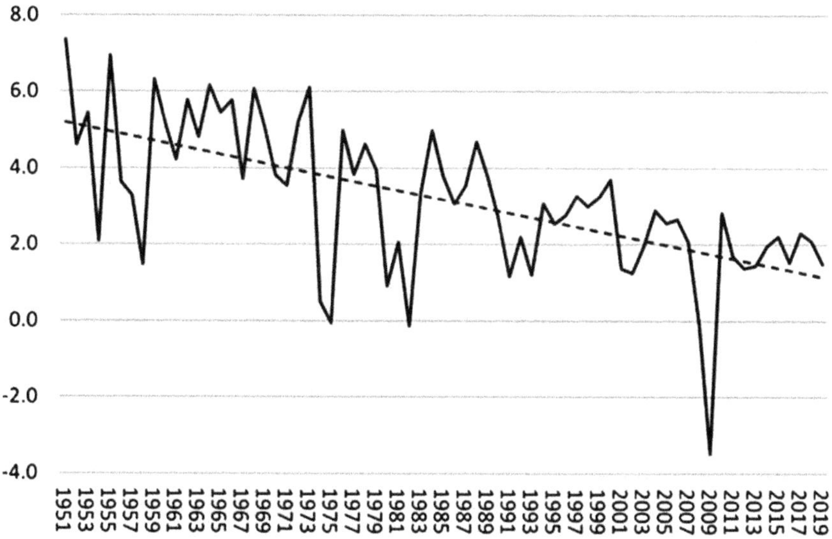

FIGURE 5.4 Annual real GDP growth (%) in imperialist countries
SOURCE: CARCHEDI AND ROBERTS (2021)

Human progress is stuck in a blind alley. Notwithstanding the latest triumphs of technical thought, the material productive forces are no longer growing [as fast]' (Trotsky, 1939).

'Machines, raw materials, workers, everything is available, not to mention the population's need for the products', and 'If notwithstanding that', unemployment cannot be lessened and income of the population increased, 'the only reason is the irreconcilable antagonism that has developed between capitalist ownership and society's need for expanding production'. Whether in the US or elsewhere, in the past or now, 'if all the actual productive possibilities were utilised' national income would be much greater than it is (Trotsky, 1939).

Further, according to Marx capitalist relations of production necessarily lead to systemic technical change. But under certain conditions of capitalism, such general tendency may be blocked or it may not be fully realized. Due to the massive presence of a reserve army of labour in part created by class differentiation of petty producers (as well as primitive accumulation), there are lots of people available to work for low wages and long hours. This means that: capitalists can make a lot of profit simply by hiring these people, so they may not be compelled to invest in technical change. The prevailing form of subsumption of labour – i.e. formal subsumption of labour – as a part of capitalist relation of production can therefore fetter the development of productive forces. Capitalists can and do indeed resort to such a strategy rather than switch to the real subsumption of labour which is associated with economic development based on systemic technological changes, and this is especially the case in rural and semi-rural areas.[35] Such a switch, which took more than hundred years in Britain, typically requires successful struggle against formal subsumption of labour. When an existing machine is not used because people can be hired for low wages and long hours, this fetters the development of productive power. This is the productive power not only of the means of production as such but also of people as labourers (they produce less; their experience with the use of technology is restricted).

It is not just the capitalist economic relations that fetter productive forces. Capitalist economic relations produce the capitalist state. And the capitalist state system fetters productive forces too.

> Capitalism achieved the twin historical merit of having placed technique on a high level and having bound all parts of the world with economic ties. Thus it pledged the material prerequisites for the systematic utilisation of all of our planet's resources. However, capitalism is in no position to fulfill this urgent task. The nisus of its expansion continues to consist of circumscribed nationalist states with their customs houses and armies. Yet the productive forces have long outgrown the boundaries of the national state, thereby transforming what was once a progressive historical factor into an unendurable restraint. Imperialist wars are nothing else that the detonations of productive forces against the state borders, which have come to be too confining for them. The programme of so-called autarchy has nothing to do with going back to a self-sufficient circumscribed economy. It only seems that the national base is being made ready for a new war. (Trotsky, 1939)

As Lenin says: 'Capitalism now finds the old national states, without the formation of which it could not have overthrown feudalism, too tight for it' (Lenin, 1915).

In short: 'Capitalist development undoubtedly creates periods of vicious turbulence during which productive forces are abandoned and destroyed' (Bowring, 2011: 148), and the fettering is expressed in the form of economic crises:

35 Formal subsumption of labour is where capitalists hire people for long hours and 'low wages' to appropriate absolute surplus value, while real subsumption is where workers work with labour-saving technology allowing capitalists to appropriate relative surplus value (see Das, 2012; 2017b: chapter 8, for details). We return to this in Chapter 9.

> Unlike the destruction caused by the plagues, droughts, wars, and precarious subsistence economies of previous centuries, the economic crises of capitalism are the product of a historically specific form of control over enormously powerful productive forces. When the economy contracts, these forces are abandoned and destroyed. Factories are mothballed, machinery is left to rust, crops remain unharvested, natural resources are left untouched, and people are deprived of productive work. This 'fettering' occurs, not because there are no needs to meet, but because needs, workers, materials, and tools cannot be put together in a way that reproduces the social relations of capitalism. (Bowring, 2011: 143)

4.3 *Capitalist Imperialism and Fettering*

It is often assumed that the relation of fettering between productive forces and production relations happens in the abstract (a-spatially) or within national societies. It is instead necessary to see such relation of fettering at a larger scale: world-economy. The claim that social relations of capitalism fetter the development or productive forces must include how relations of imperialism fetter the development of productive forces because since Marx's death capitalism, seen as a global structure of relations of production and exchange, has become imperialism (Lenin, 1916a).[36] This is something Marx did not have a chance to theorize. Scholars influenced by postmodernism and other forms of bourgeois discourse euphemistically refer to imperialism as globalization, neo-liberalism, free trade and the like. In fact, imperialism is a form of class relations: exploitative relations between metropolitan bourgeoisie, supported by their militarily power nation-states, and workers/peasants of the South, whereby the monopolized access to resources, labour, strategic location and labour of the South is utilized by different sections of the metropolitan bourgeoisie to gain competitive advantage.

As the highest stage of capitalism, imperialism fetters productive forces as capitalism as such does. 'As long as capitalism remains what it is, surplus capital will be utilised not for the purpose of raising the standard of living of the masses in a given country', that is, to develop the productive power of common people, 'for this would mean a decline in profits for the capitalists, but for the purpose of increasing profits by exporting capital abroad to the backward countries' (Lenin, 1916a). 'In these backward countries profits are usually high, for capital is scarce, the price of land is relatively low, wages are low, raw materials are cheap' (ibid.). And, 'The need to export capital arises from the fact that in

36 Lenin's views on imperialism are discussed in chapter 9.

a few countries capitalism has become "overripe" and (owing to the backward state of agriculture and the poverty of the masses) capital cannot find a field for "profitable" investment' (ibid.). On the other hand, a fundamental feature of imperialism is 'the exploitation of oppressed nations' by advanced capitalist nations which appropriate super-profits from the less developed countries (Lenin, 1916a). The appropriation superprofits occurs through the export of capital which 'sets the seal of parasitism on the whole country that lives by exploiting the labour of several overseas countries and colonies' (ibid.).[37] To the extent that imperialist exploitation involves the geographical transfer of surplus from the South to imperialist countries, that transfer cannot but fetter the development of productive forces in the South, even if it does promote some capitalist development in the South in its own interest, a process that is temporally, spatially and sectorally uneven.

Imperialism is the era of finance capital which is 'industrial capital at its highest, monopoly level which has merged with banking capital' (Lenin, 1916b). And, 'finance capital in general strives to seize the largest possible amount of land of all kinds in all places, and by every means, taking into account potential sources of raw materials and fearing to be left behind in the fierce struggle for the last remnants of independent territory, or for the repartition of those territories that have been already divided' (Lenin, 1916a). The control over land and other natural resources in the South by imperialist financial capital allows it to subject these resources to irrational use and thus to the fetter of productive forces there: irrational from the standpoint of needs of the vast majority of the population at the margins of society who want, above all, a sufficient amount of food to eat. Land and other natural resources that can produce sufficient

37 'Typical of the old capitalism, when free competition held undivided sway, was the export of goods. Typical of the latest stage of capitalism, when monopolies rule, is the export of capital' (Lenin, 1916).

The export of capital is connected to export of commodities. 'Finance capital has created the epoch of monopolies, and monopolies introduce everywhere monopolist principles: the utilisation of "connections" for profitable transactions takes the place of competition on the open market. The most usual thing is to stipulate that part of the loan granted shall be spent on purchases in the creditor country, particularly on orders for war materials, or for ships, etc.'. As well, 'the cartels add finance capital have a system peculiar to themselves, that of "exporting goods at cut-rate prices", or "dumping"' (ibid.).

'The export of capital influences and greatly accelerates the development of capitalism in those countries to which it is exported' but it is also a means of their exploitation: 'the increase in exports is connected with [many] swindling tricks of finance capital, which is not concerned with bourgeois morality, but with skinning the ox twice – first, it pockets the profits from the loan; then it pockets other profits from the same loan which the borrower uses to make purchases from [monopolies]' (ibid.).

means of subsistence – such as food-grains – are being fettered by relations of social relations imperialism (Das, 2001).

In rural areas of the Global South, as Patnaik points out, the single most important effect on agriculture of imperialist liberalization is the inverse relation between food-grains production and agricultural exports, and the ensuing threat to food security (Patnaik, 1999: 372). The export-promotion drive in agriculture in the South has led to changes in cropping patterns: cereals and pulses are being replaced by sugar cane, horticultural crops, aquaculture, and oilseeds – for example, soybean for feed export is displacing coarse grains (ibid.: 400, 407). There are several mechanisms underlying the inverse relation. The first of these is that liberalization, partly imposed by imperialism, is subjecting the economy of peripheral countries, such as India, to market demand from imperialist countries. The implication is that land and resources of the former are being bid away by the pull of demand from the latter (ibid.: 404). Consumer tastes have changed in the imperialist countries because of rising income inequality, health consciousness and environmental movements. So there are expanding demands from these countries for vegetable oils, fruits, vegetables, fibre, sea food and so on. But only a small fraction of these can be produced there (or produced profitably), given the restricted growing season in their temperate lands. These crops can, however, be produced in the developing countries such as India, given their favourable climate–soil conditions and at a very cheap cost (the price of labour power, land, etc. made artificially low), promising very high profits for global agribusiness (and some capitalist farmers in the South). Thus a growing proportion of agricultural commodities that the advanced nations need and demand comes from the les developed nations (Patnaik and Patnaik, 2016). This leads to pressure from imperialist institutions, with which sections of the bourgeoisie of the South collaborate, to open up the agricultural sector in the South (Patnaik, pp. 352–3). These commodities are sold at an artificially low price, and this low price is crucial to the maintenance of a healthy monetary system in the imperialist countries (Patnaik and Patnaik, 2016). There is also pressure from imperialist capital (and domestic capital) to reverse the post-colonial era land reform laws, which are said to be an obstacle to the flow of capital into rural areas. Indeed, the reversal of these laws paves the way for foreign companies (and also local capitalists) to own/control land, and thus enables them more easily to convert its use from food-grains cultivation to the production of agricultural commodities for export.

The neo-liberal globalizing polices of the imperialist institutions such as the IMF are, in the context of the South, and especially in their rural areas, income-deflating and inequality-enhancing. These policies, which include direct tax cuts for the super-rich but wage restraints for workers, suppressed remunerative prices for peasants and cuts in subsidies for them both, mean that in non-metropolitan contexts there is now a huge mass of people who do not have the money to buy grains. The repressed demand compounds the effect of the law of the tendency for the rate of profit to fall globally and in the (monopoly sector of the) South. This market mechanism (i.e., lack of effective demand) makes sure that the use of land and investment is diverted to agricultural exports from which imperialist nations and their businesses benefit (Patnaik, 1999: 355, 386). Arguably money for exports can be used for buying food, but there is an internal relation between export promotion and deflation of demand for food crops, so demand and supply of food shrink simultaneously (Patnaik, 1999: 405).

Moreover, the price of agricultural exports declines (and with it foreign exchange) as the number of exporting countries increases. It is true that the shift away from food-grains could be partly compensated for by a rise in yield through investment. But under the rules of imperialist institutions such as IMF, public investment which earlier played an important role in agrarian transition has been cut back (Patnaik, pp. 363, 372, 408). If the area under food-grains is being converted to non-food-grains production, and with growing pressure on the national state in the South to make land available for industrial and tertiary sector output, the required increase in agricultural yield to produce a sufficient amount of food-grains to compensate for the shift to export crops would be beyond the scale that is anyway achievable (Pushpendra, 2001: 56–7, 60). Indeed, what is observed is a *decelerating* yield, which is insufficient to compensate for the loss in area, leading to a slowing down in the growth rate of food-grain output, and falling per capita food production and food availability (Patnaik, p. 408). This suggests clearly a process of imperialism-induced fettering, stopping the rational use of natural and other resources in the South.[38]

Predatory wars are an important part of imperialism. Hundreds of capitalists and their cartels supported by their national states often try to divide up the economic world amicably among themselves, but military conflict lurks behind economic rivalry (Lenin, 1916a). Capitalism therefore 'has [now] become reduced to the absolute power of a handful of millionaires and multimillionaires who send whole nations into a bloodbath to decide whether

38 It seems to be the case that the imperialist policy package will be implemented in spite of its adverse effects on agriculture, because it serves the interests of the metropolitan capitalist class and its allies in India, including capitalist farmers and sections of the middle class whose support has been bought by unfreezing consumer imports and direct tax cuts (Patnaik, 1999; pp. 356, 366).

[this or that] group of plunderers is to obtain the spoils *of* imperialism, power over the colonies, financial "spheres of influence" or "mandates to rule", etc.' (Lenin, 1919). Wars, like the effects of environmental damage, mean the destruction of productive powers, and is an extreme example of fettering of productive forces.

5 Conclusion

A major conceptual significance of fettering is that it requires political economy to be not just about production but about production and its social relations. Social relations of production do fetter the development of productive forces. For us to better understand this insightful thesis of Marx, we have to go beyond Marx's schematic remarks as well as beyond some of its modern-day interpretations. We need to better understand a) what might fettering exactly mean and b) what exactly are the causal mechanisms of fettering? It is very important that productive forces be conceptualized to include nature and producing human beings, and not just non-human produced means of production.

Fettering of productive forces by social relations of capitalism happens when not only new means of production are not developed or existing means of production are not productively consumed in an optimal manner to create conditions for the development of new means of production. Fettering occurs also when productive power of direct producers is sapped and when improvement in natural conditions of production fails to occur because of capitalist social relations of production. There is no need to distinguish development fettering from use fettering. There is just fettering of the productive forces by the relations of production. Social relations of capitalist production and exchange fetter the development of productive powers of the means of production such as computers or machines, etc. Social relations of capitalist production fetter the productive powers of direct producers (workers who sell their labour power, and petty producers who sell products of their labour) not only by fettering the development of means of production but also by failing to meet the need of direct producers for means of subsistence without which they cannot possess and use their productive abilities. Social relations of capitalism also fetter the development of productive powers of nature by failing to improve it.

Capitalist relations fetter the development of productive forces in the same process in which these relations also develop these forces. The actual mechanisms of fettering include: private ownership and control over means of production; monopolization; crisis tendencies due to rising organic composition of capital; lack of control over production and distribution on the part of direct producers; the profit motive of production because of which direct producers' needs remain unmet causing their productive abilities to be absent or to exist in a crippled form, and nature is damaged (often irreparably), and so on. But it is not just *capitalist* relations that fetter the development productive forces. Imperialism as the highest stage of capitalism also fetters the development of productive forces, especially, in the Global South.

The fettering is relative in the sense that actual output is less than it appears to be because of the costs for planet and people. It is also relative because the net output is less than what it would be under socialist relations where nature and labour, the two sources of wealth, will not be sapped the way they are now. The slight reformulation of productive forces sees workers as productive human beings with social-ecological needs which must be met for their productive powers to be maintained and developed. This has implications for a conception of socialism that is mindful of ecological and bodily health, as discussed in chapter 10.

CHAPTER 6

Marx's *Capital* Volume 1: Relations of Property, Commodity and Value, and the State

There is a difference of opinion, sometimes subtle, concerning the status of the state in *Capital* volume 1. Jacques Bidet (2009: 68) says that in *Capital* volume 1, Marx does not offer 'a theoretical elaboration' on the state. He says that '[t]here is something missing in the discourse of *Capital*, the absence of an articulation between bourgeoisie and the state' (ibid.). In his chapter 33 Lessons on *Capital*, Harry Cleaver says, 'Marx doesn't analyze the state in the abstract but rather shows us concretely in that text where the state appears in the form of its specific apparatuses' (Cleaver, 2019: 51). Similarly, Mike Lebowitz (Lebowitz, 2009: 328–329) thinks that a concept of the state does not exist in *Capital*, but it is implicit and that 'it is possible to reconstruct Marx's concept of the capitalist state as the object and result of class struggle', as the 'latent state' of wage workers. For some (e.g. David Harvey), however, it is not just that the state is missing theoretically. Marx could not have dealt with the state theoretically: 'Conscious class strategies and state interventions are not admissible in the theoretical framework Marx has established' (Harvey, 2010a: 165).

Many decades ago, Bertell Ollman (1976: 220) had said that 'a systematic exposition of the Marxist theory of the state is more essential now than ever'. Marx's 'analysis of the relations between the state and the capitalist economy from the vantage point of such economic Relations as commodity, capital, labor and value (as found in *Capital*) was only mildly distorting of [the] real complexity' that existed 'when the state exercised minimal control over the economy' (ibid.) as during Marx's time. However, 'with the state's role so enlarged' as in the 20th century and in the 21st, 'an understanding of the state-economy relationship (and therefore of capitalism) within these limited dimensions is seriously deficient'. That is why, according to Ollman, 'Marx's political economy must be not only brought up to date but supplemented by what might be called a Marxist "economic polity"' (ibid.). A few decades after, Ollman said, 'Capital contains a theory of the state that, unlike Marx's related economic theories, is never fully worked out' (Ollman, 2003: 136).

I agree that Marx does not write *extensively* about the state, either theoretically or empirically in *Capital*. There is little explicit discussion on the state in his analysis of commodity relations, labour process, methods of exploitation, and general theory of accumulation. But his political economy does point to

 | DOI:10.1163/9789004730472_007

an *implicit* theory of the state that has to be made more explicit. This task has to be conducted more adequately than has generally been done, including even in state derivation-ism discussions.[1]

This chapter and the next two chapters constitute yet another attempt at the exploration of Marx's views on the state as they are present in that text. State theorizing inspired by *Capital* Volume 1 can help us avoid some of the problems with existing theorizing mentioned above. This chapter is divided into 4 sections. Based on Marx's class theory in *Capital* volume 1, section 1 deals with the state at the level of class society as a whole. Section 2 discusses the state and social property (or, class) relations in capitalist class society. Section 3 is focussed on capitalist commodity (value) relations and the state. I relate the state to the three attributes of the commodity in capitalism (use-value, exchange value, and value) and to the nature of the peculiar commodity (labour power). The final section outlines some implications of Marx's ideas about the state and value relations for a future world beyond value relations. The implications of Marx's *Capital* for the ability of the post-capitalist state to construct 'socialism in one country' are discussed in chapter 10.

1 Property Relations of Class Society, and the State

Production can only happen under existing relations of production (which include, above all else, the relations between those who own/control means of production and the direct producers), as we have seen in previous chapters. According to Marx (1859): the term 'relations of production' 'merely expresses the same thing in *legal terms* … the property relations within the framework of which' material productive forces operate (italics added).

Three points need to be quickly made. Firstly, with some justification, 'social relations of production' and 'property relations' as concepts can be said to apply to all forms of society, including those with communal property (e.g. primitive communism; a future communist society) and without the necessity for the state to suppress direct producers.[2] Second, as soon productive forces develop in order to allow human beings to produce a surplus, social relations of production, which in 'legal terms', are property relations, *become* class relations: the production of a surplus creates the condition for class

1 See O'Kane, 2014. See also the discussion on state derivationism in Holloway and Picciotto (1978).

2 Strictly speaking, property relations as *legal* codifications of production exist only in societies with the state – i.e. in class societies.

exploitation and class struggle (more on this below). And with this the necessity for the state arises. Thirdly, Marx's phrase 'legal terms' already points to the codification of production relations by the state and thus the importance of the state in relation to productive forces and production relations and to production as such.

Much of the Marxist state theory has been about capitalist society, which is only one form of class society. There is a need to analyse the state at the level of class relations first before analysing it at the level of, say, capitalist class relation. In *Capital* Volume 1, Marx (1887: 164) begins to develop his class theory by making the following claim:

> Wherever a part of society possesses the monopoly of the means of production, the labourer, free or not free, must add to the working-time necessary for his own maintenance an extra working-time in order to produce the means of subsistence for the owners of the means of production.

This is the case whether the property owner in question is 'the Athenian … well-to-do man …, Etruscan theocrat, … Roman citizen …, Norman baron, American slave-owner, Wallachian Boyard, modern landlord or capitalist' (ibid.). But would these types of property owner be able to maintain their monopoly over property and appropriate surplus labour from direct producers, without the assistance of the state?[3] While it is true that class societies are different one from another on the basis of 'the mode in which … surplus-labour is in each case extracted from the actual producer, the labourer' (Marx, 1887: 153), what is common to all forms of class society is that surplus labour *is* extracted. A presupposition of surplus extraction is that effective control over property is in the hands of a minority in the face of potential and actual opposition from the exploited. And such effective control is not possible without the state.

But could the author of *Capital* really have forgotten about the state's relation to class? As we will see later, Marx certainly did not. In fact, one can say that he almost began *Capital* Volume 1 with a statement about the state, although hidden in a long footnote, where he talks about the state at the level of class relations – that is, about the class-state. He begins with the idea that in certain time periods (e.g. the middle ages and ancient times), politics and religion, and not 'material interests', are said to reign supreme. But '[T]he middle ages could not live on Catholicism, nor the ancient world on politics. On the contrary,

3 After all, and as Leon Trotsky (2008: 145) rightly says, '[p]roperty is a relation among people. It represents an enormous power so long as it is universally recognised and supported by that system of compulsion called Law and the State' (italics added).

it is the mode in which' people living in these societies 'gained a livelihood that explains why here politics, and there Catholicism, played the chief part' (Marx, 1887: 58). Indeed, 'the economic structure of society ... is the real basis on which the juridical and political superstructure is raised' (Marx, 1887: 58). The state is fundamentally shaped by economic conditions/relations, or 'the mode of production'. One cannot understand the state without understanding its causal relation to class relations across class societies.[4] Every economically dominant class, or a class in the process of becoming economically dominant, seeks mastery over the state which, to use Marx's words, is the 'concentrated and organised force of society' (Marx, 1887: 532; italics added).

The class-state tries to defend the property rights of the dominant exploiting class and to make sure that this class is able to augment its property by appropriating surplus labour and in other ways (e.g. war, colonization, and so on). Marx (1887: 531–532) wrote of 'the power of the state' as an economic power in that it seeks to 'hasten ... the process of transformation of the feudal mode of production into the capitalist mode'.[5]

2 Property Relations of Capitalist Class Society, and the State

Capitalist society is a form of class society a major feature of which is commodity exchange. The sphere of the exchange of commodities is one where the principle of Property rules in the sense that 'each disposes only of what is his own' (Marx, 1887: 123). There is a need for state intervention to make sure this rule is protected. Not just that. The state is involved in the very creation of specific property rights by virtue of which 'each disposes only of what is his own' (ibid.).

There are two ways in which the state contributes to the emergence of capitalist property relations. One is class differentiation: in a society where the exchange of commodities is assisted by the state, those who are owners of private property in labour and owners of the products of their labour (i.e. small-scale producers), when unable to pay their bills, lose their property.

4 Marx (1844) says:

> '[T]he slavery of civil society is the natural foundation of the modern state, just as the civil society of slavery was the natural foundation of the state in antiquity. The existence of the state is inseparable from the existence of slavery. The state and slavery in antiquity – frank and open classical antitheses – were not more closely welded together than the modern state and the cut-throat world of modern business.'

5 In terms of the political function, which ultimately is the main function, the state's role is to keep the masses in check, as already indicated.

Some of them come to have more property than others, and some of them become net buyers of labour power, and others become net sellers of labour power. The second process in which small-scale producers lose their property giving rise to the emergence of capitalist property rights holders is what Marx calls primitive or original accumulation, which involves the state too. The state typically enables the forcible separation of direct producers from their private property and from access to communal property and contributes to the emergence of private property in its capitalist form. The state thus produces an important condition for capitalism, that is, 'the owner of money [finds] labour-power in the market as a commodity' (Marx, 1887: 119). This means that 'instead of being in the position to sell commodities in which his [or her] labour is incorporated', a person 'must be obliged to offer for sale as a commodity that very labour-power, which exists only in his [or her] living self' (ibid.). Thus, following the coercive dispossession from their property (and/or alienation from property through market mechanisms), the direct producers are now turned into new class subjects (workers for capitalists), so they are also subjected to physical coercion, criminalization and disciplinary action to make them remain dependent on the wage-relation. The newly created class of workers must be made to be accustomed to working for the capitalists and must be used to working for long hours. It is indeed not enough that the state forcibly separates direct producers from their means of production (and subsistence such as homestead or cottages) to create a proletariat. Following 'the forcible creation of a class of outlawed proletarians', it was the 'bloody discipline that turned them into wage-labourers' (Marx, 1887: 526). They were subjected to 'disgraceful action of the State which employed the police to accelerate the accumulation of capital by increasing the degree of exploitation of labour' (ibid.).

The entire capitalist mode of production itself is based on stealing and 'theft' of common people's resources by the capitalists or to-be-capitalists, assisted by the state.[6] Capital steals people: 'Nothing is more characteristic than their system of stealing men' (slaves) (Marx, 1887: 532). The genesis of capitalism is itself based on 'colossal scale thefts of state lands' (p. 512). Laws exist which serve as 'the instrument of the theft of the people's land' (p. 513). Capital engages in 'the systematic robbery of the Communal lands helped especially, next to the theft of the State domains' (ibid.).[7] This happens with – and cannot

6 Note that this theft does not include appropriation of surplus value on the basis of law of value supported by the state.

7 As we will see later, capital also steals people's labour ('extra' surplus labour) in the sense, for example, that people's need to enjoy a meal is not respected (haggling over meal times).

indeed happen without – the full support of the state. Yet it is the same state that uses force against the economically deprived and the poor to stop them from obtaining direct access to the necessaries of life. For example, the capitalist state has many laws against theft by common people, i.e. against '[t]he whole series of thefts, outrages, and popular misery, that accompanied the forcible expropriation of the people, from the last third of the 15th to the end of the 18th century' (Marx, 1887: 512).

While the state takes action against stealing (or robbing) on the part of common people, consider how it is that the state is fully in support of the capitalist, who has 'bought the use of the labour-power for a definite period' and who 'insists upon his rights', and who therefore 'has no intention of being robbed' (Marx, 1887: 137) by workers.[8] The capitalist has 'a penal code of his own' (ibid.), a penal code to stop any such robbery, a penal code that, ultimately, cannot exist without the state's support. One must ask: what is it about the state that does not allow people to steal the property of capitalists and landlords while it allows the latter classes to engage in various forms of theft which refer to the ways in which these classes steal people's land and state's own resources in various illegal and corrupt ways?

3 Capitalist Commodity and Value Relations, and the State

3.1 *The Commodity Relations and the State*

Marx (1887) memorably begins his *magnum opus*, *Capital* volume 1, with the following words. The wealth of those societies in which the capitalist mode of production prevails, presents itself as 'an immense accumulation of commodities,' so the investigation into capitalism must begin with the analysis of the (representative) commodity (Marx, 1887: 27). Could such an analysis of the commodity in the capitalist society point to an analysis of the capitalist state even if Marx does not explicitly examine the question? The answer is yes.

Capitalism is generally characterized by the free purchase and sale of commodities. A commodity has three attributes: use-value, exchange value, and (labour) value. Use-value (utility) of a commodity inheres in it. Exchange value is the proportion in which 'values in use of one sort are exchanged for those of

Capital 'steals the time required for the consumption of fresh air and sunlight' (p. 179). There are '"small thefts" of capital from the labourer's meal and recreation time, the factory inspectors also designate as "petty pilferings of minutes"' (p. 167). In pursuit of cheap labour, it is also engaged in 'child-stealing' (p. 537).

8 Workers can 'rob' the capitalists when they work less than the usual working day or when they work with less than normal intensity or when they waste any resource.

another sort, a relation constantly changing with time and place' (Marx, 1887: 27). Value (or labour value) is the fact that every commodity represents a certain amount of socially necessary abstract labour time (explained later). The state is related to each of the three aspects of the commodity.

The state is presupposed by commodity relations because of a positive (= coordinative) and a negative (= punitive) reason that Marx does not explicitly discuss. To the extent that the wealth of capitalist society exists in the form of 'immense collection of commodities', the capitalist state[9] must maintain the commodity form/status of wealth (of use-values). As inanimate objects, '[c]ommodities cannot go to market and make exchanges of their own account' (Marx, 1887: 60). There must be 'their guardians' – that is, 'their owners ... who must place themselves in relation to one another, as persons whose will resides in those objects' (ibid.). The state must ensure that commodity owners relate to one another on the basis of four basic principles. This sphere is 'a very Eden of the innate rights of [human beings]', and in this sphere 'alone rule Freedom, Equality, Property and Bentham' (Marx, 1887: 123). There is freedom 'because both buyer and seller of a commodity ... contract as free agents, and the agreement they come to, is but the form in which they give *legal expression* to their common will' (ibid.; italics added). It is the state that represents – embodies – this legal expression. There is equality because each guardian of commodity 'enters into relation with the other, as with a simple owner of commodities, and they exchange equivalent for equivalent' (ibid.). If 100 pens are worth $100, a buyer cannot force the seller to sell the pens for less than $100. The state is supposed to make sure that there is no cheating or fraud. There is respect for property because each guardian of the commodity 'disposes only of what is his own' (ibid.). There is no scope for grabbing what belongs to someone else. In other words, the state makes sure that there is respect for property. And, of course, there is 'Bentham, because each looks only to himself' (ibid.). The only force that brings the guardians of commodities 'together and puts them in relation with each other, is the selfishness, the gain and the private interests of each' (ibid.). The state, more or less, reproduces and supports this selfishness. All in all, the rule of 'Freedom, Equality, Property and Bentham' (ibid.) presupposes state action, in the sense that the state is supposed to ensure this rule.

Commodity exchange implies a division of labour in society where different producers produce different commodities.[10] This social division of labour in turn requires 'a division of labour' between society and the state in the following sense. In a society where there exists a massive and expanding division of labour, concrete labours in different places across the world are

9 Engels (1877) calls it the 'official representative of society as a whole'.

10 Social division of labour also has a spatial aspect in the form of a spatial division of labour.

inter-connected through exchange on the basis of abstract labour, and where exchange value is 'constantly changing with time and place' (Marx, 1887: 27), the state action is necessary to create conditions for society-wide coordination of the myriad commodity relations involving numerous producers, large and small. Commodity relations have a spatial – scalar – form, and this fact has implications for the state. The commodity relations happen at multiple spatial scales. The global scale is very important for capitalism: 'The production of commodities, their circulation, and that more developed form of their circulation' which is called world-embracing commerce, or trade, 'these form the historical ground-work from' which capitalism rises (Marx, 1887: 85). It follows that the state of a country protects the commodity relations that its business class enters into abroad.

It is the state, indeed, which introduces various rules to support and sustain commodity relations in the overall interest of the 'community' of commodity owners and to resolve any conflict among them. It makes sure that the guardians – the commodity owners – 'must behave in such a way that each does not appropriate the commodity of the other, and part with his own, except by means of an act done by mutual consent' and that 'they must, therefore, mutually recognise in each other *the right* of private proprietors' (Marx, 1887: 60; italics added). The relation between commodity owners as mediated by, and within, the state is a juridical relation: 'This *juridical* relation ... expresses itself in a contract, whether such contract be part of a developed legal system or not' (ibid.; italics added). It is 'a relation between two wills' (ibid.). Although, the state, or the juridical relation, is 'the reflex of the real economical relation between the two' (ibid.), state's coordinative activities are crucial to the reproduction of commodity relations, including those that involve capital and labour. There is also a need to create a geographical built environment to connect different commodity producers located in different geographical sites of concrete labour. The state seeks to fulfil this communal or society-wide need – directly through a subcontracting mechanism.[11]

Commodity exchange requires a medium of exchange, so the state 'puts in circulation bits of paper on which their various denominations ... are printed' (Marx, 1887: 83).[12] The state has to make sure that insofar as currencies 'take

11 The latter happens when private companies build the physical infrastructure for a profit which comes from hefty payments made by the state to these companies which tend to over-invoice the state.

12 'Capital is nothing more ... than money put back into production and circulation to yield more money. If money is to represent real values the same kind of State regulation of money supply and credit is called for' (Harvey, 2012: 274).

the place of gold to the same amount, their movement is subject to the laws that regulate the currency of money itself' (Marx, 1887: 83). It has to make sure that the money in circulation 'must have an objective social validity of its own': 'This compulsory action of the State can take effect only within that inner sphere of circulation which is coterminous with the territories of the community' (ibid.: 84).[13] The state acts as the lender of last resort which prevents the collapse of the monetary order and banking systems.

There is a punitive reason why the state is presupposed by – necessary for – the existence of commodity relations. The rules of commodity exchange can be violated by the guardians of commodities whose self-interest ('Benthamism') lies in expanding their command over commodities (and over money, the most abstract 'form' of commodities), so punitive actions by the state may be necessary. Commodity owners are all equal in that they all have the same trait (they all own commodities) and that they relate to one another on the basis of equality. Yet commodity relations can be unequal because some commodity owners, prior to any commodity exchange, may have more exchange value (e.g. more quantity of a given commodity or of its monetary value) than others, and that in order to expand their command over commodities and to improve their status as commodity owners, some may inflict extra-commodity relations or unequal exchange on others and defraud them, including by using monopoly power. There is therefore a need to 'guard the guardians' – i.e. to make sure that a given guardian of the commodity does not force another guardian to sell their commodity below the market price or part with their commodity against their wish. There is a need for a (political) guardian of the guardians (of economic commodities). The state is ultimately that guardian. Dominantly a site of extra-economic relations, the state must ensure that commodities are exchanged on the basis of economic relations, that is, without extra-economic coercion or without a significant quantity of extra-economic coercion. So, commodity relations are not necessarily a peaceful matter.

The state's defence of existing commodity relations on the basis of freedom and equality contribute to unfreedom and inequality. There is a massive amount of 'class inequality' between owners of capital and labour. There is also a relation of unfreedom between capital and labour, in the sense that workers are not free not to sell their labour power to the capitalist class. There is inequality, including in the form of class differentiation among commodity producers: state's defense of commodity relations based on equality produce inequality among commodity producers. Exactly in the same process the state

13 The state is also a guarantor of the stability of exchanges and therefore of the form of value (Callinicos, 1987a: 100).

is a condition for the production of inequality between the big capitalists and small-scale owners.

The dominant aim of capitalist production is not to directly meet the needs of people. 'Use-values are only produced by capitalists, because, and in so far as, they are the material substratum, the depositories of exchange-value' (Marx, 1887: 131). The capitalist's aim is 'to produce a use-value that has a value in exchange, that is to say, an article destined to be sold, a commodity'. Capitalists also have the 'boundless greed after riches' and the 'passionate chase after value' (ibid.: 107; stress added). In fact,

> it is only in so far as the appropriation of ever more *wealth in the abstract* is the sole driving force behind his operations that he functions as a capitalist ... Use-values must therefore *never be treated* as the real [or immediate] aim of the capitalist ... The restless never-ending process of *profit-making* alone is what he aims at. (ibid.; italics added)

That means that if the state supports commodity relations, it must, generally, support the commodity relations *that are capitalist* so it must also support capitalists' 'boundless greed after riches' and the 'passionate chase after value'.

3.2 *Value Relations and the State*

What determines the proportion in which one commodity is exchanged for many other commodities within a country or across countries is the social value (or simply, value) of the commodities: a socially necessary amount of abstract or homogenous labour performed under average conditions.

The labour that defines value is socially necessary labour. 'In general, the greater the productiveness of labour, the less is the labour time required for the production of an article, the less is the amount of labour crystallised in that article, and the less is its value' (Marx, 1887: 29–30). So the value of a commodity (v) 'varies directly as the quantity (q), and inversely as the productiveness (p), of the labour incorporated in it' (ibid.: 30). This productiveness is a function of the average amount of skill of the working men and women, the state of science and technology as well as the social organization of production and quality of the means of production (ibid.: 29). This productiveness is also a function of physical/natural conditions.

Now, the state is potentially related to each of these circumstances, a fact Marx abstracts from. Anything that the state can do to reduce the costs of discovery of, for example, minerals (e.g. oil drilling) will affect their value. The state can change the state of development of science and technology via its investment in education and research. The state invests resources in transforming the physical/natural environment as well (e.g. irrigating a dry area or increasing an area's geographical accessibility).

A commodity must be produced at its value, within a given geographical territory defined by the commodity circulation. It could be the area under the jurisdiction of the nation-state, and it could be the world market, which is where the law of value ultimately operates. If an enterprise spends x minutes of socially necessary average labour to produce a laptop, while the average amount of time taken to produce a laptop is x/2 minutes, that enterprise runs the risk of going out of business, unless, for example, it is subsidized by the state bridging the gap between the individual and social value. By supporting capitalist commodity relations, the state supports some capitals better than other capitals. Depending on the instrumentalist link between specific fractions of the capitalist class on the one hand and politicians and bureaucrats managing the affairs of the state on the other hand, certain capitalists can be advantaged. By investing in science and technology and through other measures, the state can create a situation where the value of commodities produced by capital under its territorial jurisdiction is reduced below the global average and where a country's global competitiveness is thus enhanced.

3.3 *The State and the 'Peculiar Commodity'*

In capitalism, an important form of commodity exchange is the one between workers and capitalists. They function 'as free persons, as independent owners of commodities; the one possessing money and means of production, the other labour-power' (p. 272). Workers (unlike petty producers) do not sell their labour – they do not sell the products of their labour. They instead sell their labour *power* or the 'capacity for labour'. This is 'the aggregate of those mental and physical capabilities existing in a human being', which they exercise whenever they produce a use-value (ibid.: 119). The labour power that *produces* commodities *is itself* a commodity.[14]

The sale and purchase of labour power requires a certain condition which has to be produced: double freedom of labour. The first aspect of this freedom is that people are economically forced to sell their labour power because they possess no means of production, a process that happens through forced dispossession and commercial class differentiation. Both of these mechanisms are related to state intervention. The state must make sure that the labour remain more or less property-less and mainly reliant on the sale of their labour power. This is a negative freedom. The second aspect of the freedom is that

14 We are abstracting from the labour of a small-scale producer working on own account.

the person must be free from any obstacle to them freely selling their labour power, and it is the capitalist state that removes the obstacles in the form of pre-capitalist regulations. This freedom, a positive freedom, exists only when the seller is the sole owner of the commodity, who does not sell himself/herself but only their ability to work for a certain number of hours every day and week.

The owner of labour power and 'the owner of money meet in the market', and there is only one difference between them: 'one is buyer, the other seller; both, therefore, equal in *the eyes of the law*' (ibid.; italics added). The state has to make sure that the labour power is a commodity and continues to remain so, that is, a person is not extra-economically forced to sell their labour power to a given buyer/employer and that a person must have the freedom to withdraw selling their labour power when they wish to.

Labour freedom, labour's commodity status, that the state generally seeks to protect, is beneficial to labour and to capital. It is better to work and live as a free labourer than an unfree/slave labourer. Because workers own their commodity labour power, they can sell it to whoever they want to and wherever they want to: if they receive lower wages from buyer b1 in one place than what the buyer b2 in another place offers, then they are free to sell it to b2. To the extent that the buyer, b1, pays lower-than-average wages and can benefit from the unfreedom and immobility of particular sellers of labour power, then he/she (b1) can have a competitive advantage over another buyer (b2). So the state makes sure that no such unfair advantage occurs in the labour market.

Individual commodity owners need rules that govern commodity exchange but such rules and mechanisms of maintaining those rules constitute a use-value which cannot be bought and sold for a profit and which cannot therefore be supplied by capitalists because of their self-interested ('Benthamite') character. This applies to the peculiar commodity (labour power). The capitalist and the worker cannot maintain the labour power in its commodity status: they cannot ensure that the labourer is able to treat 'his labour-power as his own property … by placing it at the disposal of the buyer temporarily, for a definite period of time' and that he and the owner of money deal with each other 'on the basis of equal rights' (Marx, 1887: 119; italics added). Only the state, characterized by a semblance of the separation from the private interests of workers and capitalists, can do so in the interests of the 'community' of workers and capitalists. 'Wherever free labour is the rule, *the laws* regulate the mode of terminating this contract' (Marx, 1887: 123; italics added). The fact of a free labourer is codified in state laws: '[O]nly the independent labourer, and therefore only the labourer *legally qualified* to act for himself, enters as a vendor of a commodity into a contract with the capitalist' (ibid.: 194; italics added).

There is a sense in which different types of labour are the same: leather work, scavenging, computer-typing are all equal – so leather workers, scavengers and typists are all equal – in that they represent the expenditure of a certain amount of mental and manual energy. This fact contributes to the notion of equality in society which is then reflected in state's laws about equality: all the people are equal before law. So not only does the state maintain the commodity status of the products of labour and of labour power, but also does it maintain the equal status of people involved in different kinds of labour.

Like any other commodity, labour power has value. Value of labour power is the average value of the necessary commodified means of subsistence which people need to live.[15] The value of this commodity has some peculiarity, with implications for the state. The value of labour power includes the cost of satisfying different needs (a definite quantity of muscle, brain, and the like is expended, which has to be replaced; shelter, healthcare, education, and so on) and the cost of replacing the people who die. The state plays a role in meeting some of the needs and in regulating how these needs are met. Needs are shaped by the physical environment, which is in turn changed partly by state action (e.g. policies concerning the environment). Habits and expectations and the level of civilization also shape human needs, adding a cultural element to human need. Here also the state plays a role as it partly serves as a repository of human history and memories and subjected to pressure from workers (to expand their needs).

If the state is involved in the determination of the value of labour power, it is then involved in production of labour power itself. Some of the state-aided technical change can reduce the value of labour power by shortening the time taken to produce the means of subsistence or to produce the means of production that produce the wage goods. It can affect the cost of the maintenance of labour through policies of taxation of subsistence of items and through its import policies where cheap articles produced abroad enter a national market thus lowering the cost of reproduction. By contributing to the value of labour power in non-commodified forms (e.g. state-funded schools), the state can also lower the value of the bundle of necessaries (i.e. wages that private capital pays), other things constant.

The commodity relations are characterized by the principle of not only freedom but also equality: commodity owners 'exchange equivalent for equivalent'. This general principle applies to buyers and sellers of labour power. Not only should sellers of labour power be free to sell their commodity (and that the state seeks to make sure that this happens) but also the price of their commodity, labour power (i.e. wage), should be equal to the cost of its production. Marx generally assumes in *Capital* Volume 1 that this is the case, but he is also

15 Wage is the monetary form of this value.

aware that in the real world, this is not. Millions of people receive a wage that is below the cost of production of their labour power, including the cost of food and shelter, education for children, and so on.

3.4 *The State and Commodity Fetishism*

Commodity fetishism is an important trait of capitalist society. It refers to the fact that commodities 'behave' as if being sold and bought is in an inherent part of being a useful thing, even if it is the case that '[s]o far no chemist has ever discovered exchange value either in a pearl or a diamond' (Marx, 1887: 53). Commodity fetishism means that life in capitalism is objectively based on the fact that if I have a need for a computer or a house, these must be bought (I cannot have direct access to these), which means that these must be produced and sold for a profit. Commodity fetishism means that, for example, for every potato one has, one wishes to have as many eggplants as possible from the other person one is in an exchange relation with, so these commodities effectively start relating to one another replacing the direct relation between the two producers in question. One does not care about the conditions under which the other person is living and working.

The veil of commodity fetishism is not and cannot be removed 'until it is treated as production by freely associated people, and is consciously regulated by them in accordance with a settled plan' where 'the labour power of all the different individuals is consciously applied as the combined labour power of the community' (Marx, 1887: 51–52). But the state is the biggest obstacle to this possibility because it maintains the commodity status of things that people need: it protects the private character of production and the commodity status of the products of labour.

The state reproduces a system where the production for sale for profit subordinates the production for directly meeting human needs. The state cannot ensure that society produces things that directly meet people's needs. The state is bound by the law of commodity fetishism. The state is also responsible for keeping the veil of the geographical form of commodity fetishism: because the state, in its national-geographical form, does not allow the rational and conscious mobilization of world's resources across existing national boundaries, is not possible.

3.5 *The State and Counter-tendencies to Equality and Freedom in Commodity Relations*

The sphere of purchase and sale of commodities, including labour power, is based on equality, freedom, etc. (Marx, 1887: 123). In actual practice, however, this rule is violated, and here as well the state is involved. While the state seeks to, is expected to, ensure labour freedom, it often is the case that labour is not free. In capitalism, there is unfree labour in many cases.[16] Child labour itself is unfree labour.[17]

Marx assumes that wages cover the cost of reproduction of labour power. In reality, this is the not the case (and Marx acknowledges this): wages fall below the value of labour power. And, the state is complicit in this gap. It is the case that 'during the historic genesis of capitalist production, the bourgeoisie, at its rise, wants and uses the power of the state ... to force them within the limits suitable for surplus-value making' (Marx, 1887: 523). During the historical genesis, increasing wages beyond a limit or receiving wages beyond a level invited state penalty. The state makes sure that wages remain within limits so that the capitalist class has a reasonable rate of profit. Even when real wages fall, and this happened, for example, in England in the 16th century, causing 'the condition of the labourers ... [to] become much worse' (Marx, 1887: 524), 'the laws for keeping them down remained in force, together with the ear-clipping and branding of those "whom no one was willing to take into service"' (p. 524). Whether or not the ruling classes needed any regulation of wages, it 'was unwilling in case of necessity to be without the weapons of the old arsenal' (p. 524). It was only in 1813 that 'the laws for the regulation of wages were repealed' in England (p. 525). This situation characterized not only the early stage of capitalism in Europe but also capitalism during the current times, especially in the periphery. Often millions of workers do not get a wage that conforms to the value of labour power; millions are not free to work for whoever they wish to, the facts which the state *can* do something but often fails to, because it works in the interests of *specific* capitalists who may be politically and or economically important and who benefit from such a regime of low wages and unfreedom. In addition, promoting economic globalization (free trade), the states of advanced countries trigger a race to the bottom in terms of wages. This tendency was there during Marx's time as well to some extent. In 1870s, a British politician

16 According to Brass, in the process of class struggle, capitalists may take away the freedom of hitherto free workers – 'the ability of workers to enter and withdraw from particular labour markets and labour processes', including the ability to sell the labour power as a commodity to whoever they wish to (Brass, 1994: 259). Brass suggests that 'capitalism is not only compatible with unfree labour but in certain situations actually prefers this to a free workforce' (ibid. 255; see Brass, 2022; 2011; Das, 2013a).

17 Marx treats 'the labour of those who are physically and legally minors' which can play an important role as 'a specially striking example of labour exploitation' (Marx, 1887: 194) where, in some contexts, the adult male acting as a free agent 'sells [his] wife and child. He has become a slave-dealer. The demand for children's labour often resembles in form the inquiries for ... slaves [as in America]' (Marx, 1887: 272).

remarked: '"If China ... should become a great manufacturing country, I do not see how the manufacturing population of Europe could sustain the contest without descending to the level of their competitors" (Times, Sept. 3, 1873, p. 8.)' (Marx, 1887: 430). Marx goes on to say something which is so contemporary: 'The wished-for goal of English capital is no longer Continental wages but Chinese' (ibid.).

Wages have remained within limits broadly favourable to capital, thanks partly to the state.[18] When wages rise beyond a point, the state takes step to reduce wages by, for example, raising the interest rate and creating unemployment. Similarly, even if daily or weekly wages increase, the price of labour power per hour (hourly wage) may be reduced because of capitalists prolonging the working day for a given daily wage. In addition, when the per-hour wage during the normal part of the working day is low, this 'compels the labourer to work during the better paid over-time, if he wishes to obtain a sufficient wage at all' (Marx, 1887: 386). The state engages in a case of non-doing: it does little to prevent a drop in real wages or to increase real wages.

The level of wages is partly a function of the relative power of capital and labour, a power that is mediated by the state. So complementing the state interventions aimed at regulating wages *in favour of capital* is the fact that workers' trade union activity is often restricted or even prevented by the state.[19] This has happened historically, as during Marx's time: between 1300s and 1825, workers' organization ('coalition') was treated in England as a heinous crime. '[O]nly against its will and under the pressure of the masses did the English Parliament give up the laws against Strikes and Trades' Unions, after it had itself, for 500 years, held, with shameless egoism, the position of a permanent Trades' Union of the capitalists against the labourers' (Marx, 1887: 523). More specifically, restrictions on unionization were lifted not until the time of the fully developed manufacture period when 'the capitalist mode of production had become sufficiently strong to render legal regulation of wages as impracticable as it was unnecessary; but the ruling classes were unwilling in case of necessity to be without the weapons of the old arsenal in case some emergency should arise' (p. 524). This happens in our time.[20] Labour organization

---

18 This is indicated by the decreasing ratio of wages to the value of the product (national income) that workers make. Between 1970 and 2015, the share of national income paid out to workers has decreased from about 55% to below 40% in advanced countries and from more than 50% to less than 40% in emerging economies (Dao et al., 2017).

19 '[T]he movement of the English agricultural proletariat [was] entirely crushed since the suppression of its violent manifestations after 1830' (Marx, 1887: 199).

20 Commenting on the trade union activity in the current times, an ILO (2017) report says: 'In some cases union membership is repressed for political or investment considerations. Some governments have "adopted a restrictive policy with regard to recognising

is often criminalized.[21] Coercive powers – those of police and army – are used against workers, and these powers are supplemented by capitalists' own coercive agents, legal or illegal.[22]

A peculiar character of labour power as a commodity is its 'perishability'. If a sweet potato is not sold for a couple of days, or if a machine is not sold for a few weeks, their use-value will not be significantly affected. This is not true about the labour power. If a person cannot find wage work, he/she may starve. 'If his [or her] capacity for labour remains unsold, the labourer derives no benefit from it', but there is 'a cruel nature-imposed necessity that this capacity has cost for its production a definite amount of the means of subsistence' (Marx, 1887: 122). This commodity (labour power) cannot be separated from its owner and kept in a fridge. Labour power has a bodily location: it inheres in the bearer of the commodity.[23] If it is not reproduced through regular consumption of food, clothing, medicine, and so on, its possessor, a human being, may cease to exist.[24] The state is directly or otherwise responsible for the immense emotional as well as physical suffering of the working class by not stopping the capitalist class from producing the health consequences for labour and by not making adequate interventions to ensure good health.

Marx (1887: 122) decides 'to assume provisionally, that the possessor of labour-power, on the occasion of each sale, immediately receives the price stipulated to be paid for it'. In reality, workers are paid several weeks after they perform their work. In this sense, the use-value of the labour power – labour – is given as a loan to the capitalist. There are many potential consequences of workers' loan to the capitalist. While the worker receives wages weeks after performing their work (i.e. weeks after selling its commodity – labour power), and the small-scale producers receive money for their product weeks after they sell it, they have to pay the property-owning class for the things that they

---

unions in the hope of attracting foreign investment." In addition, restrictions of various kinds and officially sanctioned, or ignored, anti-union activities remain pervasive in a large number of countries as reflected by the numerous complaints filed each year and examined by the ILO's Committee on Freedom of Association.'

21 In Marx's (1880) proposed workers' enquiry, the question #91 reads: 'Do you know of cases when the government made unfair use of the armed forces, to place them at the disposal of the employers against their wage workers?'

22 The Maruti car workers' struggle in India is a clear testimony to this: these workers have been punished basically because they have fought to establish a trade union organization that is independent of company influence (Krishnan, 2017; White, J., 2017).

23 And the body – women's body in the current society – is also the producer of future labour power.

24 Loss of work – not being hired by anyone (rejection) – hurts one emotionally too, which is why there is a strong association between depression and unemployment (Dooley et al., 1994).

need (e.g. food, medicine, and so on) at the time of buying them and even before they begin to consume a thing (people have to pay rent in advance). Thus, propertied class people, who control the means of production and subsistence, receive a credit from the masses who are always short of money. The state does little here. If the workers get paid only after having worked for 2–4 weeks, why does the state not give a loan to the worker to live for those 2–4 weeks, i.e. until they have received their wages?

4 Conclusion

State power – both in terms of what the state does and what it does not – is very much implicit in Marx's analysis of the commodity character of capitalism. The state is a necessary precondition for value relations and for capitalist property relations.

The state sustains property and commodity relations in various ways. Firstly, by using extra-economic coercion against small-scale producers (*a la* Marx) and by supporting commodity relations that subject small-scale producers to class differentiation (*a la* Lenin), the state supports the creation of the two basic classes: a class which owns/sells labour power as a commodity and a class that is the (net) buyer of this commodity and that owns the means of production in their commodity form. The state codifies the rules that support the existence of the classes based on private property relations.[25] Secondly, the state, the sphere of extra-economic coercion, makes sure that commodity exchange can freely happen, that is, that one parts with what truly belongs to one, that commodity exchange happens on the basis of the principle of 'the equivalent for the equivalent', and that there is therefore no cheating or extra-economic coercion in the sphere of economic exchange. It also affects the ways in which commodity exchange happens (e.g. investment in science which affects value; contribution to wages falling below the value of labour power, through the provision of de-commodified services). Thirdly, it tends to take steps to stop the violation of the law of commodity exchange. Fourthly, in certain cases, it itself enforces unequal exchange (or it tolerates or encourages unequal exchange on the part of commodity producers), when it is necessary in the immediate interest of capitalist class as a whole, or in the interest of a hegemonic fraction of that class, or when the long-term interest of capitalist society is at stake. Colonialism/imperialism is an expression of this tendency.

25 These rules reflect capitalist private property relations in the framework of which occur the production and sale/purchase of commodities.

Whether the owner of labour power or of any other commodity, everyone is a commodity owner and seller. In addition, all are regarded as equal before the law irrespective of what commodity – or how much of it – each owns: whether they own land as private property or whether they are poor people who own nothing but their labour power. Indeed, '[a]s the rule of law, the bourgeois state treats its citizens as free and equal owners of private property … one only acquires property by endowment, inheritance, exchange, or purchase' (Heinrich, 2004: 204–205). So state's neutrality – as the realm of extra-economic coercion – is not an illusion. Rather, it is precisely by means of this neutrality that 'the state secures the foundations of capitalist relations of domination and exploitation' (p. 205). The defence of property of everyone in a neutral manner implies that 'those who possess no relevant property beyond their own labour-power must sell their labour-power … and submit to capital' (ibid.). The state just makes sure that 'all members of society behave like owners of private property' (Heinrich, 2004: 204). It has to be independent because it has to force all members of society to recognize one another as private property owners.

In terms of freedom, the situation is better in capitalism than in precapitalist societies which lack the kind of equality and freedom that nominally exist under capitalism. Yet one cannot fetishize freedom in the sphere of capitalist exchange that the state protects. But this is exactly what most people do: prompted by the surface appearances of free exchange, they fetishize the idea that there is freedom and equality and that there is respect for private property (private property is sacrosanct), even if millions of workers experience unfreedom in the labour market and even if millions of small-scale producers lose their property through commodity exchange every year in major capitalist countries. In fact, the Heritage Foundation (2020) speaks for many when it equates economic freedom to freedom *from* government regulation, which really means freedom *to* buy and sell for profit without government intervention. Ultimately, this freedom to buy and sell is the freedom of large-scale businesses to a) buy labour power from its owners (the working class), b) to buy commodities (e.g. raw materials) from small-scale producers, and c) to sell commodities to small-scale producers and wage workers (e.g. means of production to the former, and means of subsistence to both), in a way that affects these classes adversely. The state protects this specific economic freedom, the freedom of capitalists that exists at the expense of the masses.

There *is* an internal relation between the state and the capitalist class. This idea goes against the excessive emphasis placed within (western) Marxist state theory on the separation of the political from the economic causing the so-called relative autonomy of the state. The separation of the political from the economic is more apparent than real. The idea of the separation means that individual capitalists generally do not need to exercise extra-economic coercion against other capitalists or against their workers in economic transactions.[26] This approach, in my view, while it captures a part of the reality, is deficient: it sees capitalism and its state not only from the standpoint of individual capitalists rather than as a class, but also from the standpoint of pre-capitalist societies. In pre-capitalist societies, individual owners of property (e.g. feudal lords) have political power by virtue of having control over property, a situation that is different from capitalism, where individual capitalists as capitalist property-owners do not possess public political power merely by virtue of being capitalists. But the capitalist class as a whole, by virtue of their control over property, does exercise political, cultural, and juridical functions in the lives of the masses (Eagleton, 1991: 113) in the sense that these functions are collectively performed by the collective capitalist, the state. Note that at the level of the capitalist class as a whole, the working class has no choice not to work for a wage, and it cannot choose between capitalist and non-capitalist employers.

The internal relation between the state (political power) and those who control property has important theoretical. Firstly, the internal relation thesis does not mean that capitalists and those who manage their common affairs within the state (politicians and bureaucrats) are one class. Secondly, to say that the state is the dominant part would be like saying that security officers that guard capitalists' property are the real owners of the property which the capitalists enjoy for a fee (to paraphrase a point Marx made). In fact, 'the bourgeois do not allow the state to interfere in their private interests beyond a point and give it only as much power as is necessary for their own safety and the maintenance of competition' (ibid.).

Thirdly, and related to the last point, the internal relation thesis raises the matter of the distinction between economic and political power. Those people who talk about merely economic power of capitalists do so in order 'to sidestep the question of how to transform society without the conquest of state power' (Trotsky, 1977: 121). In fact, 'the distinction between political and economic power ... [is a] terminological trap':

26 Creaven (2000; see also Wood, 2012) says that 'the structural configuration of capitalist relations of production', that is, the separation of the direct producers from access to the means of production, 'enables their routine reproduction by economic mechanisms without the continual intervention or threat of intervention of politico-military force in the class struggle' (ibid.).

> "Economic power", as such, does not exist. There is property, different forms of property. State power provides the opportunity to retain, or on the contrary, to abolish capitalist property, depending on whether state power belongs to the bourgeoisie or to the proletariat. (ibid.)

The relation between the state and private is absolutely crucial. Marx (1847) says:

> The question of property, depending on the different levels of development of industry, has always been the vital question for a particular class. In the 17th and 18th centuries, when the point at issue was the abolition of feudal property relations, the question of property was the vital question for the bourgeois class. In the 19th century, when it is a matter of abolishing bourgeois property relations, the question of property is a vital question for the working class.

Yet, many radical or Marxist scholars find no necessary relation between the two. Consider the following statement from Resnick and Wolff, two post-modernist Marxists, does not make sense:

> To own property in a particular society need not empower the owner to employ another human being or to participate in state decisions; that would depend, for example, on ideological and political conditions in that society. To be propertyless need not require a person to sell labor power; that would depend, for example, on whether propertyless persons had socially recognized access to income from other sources [such as the state]. (Resnick and Wolff, 2006: 119)

In the post-modernist Marxist view, 'the ownership of property (whether in means of production or more generally) is neither a necessary nor a sufficient condition for the wielding of power and vice versa' (Resnick and Wolff, 2006: 119).[27] In other words, the relation between the state and private property is contingent: it depends on ideology and politics. This view is mistaken.

It is true that whether a given propertyless person must sell labour power would depend on whether he/she has socially recognized access to income

27 In this view, communism (which, according to Marxism, requires that exploitative private property be abolished) is also a class society because the society as a whole will appropriate and distribute surplus labour from individuals. So social relations of production in communism and those in capitalism are both class relations.

from sources such as state, but if the state provided adequate means of subsistence to all propertyless, would there be class relations of any sort? And if the state does not and cannot do so, then the question is, why not?

Fred Block (Block, 2019) rejects Marxism's emphasis on the property-based definition of capitalism. He rejects the Marxist idea that 'the key factor in understanding any given society is the nature of the property system' (p. 1167). He suggests that one must 'avoid characterizing any particular society as being capitalist' (p. 1173), that is, a society 'defined as a regime of private property in which producers seek to profit in competitive markets' (p. 1167). The property-based view of capitalism cannot explain 'the huge differences in income inequality' among capitalist countries. He rejects therefore Marxism's view that '[w]ithout transforming that core relationship by ending private ownership of the means of production, reforms that were won today would be reversed tomorrow' (p. 1167). Block assumes that there is no internal relation between capitalist class relation and the legal and political system (i.e. the state), so the latter can be used to meet the needs of the masses. This sort of mistaken views about the relation between the state and property have specific political implications as discussed in the last chapter.

CHAPTER 7

Marx's *Capital* Volume 1: Capital Circuit, Capitalist Accumulation, and the State

According to *Capital* Volume 1, circulation, or the exchange of commodities, itself creates no value, although surplus value presupposes circulation. Nor can the redistribution of means of production itself augment the wealth of society, although the conversion of pre- or non-capitalist forms of wealth into its capitalist form can expand capitalist wealth. On the basis of circulation and creation of capitalist property from pre-capitalist or non-capitalist (small-scale owners') property, fresh wealth is ultimately produced in capitalism inside the hidden abode of capitalist production, and it is here that the state plays an important role. Capital is value-in-motion, so it is not enough for the state to merely defend capitalist property rights or commodity relations. Therefore, the state must take steps to promote capitalist accumulation in the long-term interests of the capitalist class, and especially its economically and politically hegemonic fraction.

To describe the nature of capitalism, Marx (1887: 104; 106) begins with the formula, M–C–M′, which means 'the transformation of money into commodities, and the change of commodities back again into money' plus an increment. 'Money that circulates in the latter manner is thereby transformed into, becomes capital, and is already potentially capital' (p. 104). 'This increment or excess over the original value' is called surplus value. 'It is this movement that converts it into capital' (ibid.: 106).

M–C–M′ can be further expanded to M–C(MP + LP)–P–C′–M′. The state is connected to each phase of the circuit (Fig. 7.1). The capital circuit in its expanded form can serve as a method of systematic presentation as well as a method of analysis of the role of the state.

In Sections 1–2, I discuss how the state is connected to the successive phases of the capital circuit. I discuss the state's role in relation to accumulation in Section 3. I also discuss the state's role in relation to tendencies *and* counter-tendencies towards economic crisis. In the last section, I summarize the discussion and reflect on its implications for the concepts of state capitalism and socialism.

 | DOI:10.1163/9789004730472_008

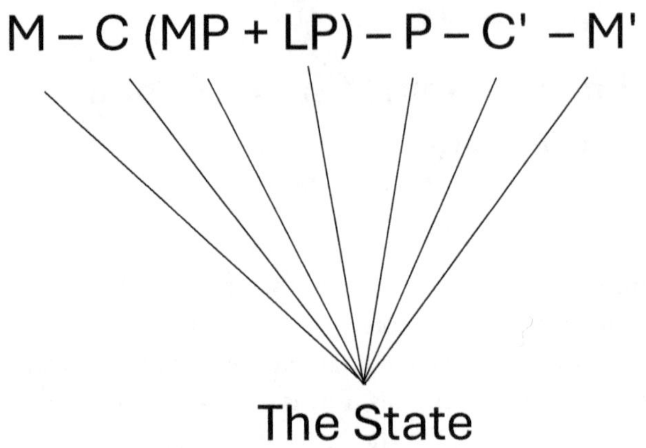

FIGURE 7.1 The capital circuit and the state
Notes: M: Money; C: commodities; MP: means of production (e.g. machines, raw materials; energy; software); LP: labour power; P: production; C: new commodities produced; M′: initial money invested plus surplus value
SOURCE: DAS (2022B)

1 The M–C (*MP + LP*) and the C′–M′ Phases of the Capital Circuit, and the State

M–C(MP + LP) means that money is invested to buy commodities (labour power and means of production). C′–M′ means that new commodities produced are sold for more money than initially invested. The state is connected to these two parts of the capital circuit.

The state makes liquid investible resources (M) available to capitalists (and especially to the big business), often at below-market rates, through various policies (e.g. low-interest loans, quantitative easing, loan waivers or forgiveness, tax-waivers,[1] etc.). Some of these policies represent simple plundering of the state treasury.[2]

1 Note that if the capitalist class does not pay any taxes, that does not have any implication for the rate of surplus value. Some people think that 'a rise in surplus value, unaccompanied by a fall in the value of labour-power, can occur through the abolition of taxes payable by the capitalist.' This is absurd, says Marx. 'The abolition of such taxes makes no change whatever in the quantity of surplus-value that the capitalist extorts at first-hand from the labourer. It alters only the proportion in which that surplus-value is divided between himself and third persons. It consequently makes no alteration whatever in the relation between surplus-value and value of labour-power' (Marx, 1887: 371).

2 Often the money received from the state (including by cheap credits) is used by capital to simply speculate rather than to invest to produce goods and services that people need, and

The state goes to wars, proxy or direct, to obtain raw materials and energy for the large-scale businesses based in the territory under its jurisdiction. The state puts resources (constant capital) in the hands of capital including by providing subsidized inputs (e.g. subsidized knowledge produced in state-funded laboratories). The state makes bulky investments in the physical infrastructure, including through its own large-scale companies.

A special type of commodity that capitalists, whether bigger or smaller, need in the production process is labour power. The state's relation to commodity labour power has been discussed in a previous chapter, and we will return to this in the next chapter.

The state helps capital access foreign markets (C′), if necessary by force. It also creates a domestic demand for what capital produces (e.g. arms manufacturing). A sphere of extra-commodity or extra-economic relations, the state is a massive source of market itself – demand for commodities that are produced for a profit. For the state to exist, a large number of goods and services (e.g. legal advice, knowledge, information about citizens, technical expertise, digitalization, surveillance technology, military equipment, and so on) are necessary. As well, through state contracts and outsourcing, the state converts these use-values into commodities and thus creates a large opportunity for capitalist investment.

2 The 'P' Phase of Capital Circuit, and the State

Following the completion of the sale and purchase of commodities, including labour power, the process of capitalist production (labour process) begins under the laws of motion of capital. It is a process in which the capitalist (or its agent) brings the means of production and the worker together to produce a use-value for sale: under capitalism, '[t]he labour-process is a process between things that the capitalist has purchased, things that have become his [or her] property' (Marx, 1887: 131). The workplace, the space of labour process, the hidden abode of production, is a sphere of certain rights of the exploiting class. These rights are defended by the state.

The main aim of capitalists is to increase their profit by reducing the cost of production, so what happens inside 'the hidden abode of production' (Marx,

in this case the state's connection to capital circuit is its connection to a shorter version of the circuit: the state helps capitalists increase their profit in the form of interest in the sphere of financialization, so M–C–P–C′–M′ is shortened to M–M′ (meaning money can simply be made from money, with assistance from the state).

1887: 123) crucially matters.[3] Apart from making available certain general conditions for production and exchange (built environment, natural resources, raw materials, scientific knowledge, and the like), the state defends the capitalist nature of labour process and capitalist exploitation. The sphere of production is a sphere of the political battle between capital and labour, one where capital exercises its despotic control (ibid.: 231–232). So all the interventions by the state aimed at reducing the bargaining power in the labour market also reduce workers' power on the shop floor.

The capitalist 'has bought the use of the labour-power for a definite period, and he insists upon his rights. He has no intention of being robbed' (Marx, 1887: 137; italics added). In capitalism, money is converted into capital 'in the most exact accordance with the economic laws of commodity production and with the right of property derived from them' (ibid.: 411; italics added). The product of labour 'is the property of the capitalist and not that of the labourer, its immediate producer' (ibid.: 131). The state defends the property right of the capitalist in the sphere of production, i.e. the right to own the products produced *by* labour and *not* by the capitalist. The right that the state defends is therefore the right to appropriate what really is not the product of one's own labour.

Under capitalism, even if there is equal exchange (all commodities, including labour power, are paid at their value), 'the laws of appropriation or of private property, the laws that are based on the production and circulation of commodities, become by their own inner and inexorable dialectic changed into their very opposite', that is, into the opposite of equal exchange (p. 412). This is for two reasons. Firstly, 'the capital which is exchanged for labour-power (as a commodity) is itself but a portion of the product of others' labour appropriated without an equivalent' (ibid.). Secondly, 'this capital must not only be replaced by its producer, but replaced together with an added surplus' (ibid.). In other words, 'what *really* takes place' between capitalists and workers is that 'the capitalist again and again appropriates, *without equivalent*, a portion of the previously materialised labour of others, and exchanges it for a greater quantity of living labour' (ibid.; italics added). This economic law of capitalist exploitation – like the law of equal exchange between commodity sellers – is codified and defended by the laws of the capitalist state. If a worker is paid the full value of the things that they and their family need to live, and if society takes 3 hours to produce all those things, the state has to defend the capitalist's right to make sure that the worker works longer than those 3 hours, that the

3 I am abstracting from mercantile and financial capitals here.

worker works, say, 8 hours, producing surplus value for capital. By maintaining the class status of a) the vast majority as workers, with little or no access to means of production, and b) the minority as capitalists who monopolize the means of production, the state makes sure that workers surrender a large part of what they produce to the capitalists. No amount of state autonomy, no degree of separation of the political from the economic, can stop the state from doing this. So, in capitalism, 'property turns out to be *the right*, on the part of the capitalist, to appropriate the unpaid labour of others or its product, and to be *the* impos*sibility*, on the part of the labourer, of appropriating his own product' (Marx, 1887: 412–123; italics added). And this sort of property right, the capitalist property right, must be coercively defended because between the right of the capitalist to the unpaid labour of the worker and the right of the worker to have full control over the product of their labour, between these two fundamental class interests and consequent class rights, which are the class interests defended by the state, there is no compatibility. The state function cannot but be shaped by this characteristic of capitalism. If the worker leaves the workplace after 3 hours, the state will consider that illegal. The state has to ensure that the value of the product produced by labour includes, not only 'the value of the capital advanced' but also 'a surplus-value which costs the worker labour but the capitalist nothing, and which none the less becomes the *legitimate property of the capitalist*' (p. 413; italics added). Thus, the state effectively goes against the rule of property discussed in the last chapter.[4] At best, as far as the state is concerned, the worker retains their property in labour power, and can sell it anew *if* they can find a buyer.

In capitalism, product of labour and labour power are commodities, but they are different types of commodity. Those who sell their labour power do not have the right to sell the products of their labour. If they exercise that right, the state will send its police to the workplace to act against them. If people receive only a part of the net product they produce under the control of capitalists, it is not injustice.

> The circumstance, that on the one hand the daily sustenance of labour-power costs only half a day's labour, while on the other hand the very same labour-power can work during a whole day … is, without doubt, a piece of good luck for the buyer, but by no means an injury [injustice] to the seller. (Marx, 1887: 136)

---

4 According to the principle of property, we may recall, 'each disposes only of what is his own' (Marx, 1887: 123).

The state accepts this: capitalist exploitation is not necessarily unjust. But it is not injustice *if and only if* we accept the law of commodity exchange: i.e. if we accept that labour power has been paid at its value, and therefore its use-value – what the capitalist, the buyer of labour power, makes of it – depends entirely on the capitalist.

Acting in the interest of the majority, the state, given its coercive power, *could* make sure that there is no exploitation in the workplace, that there is no injustice inside the sphere of production: that is, 'the [labour] process be not carried beyond the point, where the value paid by the capitalist for the labour-power is replaced by an exact equivalent' (ibid.: 137) and by a little more, in order to pay for the things that society as a whole, irrespective of whether it is capitalist or not, needs. But the state will not do this. On the contrary, it must juridically support the fact that the labour process 'be continued beyond that point' in order to become 'a process of creating surplus-value' (ibid.).

Everything in the social world exists as a product of human labour interacting with nature. The capitalist form of the wealth (value) is entirely a product of wage labour. Capitalists control property, so the world we live in *appears* to be one that has been created by capital in its own image. But, in actuality, this world is the world of ordinary people, the people who actually do the work (mostly as wage labour but also as small-scale producers). The state does everything to prop up the capitalist image. This is evident when state policies are expected to not harm capitalists and also when the state (e.g. its politicians) expects common people to see capitalists as benefactors, as jobs providers, as investors, as wealth creators, etc.

Marx says that '[a]s soon as his labour actually begins, it has already ceased to belong to him; it can therefore no longer be sold by him' (Marx, 1887: 379). The state codifies and defends the capitalist right to control the work of the worker: state action is necessary because such right of the capitalist to control the workplace is against the need and desire of the worker to perform free labour. 'The bargain concluded, it is discovered that he was no "free agent," that the time for which he is free to sell his labour-power is the time for which he is forced to sell it.' And this unfreedom is juridically justified and codified by the state. Without the state, which is the realm of unfreedom, unfreedom in the life of labour cannot exist.

In the workplace, control over workers is necessary to pre-emptively eliminate or reduce chances of resistance by workers: 'As the number of the co-operating labourers increases, so too does their resistance to the domination of capital, and with it, the necessity for capital to overcome this resistance by counterpressure' (Marx, 1887: 231). Thus, the people who do 'the work of directing, superintending, and adjusting' as agents of capital engage in despotic control over labourers subjecting them to oppressive power relations in order to increase exploitation and overcome the actual or potential resistance to that exploitation. The despotic control happens in the workplaces, with the support of the state, which represents the society-wide concentration of political power of the exploiting classes.[5] Marx's concept of 'despotic control' over workers' labour in the workplace by a tiny minority (the capitalist class, or by a special group of workers commanding in the name of the capitalist), points to that. State institutions are there to help capitalists implement its despotism in the workplace and overcome resistance from workers. No state can counter capital's despotic control over people in the workplace.

There are two major ways in which capital can increase the rate of exploitation (the ratio of surplus product to necessary product) if we assume that wages cover the value of labour power. One is technical change that raises labour productivity and makes workers produce more every hour.[6] Here the state helps by supporting technical change including by funding higher education and research, and by improving means of transportation and communication, and so on. The other method is where some capitalists mainly rely on workers working long hours (for low hourly wages); capitalists are directly affected if, for example, their access to cheaper labour is restricted by the state. Other things constant, the longer the working day, the higher the profits. This relation is particularly strong in capitalism's infancy, given the absence of productivity-raising technology.[7] Acting on behalf of capital, the state forces workers to work long hours.[8] Capital has the right to extract as much work as possible from workers because it has paid a wage that maintains the worker

---

5 That this work of directing and controlling is given over to a special class of wage labour does not make that work any less capitalistic, although the person doing the work is not a capitalist: 'An industrial army of workmen, under the command of a capitalist, requires, like a real army, officers (managers), and sergeants (foremen, overlookers), who, while the work is being done, command in the name of the capitalist. The work of supervision becomes their established and exclusive function'. (Marx, 1887: 232).

In fact, the idea and practice of hierarchy of work in the capitalist workplaces inform the internal organization (or form) of the state itself.

6 Technical change in society makes it possible for some capitalists to make *extra* surplus value, which is however temporary. Technical change in the sectors producing subsistence goods reduces the value of labour power and therefore increases relative surplus at a society-wide level.

7 'Legislation on wage-labour ... is started in England by the Statute of Labourers, of Edward III., 1349. The ordinance of 1350 in France, issued in the name of King John, corresponds with it' (Marx, 1887: 524).

8 In England, 'from the middle of the 14th to the end of the 17th century', capital, by using the state measures, tried to impose 'the lengthening of the working-day' (p. 181).

for 24 hours, and workers have the right to work normal hours. So '[t]here is here ... an antinomy, right against right, both equally bearing the seal of the law of exchanges. Between equal rights force decides' (Marx, 1887: 163–164). And this is ultimately the force of the capitalist state. The state often supports the longer working days than the shorter working days that are in workers' interest. In other words, the law of equal exchange supported by the state is violated on the basis of equal exchange, which is also supported by the state.

Long working days as well as unhealthy working conditions, job insecurity, irregular or unpredictable work hours, and the like lead to various physical and mental illnesses.[9] Capitalism is literally killing people now as it did in Marx's time. 'Capital cares nothing for the length of life of labour-power.' The states cares little too. Capital shortens 'the extent of the labourer's life, as a greedy farmer snatches increased produce from the soil by robbing it of its fertility' (Marx, 1887: 179). The state does not stop this. Sufferings of workers, including their 'physical and mental degradation' (p. 181), inflicted by capital, are contemptibly 'necessary conditions to the existence of capital' (p. 316).

The law of uneven development mediates in the way the state responds to the long working days. If capital subjects workers to excessive overwork and endangering health and cause people to die prematurely in one region/country, it can obtain fresh sources of labour from other regions/countries, especially those where capitalist development is at a lower level (e.g. rural areas or countries of the Global South) so the degeneration of the workers in the former region 'is only retarded by the constant absorption of primitive and physically uncorrupted elements from the country' (Marx, 1887: 181). The state could stop capitalists from making use of uneven development to subject workers to overwork, but it does not, and this non-doing of the state is a necessary condition for what capitalists do to workers: increasing exploitation.

In any case, with respect to the two major methods of labour exploitation, it can be said that if some capitalists make money by taking advantage of workers available to work for long hours (and for low wages), and other capitalists (e.g. bigger capitalists) resort to technical change, the state may resort to legislations to restrict the working day and to increase wages, so a level-playing field is created.[10] State action driven by inter-capitalist competition (and class struggle) and by the interests of certain (hegemonic) capitalists or capitalist fractions can in turn affect capitalist accumulation as a whole. When the state shortens the working day, this action may put pressure on all

9 A million working days were lost from work-related stress, depression or anxiety in 2016–2017 (Pfeffer, 2018).

10 This is explained in the next chapter.

capitalists to resort to technical change as a way of increasing surplus value in its relative form. Conversely, state's inability to shorten the working day allows many capitalists to resort to the appropriation of surplus value in its absolute form, producing a capitalism existing at a lower level of economic development, characterized by an absence of systemic increase in labour productivity per hour.

The state must protect capitalist private property, support commodity relations and the exploitation of labour, and create general and specific conditions for accumulation. While there is a logic to the state serving the capitalist class – this logic is to do with the class character of the capitalist state and only derivatively about the fact that it depends on taxes – the state's pro-capitalist actions often require the active intervention of capitalists. Indeed the actual ways in which the state performs its actions in support of the capitalist class and modify spontaneous operation of the laws of motion of capital are not automatic/spontaneous. They are shaped by the agency of the capitalist class, especially its ties with state actors (decision-making politicians, judges, and officials) to gain competitive advantage to avoid regulations, and to get contracts, and so on.

In terms of their political connection with state personnel, a political version of the capital circuit (M–C–M′) might be seen as functioning. Capitalists engage in what can be called a political capital circuit: M_p–C_p–M'_p (where the subscript 'p' stands for political). Capitalists invest money (M_p) to influence state actors and buy favourable interventions/policies. The latter is capitalists' political commodity, C_p. C_p helps individual capitalists or groups of capitalists remain competitive and reduces the cost of doing business, including what they might otherwise have to spend on workers' safety, environmental improvement, and the like. So capitalists with connections to the state can make more money than they invest in their instrumentalist ties (M'_p).

3 The Crisis-Ridden Capitalist Accumulation and the State

It is not enough for the state to help capitalists produce and realize surplus value. The surplus value has to be constantly reinvested. This is what accumulation means. Accumulation is in two forms: in its 'primitive' or mainly extra-economic, form (primitive accumulation) and capitalist form proper. Methods of primitive accumulation involve coercive state power, as already discussed. Capitalist accumulation occurs on the basis of concentration and centralization. To extend their businesses, capitalists reinvest the surplus value they appropriate. This is concentration. Then, some capitalists acquire businesses from other capitalists, making their businesses grow bigger. This is centralization.

The state generally allows the development of monopolies/large-scale companies including through mergers and acquisitions, and competition between/among monopolies. If credit 'soon becomes a new and terrible weapon in the battle of competition and is finally transformed into an enormous social mechanism for the centralisation of capitals' (Marx, 1887: 441), then cheap credit from the state can contribute to centralization: some companies use the cheap money to buy other companies. The state supports the fact that some commodity producers – for example, larger and more efficient capitalists – gain at the cost of other capitalists.

As the ratio of constant to variable capital rises: capitalistic accumulation produces 'a relatively redundant population of labourers, i.e., a population of greater extent than suffices for the average needs of the self-expansion of capital, and therefore a surplus-population' (Marx, 1887: 443). Capitalism 'forms a disposable industrial reserve army, that belongs to capital quite as absolutely as if the latter had bred it at its own cost' (Marx, 1887: 444), so the reserve army (un- and under-employed people) is very much a part of capitalism. 'Independently of the limits of the actual increase of population, it creates, for the changing needs of the self-expansion of capital, a mass of human material always ready for exploitation' (Marx, 1887: 444). The state makes sure that there is a reserve army of labour in situ.

The state is connected to the relative surplus population in at least two ways by its doings and not-doings. (a) It *could* take steps to make sure everyone who loses their job due to technical change in one enterprise remains employed elsewhere. It does not. It does not act to significantly counter the production of the reserve army. It does not make sure that everyone is able to work according to their abilities and for a decent wage. (b) It controls in- and out-migration generally in the long- and short-term interests of capital (or its hegemonic fractions), so capital has access to a reserve army, especially from the less developed world, a reserve army that puts pressure on wages there as well as in the (less developed areas/sectors of the) developed world.

A given state regulation impacts different capitalists (big capitalists or the capitalists using modern technologies versus smaller-scale capitalists or the capitalists not using modern technologies) differently. As far the capitalists not using modern technologies are concerned, 'Unlimited exploitation of cheap labour-power is the sole foundation of their power to compete'.[11] These

11 Marx writes: '[A]s regards labour in the so-called domestic industries and the intermediate forms between them and Manufacture, so soon as limits are put to the working-day

capitalists, often owners of smaller amount of capital, are directly affected if their access to cheaper labour is restricted by the state. As soon as the state regulations put limits 'to the working-day and to the employment of children', the enterprises using children and employing people for very long hours 'go to the wall' (Marx, 1887: 313). '[O]wing to the necessity they impose for greater outlay of capital', Factory Acts and similar other legislations 'hasten on the decline of the small masters, and the concentration of capital' (Marx, 1887: 314). As small enterprises are out-competed and are swallowed by bigger capitalist units, centralization of capital happens. The general extension of state measures to all enterprises 'for the purpose of protecting the working-class both in mind and body … hastens on the general conversion of numerous isolated small industries into a few combined industries carried on upon a large scale' thus accelerating 'the concentration of capital and the exclusive predominance of the factory system' (Marx, 1887: 328).

Thus, if the state measures force capitalists to adopt normal working days, capitalists have to make money in other ways (investing in constant capital). Making use of workers working long hours and exploitation of children cannot be the major basis for remaining competitive. Bigger capitalists are a little flexible with respect to the use of constant capital versus the use of cheap labour. State regulation means that they have to invest more in constant capital – investment in machinery, for example – to make up for the loss of cheaper labour (adults working long hours for low wages and children labour), and the bigger capitalists can make such investment.[12] In other words, while state regulation of abuses in the workplace is partly a product of workers' struggle (as discussed in the next chapter), such regulation in turn shapes the nature of capitalist production and accumulation. This happens when capitalists respond to state regulation, for example, by introducing machinery, which represents class struggle of the capitalist. Capitalist accumulation is '*artificially* helped on by' state legislations such as 'the extension of the Factory Acts to all industries in which women, young persons and children are employed'. For example, when the length of the working day is regulated by the state, this necessitates technological change 'in the place of muscles' (p. 312). Thus, state regulations contribute to the changes in the technical mode of production: 'the limitation and regulation of the working-day [by the state] give to technical

and to the employment of children [by the state], those industries go to the wall' (Marx, 1887: 313).

12 'The chief objection, repeatedly and passionately urged on behalf of each manufacture threatened with the Factory Act, is in fact this, that in order to continue the business on the old scale a greater outlay of capital will be necessary' (Marx, 1887: 313).

improvement, the anarchy and the catastrophes of capitalist production as a whole, the intensity of labour, and the competition of machinery with the labourer'. (Marx, 1887: 329). Of course, the extent to which the state actually implements policies in favour of workers is a different matter which will be discussed in the next chapter.

There is a constant tendency towards technical change expressed in the form of a rise in c/v. To this, the state contributes, directly by investing in technology that benefits the businesses, and indirectly by regulating the abuses of the worker in the workplace. The state *is* connected to the tendency towards the formation of the crisis. As mentioned, while the average rate of profit tends to drop because c/v rises faster than s/v, the opposite can also conjuncturally happen: increased rate of exploitation can counter the tendency towards the rate of profit to fall. There are various methods of increasing exploitation to which the state is connected, as we have also seen. By facilitating cheapening of constant capital and by helping capital increase the rate of exploitation, the state seeks to counter the tendency towards the crisis of profitability. Of course, over the long run, tendencies towards crisis are more powerful than the counter-tendencies.

4 Conclusion

The capitalist society is a society where wealth is produced in the form of commodities under the logic of socially necessary average labour time. For the state to contribute to such a process and to the accumulation of wealth, it is neither enough to create/sustain property rights in part by separating direct producers from their property nor is it enough that the state ensure free commodity exchange. The state must ensure that the separated means of production and subsistence are turned into capital and that the capitalists constituting the new ruling class are, like the older ruling classes, able to appropriate the unpaid surplus labour from direct producers, *even if* they pay the full value of the commodity they purchase (i.e. labour power).

The state must take steps to promote capitalist accumulation in the long-term interests of the capitalist class and especially its economically and politically hegemonic fraction(s). Following the completion of the sale and purchase of commodities, including labour power, and on the basis of capitalist property rights, all of which the state supports, the process of capitalist production (labour process) begins. The workplace (the space of labour process or the hidden abode of production) is a space of certain rights of the exploiting class. These rights are defended by the state. Therefore, the sphere of production, including the workplace, reveals important attributes of the state. The logic of capitalist social relations and production produce an imperative for the state to act.

The state is connected to the successive phases of the capital circuit (MCM′). If commodities produced are not sold (realized) then the value of the commodities is lost, so the state tries to help capitalists with the realization of value by expanding markets for commodities. The state seeks to make sure capitalist accumulation, including concentration and centralization, occurs. By facilitating cheapening of constant capital and by helping capital increase the rate of exploitation, the state seeks to counter the tendency for the average rate of profit to fall. There are several theoretical implications of the relation between the capital circuit and the state.

Firstly, if the state supports capitalist accumulation, it is not fundamentally because it depends on capitalists and on capitalist economy for its survival (that it needs taxes and loans, and so on). This view is only implicit in *Capital* volume 1. The fact that the state needs taxes and loans must be explained first in terms of state's class character. Its so-called economic dependence on capitalists and capitalists-controlled economy is a concrete expression of the fact that it is inherently a class institution, which means that in the capitalist form of class society, the state is fundamentally – it is already – a *capitalist* institution. So it must not only support capitalist property rights but also seek to promote the expansion of wealth in its capitalist form. The capitalist class relation cannot continue to exist without capitalists having capitalist property rights and right to exploit direct producers defended by the state (especially, its coercive powers against the masses). In this *concrete* sense, the capitalist state is 'constitutive' of, although not a cause of, the capitalist class relation: it codifies the class relations (exploitative production relations) into juridical relations and reproduces them politically against the resistance of the working class (and it seeks to mitigate the destructive effects of intra-capitalist class competition).[13] Given class relations, there is a need for the state (special public power). In this sense class relations are prior to the state. Once the state exists, it needs taxes and loans in a society. So it is the classness of society which explains the classness of the state that is behind state's so-called reliance on private accumulation. Consider this: the state does have all the power in the world to dispossess capitalists, take over their property and be self-reliant. Or, indeed, the state has the coercive power to take the property from a tiny minority and

13 The separation between the mode of production and class relation on the one hand and the state (which constitutes their political form) on the other is more for analytical convenience than anything else.

give it to the vast majority and help them use it collectively in order to meet their needs through society-wide planning of the use of means of production, and the majority can set aside some resources for the management of their common affairs (i.e. to do things that are necessary for the society as a whole). If the capitalist state does not do this, and therefore, if it is reliant on capitalists financially, it is because the state is, above all, a class – capitalist – institution. The state is the capitalist state *not* because it relies on the capitalist class. The state *relies* on the capitalist class *because* it is the capitalist state.

The state power is necessarily a (mediated) form of class power. That is, the relation between the two forms of power is an internal one and not an external one. The state power is the power of the exploiting classes in all pre-socialist class societies. The capitalist class controls the means of production and the surplus value, and it commands far more exchange value than the working-class people (and small-scale producers) do, and it is the class that 'controls' political power as well. The obverse side of this is the fact that proletarians (and small-scale producers) lack control over exploitative property, surplus value, and indeed over labour process, and it is also the class that lacks control over state power (and must therefore achieve state power for it to gain control over the economic aspects of class structure of society).[14] Fundamental aspects of state theory must be a part of class theory, therefore.

Secondly, the relation of the state to the capital circuit sheds light on the idea of state capitalism.[15] People use the term 'state capitalism' without making clear just what they mean by that. State railroads are state capitalism. Industries receiving state subsidies are said to represent state capitalism. Post-colonial state-led capitalist development is often called state capitalism. The former Soviet economy, according to some, was state-capitalist (Cliff, 1955). Indeed, 'the entire nationalized and plan-directed Soviet economy is supposedly also state capitalism [no matter that it was "the result of a revolution"]' (Trotsky, 1979: 340).

> The term 'state capitalism' originally arose to designate all the phenomena which arise when a bourgeois state takes direct charge of the means of transport or of industrial enterprises. The very necessity of such measures is one of the signs that the productive forces have outgrown capitalism and are bringing it to a partial self-negation in practice (Trotsky, 1991: 208).

---

14 It is not for nothing that Lenin, whose thinking is ignored or under-emphasized in much state theory, claims in *The state and revolution* that Marx 'developed his theory of the class struggle consistently, down to the theory of political power, of the state' (Lenin, 1949: 27).

15 See Sperber (2019) for a critical survey of 120 years of reflections on state capitalism and read back through the prism of class-state relations. See also Alami (2021).

As indicated already, capitalism itself creates conditions for state's economic involvement:

Monopoly capitalism has long since outgrown the private ownership of the means of production and the boundaries of the national state. ... The productive forces pound against the barriers of private property and of national boundaries [that are defended by the state]. The bourgeois governments are obliged to pacify the mutiny of their own productive forces with a police club. This is what constitutes the so-called planned economy. Insofar as the state attempts to harness and discipline capitalist anarchy, it may be called conditionally 'state capitalism.' (Trotsky, 1933).

> [U]nder state capitalism, in the strict sense of the word, we must understand the management of industrial and other enterprises by the bourgeois state on its own account, or the 'regulating' intervention of the bourgeois state into the workings of private capitalist enterprises. (ibid.)

Thus, the capitalist state can acquire attributes of 'state-capitalists', with state-managers effectively acting like capitalists.[16] One has to adequately distinguish between state capitalism and state-ism, from the standpoint of property relations or class relations.

> State capitalism means the substitution of state property for private property, and for that very reason remains partial in character. State-ism ... means state intervention on the basis of private property, and with the goal of preserving it. Whatever be the programs of the government, stateism inevitably leads to a transfer of the damages of the decaying system from strong shoulders to weak.
>
> It 'rescues' the small proprietor from complete ruin only to the extent that his existence is necessary for the preservation of big property. The planned measures of stateism are dictated not by the demands of a development of the productive forces, but by a concern for the preservation of private property at the expense of the productive forces, which are in revolt against it. State-ism means applying brakes to the development of technique, supporting unviable enterprises, perpetuating parasitic social strata. In a word, state-ism is completely reactionary in character. (Trotsky, 1991: 209)

16 This is to be distinguished from the nationalization of industries following anti-capitalist revolutions in the early parts of the 20th century.

Given the usual portrayal of the state as neoliberal state by many since the 1980s, it is difficult to believe that the state is so closely linked to the businesses as its relation to the capital circuit shows. Neoliberalism is the modern form of laissez-faire economy. What is called the neoliberal state is fundamentally *capitalist* character whatever else it may be, just like the pre-neoliberal state. The neoliberal form of the state, just like the state as such, is connected to each phase of the capitalist circuit.

Thirdly, in part because capital does not need the state's extra-economic force to make people go to work, the capitalist state is able to protect and promote a degree of freedom and equality: according to the state, all commodity owners are equal and that workers are free to work for whoever they wish to. But the equality and freedom that the capitalist state 'protects' are the *capitalist* form of equality and freedom within the sphere of exchange relations. Such equality and freedom are transformed into their opposites, i.e. inequality and unfreedom, within the sphere of property relations and production relations.[17] This is because: a) workers are not free not to work for the capitalist class as a whole, a fact which the state as the state of the capitalist class *as a whole* absolutely cannot do anything about, b) workers lack control over production and over the fruits of their labour, a fact that makes possible the appropriation of unpaid labour from sellers-cum-owners of commodity labour power. The state ensures conditions that produce substantial inequality between capital and labour.

Fourthly, the state plays an immense role in the reproduction of capitalism, and yet the state in capitalism is not the main cause of people's economic and other problems or indeed of the class relations as such. Marx (1847) says: [I]f the bourgeoisie is politically, that is, by its state power, 'maintaining injustice in property relations', it is not *creating* it. The 'injustice in property relations' which is determined by the modern division of labour, the modern form of exchange, competition, concentration, etc., by no means arises from the political rule of the bourgeois class, but vice versa, the political rule of the bourgeois class arises from these modern relations of production which bourgeois economists proclaim to be necessary and eternal laws.

17 In fact, and as mentioned earlier, *even in* exchange relations, there are inequality and unfreedom.

CHAPTER 8

Marx's *Capital* Volume 1: Labour Circuit, Class Struggle, Economic Reforms, and the State

Karl Marx (1887: 316) asks in *Capital volume 1*: 'What could possibly show better the character of the capitalist mode of production, than the necessity that exists for forcing upon it, by Acts of Parliament', the simplest of measures in the interest of workers such as the 'appliances for maintaining cleanliness and health'? Marx gives many reasons for these measures.

One is that capital needs men and women with the suitable physical and mental abilities to work and to produce surplus value, so the state steps in to ensure this. If this is the case, then why is it that so many people live with their very basic needs, including for food and healthcare, remaining unmet causing them to suffer from 'the physical and mental degradation, the premature death' etc.? (ibid.: 181; 449)? How do inter-capitalist contradictions shape state's pro-worker interventions? What role does the working class itself play? In this chapter, the focus is on how the state functions to 'help' the working class in part as a response to the working-class politics.

Partly by building on the arguments about the state's role concerning commodity and property relations in the last two chapters, I discuss, in section 1 of this chapter, the state's pro-worker interventions and the labour circuit. In Section 2, I turn to the driving forces behind the state's pro-worker measures. I argue that there *is* an objective pressure on the state (e.g. general and long-term interests of capital) to intervene on behalf of workers, and that this pressure is mediated by working-class struggle as well as inter-capitalist competition. In Section 3, I discuss the limits to what the state can do for workers under capitalism, the limits that exist because of the capitalist control over property and production, nature of capitalist accumulation and its crisis-proneness, and the capitalist state's bureaucratic functioning and its anti-worker politics. In Section 4, I offer general theoretical reflections on the ways in which the state is connected to working-class interests and struggle.

1 The Labour Circuit (C–M–C′–R–C) and the State's Pro-worker Interventions

The state intervenes on behalf of workers in the realm of exchange (e.g. labour market). This can be understood by using Marx's formula for simple commodity

 | DOI:10.1163/9789004730472_009

circulation (C–M–C). C–M–C has to be modified into C–M–C′–R–C. The state connects to each phase of the labour circuit, especially given the fact that '[i]n contradistinction … to the case of other commodities, there enters into the determination of the value of labour-power a *historical and moral element*' (Marx, 1887: 121; italics added), which, in turn, is a product of the interaction between class struggle for improvement in living conditions, and state policy (more on this in chapter 8).

Let us begin with C. The state shapes the determination of the value of the commodity labour power (C) through the minimum wage policy and its poverty-line definition that is used for its anti-poverty interventions: it influences what sorts of commodities are to be included in the value of labour power. The state, within limits, shapes the rate of employment – that is, whether, and to what extent, men and women can indeed sell their labour power for a given wage (M). Often wages fall below the value of labour power, so the state is involved in the determination of the wage (M) through, for example, its wage policy. It may also supplement the private wage with a social wage in the form of various anti-poverty and welfare measures. Through its monetary policy and other policies (including those that put a lot of money in the hands of the super-rich), the state can shape the price of wage goods (that is, it can cause inflation) and therefore the actual size of the basket of wage goods common people can access (C′).

The consumption of these commodities, mediated by un-commodified labour including especially of women at home (R), where all kinds of cost-cutting, thrifty conduct, and financial planning happen, in turn reproduces the commodity labour power (C). The state also intervenes in the sphere of reproduction, where, among other things, the commodities bought with the money wage are processed and consumed, often by women. The state has laws that regulate marriage and parental rights and control over family's property. The state has a degree of oversight over parents' role in children's education and healthcare. On the basis of all these successive phases in the labour circuit, the original C (that is used in the workplace) is reproduced anew as C. The cycle continues. In terms of a theoretical tendency, the cycle operates at the global scale. And empirically, the cycle increasingly operates at the scale of the world market with the gradual emergence of a global labour market.

The state thus connects to each phase of the labour circuit (C–M–C′–R–C). The concept of the labour circuit can now be expanded and concretized in order to shed light on state's pro-worker interventions, particularly, in the labour-market and the workplace. I will also briefly discuss state's policies in favour of small-scale producers.

The state fixes '[r]easonable wages' and 'the limits of the working-day' (Marx, 1887: 182) apart from various other measures. The minimum wage legislation, if properly implemented, can benefit workers who receive very low wages. If the mandated minimum wage is significantly above the market rate in many sectors, the minimum wage legislation could have a positive impact on the determination of the value of labour power as it puts a floor on the wage level and indeed on the actual wages paid. A lower minimum wage would have the opposite effect. The state constructs the poverty line to restrict welfare provision to the population below the poverty line. The poverty line represents state's perception of what people absolutely need to live, a perception that is determined by capitalists' interests. The state's poverty line, like the state-defined minimum wage, will have an impact on the value of labour power and on its monetary expression. A higher poverty line, if implemented, will put pressure on the buyers of labour power to pay higher wages. This can reduce the extent of the violation of the principle of 'exchange equivalent for equivalent' (Marx, 1887: 123).

In part because many workers do not receive the cost of production of labour power from private employers, millions are in poverty who receive some state assistance (e.g. subsidized food), which really amounts to subsidizing capitalist companies who fail to ensure the reproduction of their workforce.

During the infancy of capitalism, the state makes workers work long hours or supports capitalists making workers work long hours. As capitalism progresses, the state limits the working day (especially when technical change allows employers to extra more labour every hour): 'The legal limitation of the working-day puts an end to such mischief', i.e. longer working days (Marx, 1887: 385). In fact, 'Excessively long working days called forth a control on the part of Society which legally limits, regulates, and makes uniform the working-day and its pauses'. (Marx, 1887: 194). Compulsory laws for the extension of the working-day were put in place from the middle of the 14th to the end of the 17th century (ibid.). Indeed, Factory Acts came into force both in advanced countries and in the periphery. State intervention has included laws against unfree labour, and laws that restrict child labour which is a form of unfree labour, and prohibit child labour below certain age. The state may 'make elementary education a compulsory condition to the "productive" employment of children' (Marx, 1887: 274) under a certain age:

> [T]he intellectual desolation artificially produced by converting immature human beings into mere machines for the fabrication of surplus-value, ... [and] this desolation finally compelled even the English Parliament to

make elementary education a compulsory condition to the 'productive' employment of children under 14 years, in every industry subject to the Factory Acts. (Marx, 1887: 274)

2 Driving Forces behind the State's Pro-worker Measures

2.1 *Class Struggle*

State interventions (for example, Parliamentary Acts) in relation to working conditions are partly a result of class struggle between the two main classes and not 'the products of Parliamentary fancy' (Marx, 1887: 187). 'Their formulation, official recognition, and proclamation by the State, were the result of a long struggle of classes' (ibid.).

Indeed, 'in its adult condition', i.e. as capitalism develops out of original or primitive accumulation as it did in Western Europe, and as workers' organization gets stronger, workers have received 'the concessions that, growling and struggling', that capital 'has to make' (ibid.; italics added). *Acting in its own collective interest*, the working class has demanded such things as the reduction in the working day: 'The establishment of a normal working-day is the result of centuries of struggle between capitalist and labourer' (ibid.: 181). Of course, while class struggle contributes to the introduction of pro-worker measures, the nature and the impacts of the legislations can vary geographically. There were important differences between the measures taken by the French state and those by the English state, for example.[1]

What is the basis for struggle for concessions from the state? The answer partly lies in the contradictory nature of the law of commodity exchange. From capital's angle, the 'spontaneous' operation of the laws of capitalist commodity relations imposes no limit to the length of the working day. As Marx says: 'the nature of the exchange of commodities itself imposes no limit to the working day, no limit to surplus labour' which allows the capitalist to maintain 'his rights as a purchaser when he tries to make the working day as long as possible' (pp. 163–164). After all, 'the capitalist has bought the labour-power at its

1 'France limps slowly behind England. The February revolution was necessary to bring into the world the 12 hours' law, which is much more deficient than its English original. ... It once for all commands the same limit to the working-day in all shops and factories without distinction, whilst English legislation reluctantly yields to the pressure of circumstances, now on this point, now on that, and is getting lost in a hopelessly bewildering tangle of contradictory enactments. On the other hand, the French law proclaims as a principle that which in England was only won in the name of children, minors, and women, and has been only recently for the first time claimed as a general right'. (Marx, 1887: 195).

day-rate', so 'To him its use-value belongs during one working-day'. 'He has thus acquired the [state-defended] right to make the labourer work for him during one day' (Marx, 1887: 163). From the opposite angle, that is, from labour's angle, matters are different: what might begin as equal exchange ends up being unequal. If a worker works excessively long hours and if due to overwork, her longevity is reduced by, say, x%, her total wage income during her working life is not increased by x%: she still gets the wages as if she is going to live a life of normal longevity. Acting in their own interest, therefore, 'the labourer maintains his right as seller when he wishes to reduce the working day to one of definite normal duration'. So the labourer demands normal working day. Marx represents the workers' demand in the workers' voice:

> I demand, therefore, a working day of normal length, and I demand it without any appeal to your heart, for in money matters sentiment is out of place. You may be a model citizen, perhaps a member of the Society for the Prevention of Cruelty to Animals, and in the odour of sanctity to boot; but the thing that you represent face to face with me has no heart in its breast. That which seems to throb there is my own heart-beating. I demand the normal working day because I, like every other seller, demand the value of my commodity. (p. 163)

Because the law of commodity exchange imposes no limit to how much capitalists exploit workers, the state can do little except under 'compulsion from society' (Marx, 1887: 181). This compulsion is in the form of labour struggle: '[I]n the history of capitalist production, the determination of what is a working day, presents itself as the result of a struggle, a struggle between collective capital, i.e., the class of capitalists, and collective labour, i.e., the working-class' (Marx, 1887: 164). The same goes for what is a normal wage too.

It is not just that the state grants concessions (e.g. shorter working days) because of the workers' struggle. In fact, because of the political pressure from below, the state grants to the workers their right to struggle (e.g. unionization right): 'only against its will and under the pressure of the masses' did the British state (in the form of the Parliament) 'give up the laws against Strikes and Trades' Unions, after it had itself, for 500 years, held, with shameless egoism, the position of a permanent Trades' Union of the capitalists against the labourers' (Marx, 1887: 525).[2]

2 The struggle to establish unions, and especially the unions that are independent of the enterprise management, continues as the recent history of India's Maruti workers struggle shows (White, J., 2017).

While the capitalists and the state hardly grant anything without a struggle by the common people, it is also the case that capitalism creates *conditions* for such struggle, often unintentionally. It does this by promoting transportation and communication technologies to reduce the cost of movement of commodities, and removing geographical barriers to working-class unity through the spatial concentration of workers in specific localities and cities, all in its own economic interest (e.g. easy access to a labour pool). Capitalism – 'the direct and open sway of capital' – also removes non- or pre-capitalist social relations 'behind which the dominion of capital is still in part concealed'. With the 'destruction of petty and domestic industries', gone is 'the sole remaining safety-valve of the whole social mechanism', and this in turn 'generalises the direct opposition' of the masses to capital (Marx, 1887: 329). In fact, as non-capitalist ways of reproduction (e.g. family-based production, access to common property resources) vanish, workers increasingly depend on the state to meet the gap between what they need and what they receive from employers. Of course, capital and the state also promote disunity among workers by using politics of identity, including racial identity.

The introduction of a pro-labour measure and its actual implementation, generally speaking, depends on the intensity of class struggle of the masses. If workers' struggle poses a threat to property rights of capital, to wage-slavery itself, then this can induce the state to give significant concessions.

2.2 *Interests of Capital as a Whole*

There is more to the story of pro-worker measures than just workers' struggle forcing the state to intervene on their behalf. Behind the pro-worker legislations, there are often long-term capitalist interests which may coincide with the interests of workers: 'Apart from the working-class movement that daily grew more threatening, the limiting of factory labour [by the state] was dictated by the same necessity which spread guano over the English fields.' In other words, '[t]he same blind eagerness for plunder that in the one case exhausted the soil, had, in the other, torn up by the roots the living force of the nation' (Marx, 1887: 166).

Capital must be distinguished from capitals. Capital engages in the normal process of exploitation when workers surrender to capital a large part of the net product. In any society, there is an average or 'normal' rate of exploitation. And then there is excessive (= above-normal) exploitation, causing the degeneration of the working population. The excesses (abuses) inflicted on workers are a product of the mutually competing capitalists when they lower the wages below the average cost of maintenance of workers, make workers work excessively long hours of work, cut down on spending for workplace safety, and so on. 'Free competition brings out the inherent laws of capitalist production [i.e. the logic of capital], in the shape of external coercive laws having power over every individual capitalist' (Marx, 1887: 181). These external economic laws of capitalist production meet with the extra-economic laws of the state: 'Capital is reckless of the health or length of life of the labourer, unless under compulsion from society' (ibid.; italics added). This compulsion from society is represented by pro-worker state interventions against capital's recklessness of workers' health and well-being and against the violation of equal exchange in the labour market (p. 181). In general, the measures regulating the working conditions develop 'gradually out of circumstances as natural laws of the modern mode of production' (Marx, 1887: 187) in the sense that excesses of capitalism (e.g. long working day, low wages) would result in a crippled reproduction of the only source of surplus value (i.e. labour).

Thus, major concessions to workers – e.g. short working day – is not entirely due to class struggle from below: long-term interests are important explanations, especially when 'the living force of the nation' (Marx, 1887: 166) is endangered. Such endangering occurs when workers experience daily abuses. It also occurs during such things as the threat of the spread of diseases. In fact, 'the mere fear of contagious diseases which do not spare even "respectability"', that is, the bourgeoisie and well-off strata close to it, forces the state to take 'strenuous measures' (ibid.: 456).[3]

Individual capitalists are cogs in the wheel of competition. Their short-term interests – their 'recklessness' – directly destroy workers' health.[4] This fact undermines long-term interests of capitalists, thus prompting the state to intervene. The regulation of the working day is in the interest of capital and not just labour. If due to overwork and adverse working lives, people die faster, then they have to be replaced quicker, so the value of labour power will thus go up. This has a cost for the buyer/user of this labouring body, that is, the capitalist class as a whole.[5] The fact that 'the forces used up have to be replaced at a more rapid rate and the sum of the expenses for the reproduction of labour-power will be greater' implies that 'the interest of capital itself points in the direction of a normal working-day' (Marx, 1887: 179). Capitalist production leads to unfavourable effects which need state regulation:

3 In England, the state 'brought into existence from 1847 to 1864 no less than 10 Acts of Parliament on sanitation'; 'the frightened bourgeois in some towns ... took strenuous measures through their municipalities' (ibid.).

4 They cause the destruction of the environment which in turn affects workers' bodies/health.

5 This is 'just as in a machine the part of its value to be reproduced every day is greater the more rapidly the machine is worn out' (Marx, 1887: 179).

> Factory legislation, that first conscious and methodical reaction of society against the spontaneously developed form of the process of production, is ... just as much the necessary product of modern industry as cotton yam, self-actors, and the electric telegraph. (Marx, 1887: 315)

If in place of 'the unnatural extension of the working-day', and the like that Marx talks about, we put environmental damage, the logic mentioned earlier will still hold.

In other words, the state is prompted by capitalists' long-term interests to implement certain policies in favour of workers (and the environment), curbing capital's passion for profit. These policies are *ultimately* in favour of the capitalist class as a whole, more or less; or they are implemented in such a way that the capitalist class as a whole or some dominant sections of the class benefit from them. In England, the first statue of labourers was put in place in 1839. The state interventions in the form of the Factory Acts as in England 'curb the passion of capital for a limitless draining of labour-power, by forcibly limiting the working-day by state regulations, made by a state that is ruled by capitalist-and landlord' (Marx, 1887: 166). So the *general* interest of the capitalist class is crucial to the understanding of pro-worker state policies. The adverse conditions under which workers work and live and which cause illnesses and the crisis of bodily reproduction mean that capitalists can find it difficult to obtain enough people at a wage rate at which enough surplus value can be made (p. 181).

2.3 *Interests of Specific Fractions of the Capitalist Class*

The ruling class as a whole has certain long-term interests. Then elements within the ruling class have certain specific interests, and these can be mutually conflicting. Conflicts within the ruling class can help the lower-class struggle in certain cases:

> The Inquiry Commission of 1862 also proposed a new regulation of the mining industry, an industry distinguished from others by the exceptional characteristic that the interests of landlord and capitalist there join hands. The antagonism of these two interests had been favourable to Factory legislation, while on the other hand the absence of that antagonism is sufficient to explain the delays and chicanery of the legislation on mines. (Marx, 1887: 323)

If a section of the capitalist class needs the support of workers in its battle with, say, landowners, capitalists may support pro-worker legislations. In the context of Marx's England:

> [H]owever much the individual manufacturer might give the rein to his old lust for gain, the spokesmen and political leaders of the manufacturing class ordered a change of front and of speech towards the workpeople. They had entered upon the contest for the repeal of the Corn Laws [against the resistance of landowners], and needed the workers to help them to victory. They promised therefore, not only a double-sized loaf of bread, but the enactment of the Ten Hours' Bill in the Free-trade millennium. Thus they still less dared to oppose a measure intended only to make the law of 1833 a reality. (Marx, 1887: 186)
>
> The Repeal of the Corn Laws, and of the duties on cotton and other raw material; Free-trade proclaimed as the guiding star of legislation. ... [In] the same years, the Chartist movement and the 10 hours' agitation reached their highest point. They found allies in the Tories panting for revenge. Despite the fanatical opposition of the army of perjured Free-traders, ... the Ten Hours' Bill, struggled for so long, went through Parliament. (Marx, 1887: 187)

Also, inter-capitalist competition contributes to the universalization of the application of government regulations. 'The first birthright of capital is equal exploitation of labour-power by all capitalists' (Marx, 1887: 192). In addition, there is 'the cry of the [bigger] capitalists for equality in the conditions of competition, i.e., for equal restrain on all exploitation of labour' (ibid.).[6] Whenever a law (e.g. a law that limits the labour of children to 6 hours) is applicable to certain enterprises and not to other enterprises, manufacturers in the first category complain against this 'discrimination'.[7] Implied here is a general point about capitalism: 'since capital is by nature a leveller, since it

6 Marx quotes the Children Employment Commission which says that the Factory Act is unjust to the larger businesses, and by giving a stimulus to the multiplication of small workplaces, the legislation is against the 'general improvement of the people' (Marx, 1887: 321):

'It would be unjust to the larger employers that their factories should be placed under regulation, while the hours of labour in the smaller places in their own branch of business were under no legislative restriction. And to the injustice arising from the unfair conditions of competition, in regard to hours, that would be created if the smaller places of work were exempt, would be added the disadvantage to the larger manufacturers, of finding their supply of juvenile and female labour drawn off to the places of work exempt from legislation. Further, a stimulus would be given to the multiplication of the smaller places of work, which are almost invariably the least favourable to the health, comfort, education, and general improvement of the people' (Marx, 1887: 320–321).

7 For example: They allege that numbers of the parents withdraw their children from the industry brought under the Act, in order to sell them where 'freedom of labour' still rules, i.e., where children under 13 years are compelled to work like grown-up people, and therefore can be got rid of at a higher price (Marx, 1887: 273).

exacts in every sphere of production equality in the conditions of the exploitation of labour, the limitation by law of' such things as 'children's labour, in one branch of industry, becomes the cause of its limitation in others' (Marx, 1887: 272; italics added).

All in all, to the extent that the state functions in support of long-term interests of capital, such intervention is more likely when (a) people fight against the effect of exploitation and (b) there are conflicts among the ruling-class elements which means that (c) interests of the working class coincide with interests of some (hegemonic) elements of the capitalist class. State's, or state actors', including ruling political parties', own interests (e.g. votes and control over state institutions which are a source of income/wealth) also play a role. Yet the state fails to meet the needs of the working men and women in a significant and durable manner.[8] Why?

When capitalists reluctantly give in, granting such things as 'the compulsory regulation of the hours of labour', they do not give in much (ibid.). Pro-worker interventions, even if fully implemented, are only a 'meagre concession wrung from capital' (Marx, 1887: 318), and in the case of England's Factory Act, it was 'limited to combining elementary education with work in the factory' (ibid.).[9] Why?

3 Limits to State's Pro-worker Interventions, and Why?

3.1 *Capitalists' Fightback*

Even if the regulation of capitalist excesses inflicted on workers (very low wages, very long hours of work) is in the interest of long-term interests of capitalists, the latter do not still accept this 'except "under the pressure of a General Act of Parliament"' (Marx, 1887: 314). Even when pro-worker laws are introduced, capitalists resort to multiple mechanisms to get around these laws.

When a legislation is imposed on capitalists, they fight this, including through courts and political parties, on the ground that it is an 'interference with the exploiting rights of capital' (Marx, 1887: 319). Individual capitalists treat their private property rights as sacrosanct and beyond challenge, so mild

8 For example, it fails to enforce the freedom of labourers as sellers of labour power: millions of unfree labourers, including children, work in slave-like conditions. The minimum wage policy is not enforced either, and where it is, usually, the government-legislated minimum wage is lower than a wage floor set within collective agreements (Boeri, 2012).

9 Note that this was the case when capitalism was in a progressive phase relative to its current terminal decline stage. Currently, slightly pro-worker policies are characterized by the politicians of capitalist reaction (the Right) as socialist or communist.

actions against them are used to produce catastrophizing notion of the spectre of revolution: 'They [capitalists] denounced the Factory Inspectors as a kind of revolutionary commissioners' (Marx, 1887: 188).[10]

When pro-worker legislations are introduced, capitalists make changes in the labour process in response, as we have seen the last chapter. For example, if the working day is shortened, capitalists increase the speed of work that workers must do, leading to increased injury to workers, while capitalists go unpunished by the state.[11] They introduce a relay system: individual (child) workers come to work at different points in time in a 24-hour-day, and this makes it difficult for state officials (inspectors) to monitor whether any worker is working longer than the law allows.[12]

A specific form of change in the labour process is resorting to a technological fix (mechanization), which has two adverse effects on workers. One is that it is a weapon against workers' struggle: machinery replaces workers weakening their bargaining power. In addition, by enabling 'the excessive addition of women and children to the ranks of the workers, machinery ... breaks down the resistance which the male operatives in the manufacturing period continued to oppose to the despotism of capital' (Marx, 1887: 276). Besides, capital uses more efficient machines to squeeze out as much labour during the reduced working day as during the longer one.

Capitalists resort to what can be called a temporal fix. The application of the laws that restrict capitalists' freedom to exploit is staggered. Laws to prevent capitalists from hiring young children (e.g. education clauses of English

---

10 'This manoeuvre also failed. Factory Inspector Leonard Horner conducted in his own person, and through his sub-inspectors, many examinations of witnesses in the factories of Lancashire' (Marx, 1887: 188).

11 In England, 'Although, ... the Factory Inspectors unceasingly and with justice, commend the results of the Acts of 1844 and 1850, yet they admit that the shortening of the hours of labour has already called forth such an intensification of the labour as is injurious to the health of the workman and to his capacity for work'. (Marx, 1887: 283).

12 'In the ten years during which it regulated factory work, first in part, and then entirely, the official reports of the factory inspectors teem with complaints as to the impossibility of putting the Act into force. As the law of 1833 left it optional with the lords of capital during the 15 hours, from 5.30 A.M. to 8.30 P.M., to make every "young person," and "every child" begin, break off, resume, or end his 12 or 8 hours at any moment they liked, and also permitted them to assign to different persons, different times for meals, these gentlemen soon discovered a new "system of relays," by which the labour-horses were not changed at fixed stations, but were constantly re-harnessed at changing stations. ... [T]his system annulled the whole Factory Act, not only in the spirit, but in the letter. How could factory inspectors, with this complex chapter keeping in respect to each individual child or young person, enforce the legally determined work-time and the granting of the legal mealtimes?' (Marx, 1887: 186).

Factory Acts) are often staggered: these laws can allow capitalists to continue to hire younger children for a number of years, which means that the maximum age at which a child can be hired is not legally enforceable until after many years since the initial introduction of the laws.[13] In other words, if adults' working day is restricted, children are used.[14]

All in all, so soon as capital 'finds itself subject to *legal control* at one point, compensates itself all the more recklessly at other points' (Marx, 1887: 320; italics added). For example, if the working day is reduced, wages can be reduced. Just like laws against enclosures during the period of PA, *post* PA, Factory Acts that seek to ensure workers' safety in the workplace, regulate the working day, and so on remain un- or under-implemented. This is in part because of the need to cut costs, one that is expressed by the nefarious nexus of state officials/politicians and the business world and the ideology that worships the freedom of capital. The existing rules protecting nature and workers from the harmful effects of capitalist production are gutted as soon as there arises a slight political opportunity (e.g. weakness of anti-capital and anti-state organizations). All this makes for a heightened level of accumulation by exploitation.

3.2 *The Capitalist State Form and Functioning*

The nature of the functioning of the state itself limits the effectivity of pro-worker policies. Given that pro-worker policies will adversely affect capitalists, various processes (loopholes) are put in place, in the body of the legislations, to restrict the positive impact of good policies on workers. Political representatives of capital within the state, who, more or less, work on behalf of capital and who share ideas that reflect capitalist interests, make every effort, along with capitalists, to dilute the pro-worker laws and/or block their proper implementation. Every law is designed in such a way that it has many exceptions, which weaken the law. For example, 'The Factory Acts Extension Act [of England], which affects the large establishments, derogates from the Factory Act by a crowd of vicious exceptions and cowardly compromises with the masters' (Marx, 1887: 322).

13 For example, the English 'Parliament decreed that after March 1st, 1834, no child under 11, after March 1st 1835, no child under 12, and after March 1st, 1836, no child under 13 was to work more than eight hours in a factory' (Marx, 1887: 185).

14 Just as the capital uses a temporal fix, with state's help, it also uses a spatial fix. If laws to restrict capitalists' freedom to exploit are in place in one country, capitalists threaten to move their capital elsewhere in order to 'intimidate' the state and the workers.

If capital gives in to state legislation in one area, it uses the state in its own interest in another area. If the state makes 'elementary education a compulsory condition to the "productive" employment of children' (Marx, 1887: 274) under a certain age, capitalists put pressure for the laws to be relaxed in order to increase the supply of labour. If the state defines, for example, the age at which a child can work for a given number of hours, then capitalists fight to reduce that age (for them, children must work for a wage at, say, 8 and not 9) and for longer hours than shorter hours. In England, capitalists engaged in 'a noisy agitation that went on for several years', which 'turned chiefly on the age of those who, under the name of children, were limited to 8 hours' work, and were subject to a certain amount of compulsory education'. (Marx, 1887: 185–186).[15] That was not the whole story though. Marx further writes:

> At their [manufacturers'] instigation the House of Commons reduced the minimum age for exploitable children from 9 to 8, in order to assure that additional supply of factory children which is due to capitalists, according to divine and human law. (Marx, 1887: 187)

So, pro-worker laws can be mutually contradictory thanks to the fact that they partly reflect the contradictory interests of capital and labour. For example, one law shortens the working day, and another law makes available more children for exploitation by lowering the minimum wage a child can work. As well, when 'adverse circumstances prevent the creation of the industrial reserve army and, with it, the absolute dependence of the working class upon the capitalist class', capital 'rebels against the "sacred" law of supply and demand' (Marx, 1887: 448). Capital engages in its own methods of class struggle as it relies on 'forcible means' (i.e. 'State interference') (ibid.). This is a part of class struggle from above.[16] For example, the capitalist class, when necessary,

15 'According to capitalistic anthropology, the age of childhood ended at 10, or at the outside, at 11. The more nearly the time approached for the coming into full force of the Factory Act, … the more wildly raged the mob of manufacturers. They managed, in fact, to intimidate the government to such an extent that … it proposed to lower the limit of the age of childhood from 13 to 12. In the meantime the pressure from without grew more threatening. Courage failed the House of Commons. It refused to throw children of 13 under the Juggernaut Car of capital for more than 8 hours a day' (ibid.).

16 When the capitalist class hires goons to kill trade union leaders or hires strike-breakers during a strike, or when the business bosses use court orders to stop a strike, that is class struggle on their part too.

endeavours 'to prevent by every means, including State interference, the emigration of the operatives' in order to ensure the availability of a reserve army *in situ* (p. 348).[17]

The wording of the laws itself is produced in such a way that it makes it easy for the capitalists to evade them; in addition, the scope of the laws remains limited.

> Apart from their wording, which makes it easy for the capitalist to evade them, the sanitary clauses are extremely meagre, and, in fact, limited to provisions for whitewashing the walls, for insuring cleanliness in some other matters, for ventilation, and for protection against dangerous machinery. ... [There was] the fanatical opposition of the masters to those clauses which imposed upon them a slight expenditure on appliances for protecting the limbs of their workpeople, an opposition that throws a fresh and glaring light on the Free-trade dogma, according to which, in a society with conflicting interests, each individual necessarily furthers the common weal by seeking nothing but his own personal advantage! (Marx, 1887: 315–316)

The state can introduce a legislation without making available adequate financial and administrative resources to implement it, while it has a lot of money for the propertied class. The English 'Parliament passed 5 labour Laws between 1802 and 1833, but was shrewd enough not to vote a penny for their carrying out, for the requisite officials, &c' (Marx, 1887: 184). For example,

> Parliament did not vote a single farthing in aid of emigration, but simply passed some Acts empowering the municipal corporations to keep the operatives in a half-starved state, *i.e.*, to exploit them at less than the normal wages. On the other hand, when 3 years later, the cattle disease broke out, Parliament broke wildly through its usages and voted, straight off, millions for indemnifying the millionaire landlords, whose farmers in any event came off without loss, owing to the rise in the price of meat. The bull-like bellow of the landed proprietors at the opening of Parliament, in 1866, showed that a man can worship the cow Sabala without being a Hindu, and can change himself into an ox without being a Jupiter. (Marx, 1887: 407)

---

17 To keep the supply of and demand for labour to favour the capitalist class, it may support state policy of keeping people from emigrating. This happened in England 'during the catastrophe in the cotton trade' (ibid.).

If a law exists restricting the number of hours that children can work and mandating that they must receive education but if there is no mechanism to implement this law, then the law has little material effect.

> For this the legislature is alone to blame, by having passed a delusive law, which, while it would seem to provide that the children employed in factories shall be *educated*, contains no enactment by which that professed end can be secured. (Marx, 1887: 274)

Consider another example:

> The Mines' Inspecting Act of 1860 ... provides that mines shall be inspected by public officers nominated specially for that purpose, and that boys between the ages of 10 and 12 years shall not be employed, unless they have a school certificate, or go to school for a certain number of hours. This Act was a complete dead letter owing to the ridiculously small number of inspectors ... [and] the meagreness of their powers. (Marx, 1887: 323)

Without an adequate administrative machinery which costs money, and capitalists want a 'cheap state', laws are only dead letters.

> The spirit of capitalist production stands out clearly in the ludicrous wording of the so-called education clauses in the Factory Acts, in the absence of an administrative machinery, an absence that again makes the compulsion illusory, in the opposition of the manufacturers themselves to these education clauses, and in the tricks and dodges they put in practice for evading them. (ibid.: 274)[18]

18 Marx continues:

'In the year 1865 there were 3,217 coal mines in Great Britain, and 12 inspectors. A Yorkshire mine-owner himself calculates ... that putting on one side their office work, which absorbs all their time, each mine can be visited but once in ten years by an inspector. No wonder that explosions have increased progressively, both in number and extent (sometimes with a loss of 200–300 men), during the last ten years. These are the beauties of "free" capitalist production!' (Marx, 1887: 328)

'The Workshops' Regulation Act, wretched in all its details, remained a dead letter in the hands of the municipal and local authorities who were charged with its execution. When, in 1871, Parliament withdrew from them this power, in order to confer it on the Factory Inspectors, to whose province it thus added by a single stroke more than one hundred thousand workshops, and three hundred brickworks, care was taken at the same time not to add more than eight assistants to their already undermanned staff.' (p. 322)

A large number of government departments, especially those that look after welfare and environmental issues, remain typically understaffed. This was the case more than 150 years ago. This is the case now, and especially, under what is called 'neoliberalism'. To the extent that an administrative machinery is created, several mechanisms can impede the implementation of pro-worker laws. For one, while statistical information is so important for state interventions, there are officials responsible for collecting social statistics, but they might not be given 'plenary powers to get at the truth' (Marx, 1887: 7). There might not be enough people who are 'as competent' and who are 'free from partisanship' (ibid.).[19] Indeed, state officials, influenced by capitalist thinking, may not always perform their duties. Marx talks about 'the certifying surgeons, who overstated the age of the children, agreeably to the capitalist's greed for exploitation, and the sordid trafficking needs of the parents' (Marx, 1887: 272).

3.3 *Capitalist Control over Economy and Crisis-Prone Accumulation Process*

As we have seen, the relations of equal exchange impose no limit on how long individual capitalists can make people work in a day: if capitalists have bought the commodity (labour power), they can use it as much as they wish to, according to the law of commodity, which the state itself supports. And even if the state introduces pro-worker measures (e.g. 'legal limitation of the working day') due to the pressure from workers, the state, which is a class-state, cannot generally do much about macro-economic features of capitalist society (i.e. capitalist strategies) which adversely impact workers. These features or strategies include: 'the diminution of employment caused by the competition of machinery' or indeed 'by changes in the quality of the labourers employed' (Marx, 1887: 385). The state cannot do anything about these features because it is capitalists' right to use machines or a particular kind (or quality) of labour (e.g. child labour, immigrant labour, and so on). There is, of course, nothing *natural* about the state's inability mentioned earlier: for example, when the length of the working day is shortened, forced idleness (= unemployment) could be checked by spreading the working time (across workers from different sectors and areas) throughout the year, but this does not happen. This could happen if the state really was the state of the majority. While the state appears not to have money to implement pro-worker measures, it has a lot of money to implement measures in capitalists' interests.

The interests of capitalists and those of workers contradict each other. There are fundamental conflicts (that are rooted in private property and production

19 The English factory inspectors, whose reports Marx relied on so much, were exemplary though.

relations), over wealth and income or value and surplus value. Consider the limit to the rise in wages. There are two scenarios here. In one scenario, and as Marx says in chapter 25 of *Capital* volume 1, if investment (c + v) increases, without c/v increasing (much), wages can rise.

> For since in each year more labourers are employed than in its predecessor, sooner or later a point must be reached, at which the requirements of accumulation begin to surpass the customary supply of labour, and, therefore, a rise of wages takes place. (Marx, 1887: 434–435)

Indeed, as soon as the diminution of unpaid labour due to a rise in wages 'touches the point at which the surplus-labour that nourishes capital is no longer supplied in normal quantity, a reaction sets in' (ibid.: 435-436). The reaction is that: 'a smaller part of revenue is capitalised, accumulation lags, and the movement of rise in wages receives a check' (ibid.:436). 'The rise of wages therefore is confined within limits that not only leave intact the foundations of the capitalistic system, but also secure its reproduction on a progressive scale.' (ibid.: 436).

Of course, how much wages will rise is politically mediated, something Marx, more or less, abstracts from in his general law of capitalist accumulation: the rise in wages due to increase in c + v will depend on the struggle of workers, the extent to which a pro-worker wage policy or welfare policy exists, and what the state does with regards to emigration/immigration, and so on.

However, as soon as living standards increase via an increase in real wages per hour worked, other things constant, the normal rate of profit (or of exploitation) will be affected. This will put a stop to the rise in wages. One can consider state policy here too that Marx abstracts from. a) State policy itself – by putting more resources in the hands of capital, can contribute to a rise in c + v. b) The slowdown in accumulation due to a rise in wages caused by increasing c + v can affect the state's tax base which in turn may limit its ability to support workers' interests. c) Instead of c + v, we can use state policy in favour of workers and arrive at the same conclusion: the state policy can raise wages but not beyond a point (Figure 8.1). If, due to public policy, wages rise beyond a point acceptable to capital, capital may slow down investment.

In another scenario, when c + v increases and c/v also increases, the situation is worse: when c/v rises, with mechanization displacing labour, a relative surplus population is produced which adversely affects the bargaining power of the employed segments of the working class and reduces their wages: 'The constant generation of a relative surplus-population keeps the law of supply and demand of labour, and therefore keeps wages, in a rut that corresponds with the wants of capital' (Marx, 1887: 523). When the reserve army shrinks and/or wages rise beyond a limit acceptable to capital, the state does resort to

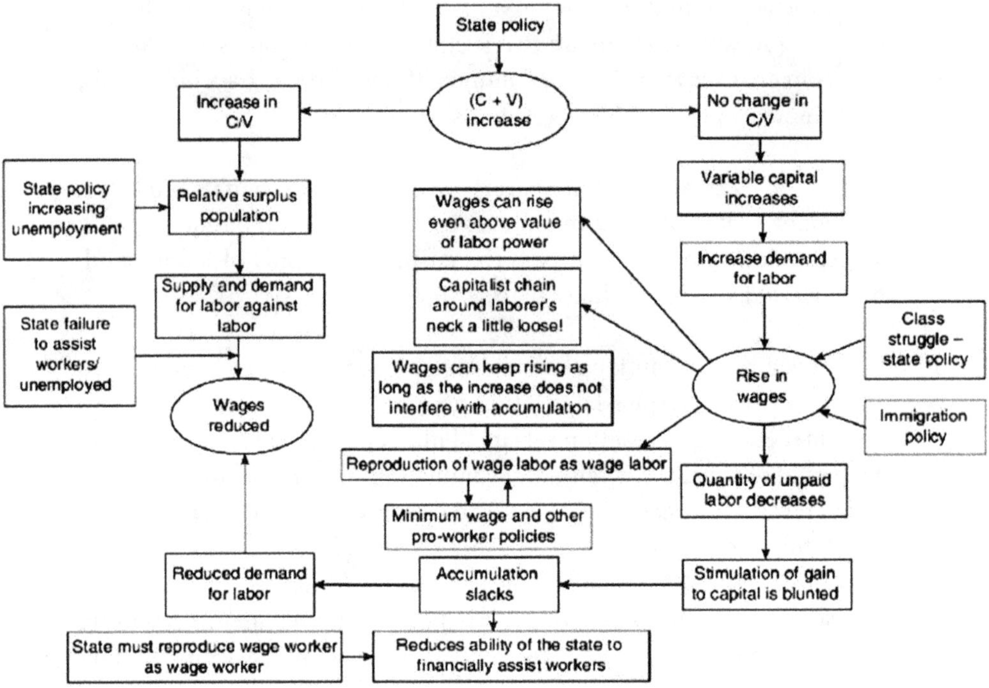

FIGURE 8.1 Marx's general theory of accumulation, class struggle, and the state
SOURCE: DAS (2022B)

several mechanisms, one of which is 'anti-inflation' measure (rise in the interest rate) and another is suppressing workers' struggle.

Of course, and once again, there is nothing absolutely natural here (in the purely economic sense): an increase in c + v combined with an increase in c/v will not adversely affect the workers, *if* the relative surplus population's needs are fully met by the state on the basis of adequate unemployment insurance and/or if they are employed by the state with decent wages, or if the state restricts the magnitude of drop in wages, and so on, but the state does not do this (Figure 8.1). For the state to do that would be to counter the very mechanism by which accumulation happens, wages are determined and the rate of exploitation kept at an acceptable level: in that sense the 'surplus population becomes … the lever of capitalistic accumulation, nay, a condition of existence of the capitalist mode of production', which the state must ultimately support at the expense of the vast majority of the population (ibid.: 444).

Even if the state somehow makes sure that wages rise, that fact, more or less, means that pro-worker legislations, just like an increase in accumulation with c/v constant, only reproduce workers as 'better-fed slaves' (Figure 8.1): a rise in wages 'only means, in fact, that the length and weight of the golden chain the wage worker has already forged for himself [or herself], allow of a relaxation of the tension of it' (Marx, 1887: 436). This would be the case whether the rise in wages is 'a consequence of accumulation of capital' or of state policy. In other words, 'just as little as better clothing, food, and treatment, and a larger peculium, do away with the exploitation of the slave, so little do they set aside that of the wage worker' (ibid.). This is the case whether the larger peculium is from private wages (wages paid by capitalists) or social wages (material resources from the state). Because the state must reproduce workers as workers, this fact sets the limits to what it can do for them (i.e. how much improvement can be granted) (Figure 8.1).

In other words, state welfare measures happen in part because of workers' struggle, but the workers that are reproduced through state welfare – just like the workers reproduced through a regime of increased wages due to a rise in c + v, with c /v constant – are the workers that ultimately produce surplus value for the capitalists. Even if workers' struggle is allowed and tolerated, the state (and capital) makes sure that 'the struggle between capital and labour [is confined] within limits comfortable for capital' (Marx, 1887: 525).

While an educated and healthy workforce is in the interest of capitalism and while that need prompts state measures in favour of workers, there is a limit to what is possible within capitalism, this irrational system of social production: '[T]he capitalist mode of production, owing to its very nature, excludes all rational improvement beyond a certain point.' (Marx, 1887: 316). It is impossible to wring from capital what labour needs for a safe and healthy working condition and healthy life, beyond a minimum level. In fact, unhealthy life and unsafe working conditions, just like un- and under-employment and precarity, 'are necessary conditions to the existence of capital' (ibid.).[20] Any significant pro-worker state policy means that '[t]he very root of the capitalist mode of

20 Let's consider this example that Marx provides:

'[T]he English doctors are unanimous in declaring that where the work is continuous, 500 cubic feet is the very least space that should be allowed for each person. ... Now, if the Factory Acts, owing to their compulsory provisions, indirectly hasten on the conversion of small workshops into factories, thus indirectly attacking the proprietary rights of the smaller capitalists, and assuring a monopoly to the great ones, so, if it were made obligatory to provide the proper space for each workman in every workshop, thousands of small employers would, at one full swoop, be expropriated directly! ... The sanitary officers, the industrial inquiry commissioners, the factory inspectors, all harp ... upon the impossibility of wringing them [500 cubic feet] out of capital. They thus, in fact, declare that consumption and other lung diseases among the workpeople are necessary conditions to the existence of capital.' (Marx, 1887: 316)

production, i.e., the self-expansion of all capital, large or small, by means of the "free" purchase and consumption of labour-power, would be attacked', so such a policy is 'brought to a deadlock' (ibid.).

During normal times, the imperative of capitalist accumulation sets a limit on what the state can do for workers. An increase in wages beyond a given point affects surplus value. Geographical mobility of capital as an accumulation strategy imposes some 'constraint', at a concrete level, on what the state can do for workers: if the state acts in workers' interest in a given country, capital may threaten to move to another country. The other aspect of the limit to what the state can do for the people is the crisis-proneness of capitalist accumulation. Capitalism is characterized by the tendency of the rate of profit to fall (TRPF), leading to reduced investment and employment. This mechanism puts a stop to the rise in wages and contributes to absolute and/or relative immiserization. Increasing the rate of exploitation, including by depressing wages below the value of labour, is a major way to counter the TRPF, and the state aids capital here. Indeed, some of the state interventions to counter the falling rate of profit aim to increase labour exploitation. Some of the state interventions seek to bailout companies in crisis, and these are ultimately paid for by the working class and small-scale producers, in the form of austerity and the like. The fact that the state cannot fundamentally rescue capitalism *from its* crisis-proneness affects workers adversely: the state indeed has little control over 'crises partial or general' which cause unemployment (Marx, 1887: 385). Or, more generally, the state qua capitalist state has little real and long-term control over the average rate of profit to fall and therefore over the extent to which it can help the workers.

As mentioned, the state has sought to improve the conditions of common people. Yet it is the case that the state fails to meet their need in a significant and durable manner. This failure is actually the state's success in keeping the masses in their place. Its failure is internally connected to what the state is.

In relation to the working class, the state falls short in two major ways (Figure 8.2). Surplus value ultimately comes from the deduction of the value of labour power from the total net value produced by the worker. State's pro-worker laws can only aim to make sure that workers get back at least as much as it takes to reproduce their labour power, that there are enough workers with adequate physical ability and mental skills, available for exploitation by the employer, that is, that 'the worker has retained his labour-power and can sell it anew' (Marx, 1887: 413).[21] This means that the state's pro-worker laws can

21 This is indeed the basis for so-called capability deprivation theory of (progressive) bourgeois scholarship such as that of Amartya Sen (Sen, 1999; Hahnel, 2002).

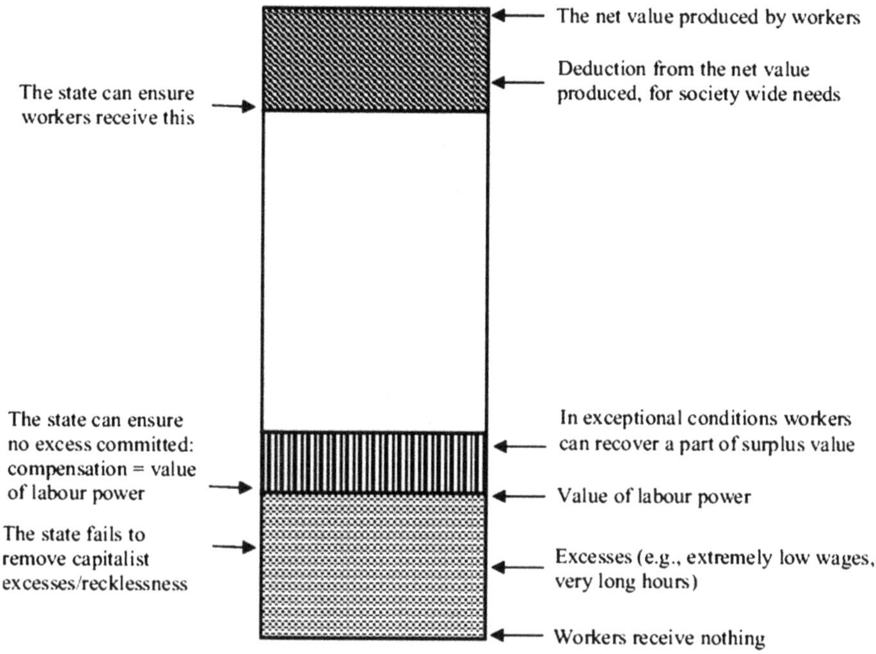

FIGURE 8.2 The state and value
SOURCE: DAS (2022B)

only be against *excesses* of capitalism. This constitutes the lower limit of state action. State laws cannot be fundamentally against the capitalist property relations, by virtue of which the excesses exist. Even then, the state falls short: it fails to eliminate the excesses, because it must meet the needs of capital. A capitalist class in a society *without* millions of people who are already in (near-)poverty and/or face the risk of being in poverty, would be a class *without* its necessary political guarantee too. This is because it would face a situation where those who are *not* poor (e.g. well-paid workers) would have a lot of bargaining power, which, in turn, would increase the bargaining power of those who *are* poor, and therefore, of *all* sections of the exploited class.[22]

The state *could* ensure that workers receive the entire value of what they produce minus the usual deductions necessary for meeting society-wide needs.[23] This is the upper limit. But the state does not and cannot, because it is the state of the capitalist class and not the workers and small-scale producers.

22 Note that this poverty may or may not include hunger/destitution.

23 Deductions will have to be made from the social product that people produce (Marx, 1875). Society will save resources for supporting people when they cannot or are not

4 Conclusion

Objective conditions and objective interests (capital's need for a suitable workforce) as such do not act. '[I]n so far as they are the personifications of economic categories, embodiments of particular class relations and class-interests classes' that are objective, (Marx, 1887: 7) people exist as classes and class fractions and engage in struggles in support of their interests. There is class struggle from below (i.e. common people's struggle). There is class struggle from above: this is in the form of what capitalists do to the working class, including through their instrumentalist ties to the state and through its own associations (e.g. chambers of commerce and the like). The class struggle from above is also in the form of the state's anti-worker economic policies and the suppression of strikes against these policies, on behalf of the capitalist class. The state is the biggest and most trusted trade union of the capitalist class that counters the trade unions and other organizations of workers.[24] As an arm of the capitalist class, the state supremely signifies class struggle from above by suppressing any significant potential or actual threat from workers to commodity relations, relations of property, and profit-making in capitalist production.

The state is related to the working class people in many ways. It 'helps' them in part as a response to the working-class struggle, as its relation to the labour

---

expected to work (e.g. women during pregnancy, children, older people, people who are ill, people who have met with an accident). A part of the total social product produced by people will need to be set aside towards the cost of the means of production (e.g. raw materials and machines and energy need to be replenished) and for the purpose of expanding the productive base (e.g. to establish new factories or labs or build a new bridge across a river). A part of the social product needs to be put aside for collective provisioning by the government (e.g. education, healthcare, and so on), for dealing with emergencies and natural calamities (e.g. storms, floods, earthquakes, pandemic) and for restoring ecological health.

24 The neo-liberal welfare cut is an instance of class struggle launched by capital and its state against the social wage that the working class had successfully fought for after the war.

A part of the wage that workers receive is the social wage benefits from the state paid from general taxation, which comes mainly from the total surplus value workers produce (Brooks, 2005). Now consider that the state provides such things as healthcare and education. Given that the labour involved in the production of these services does not directly produce surplus value, austerity can be seen as class struggle from above: struggle of capital for cuts in order to 'stop the drain on surplus value provided by the state spending' (ibid.). Such cuts can also be prompted by state's corporate welfare programme: when the state spends billions of dollars on corporate welfare, including to bail out criminal financiers that become bankrupt, a policy creates a massive deficit and then shifts the financial burden to workers in the form of cuts in welfare funding.

circuit shows. As we have seen, through its legislations and policies, the state seeks to force the capitalist class to make the conditions of workers a little tolerable by such processes as reduction of the length of the working day; it has tried to put a floor below which wages are not to fall. The state allows, or helps, people to freely sell their labour power and small-scale producers to freely sell products of their labour. It contributes to the reproduction of segments of the reserve army through unemployment insurance and similar anti-poverty measures. There have been legislations concerning health and safety at work. The working class has also received benefits in the form of subsidized health and education, and unemployment insurance. The state can positively affect the value of labour power itself.[25]

There are definite driving forces behind the state's pro-worker measures. There is an objective pressure on the state, coming from the general and long-term interests of capital-as-a-whole, to intervene on behalf of the masses. Capitalists' 'own most important interests dictate' that 'all *legally* removable hindrances to the free development of the working class' (e.g. the crippling of the quality of labour power due to overwork) be removed. Partly for this reason, Marx (1887: 7) says, he gives 'so large a space in this volume to the history, the details, and the results of English factory legislation'. And this is why it is important to re-examine Marx's discussion of the workplace legislation and to reflect on what the state does for the workers' welfare. *Capital* volume 1 reveals the economic laws of motion of capitalism. It also sheds light on the power of the working class struggle and on the conditions for, and the barriers to, the development of the working class struggle.

The long-term interests of the capitalist class, or of its hegemonic fraction/s, (and of the capitalist state)[26] may coincide with workers' own interest in better working and living conditions, and this partly drives state functions in favour of the working class. One implication of the class character of the state is that apart from the state having to meet the fundamental needs of the capitalist class, it must also respond to the struggle of the masses for concessions to gain a degree of legitimacy. There are, however, limits to what the state can

25 If the state accedes to the demand for a higher wage to allow the consumption of nutrition food or access to libraries, that need becomes a new component part of the value of labour power.

26 The state's 'own' interests are the long-term (political) interests of the capitalist class, including those that care to be met outside the formal jurisdiction of the state (e.g. securing strategic trade locations relative to foreign competitors), as these interests are mediated by the state's own internal structure and the conceptions and the interests of state actors (in favourable election results, money, power, etc.), and sometimes there can be a difference between state's interests and those of a group of capitalists.

do for workers under capitalism, the limits that exist because of the capitalist control over property and production, nature of capitalist accumulation and its crisis-proneness, and the capitalist state's bureaucratic functioning and its anti-worker politics.

These limits point to one crucial idea: the state is basically a class institution and under capitalism, it is fundamentally a capitalist institution. However, at a concrete level, in terms of its day-to-day action in a specific time and place, its capitalist character can vary a little as it is mediated/affected by the struggle of the people (workers and petty producers) in their own interests. The opposite view is not true: it is wrong to think that the state belongs to everyone equally, to all the people under its jurisdiction, but that *how* pro-people it is – i.e. to what extent it acts in the interests of everyone – is affected/mediated by the influence of the capitalist class on its functioning. Also not true is the view that the state is equidistant from capital and people (wage workers and petty producers), that it is autonomous of capital on the one hand and labour (or common people) on the other.

We have seen that the masses do not get much without a fight. It is also the case that to obtain some concessions, trade unions of a country have to often support capitalist accumulation in that country. The fact that capitalist investment in many sectors can move across countries – and this is something that can be stopped, but will not be stopped, by the nation-states working together – imposes a limit on the extent to which the state can grant workers significant concessions. All these facts together have specific political implications that are discussed in Chapter 10.

CHAPTER 9

Lenin's *Development of Capitalism in Russia* and Other Economic Writings: Commodity Production, Class Differentiation, Capitalism, and Imperialism

Vladimir Lenin, the greatest disciple of Marx and Engels, has made many valuable contributions to political economy. Lenin's (1899a) *Development of capitalism in Russia* is a model of Marx's (1887) *Capital*, for the 20th century, and an exemplar of the class approach to political economy. His writings on imperialism, including his short book *Imperialism: the highest stage of capitalism*, innovatively develop some of the themes from Marx's general law of accumulation presented in Chapter 25 of *Capital* Volume 1 and demonstrate the power of Marxist political economy when conducted at the global scale, as opposed to local and national scales (Lenin, 1916a; 1916b; 1916c). In his economic writings, Lenin makes use of empirical/statistical data which he interprets on the basis of scientific reason (theory) informed by materialist dialectics. Wedded to Marx/Engels' key tenets such as the labour theory of value, theory of surplus value and the doctrine of the proletariat-led class struggle, Lenin always draws political implications of his intellectual ideas for the radical transformation of the world, a prolonged and uneven process in which he himself actively participated as a scholar-activist. While an avowed internationalist, he is deeply sensitive to the specificities of the Global South as Marx himself was, contrary to the woke Left's eurocentrism accusation against Marx (Das, 2024d). Lenin's political economy represents great continuity from, and further development of, Marx's political economy that has been discussed in the last seven chapters.

I divide my discussion in this chapter into three parts: 1. general (epistemological) comments on Lenin's view of political economy as a field of knowledge, 2. Lenin's substantive claims in political economy, which is divided into six sections which respectively deal with: commodity production and class differentiation; capitalism as the most developed form of commodity production, and its forms, and geographically uneven development and geographical mobility that capitalism causes; capitalism's progressive character; capitalism's dark sides, including: forms of exploitation and super-exploitation of marginalized groups, as well as workers' impoverishment and rising economic inequality; capitalist imperialism; significance of workers' struggle for economic concessions; and, political economy as a guide to struggle for socialism. The final section presents my appreciation and comradely critique of Lenin's political economy.

 | DOI:10.1163/9789004730472_010

1 What Is Political Economy, and How to Study It?

1.1 *What Is Political Economy?*

Following Marx's economic doctrine,[1] Lenin says that political economy is a science of society that studies not production as such but the social relations of production and distribution as they change over time. '[P]olitical economy is the science of the historically developing systems of social production [and distribution]' (Lenin, 1898).

As a field of knowledge, political economy must examine 'the connection between, and interdependence of, the various aspects of the process taking place in all spheres of the social economy' (Lenin, 1899a: 26). In particular, it must deal with the 'question [of] … the relation of economics to politics' (Lenin, 1916b). In a 1911 plan for a lecture on the fundamentals of political economy, Lenin (1911) includes the following topics: 'The essence of the capitalist mode of production as compared with the other modes of production historically preceding it'; 'Similarity in the existence of class oppression and distinction in the forms and conditions of the class struggle'; 'Conditions for the sale of the commodity "labour-power"'; 'The production of absolute and relative surplus-value'; How '"Normal" conditions for the consumption of the commodity "labour-power" are determined by the worker's struggle against the capitalist'; and 'The strike struggle, trade unions and factory legislation in the history of the struggle for shorter working hours'.

According to Lenin, the economy, including its social (class) relations, is the basis of society: it is 'the foundation of a specific system of man's entire social life' (Lenin, 1898). '[T]he most important problems of contemporary social life are intimately bound up with problems of economic science', i.e. political economy (ibid.).

1.2 *How to Study Political Economy?*

Political economy must be based on a materialist and dialectical philosophy. This philosophy emphasizes the objective conditions of social life relative to how people think about it, which change due to contradictions in social life. 'Only the materialist conception of history can … open up the possibility for a broad, coherent, and intelligent view of a specific system of social economy' (Lenin, 1898). Marxist materialism is dialectical. How important dialectical philosophy is to Lenin's political economy could be gazed by his claim in his

1 According to Marx, as discussed in chapter 3, 'the economic' is a totality of multiple processes, namely, production, distribution, consumption and exchange, and their social relations, and interconnections.

Conspectus of Hegel's *Science of Logic*, that it is impossible to fully understand Marx's *Capital* without a thorough understanding of the *whole* of Hegel's *Logic*. 'Dialectics is a living, many-sided knowledge (with the number of sides eternally increasing), with an infinite number of shades of every approach and approximation to reality (with a philosophical system growing into a whole out of each shade)' (Lenin, 1915a). Lenin utilizes this principle in his political economy.

Political economy must be theoretical (and it must be empirically-based). For example, in his *Development of capitalism Russia*, Lenin first deals with 'the basic theoretical propositions of abstract political economy on the subject of the home market for capitalism' which then serve 'as a sort of introduction to … the factual part of' his book, and 'relieve us of the need to make repeated references to theory in our further exposition' (Lenin, 1899a: 26).

There are several aspects of his approach to theorization that are noteworthy. He makes an ontological distinction between more general (or fundamental) processes and more specific (or concrete) processes that are the manifestation of the more general processes. Therefore, according to him, political economy must examine: a) basic features of a given social economy such as capitalism which are more or less universal whose manifestations are specific, b) 'show the process (and the conditions) of its emergence, on the one hand, and the tendencies of its further development' and c) 'represent the different aspects and different manifestations of contemporary economic life as component parts of a definite system of social economy, as manifestations of the basic features of that system' (Lenin, 1898).

The reality does not deliver itself on a platter. Theory helps us understand the empirical world which in turn informs theory. The existence of an objective process (e.g. low wages) and even its acknowledgement by people do not guarantee that they understand it adequately, i.e. in terms of its root causes or conditions (e.g. wage-slavery; state support for wage-slavery). To understand a problem adequately, we require theory understood simply as statements about general causal mechanisms behind a given empirical phenomenon that are widely prevalent across times and places.[2] One can only have a 'distorted … picture of actual facts when viewed from the angle of a wrong theory' (1899: 214). A life-long student of dialectics that emphasizes the totalizing character of reality, Lenin advises that one must refrain from 'superficial generalisations based on facts selected one-sidedly and without reference to *the system of capitalism as a whole*' (Lenin, 1908; italics added), and only theory can help us

2 We return to the conception of theory (in political economy) in chapter 10.

understand that system. In using statistical data from the surveys produced by the state, one has to be mindful of the fact that these surveys are inaccurate in part because of their class biases (Lenin, 1912c). The surveys often give 'exaggerated figures of the workers' earnings' while they understate 'the amount of production and the size of the capitalists' profits' (Lenin, 1912c). This problem is partly due to the fact that all surveys 'are carried out on purely bureaucratic lines, inquiries being addressed only to the capitalists, while it is considered unnecessary to ask the workers any questions' (ibid.).

Lenin takes a class approach to the theoretical (and empirical) study of economy. This means that economic matters must be seen from the standpoint of the different classes. '[The] division of society into classes' (i.e. capitalists and landlords as well as workers and petty producers) as well as the 'change in the forms of class rule' provide the 'standpoint [for] examining all social questions – economic, political, spiritual, religious, etc.' (Lenin, 1919a). Indeed, 'A concrete analysis of the status and the interests of the different classes must serve as a means of defining the precise significance of this truth when applied to this or that problem' (Lenin, 1899a: 32). This advice is true for political economy (as it is to political theory). Political economy is indeed partisan.[3]

In a class society, there cannot be epistemic or political neutrality. 'To expect science to be impartial in a wage-slave society is as foolishly naïve as to expect impartiality from manufacturers on the question of whether workers' wages ought not to be increased by decreasing the profits of capital' (Lenin, 1913c).

For Lenin, theory requires critique which in turn informs one's theory. Theory develops partly out of criticisms of existing ideas. The ideas that Lenin often critiques include those of so-called Marxists/socialists as well as bourgeois professors.[4] Lenin is in particular critical not only of petty bourgeois or populist or Proudhonist political economy but also of what he calls 'bourgeois and professorial political economy' (Lenin, 1899b), including of the social democratic type. Lenin says:

> the *personal* qualities of present-day professors are such that we may find among them even exceptionally stupid people. … But the *social* status of professors in bourgeois society is such that only those are allowed to hold

3 Following Lenin, Althusser (1970) makes this point too.

4 'Lenin's theorizing was always built around the fights with … designated enemies … He hardly [wasted time] … on clashes with representatives of the "vulgar bourgeois political economy". His true enemies were always inside Marxism and the socialist movement' (Melnik, 2021: 45). 'Through his criticism of opponents, Lenin made his own positive contribution to the development studies' (ibid.).

> such posts who sell science to serve the interests of capital, and agree to utter the most fatuous nonsense, the most unscrupulous drivel and twaddle against the socialists. The bourgeoisie will forgive the professors all this as long as they go on "abolishing" socialism [through their lectures]. (Lenin, 1914c)

It is not just that theory helps us understand the empirical world (and ideas about it) critically. Theory also serves as a guide to action, and most of Lenin's theory was prompted by a need to politically intervene in the world. Political economy must produce ideas about what is to be done (explained below).

Lenin's specific substantive political economic claims concern: class relations and class differentiation, including in rural areas; dynamics of capitalism and its forms and stages of development; uneven (capitalist) development; obstacles to democratic politics in the epoch of capitalist and imperialist reaction; capitalist economy; imperialism and war; conditions of common people (workers and peasants), including those of women and children; and common people's impoverishment; and growing inequality in society.

2 Commodity Production and Class Differentiation[5]

A society based on commodity economy must experience class differentiation, which in turn produces home-market. When petty producers, including peasants, buy inputs and sell outputs, two classes will be produced: most of them will, gradually, lose their means of production and become propertyless (or property-poor) wage-workers, while some of them will turn into well-to-do commodity producers or proto-capitalists (e.g. rich peasants) and full-fledged capitalists (e.g. capitalist farmers). Thus 'the purely theoretical analysis of the process of the formation of ... capitalism points to the differentiation of the small producers as an important factor in this process'. In rural areas, this means:

> 1) the transformation of the peasantry into a rural bourgeoisie (ownership of commercial and industrial establishment), and 2) the transformation of the peasantry into a rural proletariat (sale of labour-power ...). (Lenin, 1899a: 111)

5 While Lenin's political economy covers both industry and agriculture, this chapter is focussed on his political economy of agrarian capitalism and capitalism as such, and does not deal with political economy of industry in great details.

Small scale production faces still competition from the capitalists. 'Every advance in science and technology inevitably and relentlessly undermines the foundations of small-scale production in capitalist society' (Lenin, 1908). Small scale producers cannot normally compete with large scale commercial producers. 'The technical and commercial superiority of large-scale *production* over small-scale production not only in industry, but also in agriculture, is proved by irrefutable facts' (Lenin, 1908).

While both petty producers and wage workers perform labour, that does not mean they belong to one category. 'It is not labour that is a definite category of political economy, but only the social form of labour, the social organisation of labour, or, in other words, the mutual relations of people arising out of the part they play in social labour.' (Lenin, 1902a). Class differentiation involves two processes: *differentiation of property* (some people come to possess more property than others and the majority ultimately become propertyless), and *dissolution of petty production*. In rural areas:

> The old [pre-capitalist] peasantry is not only "differentiating," it is being completely dissolved, it is ceasing to exist, it is being ousted by absolutely new types of rural inhabitants – types that are the basis of a society in which commodity economy and capitalist production prevail. (ibid.: 174)

The two new rural classes – rural bourgeoisie and proletariat – that are produced due to class differentiation of the peasantry, at the expense of the middle peasantry, share a common feature: 'the commodity, money character of their economy'. They are both involved in commodity circulation.

The rural bourgeoisie, or the well-to-do peasantry, the first new type of class, includes: 'the independent farmers who carry on commercial agriculture in all its varied forms' as well as 'the owners of commercial and industrial establishments, the proprietors of commercial enterprises, etc.' (Lenin, 1899a: 176). The well-to-do-peasantry's distinguishing mark is that they hire wage-labour even if they also employ family labour. They hire wage worker to get the work done because the family labour is not enough: 'The size of the farm, in the majority of cases, requires a labour force larger than that available in the family, for which reason the formation of a body of farm labourers, and still more of day labourers, is a necessary condition for the existence of the well-to-do peasantry' (ibid.). The well-to-do-peasant 'rents or buys land' or '"gathers" land' that is abandoned by the poor peasant, and 'owns many animals, fertilises his soil, introduces improvements., etc.' (Lenin, 1989a: 103). They produce for the market. The conditions of the well-to-do peasantry, a minority of the rural population, are 'considerably above the average' (ibid.: 144). They 'not only cover all their expenditure by independent farming, but also obtain a surplus', although they are not rich enough – they do not accumulate enough capital to be able to avoid manual labour (ibid.).

When the well-to-do-peasantry makes a profit, this profit is 'either directed towards commercial operations and usury' or 'invested in the purchase of land, farm improvements, etc.' (ibid.: 177). 'Numerically, the peasant bourgeoisie constitute a small minority of the peasantry', although its relative numerical strength 'fluctuates considerably' in the geographic space (ibid.). But as far as their economic weight is concerned – when economic weight is seen as the 'quantity of means of production' produced by the peasantry, 'the total amount of produce raised by the peasantry', and so on – 'the peasant bourgeoisie are undoubtedly predominant. They are the masters of the contemporary countryside' (ibid.).[6] 'From among these well-to-do peasants a class of capitalist farmers is created' (ibid.: 176).

The richer peasant families tend to have larger families.[7] This partly 'indicates the lesser desire of the well-to-do peasantry to divide up the land, which is an important means of production. The "family co-operation" ... is thus the basis of capitalist co-operation' (ibid.). As peasants' economic strength increases, they 'resort in the greatest measure to the employment of hired labour' (ibid.). This is 'despite the fact that the most affluent peasants are best provided with workers in their families. Here, too, family co-operation is the basis of capitalist co-operation' (ibid.: 108).

The other new type of class produced by class differentiation is the proletariat. In rural areas, the proletariat 'covers the poor peasants' and those that 'are completely landless' (ibid.: 177). Their conditions are characterized by 'insignificant farming on a patch of land, with the farm in a state of utter ruin' as well as by their 'inability to exist without the sale of labour-power' and 'an extremely low standard of living' (ibid.). 'The rural proletarian, by comparison with the middle peasantry, consumes less, and, moreover, consumes food of worse quality (potatoes instead of bread, etc.), but buys more' (ibid.: 181). There is also a major difference between the poor peasant component of the rural proletariat and the well-to-do-peasant peasant: the poor peasant leases

6 'When we said above that the peasant bourgeoisie are the masters of the contemporary countryside, we disregarded the factors retarding differentiation: bondage, usury, labour-service, etc. Actually, the real masters of the contemporary countryside are often enough not the representatives of the peasant bourgeoisie, but the village usurers and the neighbouring landowners' (ibid.: 186).

7 '[W]hen classifying households according to economic strength, or to size of farm, we always get larger families among the well-to-do strata of the peasantry' (ibid.: 94).

out land or abandons the land or 'runs his most wretched farm with an insignificant number of animals' (ibid.: 103).

In between the well-to-do peasants and the rural proletariat are the middle peasantry. 'It is distinguished by the least development of commodity production' (ibid.: 181). The middle peasants performing 'independent agricultural labour' cover their 'maintenance in perhaps only the best years and under particularly favourable conditions' so their 'position is an extremely precarious one' (ibid.). 'Every crop failure flings masses of the middle peasants into the ranks of the proletariat' (ibid.). Majority of middle peasants 'cannot make ends meet without resorting to loans, to be repaid by labour service, etc., without seeking "subsidiary" [wage] employment on the side' (ibid.). 'In its social relations this group fluctuates between the top group [peasant bourgeoisie], towards which it gravitates but which only a small minority of lucky ones succeed in entering, and the bottom group, into which it is pushed by the whole course of social evolution' (ibid.). '[T]he peasant bourgeoisie *oust* not only the bottom group, but also the middle group, of the peasantry' (ibid.).

'The small proprietors', those who operate mainly with their family labour, 'obtain a net income considerably below the wages of the hired workers employed in the big establishments.' (ibid.: 354). '[U]nder commodity economy, the small producer inevitably falls into dependence upon merchant's capital by virtue of the purely economic superiority of large, mass-scale marketing over scattered, petty marketing' (ibid.: 361).

To the extent that modern society is based on commodity production, and to the extent that commodity producers exist, their economic conditions depend on the freer development of commodity production: 'In modern society it is impossible to exist without selling, and anything that retards the development of commodity production merely results in a worsening of the conditions of the producers' (ibid.: 155). A major impact of class differentiation does therefore mean that the poor peasantry's life may be worse than the rural proletariat's.[8] But this conclusion does not mean that Lenin's political economy would '"stand for" dispossessing the peasantry of the land' (ibid.: 170). On the contrary, 'All that follows from what has been said is that we "stand for" abolishing all restrictions on the peasants' right freely to dispose of their land' and 'to leave the village community' (ibid.), or one might add, to get a good price for their products. 'Only the peasant himself can be the judge of whether it is more advantageous to be a farm labourer' (ibid.).

8 Indeed, when peasants are not able to produce efficiently and/or not sell their products for a good price, their living conditions can be worse than those of landless workers.

The fact that peasants are completely subordinated to the market is expressed in the fact that they are dependent on the market for both personal consumption and the means of farming as well as the payment of taxes to the state (ibid.: 172). The peasants are subjected to all those mechanisms, 'all those contradictions which are inherent in every commodity economy and every order of capitalism: competition, the struggle for economic independence, the grabbing of land (purchasable and rentable), the concentration of production in the hands of a minority, the forcing of the majority into the ranks of the proletariat, their exploitation by a minority through the medium of merchant's capital and the hiring of farm labourers' (ibid.). There is a double transformation of petty commodity production: 'the dialectics of commodity production' transforms '"working with our own hands" into working with others' hands, into exploitation' (ibid.: 351). 'The sum-total of all the economic contradictions among the peasantry constitutes what we call the differentiation of the peasantry.' (ibid.: 173). In fact, under capitalism, 'There is not a single economic phenomenon among the peasantry that does not bear this contradictory form, … i.e., that does not express a struggle and antagonism of interests, that does not imply advantage for some and disadvantage for others' (ibid.: 172). This is the case whether it is the renting or purchase of land, development of agricultural industries, or technical progress of farming, etc. (ibid.).

If there were no class differentiation, the existence of the peasants would 'represent a fairly even type of poverty-stricken cultivators, among whom only usurers would stand out, and they only to the extent of money owned and not to the extent and organisation of agricultural production' (ibid.: 185). But that is not the case. Some peasants live better than other peasants, as already indicated, as discussed.

Some processes (e.g. the use of labour service; usury, etc.) retard class differentiation while other processes quicken class differentiation. One of the latter is the combination of industry with agriculture. On the one hand: the combination of industry with agriculture aggravates and accentuates 'the differentiation of the peasantry: the prosperous and the well-off peasants open workshops, hire workers from among the rural proletariat, and accumulate money for commercial and usurious transactions' (ibid.: 376). On the other: '[t]he peasant poor … provide the wage-workers, the handicraftsmen who work for buyers up, and the bottom groups of petty-master handicraftsmen, those most crushed by the power of merchant's capital' (ibid.). In these ways, 'the combination of industry with agriculture consolidates and develops capitalist relations, spreading them from industry to agriculture and vice versa' (ibid.: 376–377).

Connected to, and following, the process of the combination of industry with agriculture, is the separation between the two under capitalism. This 'takes place in connection with the differentiation of the peasantry, and does so by different paths at the two poles of the countryside' (ibid.: 377). At one pole of the countryside are 'the well-to-do minority [who] open industrial establishments, enlarge them, improve their farming methods, hire farm labourers to till the land, devote an increasing part of the year to industry'. And, 'at a certain stage of the development of the industry' these well-to-do commodity producers 'find it more convenient to separate their industrial from their agricultural undertakings, i.e., to hand over the farm to other members of the family, or to sell farm buildings, animals, etc.', and to become merchants, etc. (ibid.). 'At the other pole of the countryside the separation of industry from agriculture consists in the fact that the poor peasants are being ruined and turned into wage-workers (industrial and agricultural)', as they are compelled to abandon the land and independent industrial labour (e.g. artisanal work) because farming and independent industrial labour are not profitable (ibid.). 'At this pole', therefore, 'it is not the profitableness of industry, but need and ruin, that compels the peasant to abandon the land, and … independent industrial labour', so 'the process of the separation of industry from agriculture is one of the expropriation of the small producer' (ibid.: 378).

Class differentiation is linked to the formation of the home market. Signifying 'the transition from simple commodity production to capitalist production (and constituting the necessary condition for this transition)', the process of the separation of the direct producer from the means of production – i.e., their expropriation – '*creates* the home market' (Lenin, 1899a: 67–68; italics in original).[9] This occurs in two ways. 'On the one hand, the means of production from which the small producer is "freed" are converted into capital in the hands of their new owner, serve to produce commodities and, consequently, are themselves converted into commodities' (ibid.: 68). That is, when a section of the petty producing class is transformed into the bourgeoisie, this 'creates a market mainly for means of production' (ibid.: 166). 'On the other hand, *the means of subs*istence of the small producer', who is not expropriated, 'become the material elements of the variable capital, i.e., of the sum of money expended by the employer … on hiring workers', as these means of subsistence are converted into commodities and thus create a home market for articles of consumption' (ibid.: 68; 166).

'The *differentiation of the peasantry* [thus] *creates a home market for capitalism* by converting the peasant into a farm labourer, on the one hand, and into a small-commodity producer, a petty bourgeois, on the other' (ibid.: 155;

9 Lenin discusses the formation of the home market by closely following Marx and by disregarding, like Marx does, the *foreign* market.

italics in original).[10] Among the petty producers who possess limited amount of means of production ('the bottom groups'), their ability to engage in productive work is transformed into commodity labour power, while the means of production possessed by wealthier peasants are transformed into capital, i.e. money invested to make more money. 'Both these transformations result in precisely that process of the creation of a home market which theory has established for capitalist countries in general' (ibid.). The processes of the formation of the home market due to class differentiation in the rural context apply to urban areas too.

Class differentiation is a dynamic process. In a society with commodity production under private property, petty bourgeois strata are constantly produced. They are also constantly pauperized and proletarianized. In capitalism, '[A] number of new "middle strata" are inevitably brought into existence again and again by capitalism (appendages to the factory, work at home, small workshops scattered all over the country to meet the requirements of big industries, such as the bicycle and automobile industries, etc.). These new small producers are just as inevitably being cast again into the ranks of the proletariat' (Lenin, 1908).[11]

While the general tendency in commodity-producing society where there is private property is towards proletarianization of the vast majority on the basis of class differentiation,[12] small-scale production does not completely vanish. To the extent that it does, it 'maintains itself ... by constant worsening of diet, by chronic starvation, by lengthening of the working day, by deterioration in the quality' of its means of production (ibid.). The process is the same whether it is agriculture or industry. The small producer finds it difficult to compete with the large-scale producers, and especially those using machines, so:

> The small producer tries to make up for these unfavourable conditions by working longer hours and with greater intensity. Under commodity production, the small producer both in agriculture and in industry carries on only by cutting down his requirements. (1899a: 353)

10 [I]n capitalist production the basis for the formation of a home market is the process of the disintegration of the small cultivators into agricultural entrepreneurs and workers.' (ibid.: 70).

11 In a major political writing, Lenin (1920) says: 'Capitalism would not be capitalism if the proletariat *pur sang* were not surrounded by a large number of exceedingly motley types [exiting] between the proletarian and the semi-proletarian'.

12 We may recall from chapter 2 Marx's point that by taking away property from small-scale producers, the bourgeoisie has simplified class antagonisms.

Small scale production does not just produce suffering for individual producers. The maintenance of petty production, because of its inefficient nature, represents a wastage at the level of society too: 'an immense amount of social labour is … being wasted owing to the preservation of senseless, backward and scattered small production, particularly in agriculture and in commerce!' (Lenin, 1914d).[13]

Apart from class differentiation, another aspect of the development of commodity production and of commodity economy, is the social division of labour which refers to the fact that different parts of society produce different commodities for exchange. This also contributes to the formation of a home market (Lenin, 1899). Commodity production takes the form of 'various forms of processing raw materials (and various operations in this processing) separating from agriculture one after another and becoming independent branches of industry, which exchange their products (now commodities) for the products of agriculture' (ibid.: 67).

3 Capitalism as the Highest Form of Commodity Production, and Its Social and Spatial Forms and Effects

3.1 *Forms of Capital and Capitalism and Stages of Capitalist Development*

In many contexts, capitalism develops out of commodity production, and attendant class differentiation, and represents the highest form of commodity production. Capitalism in turn takes different forms at different points in time and in different countries. Capitalism can be more or less egalitarian (with some concessions gives to common people). It can be more or less democratic. It can co-exist with variable presence of the remnants of feudal social relations of production (and culture). It exists in more technologically-economically 'backward' form and in more developed form. Capitalism exists in non-monopoly ('competitive') and in 'monopoly' forms.

Another crucial differentiation is the varying levels of property-lessness of direct producers. There can be no capitalism without the proletarians, and this is why '[t]he use of hired labour is the chief signifier of capitalism'.[14] Labour

13 Consider how close is Lenin's argument to Marx's (1887: 539). '[Petty production is] where the labourer is the private owner of his own means of labour set in action by himself: the peasant of the land which he cultivates, the artisan of the tool which he handles as a virtuoso'. As we have seen in chapter 5, Marx thinks, and rightly so, that small scale production fetters the development of productive forces.

14 'Capitalism is that stage in the development of commodity-production in which labour power, too, becomes a commodity. The main tendency of capitalism is to apply the

is available for hire when the direct producer is separated from the means of production. Yet, one must not have 'too stereotyped an understanding of the theoretical proposition that capitalism requires the free, landless worker'. 'This proposition is quite correct as indicating the main trend, but capitalism penetrates into agriculture particularly slowly and in extremely varied forms' (Lenin, 1899a: 178). If workers have some land from the state or some such resource to supplement their wage income, that very often serves the interests of the employers, including (especially) in rural areas (ibid.).

As a logic of accumulation, capital itself exists in *different* forms which are united by the *single* drive to invest money to make more money.[15] Trading capital and productive capital (e.g. agrarian or industrial capital) 'are of the same kind' and they are similar to merchant and usurer capital (Lenin, 1898). There is also a contradiction here: generally, the greater the development of merchant's and usurer's capital, the smaller the development of productive capital (i.e. of capitalist production itself), and the slower the degree of class differentiation among petty producers. As 'the development of commerce proceeds' which undermines the monopoly of rural merchants including the village shopkeeper, and as 'forms of credit that accord with' the standards of advanced capitalist countries develop, thus 'displacing the village usurer', the differentiation of the peasantry becomes deeper and more extensive (Lenin, 1899a: 185–6).[16]

As capitalism as the highest form of commodity-producing society evolves over time, 'infinitely diverse combinations of elements of this or that type of capitalist evolution is possible' (Lenin, 1899a: 33). Capitalism develops when feudal type property owners turn into capitalists. And it develops when petty producers are differentiated through market-mechanisms into capitalists and wage workers. 'Capitalism arose and is constantly arising out of small production' (Lenin, 1908b).

In developing from commodity production, capitalism evolves through manufacture to machine-based large-scale production then to imperialism (world-capitalism) (the latter is discussed below). In the case of capitalist industry

sum-total of labour-power in the national economy to production only after it has been sold and has been purchased by the employers' (ibid.: 581).

15 This is indicated by Marx's general formula of capital. 'M–C–M' is … in reality the general formula of capital as it appears prima facie within the sphere of circulation' (Marx, 1887: 108).

16 'Another important phenomenon in the economy of our countryside that retards the differentiation of the peasantry is the survivals of corvée economy, i.e., labour service' (ibid.). While this is broadly true, as mentioned earlier, unfree labour can be produced out of free labour to be made use of by capital in order to subject labour to greater amount of exploitation than nominally free labour and to weaken resistance.

specifically: 'the main trend of small commodity-production is towards the development of capitalism, in particular, towards the rise of manufacture', and manufacture grows into 'large-scale machine industry' (ibid.: 541–542). 'There are three main stages in this development: small commodity-production (small, mainly peasant industries); capitalist manufacture; and the factory (large-scale machine industry).' (ibid.: 541), therefore. (And the final state is imperialism).[17]

These three main forms of capitalist production also differ one from another. They differ in terms of scale of production. During the small commodity-production and manufacture stages, capitalist enterprises are small-scale. 'Capitalist relationships arise in the small industries' which are 'in the form of workshops employing wageworkers and of merchant's capital' (ibid.: 543). As in agriculture, so in industry: From these small establishments, '*only a few* large ones emerge', as large-scale machine industry outcompetes 'the small establishments' (ibid.; italics added).

The three main forms of capitalist production also differ 'in their systems of technique' (ibid.: 543). Prior to the introduction of large-scale production, capitalism is generally characterized by 'almost complete stagnation in technique' (ibid.: 543). 'Small commodity production is characterised by its totally primitive, hand technique that remained unchanged almost from time immemorial' (ibid.: 543).[18] 'Manufacture introduces division of labour, which effects a substantial change in technique and transforms the peasant into a factory-hand, a "labourer performing one detailed operation."' (ibid.: 543). 'But production by hand remains, and, on its basis, progress in methods of production is inevitably very slow. Division of labour springs up spontaneously and is passed on by tradition just as peasant labour is' (ibid.). Then, 'Large-scale machine industry alone introduces a radical change, throws manual skill overboard, transforms production on new, rational principles, and systematically applies science to production' (ibid.: 26).[19] Introduction of machinery under capitalism requires and leads to an expansion of production and concentration of capital.[20] Only

17 On the recent attempts at the periodization of capitalism, see Callinicos (2001) and McDonough (1995).

18 'The small producer in industry remains a peasant who follows tradition in his methods of processing raw material' (ibid.: 543).

19 '[I]n industries subordinated to the factory we observe a complete technical revolution and extremely rapid progress in the methods of machine production' (ibid.: 543).

20 In agriculture, machines can help enterpreneurs overcome the obstacles posed by nature to production: 'The machine has enabled the work to be carried on irrespective of atmospheric temperature' for example, when it comes 'butter production (the machine requires less labour, space, and ice, as well as fewer utensils), and has led to the

larger-scale capitalists (e.g. capitalist farmers) have the capital to introduce machinery.

> The introduction of machinery, on the one hand, calls for capital on a big scale ...; on the other hand, machines pay only when there is a huge amount of products to be dealt with; the expansion of production becomes a necessity with the introduction of machines.

The wide use of machines is therefore indicative of the concentration of production, including in agriculture and industry. Introduction of machines in turn creates a home market for commodities and requires a large number of workers.

> machines *create* a home market for capitalism: first, a market for means of production (for the products of the machine-building industry, mining industry, etc., etc.), and second, a market for labour-power. (ibid.: 232)

Connected to the difference in scale and technique is another difference between the different forms of capitalist development: sharpness of class opposition. The manufacture stage is associated with the rise of the classes of big capital and a large mass of labour. 'The gulf between the one who owns the means of production and the one who works now becomes very wide' relative to the stage of small-scale commodity production prior to manufacture (ibid.: 544). '"Wealthy" industrial settlements spring up, the bulk of whose inhabitants are poor working people. A small number of merchants, who do an enormous business buying raw materials and selling finished goods, and a mass of detail workers living from hand to mouth – such is the general picture of manufacture'. However, intermediate groups come to exist: 'the multitude of small establishments, the retention of the tie with the land, the adherence to tradition in production and in the whole manner of living – all this creates a mass of intermediary elements between the extremes of manufacture [i.e. big capital and labour] and retards the development of these extremes' (ibid.). In contrast, 'In large-scale machine industry all these retarding factors disappear; the acuteness of social contradictions reaches the highest point' (ibid.). Once large-scale machine-based industrial capitalism develops, 'all the dark sides of capitalism' come to be concentrated (ibid.). Indeed: the capitalist machine

---

concentration of production' (ibid.: 267). Similarly, 'the rapid development of elevator construction in recent years means as big a victory for capital and degradation of the small commodity-producer in the grain business' (ibid.: 270).

'gives a tremendous impulse to the greatest possible prolongation of the working day; women and children are drawn into industry; a reserve army of unemployed is formed (and must be formed by virtue of the conditions of factory production), etc.' (ibid.: 229). There are also geographical/scalar differences between the stages/forms of capitalist development (as discussed below).

There are cultural differences between the stage of large-scale capitalist industrial development and the preceding stages. Capitalism at its pre-manufacture stage where the demand for products is local is characterised by the greatest economic stability, but this stability is tantamount to not only stagnation in technique but also 'the preservation of patriarchal social relationships tangled up with all sorts of survivals of medieval traditions' (ibid.: 545).

Large-scale industrialization is associated with, and bring into existence, 'the socialisation of labour' that is 'effected on a vast scale by the factory', the new site of capitalist production (ibid.: 544). With is material transformation comes 'the transformation of the sentiments and conceptions of the people it employs (in particular, the destruction of patriarchal and petty-bourgeois traditions)'. Socialization of production and changes in sentiments 'cause a reaction: large-scale machine industry, unlike the preceding stages, imperatively calls for the planned regulation of production and public control over it (a manifestation of the latter tendency is factory legislation)' (ibid.). Capitalism 'increases literacy among the population, heightens their understanding, and gives them civilised habits and requirements' (ibid.: 576).

'The "instability" of large-scale machine industry', the fact that it develops spasmodically, 'has always evoked, and continues to evoke, reactionary complaints from individuals who continue to look at things through the eyes of the small producer and who forget that it is this "instability" alone that replaced the former stagnation by the rapid transformation of methods of production and of all social relationships' (ibid.: 545).

Large-scale industry 'creates a special class of the population', i.e. the proletariat, that is 'totally alien to the old peasantry and differing from the latter in its manner of living, its family relationships and its higher standard of requirements, both material and spiritual' (ibid.: 546).

'In the small industries and in manufacture we always find survivals of patriarchal relations and of diverse forms of personal dependence, which, in the general conditions of capitalist economy, exceedingly worsen the condition of the working people, and degrade and corrupt them' (ibid.). 'Large-scale machine industry, which concentrates masses of workers who often come from various parts of the country, absolutely refuses to tolerate survivals of patriarchalism and personal dependence, and is marked by a truly "contemptuous attitude to the past."' (ibid.). 'It is this break with obsolete tradition that is one of the substantial conditions which have created the possibility and evoked the necessity of regulating production and of public control over it' (ibid.).

'[T]he capitalist factory places these categories of the working population in particularly hard conditions', so 'for them it is particularly necessary to regulate and shorten the working day, to guarantee hygienic conditions of labour, etc.' (ibid.: 547).[21] 'By destroying the patriarchal isolation of these categories of the population who formerly never emerged from the narrow circle of domestic, family relationships, by drawing them into direct participation in social production, large-scale machine industry stimulates their development and increases their independence, in other words, creates conditions of life that are incomparably superior to the patriarchal immobility of pre-capitalist relations' (ibid.).

The different stages of capitalist development vary in terms of their progressive implications for common people. This is discussed below. While the stages of capitalist development differ in many ways, they are also inter-connected. 'The connection and continuity between the forms of industry mentioned is of the most direct and intimate kind.'

> Perhaps one of the most striking manifestations of the intimate and direct connection between the consecutive forms of industry is the fact that many of the big and even the biggest factory owners were at one time the smallest of small industrialists and passed through all the stages from [small-scale capitalism] to "capitalism."

Besides, common to the different stages of capitalism is the fact that capitalism is dominantly based on production and circulation of commodities. The capitalistically produced product has to be sold too in the market so that the capitalist can get back the money invested plus surplus value appropriated from wage labour: that is, realization must happen. '[T]he realisation of the product in capitalist society (and, consequently, the realisation of surplus-value)' requires that: '1) the social product, like the individual product, resolves itself in terms of value into three parts', i.e. 'constant capital + variable capital + surplus-value', and '2) in its natural form it must be divided into two big departments: means of production (consumed productively) and articles of consumption (consumed personally)' (ibid.: 43).[22] Capitalist circulation of

21 '[B]ut endeavours completely to ban the work of women and juveniles in industry, or to maintain the patriarchal manner of life that ruled out such work, would be reactionary and utopian' (ibid.).

22 'The home market appears when commodity economy appears; it is created by the development of this commodity economy, and the degree to which the social division of

commodities, of course, does not exclude cheating and fraud; the latter exist thus violating the principle of the exchange of the equivalent for the equivalent.

Contrary to much political economy which explains profits in terms of cheating and fraud, Lenin, like Marx, explains it in terms of the law of value without ignoring cheating and fraud:

> to explain the profits of the industrial capitalists we must assume that labour-power is sold at its real value. Similarly, to explain the role of the buyer-up we must assume that he buys and sells goods in accordance with the general laws of commodity exchange. Only these economic causes of the domination of merchant's capital can provide the key to an understanding of the variety of forms which it assumes in real life, and among which we constantly meet (there can be no doubt of that) the plainest fraud.

As if to critically respond to all those who emphasize cheating and fraud at the expense of commodity relations in capitalism, Lenin says:

> To proceed otherwise, … that is, to confine oneself to enumerating the various tricks of the "kulaks," and on these grounds completely to brush aside the economic nature of the phenomenon would be to adopt the viewpoint of vulgar economics.

3.2 *Geographically Uneven Development and Geographical Mobility in Capitalism*

Capitalism produces new forms of uneven development, temporally, spatially and sectorally. Spatially uneven development causes migration across and inside countries.

---

labour is ramified determines the level of its development; it spreads with the extension of commodity production from products to labour-power, and only in proportion as the latter is transformed into a commodity does capitalism embrace the entire production of the country, developing mainly on account of means of production, which occupy an increasingly important place in capitalist society. The "home market" for capitalism is created by developing capitalism itself, which deepens the social division of labour and resolves the direct producers into capitalists and workers. The degree of the development of the home market is the degree of development of capitalism in the country' (ibid. 69).

'The home market for capitalism is created by the parallel development of capitalism in agriculture and in industry, by the formation of a class of rural and industrial employers, on the one hand, and of a class of rural and industrial wage-workers, on the other' (ibid.: 590).

Uneven development of capitalism in a temporal sense refers to the fact that 'periods of prosperity alternate with periods of crisis' (ibid.: 597). In a sectoral sense, uneven development refers to the fact that 'the development of one industry leads to the decline of another', that 'there is progress in one aspect of agriculture in one area and in another aspect in another area' and, that 'the growth of trade and industry outstrips the growth of agriculture, etc.' (ibid.: 597). In fact, because of its very anarchic or capricious nature, 'capitalism in agriculture (as in industry) cannot develop evenly' and that 'techniques are transformed in some operations and not in others' (ibid.: 314). Capitalist development is governed 'by market requirements that are capricious and not always known to the producer', so it becomes 'onesided and lopsided' (ibid.: 314), including in capitalist agriculture, in part because of its nature-dependent character which varies enormously in space. Yet, one cannot say that 'this disproportionate, spasmodic, feverish development is not development' (ibid.: 597).

Uneven development is also geographical. 'In one place (in one country, in one area, on one farm) it [i.e. capitalism] pushes forward one aspect of agriculture or industry, in another place another aspect, etc.' (Lenin, 1899a: 314). Capitalism involves anarchic commodity production and class differentiation (in rural and urban areas). The degree of class differentiation of petty producers including those in rural areas, and therefore of the development of capitalism, varies across different localities (Lenin, 1899a: 140). Commodity production has a causal tendency to produce class differentiation among commodity producers and to centralize production. This causal *tendency* is expressed in the main empirical *trend*. Yet, this main trend assumes different forms.[23] For example, while the petty producers *are* differentiated into different classes, the relative importance of the well-to-do commodity producers to the vast majority 'assumes different forms' under different conditions of production (Lenin, 1899a: 145).

While one reason for uneven spatial development is the geography of class differentiation, another reason, related to the first, is the fact that different localities in a country are differentially connected to the national and global markets. 'Directly connected with division of labour in general is … territorial division of labour – the specialisation of certain districts in the production of some one product, of one sort of product and even of a certain part of a product' (ibid.: 431). While it is the case that the 'close connection with the home and foreign markets' of different localities could [cause] the economic development of these localities [to] proceed so rapidly' (ibid.: 258), it is also

23 In the rural context, 'The main trends of peasant differentiation are one thing; the forms it assumes, depending on the different local conditions, are another' (ibid.: 145).

the case that different localities or regions of a country, which are involved in commodity production and commercial specialization, are not equally connected to the world market.

There are geographical/scalar differences between the different forms of capitalist development. At the pre-manufacture stage of capitalism, when it emerges from simple commodity production, production and exchange are more localized: 'the market is extremely narrow, the distance between the producer and the consumer is short, and the insignificant scale of production easily adapts itself to the slightly fluctuating local demand' (ibid.: 544). In contrast, 'The manufactories work for a big market – sometimes for the whole country – and, accordingly, production acquires the instability characteristic of capitalism, an instability which attains the greatest intensity under factory production' (ibid.).

The settled and isolated character of the population is typical of the first two stages of capitalist development. 'The small industrialist, remaining a peasant, is bound to his village by his farm. The artisan under manufacture is usually tied to the small, isolated industrial area which is created by manufacture' (ibid.: 548). Large-scale capitalist development is characterized by mobility of capital and people, however.

During the pre-machine stage of capitalism, 'Intercourse between the various industrial areas is rare. The transfer of industry to other areas is due only to the migration of individual small producers, who establish new small industries in the outlying parts of the country' (ibid.: 548). 'Large-scale machine industry' in contrast, 'necessarily creates mobility of the population' (ibid.: 548) (more below). '[C]ommercial intercourse between the various districts grows enormously; railways facilitate travel. The demand for labour increases on the whole – rising in periods of boom and falling in periods of crisis, so that it becomes a necessity for workers to go from one factory to another, from one part of the country to another' (ibid.).

Capitalism connects rural areas to urban areas 'by the transplantation of largescale capitalist industry to the rural districts' (Lenin, 1899a: 28). Capitalism thus urbanizes villages by extending the nexus of commerce, which is aided by the development of transport and communications under capitalism. Indeed, the more extensive development of commerce brings 'the country closer to the town, eliminating the primitive village markets' (Lenin, 1899a: 185–6). Capitalism thus expands urban population leading to structural transformation: 'the percentage of urban population is constantly growing' which means that with the growth of large-scale machine industry, 'the population is being diverted from agriculture into commercial and industrial occupations' (ibid.: 551; 561). 'The population of towns that are important industrial and commercial centres is growing much more rapidly than the urban population generally' (ibid. 561). '[T]he industrial population grows at the expense of the agricultural from the fact that in industry variable capital increases absolutely (the growth of variable capital means a growth of the number of industrial workers and a growth of the total commercial and industrial population), whereas in agriculture the "variable capital required for the exploitation of a certain plot of land decreases absolutely."', except when the total amount of land under agriculture increases (Lenin, 1899a: 562).

'Largescale machine industry creates a number of new industrial centres, which grow up with unprecedented rapidity, sometimes in unpopulated places, a thing that would be impossible without the mass migration of workers' (548). 'Hence, workers leave not only because they do not find "local occupations at hand," but also because they make for the places where conditions are better' (ibid.: 549).

Capitalist uneven development produces different types of urban or urbanizing areas are actively produced by capital in its search of cheap labour: industrial towns, which are 'the greatest concentration of both workers and establishments'; the suburbs – 'the suburbs of large towns are very often big industrial centres'; factory villages; and "handicraft" villages (Lenin, 1899a: 519).[24]

Geographically uneven development gives rise to, and is shaped by, migration. This happens within countries. There is a connection between migration and the class differentiation of commodity producers: the development of the migration movement gives 'a tremendous impetus to' class differentiation, including of the peasantry (ibid.: 182). Also, it is mainly the middle peasants who tend to leave their villages 'which are "the areas of emigration"' and it is mainly the well-to-do peasantry and the proletariat including poor peasants who tend to remain at home (ibid.: 182–183). Thus, migration is accelerating the differentiation of the peasantry in the areas of emigration and is carrying the elements of differentiation to the new places (1899a: 182–183).

Uneven development gives rise to, and is shaped by, migration from poorer countries to more developed ones too. People are pulled by better conditions of advanced countries and pushed out of the bad conditions in poor countries. 'Capitalism has given rise to a special form of migration' (Lenin, 1913k). 'The rapidly developing industrial countries, introducing machinery on a large scale and ousting the backward countries from the world market, raise wages at home above the average rate and thus attract workers from the backward

24 'Besides the concentration of production in very large establishments, the concentration of production in separate factory industrial centres and the different types of factory centres are also important in characterising large-scale machine industry' (Lenin, 1899a: 518).

countries' (ibid.). The economic motive for mobility is paramount: 'There can be no doubt that dire poverty alone compels people to abandon their native land, and that the capitalists exploit the immigrant workers in the most shameless manner' (ibid.). And coincidentally, emigration from advanced – imperialist – countries decreases.[25] Migration produces economic advantages for workers. It 'raises the wages not only of the wage-workers who migrate, relative to their wages in the origin places, but also of those who stay behind' (Lenin, 1899a: 578). Migration has political advantages too as explained below.

4 Capitalism as a Transient Progressive Social Form Production

The progressive character of capitalism lies in the fact that large-scale capitalist industry promotes socialization of production and of labour (even if its shell is private property). There are 'elements of the capitalist process which is increasingly socialising production in the country, and with it those who participate in production' (ibid.: 549–550). These elements include: 'production for an enormous national and international market', including the market for both means of production and means of consumption; 'development of close commercial ties with various parts of the country and with different countries for the purchase' of means of production such as 'raw and auxiliary materials'; and 'enormous technical progress'; concentration of production and of the population in colossal enterprises; and 'creation of mobility of the population' which causes intermingling among people, and so on.

Capitalism is a progressive social form because relative to pre-capitalist societies it increases 'the productive forces of social labour' (Lenin, 1899a: 596). This is true about capitalism in general. This is also true about agricultural capitalism which, once it arrives, has a tendency to undermine 'the age-old stagnation of our agriculture', and

> it has given a tremendous impetus to the transformation of its technique, and to the development of the productive forces of social labour. A few decades of "destructive work" by capitalism have done more in this respect than entire centuries of preceding history. (ibid.: 314)

25 'One of the special features of imperialism ... is the decline in emigration from imperialist countries and the increase in immigration into these countries from the more backward countries where lower wages are paid' (Lenin, 1916a).

Capitalism develops intensively and extensively: 'the process of the formation of a market for capitalism has two aspects, namely, the development of capitalism in depth, i.e., the further growth of capitalist agriculture and industry in the given, definite and enclosed territory – and the development of capitalism in breadth, i.e., the extension of the sphere of the capitalist domination to new territory' (Lenin, 1899a: 594).

'Capitalism ... replaces the minute medieval divisions among cultivators by a major division, embracing the whole nation, that divides them into classes occupying different positions in the general system of capitalist economy' (ibid.: 316). Capitalism also undermines personal dependency of the direct producers on the propertied class as it cuts 'at the root of labour-service' (ibid.).

> Capitalism ... destroys the primitive forms of bondage and personal dependence, develops in depth and in breadth the contradictions which in a rudimentary form are also to be observed among the community peasantry – and thus paves the way for their resolution. (ibid.: 383)

Large-scale industry produces mobility which allows inter-mingling of people. It is wrong to 'idealise local occupations and condemn migration to industrial districts, ignoring the progressive significance of the mobility of the population created by capitalism' (ibid.: 549). '[O]nly reactionaries can shut their eyes to the *progressive* significance of this modern migration ...' (Lenin, 1913k).

'Capitalism destroys local seclusion and insularity' (ibid.: 316). 'The mass of cultivators were formerly tied to their place of residence by the very conditions of production, whereas the creation of diverse forms and could not but cause the movement of enormous masses of the population throughout the country' (ibid.: 316). 'Like the diversion of the population from agriculture to the towns, non-agricultural migration is a progressive phenomenon. It tears the population out of the neglected, backward, history-forgotten remote spots and draws them into the whirlpool of modern social life'. (ibid.: 576). The transformation brought about by large-scale machine-based capitalist production in the conditions of common people's life includes 'the drawing of women and juveniles into production', which is a progressive process (ibid.: 546).[26]

Pre-capitalist systems of production and exchange are more localized. In contrast, capitalist production and exchange tend to be more global and therefore more progressive as it breaks down pre-capitalist isolation.

---

26 Note that small-scale production also makes use of women and children to compete with the more efficient large-scale industry, as Lenin himself says.

> Under the old modes of production, economic units could exist for centuries without undergoing any change either in character or in size, and without extending beyond the landlord's manor, the peasant village or the small neighbouring market for the rural artisans and small industrialists (the so-called handicraftsmen). (ibid.: 66)

The capitalist system of production and exchange is different:

> The capitalist enterprise, on the contrary, inevitably outgrows the bounds of the village community, the local market, the region, and then the state. Since the isolation and seclusion of the states have already been broken down by commodity circulation, the natural trend of every capitalist industry brings it to the necessity of "seeking a foreign market." (ibid.: 66)

Echoing the *Communist Manifesto*, Lenin says that: 'capitalism cannot exist and develop without constantly expanding the sphere of its domination, without colonising new countries and drawing old non-capitalist countries into the whirlpool of world economy' (ibid.: 594).

Here lies the progressive character of capitalism:

> the necessity of seeking a foreign market by no means proves that capitalism is unsound ... Quite the contrary. This necessity demonstrates the progressive historical work of capitalism, which destroys the age-old isolation and seclusion of systems of economy (and, consequently, the narrowness of intellectual and political life), and which links all countries of the world into a single economic whole. (ibid.: 67)

Capitalism is also a progressive social form because it brings into being its grave digger – the world working class – the greatest anti-capitalist subjective factor. From a political angle, advanced countries such as those in Europe are 'advanced' in a political and cultural sense, 'not *thanks* to, but *in spite of*, the bourgeoisie, for it is only the proletariat that is adding to the million-strong army of fighters for a better future' (Lenin, 1913b). The proletariat, which is 'the *sole advanced* class' is the only class that 'preserves and spreads implacable enmity towards backwardness, savagery, privilege, slavery and the humiliation of man by man' (ibid.).

Lenin (1899a: 598) sums up the progressive character of capitalism rooted in the multiple processes of socialisation of labour by capitalism, in both economic and spatial senses, in the following lines. Capitalism is a progressive system economically:

> Firstly, the very growth of commodity-production destroys the scattered condition of small economic units that is characteristic of natural economy and draws together the small local markets into an enormous national (and then world) market. Production for oneself is transformed into production for the whole of society …
>
> Secondly, capitalism replaces the former scattered production by an unprecedented concentration both in agriculture and in industry.
>
> Thirdly, capitalism eliminates the forms of personal dependence that constituted an inalienable component of preceding systems of economy. … Compared with the labour of the dependent or bonded peasant, the labour of the hired worker is progressive in all branches of the national economy.
>
> Fourthly, capitalism necessarily creates mobility of the population [that creates enhanced interaction among people], something not required by previous systems of social economy and impossible under them on anything like a large scale.
>
> Fifthly, capitalism constantly reduces the proportion of the population engaged in agriculture (where the most backward forms of social and economic relationships always prevail), and increases the number of large industrial centres.

Then, there are social-cultural aspects of capitalism's progressive character.

> Sixthly, capitalist society increases the population's need for association, for organisation, and lends these organisations a character distinct from those of former times. While breaking down the narrow, local, social-estate associations of medieval society and creating fierce competition, capitalism at the same time splits the whole of society into large groups of persons occupying different positions in production, and gives a tremendous impetus to organisation within each such group.
>
> Seventhly, all the above-mentioned changes effected in the old economic system by capitalism inevitably lead also to a change in the mentality of the population. The spasmodic character of economic development, the rapid transformation of the methods of production and the enormous concentration of production, the disappearance of all forms of personal dependence and patriarchalism in relationships, the mobility of the population, the influence of the big industrial centres, etc. – all this cannot but lead to a profound change in the very character of the producers.

However, 'Recognition of the progressiveness of this role is quite compatible (as we have tried to show in detail at every stage in our exposition of the facts) with the full recognition of the negative and dark sides of capitalism, with the full recognition of the profound and all-round social contradictions [discussed below] which are inevitably inherent in capitalism, and which reveal the historically transient character of this economic regime.' (ibid.: 596). Indeed, 'the greater the development of capitalism, the stronger becomes the contradiction between this collective character of production and the individual character of appropriation' (ibid.: 598).

5 Capitalist (Super-)Exploitation, Economic Inequality, and Impoverishment

5.1 *Forms of Exploitation*

Capitalism is the main reason for impoverishment of common people, including women and children. This is because capitalism is an exploitative society. Lenin is (somewhat) critical of the concept of '"exploitation" in general': 'it is precisely the exploitation of wage-labour that forms the basis of the whole predatory system of today'. It is 'the exploitation of wage-labour that leads to the division of society into irreconcilably opposed classes and class struggle, and 'only from the point of view of *this* class struggle can all other manifestations of exploitation be consistently gauged, without lapsing into vagueness and abandoning all principles' (Lenin, 1902a). While capitalism is exploitative, some groups of workers such as women and children are subjected to above-average exploitation. This happens both in the petty production sector and in large-scale industry.

Capitalism is characterized by primary exploitation (appropriation of surplus labour in the sphere of production) and by 'derivative exploitation' that happens in spheres outside of production. Workers are subjected to primary exploitation in its absolute when the working day is prolonged. They are subjected to exploitation in its relative form when on the basis of productivity-enhancing technical change, they produce more value and surplus value every hour. 'Capital organises and rationalises labour within the factory for the purpose of increasing the exploitation of the workers and increasing profit' (Lenin, 1914a).

The sphere of petty production (in agriculture) faces stiff competition from the capitalist sector.

Yet, the continued existence of petty production is made possible because 'a *larger* amount of work' is squeezed out of the worker in the petty production sector, i.e. from self-employed people, 'than is squeezed out of the worker in large-scale production' (Lenin, 1913i). Indeed, due to competition from the capitalist sector, the petty producer (e.g. the peasant) 'is unable to keep going without almost working himself to death and compelling his children to work as hard' (Lenin, 1913j). In rural areas, 'In the busy season the peasant suffers from a shortage of workers; he can hire workers only to a small extent; he is compelled to employ the labour of his own children to the greatest extent' (Lenin, 1913j).

Women do a lot of work in petty production sector as in the capitalist sector. 'Millions upon millions of women' in working families such as 'poor townspeople, artisans, workers, employees and petty officials' live (or, rather, exist) as "domestic slaves", striving to feed and clothe their family on pennies, at the cost of desperate daily effort and "saving" on everything – except their own labour' (Lenin, 1913h). 'It is these women that the capitalists most willingly employ as home-workers, who are prepared for a monstrously low wage to "earn a little extra" for themselves and their family, for the sake of a crust of bread.' (ibid.).

Apart from 'the expropriation of the small producers' (ibid.: 321),[27] the introduction of machines, by ousting the worker, expands the reserve army of labour. The reserve army is a necessary product of capitalism. The mass-scale employment of machinery *presupposes* the existence of a mass of wageworkers (Lenin, 1899a: 232). 'The formation of a vast reserve army of unemployed, ready to undertake any kind of work, becomes a condition for the existence and development of large-scale machine industry' (ibid.: 545). A reserve army is necessary requirement, and a necessary product, of large-scale machine-based capitalism. Capitalism 'can only develop in spurts, in alternating periods of prosperity and of crisis', so 'the workers are drawn into the factory in masses during a boom period, and are then thrown out.' (ibid.: 545):

> an army of many millions of wageworkers ready at the first call to satisfy the maximum demand of the employers in agriculture, lumbering, building, commerce and in the manufacturing, mining, and transport industries, etc. We say the maximum demand, because capitalism can only develop spasmodically, and consequently, the number of producers who need to sell their labourpower must always exceed capitalism's average demand for workers. (ibid.: 584)

27 'The increase in the number of peasants thrown into the ranks of the industrial and rural proletariat, and the increase in the demand for wage-labour, are two sides of one medal' (ibid.: 584).

The reserve army of labour is a lever for increasing exploitation. This is true in both industry and agriculture, but 'the specific features of agriculture merely give rise to special forms of this phenomenon' of the reserve army (ibid.: 321). In agriculture, for example, 'The working period is the period in which labour is applied to the product; the time of production is the time during which the product is in production, including the period in which labour is not applied to it. The working period does not coincide with the time of production in very many industries, among which agriculture is merely the most typical, but by no means the only one' (ibid.: 322). So, 'the only conclusion that follows from the specific features of agriculture ... is that the position of the agricultural worker must be even worse than that of the industrial worker.' (ibid.).

Introduction of machines – technological change – has specific consequences for women and children. One consequence is 'the growing employment of female and child labour' (Lenin, 1899a: 234) in place of male adults because the labour power of children and women is usually cheaper to buy. Secondly, 'The more child labour is exploited the worse, undoubtedly, is the position of the [adult] worker, and the harder his life' (Lenin, 1913j). 'Often [child workers] work merely for their food and clothing' (Lenin, 1899a: 234). Thirdly, the employment of machinery has adverse health impacts (as explained below). Thus the introduction of technical change, via increased employment of women and children can increase the rate of exploitation of the working class as a whole.

5.2 *Forms of Impoverishment in Capitalism and Rising Economic Inequality*

Because of primary exploitation in its absolute and relative forms, and derivative exploitation, and market relations (of competition, centralization, class differentiation, etc.) – and to these, one might add coercive dispossession – capitalist development results in absolute and relative impoverishment (the phenomenon where people's needs remain unmet), worsening health conditions of workers (and petty producers) and in rising inequality, especially between large-scale business owners, and common people.

A fundamental reason for the poor conditions of workers is unemployment/under-employment which is rife, as we have seen. Wages do not rise, or when they do, they increase 'much more slowly than the necessary expenditure of labour power' (Lenin, 1912a). Wages are generally low relative to the value of labour power, and they are low relative to the cost of living steadily rising (decline in real wages). 'Food, clothing, fuel and rent have all become more expensive. The worker is becoming impoverished *absolutely*, i.e., he is actually becoming poorer than before; he is compelled to live worse, to eat worse, to suffer hunger more, and to live in basements and attics' (Lenin, 1913e). 'Want among the workers is becoming more and more distressful and intolerable' (Lenin, 1914d).

The diet of the people deteriorates as capitalism develops (Lenin, 1912b). Lack of income forces people to eat cheap food (margarine not butter; meat from boiled diseased animals, etc.). Not only are people unable to buy good food. They also incur additional costs due to injuries in the workplace. For example, many workers – including women and children – experience accidents in the workplace: 'The employment of young women and children at machines naturally results in a particularly large toll of injuries' (Lenin, 1899a: 235). Lenin implies that wages are not increased as a compensation for the injury to women's and children's working bodies.[28]

Unemployment/under-employment of workers and low wages mean low income for everyone dependent on wages for living, including some workers who many own small amount of means of production. Workers' low income and petty producers not being able to earn an adequate remuneration for their work due to stiff competition from the capitalist sector – these two processes explain low income of common people, and their bad diet which has adverse health impacts.

On the one hand, capital 'throws the whole of its crushing weight upon the ruined small producers and the proletariat, constantly threatens to force the conditions of the workers down to starvation level and condemn them to death from starvation', and on the other hand: 'the wealth of the capitalists is increasing at a dizzy rate' (Lenin, 1912a). While working-class families produce all the consumers' goods, they take only a small part of 'this vast amount of wealth' (Lenin, 1914d). The remainder 'is pocketed by the capitalists, who, with all their apologists and hangers-on, constitute only' a very small part of the population' (ibid.).

The inequality between capital and labour is expressed in the form of workers' impoverishment. As mentioned already, workers become 'impoverished *absolutely*.' (Lenin, 1912a). They also experience impoverishment in its relative form: 'the *relative* impoverishment of the workers, i.e., the diminution of their *share* in the national income, is still more striking'. This means that workers' *comparative* share in capitalist society, which is fast growing rich, is dwindling because the millionaires are becoming ever richer'. 'Wealth in capitalist society

28 On capitalism and its adverse impacts on workers' health, see Das (2023c).

is growing at an incredible rate – side by side with the impoverishment of the mass of the workers' (Lenin, 1912a). Workers' productivity is rising but 'the worker's pay is not increased [proportionately], and, if wages do rise, they rise 'at the very most ... *only for a short period* at that' (Lenin, 1914a). The inequality between capitalists and common people is much greater than official statistics suggests. This is in part because 'Capitalists are not inclined to be frank about their incomes' (Lenin, 1913e).[29] While the worker has to support their family with a salary that is meagre relative to 'high rents and high food prices', the capitalists who hold the shares grow 'rich *for not* working' (Lenin, 1913e). 'The wealth of the bourgeoisie is growing. So are the poverty and want of the proletariat and of the mass of small proprietors, peasants, artisans and petty traders, who are being ruined' (Lenin, 1912b).

Workers do all the work but live on meagre salary, while capitalists do little work but pocket a large part of what workers produce. And to the extent that capitalists do any work, their income from it is disproportionately more than the contribution of their work: 'If any of the magnates did a bit of "work" *as a director*, he received *special* remuneration in the form of a ministerial salary and bonuses' (Lenin, 1913e). Most of them are coupon clippers.[30]

Inequality rises between capital and labour, between big capital and smaller-scale capital, and between (big) capital and petty producers. Big capital, gathering around itself small sums of shareholders' capital from all over the world, has become more powerful still. Through the joint-stock company, the millionaire now has at their disposal not only his own million, but additional capital gathered from petty proprietors (Lenin, 1913e). The increase in the number of small-scale owners is not a necessary indicator of the reduction in economic inequality among those who own money capital. Indeed, 'in all capitalist countries, concentration of production is going on, i.e., its concentration to an ever greater extent in a small number of large and very large undertakings' (Lenin, 1912d). 'The professors who defend capitalism chatter about the increase in the number of property-owners when they see a growth in the number of small shareholders. What actually happens is that the power (and the income) of the millionaire magnates *over* the capital of the "small fry" is increased' (Lenin, 1913e).

29 See Das (2024e) on the Marxist theory of inequality, including Lenin's views.

30 '[I]mperialism is an immense accumulation of money capital in a few countries. ... Hence the extraordinary growth of a class, or rather, of a stratum of rentiers, i.e., people who live by "clipping coupons", who take no part in any enterprise whatever, whose profession is idleness' (Lenin, 1916).

Lenin's political economy sees economic inequality from the standpoint of class relations, which are the major reason for the differences in income: 'There cannot be, nor is there nor will there ever be "equality" between the oppressed and the oppressors, between the exploited and the exploiters.' (Lenin, 1919c). Class inequality is related to oppression of women.

> There cannot be, nor is there nor will there ever be real "freedom" as long as there is no freedom for women from the privileges which the law grants to men, as long as there is no freedom for the workers from the yoke of capital, and no freedom for the toiling peasants from the yoke of the capitalists, landlords and merchants. (Lenin, 1919c)

Capitalism is thus a deeply unequal society in terms of class relations. Socialists recognize inequality in natural abilities (e.g. 'physical strength and mental ability'), but that is not their concern, and in fact, 'it is absurd to expect *equality* of strength and abilities in socialist society'.

6 Imperialism as the Highest Stage of Capitalism, and National Exploitation

Capitalism has a tendency to be a global system of social-economic relations. While Marx recognizes this, he does not have a developed theory of imperialism, a gap in Marxism that Lenin fills.[31] Capitalism at its highest stage develops into imperialism which promotes wars, war-mongering and reaction and subordination and exploitation of the Global South. Class exploitation and national exploitation co-exist.

'Colonial policy and imperialism existed before the latest stage of capitalism, and even before capitalism.' (Lenin, 1916a). Modern-day imperialism is different as it is based not only capitalist production and exchange but also in monopoly capitalism dominated by financial capital. 'Capitalism is commodity production at its highest stage of development, when labour power itself becomes a commodity', and imperialism is the highest stage of capitalism itself reached only in the twentieth century' (ibid.). Imperialism is the capitalism as it operates at the world-scale. 'Capitalism now finds the old national states,

31 Pradella (2023) says: for Marx, capitalism is inherently an ever-expanding global system as it was for Lenin: 'What, for Marx, was later defined as imperialism is the concrete form of the process of "globalisation" of the capital of the dominant states'.

without the formation of which it could not have overthrown feudalism, too tight for it' (Lenin, 1915b).

As a *specific stage* of capitalism, imperialism has certain *fundamental* economic features which indicate its functioning and its consequences. Among the fundamental features of imperialism are the following, as Lenin points out in one of his most famous books (Lenin, 1916a):

> the concentration of production and capital has developed to such a high stage that it has created monopolies which play a decisive role in economic life; (2) the merging of bank capital with industrial capital, and the creation, on the basis of this "finance capital", of a financial oligarchy; (3) the export of capital as distinguished from the export of commodities [acquiring] exceptional importance; (4) the formation of international monopolist capitalist associations which share the world among themselves, and (5) [the completion of] the territorial division of the whole world among the biggest capitalist powers is completed [as a consequence of 3 and 4 above].

'[C]apitalism only became capitalist imperialism at a definite and very high stage of its development, when certain of its fundamental characteristics' such as free competition 'began to change into their opposites ... Economically, the main thing in this process is the displacement of capitalist free competition by capitalist monopoly' (Lenin, 1916a). '[I]n its economic essence imperialism is monopoly capitalism' (ibid.).[32] And, imperialism is characterized by the supremacy of financial capital which is 'industrial capital at its highest, monopoly level which has merged with banking capital' (ibid.).[33]

---

32 In the imperialist stage of capitalism, 'production has assumed such big, immense proportions that *free competition gives way to monopoly*. That is the *economic* essence of imperialism' (Lenin, 1919b).

33 'It is characteristic of capitalism in general that the ownership of capital is separated from the application of capital to production, that money capital is separated from industrial or productive capital, and that the rentier who lives entirely on income obtained from money capital, is separated from the entrepreneur and from all who are directly concerned in the management of capital. Imperialism, or the domination of finance capital, is that highest stage of capitalism in which this separation reaches vast proportions. The supremacy of finance capital over all other forms of capital means the predominance of the rentier and of the financial oligarchy' (Lenin, 1916a).

Lenin's point is: there are different fractions of capital but there is merger and interlocking among them:

'[A] personal link-up ... is established between the banks and the biggest industrial and commercial enterprises' which indicates 'the merging of one with another through

'To acquire full monopoly, all competition must be eliminated, and not only on the home market (of the given state), but also on foreign markets, in the whole world' (Lenin, 1916b).[34] There are two ways in which imperialism eliminates competition in foreign markets. One is through economic mechanisms. These include: the creation of 'a rival's financial dependence' and 'acquisition of [their] sources of raw materials and eventually of all [their] enterprises' (ibid.). As well, 'Big finance capital of one country ... [buys] up competitors in another, politically independent country' (ibid.). 'Economic "annexation" is *fully* "achievable" without political annexation and is widely practised' (ibid.).[35] However, imperialist businesses and states acting on their behalf 'do not confine themselves to economic means of eliminating rivals, but constantly resort to political, even criminal, methods' (ibid.). This suggests that the existence of capitalist monopolies characteristic of capitalist imperialism does not occur on the head of a pin but on an uneven surface of nation-states or national space-economies. There are monopolist businesses and monopolist nation-states/countries: imperialism is characterized by 'monopolist associations of capitalists in all capitalistically developed countries' and by 'the monopolist position of a few very rich countries, in which the accumulation of capital has reached gigantic proportions' (Lenin, 1916a).

Imperialism's features include certain mechanisms as mentioned above, the operation of which produce certain consequences (Lenin, 1916c). There are five of them, the first three concern of which decay of capitalism:

> The fact that imperialism is parasitic or decaying capitalism is manifested first of all in the tendency to decay, which is characteristic of *every* monopoly under the system of private ownership of the means of production.[36] Secondly, the decay of capitalism is manifested in the

---

the acquisition of shares, through the appointment of bank directors to the ... Boards of Directors ... of industrial and commercial enterprises, and vice versa' (Lenin, 1916a).

34 'Monopolist capitalist associations, cartels, syndicates and trusts first [divide] the home market among themselves and [obtain] more or less complete possession of the industry of their own country' and then they acquire control over the world market which capitalism created long ago and to which 'the home market is inevitably bound up', so domestic monopolies grow into international cartels' (Lenin, 1916a).

35 '[There are] dependent countries which, politically, are formally independent, but in fact, are enmeshed in the net of financial and diplomatic dependence' (Lenin, 1916a).

36 'Since monopoly prices are established, even temporarily, the motive cause of technical and, consequently, of all other progress disappears to a certain extent and, further, the economic possibility arises of deliberately retarding technical progress. Certainly, monopoly under capitalism can never completely, and for a very long period of time, eliminate competition in the world market ... Certainly, the possibility of reducing the

> creation of a huge stratum of rentiers, capitalists who live by "clipping coupons".[37] Thirdly, export of capital is parasitism raised to a high pitch.

There are two other consequences of the operation of the structure of relations that constitute imperialism. One is 'the exploitation of oppressed nations – which is inseparably connected with annexations – and especially the exploitation of colonies [or semi-colonies or even nominally independent nations] by a handful of "Great" Powers' (ibid.). In fact, 'world's greatest capitalist powers [pursue] a policy of incessant economic rivalry aimed at achieving world supremacy, subjugating the small nations' (Lenin, 1917a). Under imperialism, class exploitation and national exploitation co-exist.

The imperialist exploitation of the less developed nations occurs through the appropriation of super-profits from less developed nations (i.e. through super-exploitation, mentioned earlier), the profits that 'are obtained over and above the profits which capitalists squeeze out of the workers of their "own" country' (Lenin, 1916a). Or, their superprofits are 'a surplus of profits over and above the capitalist profits that are normal and customary all over the world' (Lenin, 1916c). The appropriation superprofits occurs through the export of capital which 'sets the seal of parasitism on the whole country that lives by exploiting the labour of several overseas countries and colonies' (Lenin, 1916a). To remain competitive in the world economy, imperialist countries exploit and subjugate the less developed nations, including their 'cheaper' land and natural resources. And such exploitation is helped by the support of middle class

---

cost of production and increasing profits by introducing technical improvements operates in the direction of change. But the tendency to stagnation and decay, which is characteristic of monopoly, continues to operate, and in some branches of industry, in some countries, for certain periods of time, it gains the upper hand' (Lenin, 1916a).

Indeed, this tendency towards stagnation – which demonstrates how social relations can fetter productive forces – does not however preclude 'an extraordinarily rapid development of capitalism in individual branches of industry, in individual countries, and in individual periods' (Lenin, 1919c). Productive forces are fettered but unevenly.

37 The coupon clipping is expressed, among other things, in speculation activity, which is evident on the ground. 'Speculation in land situated in the suburbs of rapidly growing big towns is a particularly profitable operation for finance capital. The monopoly of the banks merges here with the monopoly of ground-rent and with monopoly of the means of communication, since the rise in the price of land and the possibility of selling it profitably in lots, etc., is mainly dependent on good means of communication with the centre of the town; and these means of communication are in the hands of large companies which are connected with these same banks through the holding system and the distribution of seats on the boards' (Lenin, 1916a).

people in advanced countries, including trade union leaders who are bribed by capital (discussed earlier).[38]

The other consequence of imperialism, related to the first four, is reaction, the opposite of democracy: "finance capital strives for domination, not freedom". Political reaction *all along* the line is a characteristic feature of imperialism. Corruption, bribery on a huge scale and all kinds of fraud' (Lenin, 1919c). Capitalism has been progressive by creating objective and subjective conditions for socialist society but it has now turned into a reactionary social form, at least since the early part of the 20th century when the global capitalist system became blatantly and brutally imperialist. Reaction is expressed in the form of authoritarianism and militarism.

In developed countries such as those in Europe, capital fears 'the growth and increasing strength of the proletariat' (Lenin, 1913b). So, it 'comes out in support of every thing backward, moribund and medieval' and it joins 'with all obsolete and obsolescent forces in an attempt to preserve tottering wage-slavery' (ibid.). It 'is prepared to go to any length of savagery, brutality and crime in order to uphold dying capitalist slavery' (ibid.). This tendency to fear the proletariat and therefore to turn to reaction also in evidence in less developed nations. Indeed, 'Both in foreign and home policy imperialism strives towards violations of democracy, towards reaction. In this sense imperialism is indisputably the "negation" of *democracy in general*' (Lenin, 1916b). Being a "negation" of democracy in general, imperialism is *also* a "negation" of democracy in the national question (i.e., national self-determination)' (ibid.).

Imperialism, as *the highest stage of capitalism*, is associated with annexation and militarism, but it is wrong to see – as Kautsky does – imperialism *merely* as a government policy, including annexation or militarism, and it is wrong to reduce imperialism to one state bullying another: 'the philistine regards annexation (i.e., acquisition of foreign territories against, the will of their people, *i.e.*, violation of self-determination) as equivalent to the "spread" (expansion) of finance capital to a larger economic territory' (Lenin, 1916b).

Hundreds of cartels supported by their states often try to divide up the economic world amicably among themselves, but military conflict lurks behind

38 More than any classical Marxist's, it was Lenin's political economy that has inspired research on imperialism. For a survey on ideas about imperialism, see Brewer (1990) and Callinicos (2009). On the conceptualization of imperialism in relation to globalization, see Kiely (2005) and Berberoglu (2022). On the connection between imperialism and economic development in the South, see the classic, Warren (1980). For a (critical) discussion on Lenin's theory of imperialism and/or on its further development, see Blaut (1995); Carchedi and Roberts (2021); McDonough, 1995, Patnaik (2014); Panitch (2014); Roberts (2019; 2024); Sakellaropoulos and Sotiris (2015); and Willoughby (1995).

economic rivalry (Lenin, 1916c). Capitalism therefore 'has [now] become reduced to the absolute power of a handful of millionaires and multimillionaires who send whole nations into a bloodbath to decide whether [this or that] group of plunderers is to obtain the spoils *of* imperialism, power over the colonies, financial "spheres of influence" or "mandates to rule", etc.' (Lenin, 1919b).

Imperialism and wars/war-mongering are internally connected. 'Armaments are considered a national matter, a matter of patriotism; it is presumed that everyone maintains strict secrecy. But the shipyards, the ordnance, dynamite and small-arms factories are *international enterprises*, in which the capitalists of the various countries work together in duping and fleecing the public of the various countries' (Lenin, 1913d). Elected politicians managing the affairs of the state 'are almost all shareholders in these firms' and they work hand in glove' (ibid.). Lenin (1913d) says: 'syndicates of internationally associated capitalists are pushing the nations into war. ... The capitalist press and the [capitalist] political leaders ... have been ... clamouring for more armaments – that is so profitable for the industrialists manufacturing military supplies!'.

7 Workers' Struggle for Improvements within Capitalism, and for Socialism

7.1 *Workers' Struggle for Concessions*

Capitalism creates conditions for, and impedes, workers' struggle. Workers' struggle does improve their conditions but within narrow limits set by wage-slavery that characterizes capitalism.

Workers' resistance requires hard work and sacrifices (e.g. loss of wages). 'Only as a result of this resistance, despite the tremendous sacrifices the workers have to make in the struggle, are they able to maintain anything like a tolerable standard of living' (ibid.). Thus, workers conditions can be better in some countries and some regions in a country than in others because of 'a higher standard of culture', '*freedom of strikes* and association', greater 'political liberty', presence of 'millions of trade unionists' in the former countries or regions (ibid.). Of course, uneven capitalist economic development is a reason for such variation too.

The difficult economic conditions to which capital pushes workers forces them to resist. 'The workers' resistance springs from their very conditions of life – the sale of labour-power' (Lenin, 1914b). By developing means of transportation and communication, by geographically concentrating workers in cities, and by proletarianizing large masses of (rural) petty producers, capitalism creates also conditions for class struggle against it. Uneven development that capitalism creates between rural and urban areas and across nations thus causes migration of people which weakens geographical isolation. This is the case internationally as it allows people from different countries to inter-mingle. This is the case within a country too:

> Unless the population becomes mobile, it cannot develop, and it would be naïve to imagine that a village school can teach people what they can learn from an independent acquaintance with the different relations and orders of things in [different parts of a country], in agriculture and in industry. (Lenin, 1899: 251)[39]

For example, 'Migration to the town elevates the peasant as a citizen, releasing him from the host of patriarchal and personal relationships of dependence and social-estate divisions so strongly entrenched in the rural districts' (Lenin, 1913k). 'Migration to the towns loosens the old patriarchal family ties and places women in a more independent position, on an equal footing with men' (Lenin, 1899a: 578). At the international scale, as well, 'Advanced capitalism drags [workers] forcibly into its orbit, tears them out of the backwoods in which they live, makes them participants in the world-historical movement and brings them face to face with the powerful, united, international class of factory owners' (Lenin, 1913k).

However, the relation between workers' struggle against capitalism and their economic conditions is complicated because of two processes. Firstly, even if wages rise, wages do not rise much, 'even with the most stubborn and *most* successful strike movement' (Lenin, 1912a). Secondly, workers do not always succeed in resisting capital: So, 'The cost of living, which has been rising rapidly in recent years, often nullifies all the workers' efforts' to improve their conditions through strikes, etc. (1914b). '[I]n all countries there have been cases, even whole periods in the life of nations, when the failure of the workers to fight back has led to their being reduced to incredible poverty and all the horrors of starvation' (ibid.).

Why such failure? Capital not only makes workers' economic conditions difficult. It also makes their resistance against these conditions difficult in the selfsame process: 'capital is becoming more and more concentrated', and its 'associations are growing', while 'the number of destitute and unemployed people is increasing, and so also is want among the proletariat', as a result of which

39 '[U]nless the population is mobile … there can be no question of its developing understanding and initiative' (ibid.: 251).

'it is becoming harder than ever to fight for a decent standard of living' (ibid.). While by encouraging international migration, capital creates conditions for working class struggle, it also creates obstacles. In order to divide the masses, capital pits migrants of one national or other cultural identity against those with another: 'The bourgeoisie incites the workers of one nation against those of another in the endeavour to keep them disunited' (ibid.). The bourgeoisie also makes use of state's coercive forces (e.g. police) against workers involved in resistance.

It also bribes, or otherwise influences, workers' leaders, directly or through bourgeois political parties, to discipline rank-and-file workers. To the extent that class struggle requires international unity of world's workers, bribing of trade union leaders in imperialist countries creates an obstacle to such unity and supports imperialist exploitation – or, super-exploitation – of the workers of the less developed nations. Imperialist capitalists use some of their super-profit obtained from such super-exploitation, 'to bribe the labour leaders and the upper stratum of the labour aristocracy ... in a thousand different ways, direct and indirect, overt and covert'. (Lenin, 1916a). Superprofits are used 'to create something like an alliance ... between the workers of the given nation and their capitalists *against* the other countries' (Lenin, 1919c), and therefore break the principle of socialist internationalism. Imperialism produces '*opportunists* (social-chauvinists)' out of 'a section of the petty bourgeoisie and of a certain strata of the working class who *have been bribed* out of imperialist superprofits and converted to *watchdogs* of capitalism and *corruptors* of the labour movement', and these opportunist collaborate with 'the imperialist bourgeoisie' to maintain imperialism 'on the backs of Asia and Africa' (Lenin, 1916c). Indeed, 'A privileged upper stratum of the proletariat in the imperialist countries lives partly at the expense of hundreds of millions in the [less developed] nations.' (Lenin, 1919c).[40]

7.2 *Workers' Struggle for Socialism*

Lenin's political economy of capitalism produces ideas about what is to be done about it: it points to the significant reforms under capitalism that workers must fight for and to the obstacles that exist towards such struggle. His political economy also points to the transitional measures that a proletarian party can/must take following the overthrow of capitalism as a part of a more or less uninterrupted struggle to establish communism.

40 In fact, by using labour aristocracy, etc., imperialism needs and creates imperialist ideology which 'penetrates the working class. No Chinese Wall separates it from the other classes' (Lenin, 1916a).

Capitalism has some essential/fundamental features (wage slavery, competition, exploitation, imperialism, etc.). It also has derivative features or symptoms (e.g. excessively difficult economic conditions; capital's attacks on democratic rights), or it coexists with pre-capitalist relations which impede its fuller development. Such a view of capitalism points to the need for 1) a fight for land by peasants, including those who are oppressed by pre-capitalist landlords, and 2) a fight of workers and petty producers' for liberty and for economic concessions (e.g. progressive taxation, increased remuneration, etc.), a fight that must be a part of, and linked to, 3) a fight for socialism, or against wage-slavery itself.

Given his stress on imperialism and on the fact that class exploitation coexists with national exploitation, Lenin emphasizes oppressed nations' right to self-determination, both economically (vis a vis economic annexation) and politically. In fact, imperialism represents – creates opportunities for – transition to socialism:

> When a big enterprise ..., on the basis of an exact computation of mass data, organises according to plan the supply of primary raw materials to the extent of two-thirds, or three-fourths, of all that is necessary for tens of millions of people; when the raw materials are transported in a systematic and organised manner to the most suitable places of production, sometimes situated hundreds or thousands of miles from each other; when a single centre directs all the consecutive stages of processing the material right up to the manufacture of numerous varieties of finished articles; when these products are distributed according to a single plan among tens and hundreds of millions of consumers ... then it becomes evident that we have socialisation of production, and ... that private economic and private property relations constitute a shell which no longer fits its contents, a shell which must inevitably decay if its removal is artificially delayed, a shell which may remain in a state of decay for a fairly long period (if, at the worst, the cure of the opportunist abscess is protracted), but which will inevitably be removed. (Lenin, 1916a)

That shell, which fetters further development of productive forces and their rational use for the benefit of humanity, will be removed through a revolutionary fight against capitalism.

This revolutionary fight against capitalism has many aspects. 'Unlike the anarchists, the Marxists recognise struggle for reforms, i.e., for measures that improve the conditions of the working people without destroying the power of the ruling class' (Lenin, 1913a). The fight for reforms is not automatically reform*ism*. Reformism is that which restricts 'the aims and activities of the working class to the winning of reforms' (ibid.). 'Reformism is bourgeois deception of the workers', a deception that makes workers forget that 'despite individual improvements' that workers may experience, they 'will always remain wage-slaves, as long as there is the domination of capital' (ibid.).[41] This is why 'Marxists wage a most resolute struggle against the reformists' (ibid.).

The interaction of objective reality of capitalist political economy and workers' existing consciousness produce two kinds of workers. Some run after petty concessions *only*. They possess reformist or trade union consciousness. Other workers (a smaller group) have graduated from such consciousness and possess class consciousness (Lenin, 1902b: 17–18). The class-conscious workers are those who 'have assimilated Marx's theory, i.e., realised the inevitability of wage-slavery so long as capitalist rule remains, will not be fooled by any bourgeois reforms' (Lenin, 1913a). Class conscious workers understand that as long as there is capitalism, 'reforms cannot be either enduring or far-reaching' (ibid.). On the basis of such understanding, they 'fight for better conditions and use them to intensify the fight against wage-slavery'. Thus, 'having seen through the falsity of reformism', class conscious workers 'utilise reforms to develop and broaden their class struggle' (ibid.).

Lenin's political economy of class differentiation leads him to conclude that petty production is not viable and also that and that while the peasantry can be revolutionary against pre-capitalist system, it cannot play a leading role in the socialist fight against capitalism because of their proprietary class status:

> On the one hand, the tremendous survivals of corvée economy and all kinds of survivals of serfdom, with the unprecedented impoverishment and ruin of the peasant poor, fully explain the deep sources of the revolutionary peasant movement, the deep roots of the revolutionary character of the peasantry as a mass. On the other hand, in the course of the revolution, the character of the various political parties, and the numerous ideological-political trends reveal the inherently contradictory class

41 'The liberal bourgeoisie grant reforms with one hand, and with the other always take them back, reduce them to nought, use them to enslave the workers, to divide them into separate groups and perpetuate wage-slavery. For that reason reformism, even when quite sincere, in practice becomes a weapon by means of which the bourgeoisie corrupt and weaken the workers. The experience of all countries shows that the workers who put their trust in the reformists are always fooled' (ibid.). The reformists, the upper layers of labour aristocracy, try 'to divide and deceive the workers, to divert them from the class struggle by petty concessions' (Lenin, 1913a).

> structure of this mass, its petty-bourgeois character, the antagonism between the proprietor and the proletarian trends within it. (Lenin, 1899: 31)

So, the petty producers must adopt the attitude not of a small proprietor (an attitude that overlaps with that of the bourgeoisie) but 'the point of view of the revolutionary proletarian' (Lenin, 1908). 'The majority of the peasants live in poverty, are ruined and become proletarians, while the minority trail after the capitalists and help keep the masses of the rural population dependent upon the capitalists. ... Only an independent organisation of wage-workers which conducts a consistent class struggle can wrest the peasantry from the influence of the bourgeoisie and explain to them the absolute hopelessness of the small producers' position in capitalist society' (Lenin, 1913g). According to Lenin, once again, 'it is precisely the exploitation of wage-labour that forms the basis of the whole predatory system of today' that is called capitalism (Lenin, 1901). He fully accepts Marx's economic theory which 'has explained the true position of the proletariat in the general system of capitalism' (Lenin, 1913c). 'The chief thing in the doctrine of Marx is that it brings out the historic role of the proletariat as the builder of socialist society' (ibid.). 'The leading role of the proletariat has been fully revealed. It has also been revealed that the strength of the proletariat in the process of history is immeasurably greater than its share of the total Population' (Lenin, 1899: 31). Of course, there are capitalists that are more democratic and that are more reactionary, so the proletariat in its pursuit of power must not ally itself with any faction of the bourgeoisie, even in the name of fighting the lesser evil.

Lenin's examination of the 'abuses' in the capitalist workplace leads him to reach the following conclusion: 'Exposing the capitalists is the first step towards curbing the capitalists. Exposing the orgy of pillage is the first step in our fight against the pillagers.' (Lenin, 1917b). Exposing the capitalists requires a careful study of capitalism based on Marxist theory. 'Every worker ... working in a bank, factory or commercial house, ... every engineer, statistician, accountant – all should ... collect accurate, even fragmentary, and, if possible, documented data concerning [capitalist] orgy of pillage, i.e., concerning prices and profits' (Lenin, 1917b).

The fact that capitalists organise and rationalise labour within the factory to increase exploitation of the workers (Lenin, 1914a) has political implication: the rational organization of social labour under capitalism 'is preparing the time when the proletariat will take over all social production and appoint its own workers' committees for the purpose of properly distributing and rationalising all social labour' (ibid.).[42] As well, 'Large-scale production, machinery, railways, telephone – all provide thousands of opportunities to cut [production time enormously]'. (ibid.).

Capitalism will not be capitalism if it develops evenly across nations. This fact has a political implication. Different countries will overthrow capitalism at different points in time. So following the overthrow of capitalism, the actual introduction of socialist measures must be mindful of country-specific conditions and of the fact that for some time a country that has overthrown capitalism will be an island in a world of capitalism.[43] What the proletariat, the advanced class, does in developed countries will be different to a certain extent from what it does in poorer countries. 'Under no circumstances can the party of the proletariat set itself the aim of "introducing" socialism in a country of small peasants so long as the overwhelming majority of the population has not come to realise the need for a socialist revolution' (Lenin, 1917c). Lenin takes the truth of the law of value seriously, a law which works at the international scale and according to which all countries, developed and developing, are inter-locked, and this makes the successful construction of socialism in one country impossible.[44] However, that does not mean that following a successful overthrow of capitalism in a country, including a poor country, certain revolutionary measures cannot be taken: 'only bourgeois sophists, hiding behind "near-Marxist" catchwords, can deduce from this truth a justification of the policy of postponing immediate revolutionary measures, the time for which is fully ripe' (ibid.).[45]

The proletarian state may be compelled to introduce 'new economic policy', or NEP, where a degree of capitalist development under strict state supervision is allowed until the international balance of power in favour of world socialism

42 'Capitalism is thus creating a condition where "workers" committees, assisted by the workers' unions, will be able to apply these principles of rational distribution of social labour when the latter is freed from its enslavement by capital' (ibid.).

43 A similar point is made in the *Communist Manifesto*, as discussed in Chapter 2.

44 'Regarded from the world-historical point of view, there would doubtlessly be no hope of the ultimate victory of our revolution [i.e. construction of a successful socialist society in a post-revolution society] if it were to remain alone, if there were no revolutionary movements in other countries. When the Bolshevik Party tackled the job alone [in Russia], it did so in the firm conviction that the revolution was maturing in all countries and that in the end – but not at the very beginning – no matter what difficulties we experienced, no matter what defeats were in store for us, the world socialist revolution would come – because it is coming; would mature – because it is maturing and will reach full maturity. I repeat, our salvation from all these difficulties is an all Europe revolution' (Lenin, 1918).

45 '[These] measures ... *have been* frequently *resorted to during the war by a number of bourgeois states* [themselves], ... which are absolutely indispensable in order to combat impending total economic disorganisation and famine' (ibid.).

tilts towards the world working class. 'Such measures as the nationalisation of the land, of all the banks and capitalist syndicates, or, at least, the *immediate* establishment of [workers' control] … over them – measures which do not in any way constitute the "introduction" of socialism – must be absolutely insisted on, and, whenever possible, carried out in a revolutionary way' (Lenin, 1917c). These measures are 'only steps towards socialism, and which are perfectly feasible economically' (ibid.), which the party of the revolutionary proletariat will never refrain from taking. The party will thus never 'hesitate to lay hands on the fabulous profits of the capitalists and bankers, who are enriching themselves on the war in a particularly scandalous manner' (ibid.).

Lenin's class-based political economy leads him to conclude that 'the abolition of classes as the socialist agenda means placing *all* citizens on an *equal* footing with regard to the *means of production* belonging to society as a whole. It means giving all citizens *equal* opportunities of working on the publicly-owned means of production, on the publicly-owned land, at the publicly-owned factories, and so forth' (Lenin, 1914c). It is 'absurd to expect *equality* of strength and abilities in socialist society. In brief, when socialists speak of equality they always mean *social* equality, equality of social status, and not by any means the physical and mental equality of individuals' (ibid.).

Lenin's political economy, informed by materialist dialectics, convinces him about the need for temporary revolutionary political compromises in a society full of class-contradictions (Das, 2018b). His advocacy for NEP is an example which involves giving concessions to profit-seeking commodity producers, including both petty producers and big capital. 'We have reiterated … our readiness to give foreign capital the most generous concessions and guarantees. But we do not propose to be strangled to death for the sake of peace' (Lenin, 1920a). 'I know of no reason why a socialistic commonwealth like ours cannot do business indefinitely with capitalistic countries. We don't mind taking their capitalistic locomotives and farming machinery, so why should they mind taking our socialistic wheat, flax and platinum. Socialistic corn tastes the same as any other corn, does it not?' (ibid.).

8 Conclusion

Lenin is not just a political theorist and socialist revolutionist. He is also great political economist, and his political economy informs his political practice.[46] Lenin's political economy follows closely that of Marx. Yet, according to him:

46 Harding (1977) signals the importance of Lenin's economic writing, which are generally neglected, for understanding his politics (and, I would add, his political theory).

'We do not regard Marx's theory as some thing completed and inviolable; on the contrary, we are convinced that it has only laid the foundation stone of the science which socialists *must* develop in all directions if they wish to keep pace with life' (Lenin, 1899c). This is why he is able to develop some of Marx's ideas in new ways. Even his critics recognize his contributions to political economy, however one-sidely or reservedly (Howard and King, 1988). 'Lenin's political economy, while neither unchanging nor wholly original, can be understood as the product of a Marxian thinker, whose revolutionary activity was theoretically informed' (Howard and King, 1988). His political economic claims made 100–125 years ago are significantly relevant to the contemporary world.

Among his greatest contributions to political economy remain his thinking about class differentiation and capitalist agriculture, apart from imperialism.[47] '[A]s the acknowledged expert on agriculture, it had fallen to Lenin to counter the revisionists' claims that the Marxian "laws of motion" were inoperative in this sector' (Howard and King, 1988: 502; Milios, 1999).[48] Processes of class differentiation that Lenin studied are quite evident in contemporary society where relatively small-scale or economically weaker producers (e.g. small- and medium-scale urban businesses; peasants/farmers) become economically unviable.[49] The pace of class differentiation may be slow or quick, but the tendency does exist leading to the centralization of capital in the hands of a few.

Lenin's insights on common people's impoverishment are important part of Marxist theory of poverty and inequality (Das, 2024e; 2024f). His political

47 'The claim that Russian agriculture had already become capitalist was arguably the most controversial element of Lenin's development studies. But it conformed to his general message: the economic development of Russia was subject to principles of capitalist accumulation, and the presence of pre-capitalist sectors could not alter that path' (Melnick, 2021: 46).

48 Like all classical Marxists, Lenin has been subjected to many unfair criticisms (Das, 2023a). For example, one author finds 'considerable shortcomings compared to Marx's work, sufficiently so and with such a pattern as to suggest that Lenin is taking a step backwards to an economics of production à la Ricardo.' (Zarembka, 2003). This critic forgets, among other things, that Lenin was opposed to political economy being a *study of production* as such. This critic is also unnecessarily harsh towards Lenin whose political economy informed his revolutionary practice, when the critic says: 'the revolutionary success of 1917 gave Lenin's political economy an imprimatur much beyond its actual intellectual weight' (Zarembka, 2003: 299). Another critic says that 'the economic content of socialism in Lenin is not exactly the same as that in Marx' (Chattopadhyay, 1991). Given, once again, the link between Lenin's political economy of capitalism and his view of socialism, one might conclude that according to this critic, Lenin's political economy is problematic. On other critical assessments of Lenin's work, see also Jeong (2011).

49 This is the case both in richer and poor countries as well as richer countries such as US and Canada. This process became especially acute during Covid.

economy is admirably armed with an extraordinary sense of geographical imagination that emphasizes: uneven character of capitalist development and resultant mobility of capital and people at sub-national, national and global scales of capitalist production and exchange, urbanization and ruralization of capital, creation of hierarchy of nations, the relation between imperialist speculation and suburbanization, imperialist conflicts over the environment (e.g. raw materials), etc. He was concerned about the less developed world such as African nations (Pateman, 2022). He was also deeply interested in the developed nations such as the US, both intellectually and politically (Lenin, 1917d). In fact, 'the world of globalised capitalism ... make[s] Lenin's questions relevant once again', even if not in every detail (Küttler, 2023: 528).

Given the current denial of imperialism as an objective process and as a concept, Lenin's work on imperialism remains a critical intellectual resource. Panitch, who is critical of Lenin's theory of imperialism, is able to say: 'there was unquestionably a certain symmetry between Das Kapital's famous description of capital as having come "into the world dripping from head to foot, from every pore, with blood and dirt" and Lenin's expectation that it was in the process of leaving the world in the same way' (Panitch, 2014: 22). Contrary to imperialism-deniers[50] or those who underemphasize imperialism by saying the world economy is dominated by trans-national capitalist class and trans-national capitalist state (e.g. Robinson, 2007) or who say imperialism can be tamed by better government policy of advanced countries (e.g. Harvey, 2003),[51] it is the case that: 'Almost 100 years after it was written, Lenin's classic Marxist theory of imperialism, principally articulated in his book *Imperialism: The Highest Stage of Capitalism*, remains the best framework to understand capitalism's international political economy' (King, 2014). His theory of imperialism draws attention to capitalist competition and capitalist exploitation at the global scale. Imperialism involves the exploitation of workers and petty producers of the nations of the South with weak military powers, by the monopolies of the technologically and economically advanced nations supported by their militarily powerful states, a process that is mediated, to a variable degree, by competition among monopolies of advanced nations. The

50 On the topic of the denial of imperialism, see Foster (2019).

51 In *New Imperialism* Harvey (2003: 75) suggests: 'The United States could downgrade if not turn away from its imperialist trajectory by engaging in a massive redistribution of wealth within its borders and redirection of capital flows into the production and renewal of physical and social infrastructures ... A massive counterattack within the US as well as in the other core countries of capitalism against the politics of neoliberalism and the cutting of state and social expenditures might be one of the only ways to protect capitalism internally from its self-destructive and crisis prone tendencies'.

tendency of capitalism to draw non-capitalist countries into the whirlpool of capitalist world economy that Lenin draws attention to explains, for example, why the imperialist US showed so much aggressive attitude towards the former USSR and why it shows such an attitude today towards the dominantly non-capitalist China. Lenin's claim about imperialism and geopolitical struggle for control over land and raw materials is extremely relevant to our world.[52]

Consider the imperialist nations' attempt to control the supply of critical minerals including those needed for their green industry: 'The concern of the American state is not simply that it does not produce and control these vital resources, but rather that China, the principal target of its geostrategic ambitions, does' (Black, 2022). Similarly, Russia 'plays a leading role in the production of a variety of key minerals, holding an important piece of global reserves. In understanding the broader drive of the United States to dominate Eurasia and subjugate Russia, the role of these key resources cannot be overlooked' (ibid.).

Lenin's claim that politically 'independent' nations can be subjected to imperialism – economic annexation – is well known to everyone who knows about what is done by the imperialist institutions such as World Bank and IMF and the regime of economic sanctions to the South. In emphasizing the imperialist character of capitalism, and seeing imperialism as the era of finance capital, Lenin steers clear of what is now called 'the financialization thesis', which says that a new financialized capitalism has arrived that 'operates in a completely different fashion compared to traditional capitalism' (Mavroudeas

52 'The more capitalism is developed, the more strongly the shortage of raw materials is felt, the more intense the competition and the hunt for sources of raw materials throughout the whole world, the more desperate the struggle for the acquisition of [spheres of influence]', the aim of this being both guaranteed access to raw materials vis a vis global competitors and to protect capitalist property rights from takeover by the state' (Lenin, 1916a).

'Finance capital is interested not only in the already discovered sources of raw materials but also in potential sources, because present-day technical development is extremely rapid, and land which is useless today may be improved tomorrow if new methods are devised (to this end a big bank can equip a special expedition of engineers, agricultural experts, etc.), and if large amounts of capital are invested. This also applies to prospecting for minerals, to new methods of processing up and utilising raw materials, etc., etc. Hence, the inevitable striving of finance capital to enlarge its spheres of influence and even its actual territory. ... [F]inance capital in general strives to seize the largest possible amount of land of all kinds in all places, and by every means, taking into account potential sources of raw materials and fearing to be left behind in the fierce struggle for the last remnants of independent territory, or for the repartition of those territories that have been already divided' (Lenin, 1916a).

and Papadatos, 2018: 451–452).[53] For Lenin, as we have seen, financial capitalists and industrial or productive capitalists are not two entirely different and independent sets.

Contrary to many political economists during his time ('populists') and contrary to many political economists and social thinkers today (e.g. Federici), Lenin emphasizes the progressive character of capitalism and yet he is scathing in his criticisms of capitalism. Once again, recognition of capitalism's progressiveness is quite compatible with the full recognition of its 'negative and dark sides' and with the full recognition' of its 'profound and all-round social contradictions', which 'reveal the historically transient character of this economic regime.' (Lenin, 1899a: 596).

Lenin indeed points to the fundamental relations of exploitation and inequality in capitalism: exploitation of women by men; exploitation of workers by capitalists; exploitation of petty producers by capitalists, landlords, merchants and money-lenders; exploitation poorer countries by imperialist countries, and rural-urban inequality. Very few political economists can match the grandeur of theoretical imagination that Lenin possesses. Lenin's political economy is arguably broader than Marx's because of: its emphasis on agrarian and rural aspects of capitalism and on the ways in which capitalism develops out of class differentiation of commodity producers; its theorization of imperialism'; and the fact that he generally thinks about the relation between political economy and class struggle. A large part of Lenin's political economy of rural/agricultural production is relevant to commodity economy and to capitalism as such. While Marx assumes that all labour is wage-labour, Lenin gives due importance to both wage labour and the labour of petty producers.

Lenin's political economy is a powerful antidote to the current obsession with what some scholars call 'accumulation of dispossession', which includes, among many other things, the extra-economic ways in which direct producers are divorced from their means of production. According to some (e.g. Harvey, 2006), accumulation by dispossession is the dominant form of capitalism.[54]

53 In other words, it is the idea that 'over the past three decades at least, modern capitalism has undergone a radical transformation, with the financial system, through a series of innovative mechanisms, conquering the commanding heights of capitalism and transforming the whole system in line with its own prerogatives' (ibid.).

54 Harvey's chaotic theory of dispossession has fuelled much discussion in contemporary political economy. For a critique of this theory, see Das (2017c). Das (forthcoming) presents a detailed discussion of Marx's own theory of primitive accumulation, its modern versions advocated for by Marxists including Harvey, a critique of these views, and a reconstruction of Marx's original theory (from the standpoint of capitalist relations of production and exchange).

Yet, what Marx calls primitive accumulation *is* an on-going process, which coexists with class differentiation by economic means that Lenin himself correctly stresses. But Lenin almost always neglects primitive accumulation.[55]

Lenin rightly thinks that crises are 'not a thing of the past' and that prosperity is followed by a crisis, and that while 'the forms, the sequence, the picture of particular crises' change, crises remain 'an inevitable component of the capitalist system'. Yet, his crisis theory is inadequate. In his review of Marx's ideas, Lenin does acknowledge Marx's view that:

> A rise in the productivity of labor implies a more rapid growth of constant capital as compared with variable capital. Inasmuch as surplus value is a function of variable capital alone, it is obvious that the rate of profit (the ratio of surplus value to the whole capital …) tends to fall. Marx makes a detailed analysis of this tendency and of a number of circumstances that conceal or counteract it. (Lenin, 1914e)

But Lenin quickly moves on without indicating in this article or elsewhere what *he* makes of Marx's famous law of the tendency towards the rate of profit to fall (LTRPF) which Marx considers to be the most important law of political economy. Lenin offers a view of crisis that appears to be over-productionist or under-consumptionist: For example he says: 'Industry *could* produce hundreds of thousands of motor vehicles but the poverty of the *masses* hampers development and brings about crashes after a few years of "brilliant" growth.' (Lenin, 1913f). Elsewhere he says: 'In social production as a whole, chaos continues to reign and grow, leading to crises when the accumulated wealth cannot find purchasers, and millions of workers starve because they are unable to find employment' (Lenin, 1914a).[56] Further, in a plan for a talk on crisis, Lenin (1904) includes the following components (italics added):

55 'Rather than focusing on coercion to create commodity production, Lenin says that the extent of the market is "inseparably connected with the degree of specialization of social labor," and that "this specialization, by its very nature, is as infinite as technical developments". Lenin underplays the question of coercion in market creation, while highlighting the possible role of technical change' (Zarembka, 2003: 282–283). In my view, Lenin is right not to *focus* on coercion to create commodity production but he is incorrect to almost entirely neglect it.

56 In his *Development of capitalism*, Lenin (1899a) writes about the contradiction in capitalism: 'It is this expansion of production without a corresponding expansion of consumption that corresponds to the historical mission of capitalism and to its specific social structure: the former consists in the development of the productive forces of society; the latter rules out the utilisation of these technical achievements by the mass of the population. There is an undoubted contradiction between the drive towards the unlimited

> What is a crisis? – Stoppage in industry, unemployment, hitch in marketing, *overproduction* ... 2. Overproduction, under consumption ...
> Competition, its international character, drive for markets, gigantic growth of production.
> Reduction in demand for living labour: intensification, machines, women and children, skilled and unskilled workers.
> ... Supply grows, marketing tight.

In this plan, there is nothing on Marx's LTRPF.

In explaining Marx's concept of surplus value, Lenin brings up what he calls overproduction:

> By speeding up the supplanting of workers by machinery and by creating wealth at one extreme and poverty at the other, the accumulation of capital also gives rise to what is called the "reserve army of labor" ... which assumes the most diverse forms and enables capital to expand production extremely rapidly. In conjunction with credit facilities and the accumulation of capital in the form of means of production, this incidentally is the key to an understanding of the *crises* of overproduction which occur periodically in capitalist countries – at first at an average of every 10 years, and later at more lengthy and less definite intervals. (Lenin, 1914e)

In his *Development of capitalism in Russia*, Lenin says: 'Another feature of the development by capitalism of the social productive forces is that the growth of the means of production (productive consumption) outstrips by far the growth of personal consumption', both 'in agriculture and in industry' (ibid.: 597).[57]

Lenin also says little about how capitalism at the national scale is itself a barrier to the development of productive forces. For example, given the massive presence of a reserve army of labour in part created by class differentiation of petty producers that he has so eloquently explained, capitalists can resort to the formal subsumption of labour, as we have seen in chapter 5. Like most Marxists of the world, he assumes that once there are commodity relations and wage labour, capitalism will automatically become developed capitalism

---

extension of production inherent in capitalism, and the limited consumption of the masses of the people (limited because of their proletarian status)' (p. 56).

57 'This feature springs from the general laws of the realisation of the product in capitalist society, and fully conforms to the antagonistic nature of this society.' (Lenin, 1899a: 597–598).

based on systemic technical changes. He says that 'once social economy is based on the division of labour and the commodity form of the product, technical progress must inevitably lead to the strengthening and deepening of capitalism' (Lenin, 1893).[58] He also claims that 'The competition that is the product of capitalism, and the producers' dependence 'on the world market' make 'the transformation of technique a necessity' (Lenin, 1899a: 229). Lenin recognizes that when a less developed country is less developed relative to what it can accomplish, it is because of pre-capitalist relations; he does not, however, recognize some of the important ways in which capital itself – as a class relationship rooted in the relations of production – is a barrier to the further development of productive forces. He does think that relative economic development during the pre-capitalist epochs of a country, 'the development of social economy under capitalism must be considered as extremely rapid' but that if 'we compare the present rapidity of development [in a country] with that which could be achieved with the general level of technique and culture as it is today', then we will see that 'the present rate of development of capitalism ... really must be considered as slow'. This is because of 'an abundant survival of ancient institutions that are incompatible with capitalism'. So, obstacles to capitalist development are pre-capitalist relations rather than capitalism, according to Lenin.[59] Lenin recognizes that 'low wages are one of the most important obstacles to the introduction of machines', and yet he appears

58 Lenin does not ignore the fact that capitalism develops through different stages:
'the difference between them [i.e. stages] boils down to different stages of technical progress. In the lower stages of the development of capitalist technique – simple co-operation and manufacture – the production or means of production as means of production does not yet exist: it emerges and attains enormous development only at the higher stage – large-scale machine industry' (ibid.). He, however, assumes that the lower stage automatically develops into the higher stage.
'Fighting Narodniks, he insisted that political and institutional "peculiarities" were but temporary impediments to the spread of the virus of commodity production. There is no place for a modernization theory in Lenin. He conceived "industrialization as a transition from one (the underdeveloped) capitalist form to another (the developed)..." ' (Milios quoted in: Melnik, 2021: 45). While emphasizing such a transition, he like Marx, under-stressed the mediated character of that transition: how workers' struggle against the lower form of capitalism creates a condition for a higher stage where labour-saving technology is systemically used. In this sense there is some relevance to Zarembka's (2003: 283) point that in Lenin's thinking 'there is no theory of technical change ... beyond saying that competition drives the need for cost re-ductions'.

59 It could be said that while as a general explanation of relative absence of development this inadequate, the explanation is not without merit in a context where capitalism is still at its early stage of development and where capitalism coexists with pre-capitalist relations of production.

to ignore the fact that the transition from formal subsumption (a lower stage of capitalism) to real subsumption of labour, to a more developed stage of capitalism, or to 'the machine period of capitalism' is a mediated process.[60] In spite of these problems, Lenin's contributions to political economy are priceless.

---

60 There is also little recognition of ecological problems created by capitalism or of the role of the state in the 'economic management' of capitalism including its crises (except in terms of his comments on regressive taxes).

CHAPTER 10

Theoretical and Practical Implications of Marxist Political Economy

The aim of theoretical ideas is to provide explanations of the world in a way that is relatively independent of concrete conditions, i.e. specific conjunctures or of specific times and places, while theoretical ideas are not un-informed by concrete conditions. A given theoretical idea points to another idea or to another set of ideas; a given theoretical idea may support another idea or oppose it. As well, every theoretical idea, more or less, points to practical implications – that is, the questions of what is to be done about the world that the theory explains. If theoretical ideas did not have practical implications, a lot of energy would not be spent by bourgeois scholars to refute Marxist ideas.

> There is a well-known saying that if geometrical axioms affected human interests attempts would certainly be made to refute them. Theories of natural history which conflicted with the old prejudices of theology provoked, and still provoke, the most rabid opposition. No wonder, therefore, that the Marxian doctrine, which directly serves to enlighten and organise the advanced class in modern society [i.e. the proletariat], indicates the [revolutionary] tasks facing this class ... – no wonder that this doctrine has had to fight for every step forward in the course of its life. (Lenin, 1908)

The theoretical implications of the political-economic ideas of Marx and Lenin as present in their selected key texts for further understanding the capitalist world have been discussed in final sections of each of the chapters starting with chapter 2. I will summarize these implications in this chapter. But this chapter will also draw the practical/political implications of Marx's and Lenin's political economy.

1 A General Map of Marx's and Lenin's Political Economy as a Field of Study

The political economy discourse since the time of Marx and Lenin has had many problems as it offers a range of problematic revision*ist* claims (Lenin,

 | DOI:10.1163/9789004730472_011

1908; Das, 2023a). These include denial of, or underemphasis on, a series of facts/processes in the capitalist society (as discussed in Chapter 1). The political economic theoretical idea that are present in the key texts of Marx and Lenin respond to many of these problems and advance an alternative approach. Claims in Marxist political economy, some of which are presented in Table 10.1 below, fall under the following three broad categories: claims about what exists and why; claims that are critical of the capitalism and of ideas about it; and claims about what is to be done politically about the adverse consequences of capitalism for common people.

Marxist political economy is a scientific study of production and social relations of production, which become class relations in surplus-producing societies, in relation to distribution, exchange and consumption. It is also a study of the relation that economy has with politics, and culture, from a class standpoint.[1] The most important problems of society are intimately bound up with problems of the field of political economy (as Lenin has said).

Informed by materialist dialectical philosophy, Marxist political economy is conducted theoretically. This philosophy prioritizes a relational and processual view of society in which things are seen as processes and processes (see Ollman, 2003; Das, 2017b: 175–211). It emphasizes the material and objective conditions of social life, which change due to contradictions in these processes/relations that define social life. It emphasizes the fact that capitalism has many-sides which are constantly changing. It emphasizes the totalizing nature of capitalism. Armed with this philosophy, the Marxist political economic theory of society begins with (a) the structure of *social relations* (particularly of relations of production and 'attendant' level of the development of productive forces), the social relations that set up (b) certain *mechanisms* (= ways of acting) which in turn produce (c) certain *effects* such as impoverishment of people (which are objectively and subjectively *experience*d by them in different places).[2]

1 In his famous 'Preface' to *A contribution to the critique of political economy*, Marx says that as compared to knowledge claims about economic matters, i.e. 'the material transformation of the economic conditions of production', making claims about the political aspects of society 'with the precision of natural science' is difficult.

2 Can one explain an apple falling without explaining it in terms a general mechanism called gravity? But explaining why the apple falls is not the same as explaining why a space vehicle falls or why rain drops fall. The gravity, when it is expressed in different contexts (that is, when it is combined with different contingent, concrete, things), produces apples falling, space vehicles falling, rain drops falling and so on.

Suppose one wishes to examine why/how x happens. To explain this theoretically, one will have to first conceptualize x (including its causal powers and liabilities) as a form of y

TABLE 10.1 Selected relational and processual claims in Marxist political economy

- Objectivity of political-economic processes relative to how they are mentally constructed
- Dialectical relation between economic processes and extra-economic processes (politics and culture)
- Determining influence of class relations on economic, political and cultural phenomena
- Primacy of production and production relations over other (economic) processes
- Dialectical relation between productive forces and production relations
- Importance of the concept of labour, including its social relations/organization
- Foundational value of value relations
- Dominance of exchange relations over physical coercion and cheating/fraud
- Tendency towards class differentiation of commodity producers
- Similarity/difference between pre-capitalist and capitalist forms of production/exchange
- (Twin methods of) exploitation of wage-labour in the sphere of production
- Methods of secondary exploitation
- Tendency towards economic crises due to the growing organic composition of capital
- Increasing scalar and spatial scope of commodity production and of capitalism over time
- Dominance of global-scale relations/processes over local and national relations/processes
- Imperialism as a major obstacle to the development of the South and to world-peace
- Absolute and relative impoverishment of direct producers (workers and petty producers)
- Obstacles to improvements in nature and in conditions of direct producers due to the fettering effects of capitalist social relations of production
- Incompatibility between economic interests of direct producers and those of capitalists
- *Inherently* class/capitalist nature of the state in capitalist forms of society
- Limits to the power of the capitalist state to solve problems created by capitalism
- Importance of, and limits to, workers' (trade union) struggle
- Unique revolutionary role of the proletariat relative non-proletarian suffering masses
- Objective necessity of the revolutionary overthrow of capitalist economic relations

Note: Not all of these ideas receive equal emphasis in this book.

Theory of political economy makes an ontological distinction between more general processes in (capitalist) society and more concrete processes. Political economy must examine: a) basic features of a given social economy such as capitalism which are more or less universal, b) the process (and the conditions) of the emergence of capitalism, and the tendencies of its further development, c) represent the different aspects of contemporary economic life as component parts of a definite system of social economy, as manifestations of the basic features of the capitalist system (e.g. production, exchange, competition, exploitation and inherently capitalist nature of state). We may recall Lenin's (1919a) statement that political economy is a way of examining 'all social questions – economic, political, spiritual, religious, etc.', in their inter-relationships. Of course, the economic processes have primacy over the non-economic processes.

The empirical reality (e.g. economic inequality or the phenomenon of low wages) does not deliver itself on a platter. Theory only can help us adequately understand the empirical world, including its multiple layers some of which may not be apparent, which in turn informs theory. It must be conducted empirically, although this is not a part of the discussion in this book. Theory in Marxist political economy seeks to refrain from shallow generalisations based on facts selected one-sidedly and without reference to *the system of capitalism as a whole* (or as a totality), and only theory can help us understand that *system* by helping us inter-connect the different parts of it.

Marxist political economy takes a class approach to the theoretical (and empirical) study of economy. In terms of theory, economic matters must be seen from the standpoint of opposed classes (as explained below). In a class society, there cannot be epistemic or political neutrality. A fundamental distinction between Marxist political economy and non-Marxist political economy is this: while the latter defends wage slavery and dictatorship of the bourgeoisie, including under conditions which make conditions of the slave tolerable, the former has declared relentless war on that slavery, as a part of what Engels calls an 'ideological class struggle' against capitalism. As Lenin says in *What is to be done?*, ideas and thinkers are either bourgeois or socialist because ideas are, more or less, either socialist or bourgeois: 'There is no middle course ... in a society torn by class antagonisms' (Lenin, 1901). An idea/'ideologist' that is in between must choose sides, although petty

(which has its causal powers and liabilities). The explanation of y, along with an explanation of some matter that is contingently linked to y, will lead to the explanation of x to show that: x occurs when some general properties of society that apply to many things including x (these general properties are those of y) are combined with things that are more concrete than y.

bourgeois political economy vacillates between the two. There are *three* kinds of political economy: bourgeois, petty-bourgeois, and Marxist/socialist. To belittle the socialist political economy means to strengthen bourgeois political economy, therefore.

Theory in Marxist political economy – as theory in general – requires critique which in turn informs one's theory (and practice). Theory develops partly out of criticisms of existing ideas, including those of who call themselves Marxists/socialists as well as of bourgeois ideologists (e.g. professors).[3] It is not just that theory helps us critically understand the empirical world (and ideas about it). Theory also serves as a guide to action. Lenin's famous dictum of 'Without Revolutionary theory, there can be no Revolutionary Movement' (Lenin, 1901), applies to theory in political economy.

Combining Marx's map of political economy in the 'Introduction' to *Grundrisse* and Lenin's plan for political economy, one can draw the following integrated plan for the study of political economy:

the general, abstract determinants of production and distribution which obtain in more or less all forms of society, including all forms of class society;

dialectics of relation between forces and relations of production, including the ways in which the latter fetter the development of the former;

class differentiation of producers in commodity-producing society, and extra-economic dispossession of petty-producers, creating conditions for capitalist commodity production based on the law of value;

the essence of the capitalist mode of production as compared to the pre-capitalist modes of production; similarity and differences involving various forms of class relation and various forms and conditions of class struggle;

the categories which make up the inner structure of the bourgeois society and on which rest the fundamental classes such as capital, wage labour, landed property;

the major social classes (capitalists, including mercantile and money-lending capitalists, workers, rent-appropriating landlords, and petty producers) and their inter-connections;

circulation and credit system;

production of absolute and relative surplus-value, and how labour power, wages and workers' conditions are determined by their struggle against

3 On the connection between critique and theorizing, see Das (2014; 2023d).

the capitalist class, and in particular, how workers' struggle, under certain conditions, compel the state to introduce legislation in the workers' favour; exploitation of workers and petty producers compounded by oppression of marginalized groups within these classes;

progressive nature of capitalism, including large-scale urbanized machine-based production, as it creates objective and subjective conditions for socialist struggle and socialist society;

the geographical forms of society, including: the city and rural areas; capitalism producing uneven development, economic inequality, and spatial mobility of people;

the international relation of production; international division of labour; export and import; the world market and crises that originate in one nation and spread globally; imperialist nature of capitalism causing national exploitation which reinforces class exploitation.

Finally, since economic processes are deeply linked to political power, one must examine concentration of political power of the bourgeoisie in the form of the state;[4] Then there are processes shaped, by or connected to the state, such as: the 'unproductive' classes such as civil servants. Taxes. State debt. Public credit. The population which is held together by the state on the basis of an ideology such as nationalism. The colonies that colonizing states create and possess, and with this process, the redivisions of the world market that come with it. Emigration which the state controls in the interests of its business class.

Some of these ideas in Marx's and Lenin's plans for political economy have been explored in chapters 2–9 based on their selected key texts. While Table 10.1 presents the relational and process-based claims at a more general level, Figure 10.1 presents key concepts as pillars of theory construction within Marxist political economy. Both Table 10.1 and Figure 10.1 along with the accompanying discussion aim to demonstrate some of the power of Marxist political economic thought.

In the remainder of this chapter, I provide a summary of the discussion in these chapters. More importantly, I discuss the practical implications of the ideas presented for the conception of socialism and for socialist struggle.

4 That is, in terms of the internal relation between the state on the one hand and the relations of property, commodity, value, and the production process, in capitalist society.

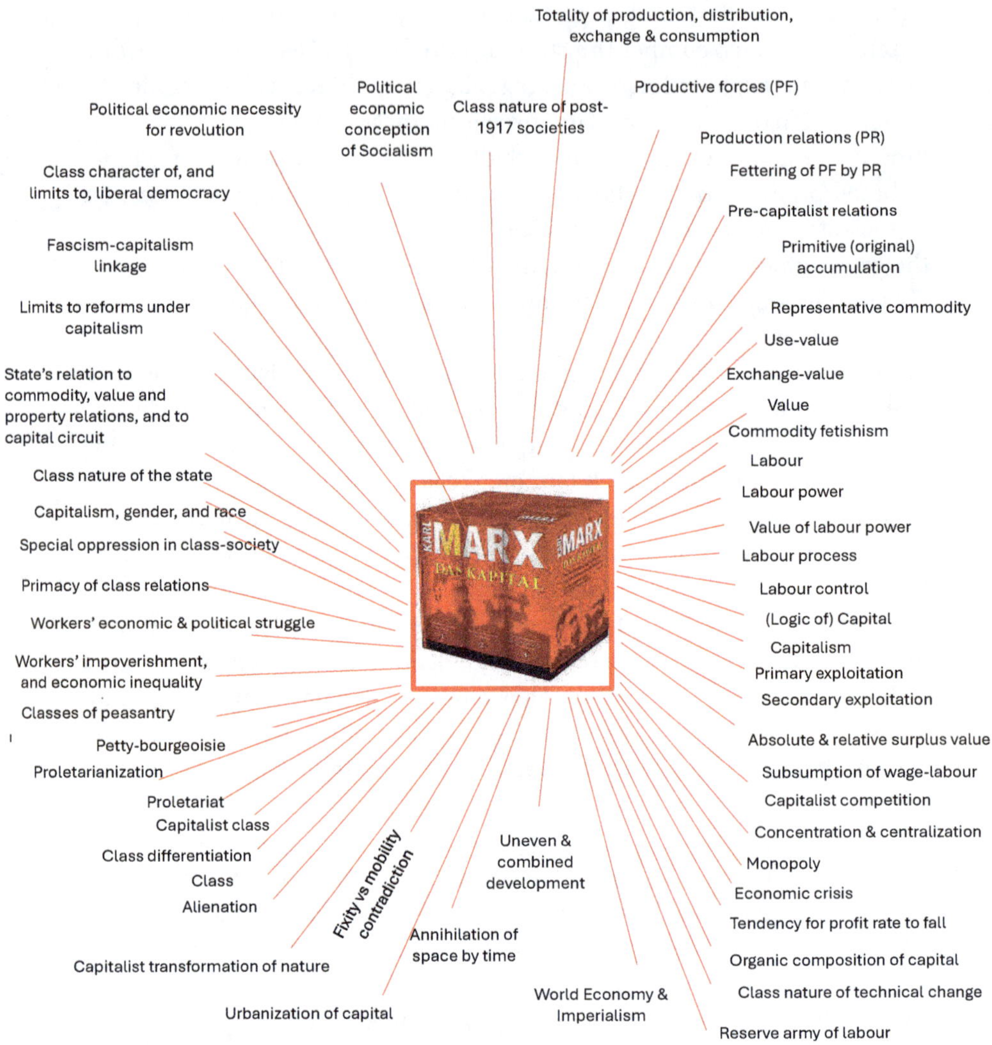

FIGURE 10.1 Selected key concepts in Marxist political economy
SOURCE: ADAPTED FROM DAS (2022D)

2 Political Economy of the Relation between the Economic and the Extra Economic

The economic realm comprises production, distribution, exchange and also consumption, and their reciprocal interrelations. Across all forms of society, production has certain common traits. Production always occurs under certain social relations of production. Relations of production become property relations, which are different in different class societies such as feudalism and capitalism.

Production as a process, *together with* its relations (i.e. class and intra-class relations) and forces, has the ultimate primacy, at least at the level of society as a whole and over a long time period, over other elements of the economic realm and their attendant social relations;[5] of course, these latter elements and their relations shape production and production relations.[6] Means of production and means of subsistence – have to be produced in the first place for them to be distributed/ redistributed, exchanged and consumed. If in a society, different social relations (or social forms) of production coexist, one type generally dominates. Production has a dominant and determinant influence on other moments of economy and on non-economic processes. This is contrary to much of the current political economy.

Marx's view on the dominance of production can be used to correct all those who trace economic crisis to distribution or consumption rather than to the dynamics of production. Marxist political economy rooted in Marx and Lenin can be conceptually put to good use against all those (e.g. David Harvey) who mistakenly over-emphasize modern-day forms of primitive accumulation at the expense of the dynamics of actual production and who indeed appear to analytically *divorce* primitive accumulation from the ways in which production is affected by it. For redistribution of assets to happen, assets have to exist and produced in the first place.

There are political implications of Marx's discussion on the economic realm in his introduction to *Grundrisse*, including the two types of distribution (distribution of means of production and distribution of means of subsistence) and the idea that it cannot be separated from production. Marx points out that bourgeois economists' aim is to present production as distinct from distribution

5 The question of primacy of productive forces over relations does not arise because production always must happen in a framework provided by social relations of production which, because they are unequal and exploitative, are always fraught with possibilities of class struggle. As Lebowitz (1992: 126) says: 'all development of the productive forces occurs within and through a specific set of social relations'. However, while Lebowitz blames this one-sided stress on productive forces in the work of Cohen and others on Marx's *Capital*, which, according to Lebowitz, is characterized by the 'neglect of the worker as subject', I do not think such a conclusion is warranted. As I show in chapters 6–8, there is plenty of advocacy in Marx's *Capital* Volume 1 for the role of human agency and state intervention, including in relation to the development of means of production and enhancement of workers' wellbeing as an aspect of their productive power.

6 The idea that production and its relations dominate other aspects of the economic realm does not mean that it is the technological change as an aspect of production that dominates.

and to regard only distribution relations as historical, but not production relations. According to this mistaken approach, which sees distribution as the distribution not of the means of production but simply as income, or, means of subsistence, production relations in bourgeois society are written in stone and are unchangeable, but a few changes can be made with respect to distribution. For socialism to come, Marxist political economy insists, the distribution of means of production has to drastically change such that one small group does not monopolize the means of production and thus control the labour of another group. A distributive socialism that merely prioritizes the distribution of access to food or shelter (or of money as a medium of exchange) cannot bring socialism. For social*ism* requires the social*ization* in common people's political economic conditions. That is, it requires socialization – democratization – of the means of production, and the ecologically sustainable use of those means of production by the collective of common people with the purpose of meeting their needs rather than prioritizing profit and/or state power at the expense of the common people, the vast majority of humanity.

Conceptions of the producing individual are an important part of a society's extra-economic realm. Marx's idea is that production outside of society – production outside of social relations – is an impossibility. What an individual does or accomplishes is a production is a massive network of social relations. Yet, bourgeois society is justified on the basis of the idea that bourgeois relations protect the sanctity of the individual, which is then connected to the principles of freedom, equality, etc. That the so-called sanctity of the individual is another name for the justification of the individual right to buy and sell for profit or for personal gain is forgotten. It does not care about the fact that such buying and selling, which is a deeply social act, kills millions of individuals in wars or due to the artificial shortage of food, housing, healthcare, etc. (Das, 2018c). Under capitalist reaction, the concept of the isolated individual is being utilized for a political purpose. Right-wing individualism is extended to members of the ruling class. Social problems of poverty etc. are explained in terms of people's alleged laziness or lack of entrepreneurship while capitalists are seen as individuals whose wealth is because of their own hard work and as benefactors to the whole society – as job providers, wealth-creators, etc. An ideological fight against the right-wing movement requires the demolition of this fetishistic concept of the individual.

Not only do production and its relations dominate distribution, exchange and other aspects of the economic realm. Production and its relations also dominate the extra-economic aspects of life: once again, 'mode of production of material life conditions the general process of *social, political, and intellectual life*' (Marx, 1859). For example, art and mythology, which are important parts of the extra-economic realm, more or less, reflect the economic under-development of society. So to make mythology fit the facts of a relatively more developed society is a mistake. The Right-wing does exactly this in these post-truth times (Das, 2023e). Treating mythological stories about deities as true, right-wingers produce a cultural politics of eternity that glorifies the past, a past that has been apparently ruined by outsiders or minorities, etc. Since religion inspires much mythology, one can imagine how beliefs and practices of, say, religious supremacism, can be boosted by treating the religious mythologies of the majority religion group of a multi-religion nation to be true which speak of a golden period of the nation in the past that has been sullied by intruders whose religion happens to differ from that of the majority.

Right-wing people see the relation between art/mythology and economy upside down: they think mythological descriptions of society in the past accurately reflect that society. In mythology, if there were aeroplanes or if babies were born from outside of the womb, then the right-wing thinks that the technology of aeroplanes and invitro fertilization was a reality thousands of years ago. However, to the extent that a nation possesses a mythological literature that is inspiring in the sense Marx understands it – in the sense that it imagines a much better society including a much higher level of economic development than the existing one – this very fact can be a reason for 'national pride' in the Global South context, i.e. in the context where imperialism inferiorizes the level of cultural development in the nations of the South.

3 Political Economy of Class Society

People (or human beings or individuals) should be seen in terms of classes (or class-fractions), and not merely as people or as human beings as such.[7] Of course, in the context of *national* oppression, people may be seen in terms of cultural-geographical aggregate, i.e. nation, which, in turn, are to be seen in terms of the opposed classes (and class-fractions) that constitute the nation. The concept of the nation as *a* people with a loyalty to a territory and with some common cultural traits and history has a progressive character in the imperialized countries of the world, while the same concept of the nation in

7 This is the case although it must be acknowledged that all human beings have certain common interests (e.g. need for food, need for respect, etc.), the common interests that can properly. The fact that all the people, irrespective of their objective class positions, have some common interests or they have certain other common attributes cannot, however, explain the massive social-ecological problems humanity confronts.

imperialist countries can be reactionary. Similarly, within each class, there can be oppression based on non-class relations; as well the ruling classes can make use of non-class oppression to extract more work from the direct producers.

Classes as (large) *groups* of men and women presuppose *relationships* between classes: what one class is it is because of its relation to another class. These relations are objective and antagonistic. Objective conditions that define the lives of classes – labour's needs and capital's needs – do not act on their own. People, as classes and class fractions, constantly engage in struggles (overt or covert) in support of their economic and non-economic interests. There is class struggle from below (i.e. common people's struggle). There is class struggle from above: this is in the form of what capitalists do to the common people, including through their instrumentalist ties to the state and through its own associations (e.g. chambers of commerce and the like).

To take a class approach to political economy is to accept that class relations are historically dynamic. As Lenin's political economy emphasizes, a society based on commodity economy where means of production and subsistence are bought and sold in the market must experience class differentiation, which produces home-market.[8] When petty producers, including peasants, buy inputs and sell outputs, gradually most of them will lose their means of production and become propertyless (or property-poor) wage-workers, while some of them will turn into well-to-do peasantry or proto-capitalists (e.g. rich peasants) or into full-fledged capitalists (e.g. capitalist farmers). The fact that both petty producers and wage workers perform labour does not mean they belong to one class. There is a world of difference between labour by the petty producer which owns means of production and labour performed by the wage worker. To return to Lenin: 'It is not labour that is a definite category of political economy, but only the social form of labour' (Lenin, 1902a).

While the general tendency in societies where capitalism is developing or deepening is towards proletarianization of the vast majority on the basis of class differentiation, small-scale production does continue to exist. Petty producers cannot normally compete with large scale commercial producers which possess engage technical and commercial superiority. To the extent that petty producers continue to exist, they maintain themselves by under-feeing themselves and their families and by working long hours.

8 Lenin's political economy has inspired a large amount of research on class differentiation (e.g. Cousins, 2022; Byres, 2006; Harriss-White, 2022; Zhang, 2015), some of which (e.g. Van der Ploeg, 2018) is critical of aspects of Lenin's theory. Patnaik (2015) argues against the Marxist idea that: 'whenever production is for the market, a process of differentiation among producers, creating conditions for the emergence of capitalism, must necessarily take place.'

The maintenance of petty production does not only represent massive economic suffering. Because of its inefficient nature, it also represents a wastage at the level of society: an immense amount of social labour is wasted owing to the preservation of senseless, backward and scattered small production. As Marx (1887: 539) says: the petty mode of production presupposes the scattering of the means of production, so it is 'compatible only with a system of production, and a society, moving within narrow and more or less primitive bounds'. The solution to the problems created by capitalism is not a society based on everyone being a commodity producer not only because small-scale production represents wastage of social resources but also because commodity production generally will lead to class differentiation among the producers. The Proudhon style thinking is seriously limited. Given the exploitative nature of capitalist property rights defended by the state and given that it defends commodity relations that do result in class differentiation and inequality, it is futile to think about social justice, in the Proudhon style, on the basis of merely 'the juridical relations that correspond to the production of commodities' (Marx, 1887: 64) and on the basis of the idea that 'the production of commodities [by small-scale producers] is a form of production as everlasting as justice' (ibid.).

4 Political Economy of Capitalist Class Society

The capitalist society is a society under the rule of capital (money invested in production and exchange to make more money). The capitalist owns property (means of production) as personal property, but this property is created by numerous members of a society. Therefore, capital as a relationship of power is a social power.

Capitalism develops out of commodity production, and attendant class differentiation (or from extra-economic dispossession of direct producers). Capitalism takes different forms at different points in time and in different countries. Capitalism can be: more or less egalitarian (with some concessions gives to common people) and more or less technologically-economically developed. Capitalism exists in non-monopoly ('competitive') and in monopoly forms.

As a logic of accumulation, capital exists in *different* forms which are united by the *single* drive to invest money to make more money.[9] Trading capital and industrial (or productive) capital are of the same type and they are similar to merchant and usurer capital. Common to the different forms of capital and of

9 This is indicated by Marx's general formula of capital. 'M–C–M' is … in reality the general formula of capital as it appears prima facie within the sphere of circulation' (Marx, 1887: 108).

capitalism is the *differentia specifica* of capital/capitalism: commodity form of wealth, appropriation of surplus value from wage labour and incessant augmentation of capital. It is also the case that the greater the development of merchant's and usurer's capital, the smaller the development of industrial or productive capital (= capitalist production), and the slower the degree of class differentiation among petty producers.[10] While capitalist production shares with pre-capitalist systems of production some traits (private property; exploitation, etc.) and while capitalism exists in different forms, it is wrong to smuggle in bourgeois relations as the inviolable natural laws that apply to all forms of production and all forms of society.

The direct producers under capitalism can vary in terms of their propertylessness. There can be no capitalism without the proletarians, and this is why the use of hired labour is the chief feature of capitalism. Labour is available for hire when the direct producer is separated from the means of production. Yet, it is not absolutely necessary that that capitalism requires 'the free, landless worker'. The latter is the main trend but it is also true that if workers have some resource of their own or form the state to supplement their wage income, that is very often to the interests of the capitalists.

Capitalism as the highest form of commodity-producing society evolves over time. In developing from commodity production, capitalism evolves through manufacture to machine-based large-scale production then to imperialism (world-capitalism). The three main forms of capitalist production differ. They differ in terms of scale and technique of production. During the small commodity-production and manufacture stages, capitalist enterprises are relatively small-scale. The three main forms of capitalist production also differ in their systems of technique. Prior to the introduction of large-scale production, capitalism is generally characterized by near-complete stagnation in technique. Connected to the difference in scale and technique is another difference: the gulf between capitalists and workers gets sharper as

10 'If then we treat this mode of production as one eternally fixed by Nature for every state of society, we necessarily overlook that which is the differentia specifica of the value form, and consequently of the commodity form, and of its further developments, money form, capital form, &c.' (Marx, 1887: 58). Further:

'… the differentia specifica … of capitalistic production' is the appropriation of surplus value. 'Labour power is sold today, not with a view of satisfying, by its service or by its product, the personal needs of the buyer. His aim is augmentation of his capital, production of commodities containing more labour than he pays for, containing therefore a portion of value that costs him nothing, and that is nevertheless realised when the commodities are sold. Production of surplus-value is the absolute law of this mode of production' (Marx, 1887: 434).

capitalism moves from small-scale production through manufacture to large-scale machine-based production.

According to Marxist political economy, economic relations in capitalism are normally based on commodity exchange, even if cheating and fraud do exist. But some political economists emphasize cheating and fraud and coercive power relations at the expense of the exchange of the equivalent for the equivalent. First of all, as Marx says, the entire capitalist class cannot be defrauded. Besides, to explain the profits of the capitalists, one has to assume that labour-power and other commodities are sold at their real value. So, to confine oneself to enumerating the various tricks that capitalists employ and thus to completely brush aside the economic nature of the phenomenon, would be to adopt the viewpoint of vulgar economics, says Lenin. A potential practical implication of this over-emphasis on cheating and fraud in capitalist economy is that a better form of capitalism, one where cheating and fraud do not exist, is possible on the basis of state regulation, community or civil society action from below (e.g. anti-corruption movement), etc.

Marx's and Lenin's political economy is a powerful antidote to the current obsession with what is called 'accumulation of dispossession', which includes the extra-economic ways in which direct producers are divorced from means of production, with some (e.g. Harvey, 2006) saying that accumulation by dispossession is the dominant tendency of capitalism (see Das, 2017c for a critique). Yet, what Marx calls primitive accumulation *is* an on-going process, which coexists with class differentiation by economic means.

Commodity relations have a spatial – scalar – form. When capitalism is prior to large-scale machine-based production, production and exchange are more localized. The scalar-ity increases with the deepening of commodity relations, reaching the highest stage under capitalism. The scale of capitalist production and exchange has increased from the local to the national and the global. At the global scale, capitalism, in fact, originated in a few countries, and then spread. In its very origin, capitalism has been a global phenomenon. Driven by competition, the bourgeoisie is forced to look for a global market. If a country can produce things at a lower price, it can break open the markets of foreign countries.

Capitalist commodity relations give rise of uneven development.[11] The commodity economy leads to class differentiation which itself has a geography, which in turn leads to uneven development of capitalism. By its very anarchic

11 The academic literature examines unevenness of industry, including the spatial division of labour (Massey, 1995; Harvey, 2006; Das, 2017b; 2022d for a critique of some of this literature and for an alternative approach).

or capricious nature, capitalism in agriculture (as in industry) cannot develop evenly. Another reason is the fact that different localities in a country are differentially connected to the national and global markets. Capitalist uneven development occurs across nations, and inside nations, including between cities and villages. Inside nations, the different types of urban or urbanizing areas are actively produced by capital in its search of cheap labour: industrial towns; the suburbs; factory villages; and handicraft villages, etc.

Uneven development of capitalism is not only geographical. It is also temporal: this is the fact that periods of prosperity of a nation alternate with periods of crisis; the development of one branch of production leads to the decline of another.

Marx says, relations existing in earlier forms of society (e.g. communal property) will often be found within the bourgeois society only in an entirely stunted form. Marx here anticipates Trotsky's (1930) idea that development is both uneven and combined: the past relations coexist and interact with present relations within a social formation that is dominantly capitalist. Modern technology borrowed by a less developed country from an advanced country is well adapted and developed in a backward economy, or it can be stunted or caricatured. We may recall Trotsky's point that:

> Unevenness, the most general law of the historic process, reveals itself most sharply and complexly in the destiny of the backward countries. Under the whip of external necessity their backward culture is compelled to make leaps. From the universal law of unevenness thus derives another law which …, we may call the law of *combined development* – by which we mean a drawing together of the different stages of the journey, a combining of the separate steps, an amalgam of archaic with more contemporary forms. (Trotsky, 1930)

Capitalism connects rural areas to urban areas by the transplantation of largescale industry to the rural areas. Thus ruralization and urbanization of capital coexist. This potentially creates urban regions: a big city and its surrounding rural and semi-rural areas. The more extensive development of commerce brings rural areas into close interaction with the cities and weakens rural markets. Capitalism thus expands urban population at the expense of the agricultural population.

Uneven development in turn gives rise to, and is shaped by, mobility of both capital and common people. This happens within countries. Uneven development also gives rise to, and is shaped by, migration from poorer countries to more developed ones. Migration produces economic advantages for workers.

It raises the wages the wage-workers migrants, relative to their wages in the origin places, but also of those who stay behind in origin areas.

5 Political Economy of Imperialism as the Highest Stage of Capitalism

Capitalism at its highest stage develops into imperialism which promotes wars, war-mongering and reaction (authoritarianism) and subordination-exploitation of the Global South by imperialist nations. Modern-day imperialism is based not only in capitalist production and exchange but also in 'monopoly capitalism', representing the merging of bank capital with industrial capital. These structural features of imperialism produce certain consequences. The first three of these include:

> The fact that imperialism is parasitic or decaying capitalism is manifested first of all in the tendency to decay ... Secondly, the decay of capitalism is manifested in the creation of a huge stratum of rentiers, capitalists who live by "clipping coupons". Thirdly, export of capital is parasitism [of imperialist nations] raised to a high pitch.

There are two other consequences of the operation of the structure of relations that constitute imperialism. One is the exploitation of poorer nations, including those that have nominal political sovereignty, by a handful of "Great" Powers, through the appropriation of super-profits from less developed nations on the basis of the export of capital to these nations.[12] Under imperialism, class exploitation and national exploitation thus co-exist.

12 In part inspired by Lenin (and also by Marini, 2022), there has been much discussion on imperialism and super-exploitation (the latter is when wages fall below the value of labour power). According to Smith (2016), the whole imperialist system has increasingly come to depend on the 'super exploitation' of impoverished workers in the 'developing world' where more than 80% of manufacturing workers live in the 21st century, the super-exploitation that exists not because of low labour productivity but because of *'wage differences [that] are significantly affected by coercive suppression of labor mobility' due to restrictions imposed on it and also because of* authoritarian regimes in the South (p. 240). Apart from the methods of appropriation of surplus value in its absolute and relative forms, it is the '[r]eduction in the value of labour power by suppressing consumption levels (or what amounts to the same thing, shifting production to countries where workers' consumption levels and the value of labour power is much lower) is a distinct, third way to increase surplus value, and it has attained incredible importance during the neoliberal era, the driving force of its greatest transformation' (Smith, 2018). While 'every

To remain competitive in the world economy, imperialist countries exploit and subjugate the less developed nations, including their 'cheaper' land and natural resources. And such exploitation is helped by the support of middle class people in advanced countries, including trade union leaders who are bribed by capital. The decaying nature of global capitalism combined with the exploitation of the poorer nations by the imperialist nations relates to the topic of fettering (explained below).

The other consequence of imperialism is reaction, which is the opposite of democracy, domestically and globally. Reaction is expressed in the form of authoritarianism and militarism. One reason is that finance capital driving imperialism strives for domination. In the process, corruption, bribery and fraud are resorted to.

While imperialism, as *the highest stage of capitalism*, is associated with annexation and militarism, it is wrong to see – as Kautsky does – imperialism *merely* as a government policy, including annexation or militarism, and it is wrong to reduce imperialism to one state bullying another. There are fundamental economic features of imperialism which condition and lead to political domination aspects.[13] Imperialism, as the highest stage of capitalism, involves

---

capitalist dreams of becoming a monopolist', this remains only a dream for capitalists in less developed countries so 'they have no choice but to rely exclusively on the extraction of surplus value from their own workers by super-exploiting them up to and beyond the limits – or rather, to rely on what's left to them after monopolists and imperialists have taken their share' (ibid.).

While Smith's idea that the exploitation of the workers of the South is less through an expansion of absolute and relative surplus value and more through super-exploitation, and that super-exploitation is the dominant feature of imperialism (Roberts, 2016b; Burns, 2024) is problematic, the fact of super-exploitation in the South cannot be denied. Besides, super-exploitation is not just in the South. It is in the imperialist heartland too: 'Zero-hour' contracts, where workers are at the beck and call of employers at all hours for minimal pay, now affects two million workers in Britain.' (Roberts, 2016b).

According to Roberts (2024), 'roughly 5–10% of G7 workers are being "super-exploited", while in the BRICS it's about 25–30%. But that still means that 70% of workers in the BRICS, while earning way less per day than G7 workers, are not earning below the value of their labour power on a national basis. Exploitation of workers in the Global South is huge, but super-exploitation as such is not the main cause'.

On other works on super-exploitation, see Higginbottom (2023); Katz and Fidler (2018); Latimer (2021); Osorio and Reyes (2024); Valencia and Felix (2022). On the topic of how migration of people from the less developed world to the developed world is part of super-exploitation of the less developed world by imperialist monopoly capital, see Pröbsting (2015).

13 Imperialism has specific economic features. Carchedi and Roberts define imperialism 'as *the persistent and long-term net appropriation of surplus value by the high-technology advanced capitalist countries transferred from the low-technology dominated countries*'

the exploitation of the imperialized world (the countries of the South with weak military powers), and especially, their workers and petty producers, by the monopolies of advanced nations supported by their states, a process that is mediated by competition among monopolies of advanced nations. The tendency of capitalism to draw non-capitalist countries into the whirlpool of capitalist world economy explains, among other things, the aggressive attitude of the imperialist nations – the largest imperialist power (the US) and its allies – towards the former USSR. It also explains such aggressive attitude of imperialist nations today towards the dominantly non-capitalist China and towards Russia which has inherited a massive military infrastructure as well as large territory rich in natural resources from the USSR. When these countries as the targets of imperialism fight back to protect their national interests, they are often called 'imperialist' or autocratic, etc.

In this context it should be said that it is wrong to see countries such as Russia and China as imperialist, as some do. To be imperialist, a country must be economically developed capitalist countries dominated by big monopolies. 'Even the poorest imperialist state, Spain (income [in GDP per capita] $25,555), earns nearly *double* the top-earning Third World state Argentina ($13,432) and Chile ($13,416) and *three times* Mexico, Brazil and China, Russia and Turkey's (King, 2014). Then, to be imperialist, a country must be dominated by big monopolies. The less developed countries, including Russia and China, account for about 85% of the global population but just 21% of listed companies. The overwhelming majority of these firms in the South are domestically oriented financial companies or those that deal in natural resources such as oil or in utilities. Consider Russia. '"The Russia[n] economy remains dependent on oil and gas that make up more than half its exports before the war started".

---

through four mechanisms: 'currency seigniorage; income flows from capital investments; unequal exchange through trade; and changes in exchange rates' (Roberts, 2024; italics in original).

The greater use of technology and thus higher labour productivity in imperialist countries enable them 'to sell their goods in world markets at costs below the international average'. The capitalists in the less developed world try to compensate for their lower technical level and productivity by paying low wages thus increasing the rate of exploitation. 'So the higher rate of exploitation in the South, whether by super-exploitation or not, is a reaction to the failure to compete against the North.' (Roberts, 2019).

There *are* political aspects imperialist domination of the majority of world i.e. in particular, military power and political control of international institutions (UN, IMF, World Bank etc.) (Roberts, 2024). The economic power between imperialist and imperialized nations 'is *determinant* [or, determining] because it is the condition of existence of the military and ideological power and the latter is *determined* because it is the condition of reproduction (or supersession) of the former' (Carchedi and Roberts, 2021).

Other Russian companies deal in grain, chemicals and metals' and they do not export advanced technology earning super profits. 'That means that far from extracting surplus value [profit] through trade with other countries, instead, the more advanced capitalist economies and their multi-nationals get net transfers of surplus value from Russia'. The leaders of a relatively less developed country such as Russia may think their country is an imperialist power, but 'the economic reality is that Russia is just a large peripheral economy outside the US-led imperialist bloc like Brazil, China, India, South Africa, Turkey, Egypt etc. – if with a larger military than most' (Roberts, 2022).

Lenin's claim about imperialism and struggle for control over land and raw materials is extremely relevant to our world. Consider the imperialist nations' attempt to control the supply of critical minerals including those needed for the green industry, the minerals in the production of which many non-imperialist nations such as Russia and China play a leading role. Politically 'independent' nations can be subjected to imperialism via 'economic annexation'. Consider what is done by the imperialist institutions such as World Bank and IMF to the South (i.e. imposition of neoliberal policies, including privatization of state-owned enterprises) and the regime of economic sanctions against many nations of the South. Imperialist attacks in their economic, political/military, etc. forms, are prompting anti-imperialism in many parts of the world. The struggle against capitalism will not succeed unless it is also a struggle against imperialism. The struggle against imperialism will not succeed unless it is also a struggle against capitalism. And, the struggle against capitalism and capitalist imperialism will not succeed unless workers leading the petty producers are united across the imperialist and imperialized nations.[14]

6 Political Economy of the Progressive and Dark Sides of Capitalism/Imperialism

6.1 *Capitalism's Progressive Tendencies*

Capitalism is a progressive society relative to pre-capitalist systems because it develops the productive forces. It is also progressive because it creates objective and subjective conditions for a future society that is superior to capitalism.

14 Such struggle must include the struggle against its imperialist institutions such as the World Bank, etc. The right to self-determination today partly means the liberation from the control of these institutions.

Marxist political economy's conceptualization of global capitalism as imperialism points to 'the fundamental importance of building a real solidarity between class struggles in imperialist countries and anti-colonial resistance in colonised and dependent countries' (Pradella, 2023).

The progressive character of capitalism lies in the fact that large-scale capitalist industry promotes socialization of production (although under the shell of private property). Socialization in capitalism includes: development of close commercial ties with various parts of the country and with different countries, with people in one country/region consuming articles of final consumption or making use of means of production drawn from other countries/regions; enormous technical progress due to the revolutionization of means of production; concentration of production and of the population in enormously large enterprises where thousands of men and women work together; both technical changes and large-scale production having resulted in a rise in labour productivity; enhanced degree of control over nature and over adverse natural conditions; and so on.

With these progressive material changes come cultural changes, including the transformation of the sentiments and mental conceptions of the people. Capitalism requires and increases literacy among people, heightens their understanding of the world, and gives them 'civilised habits and requirements' as reflected in the improvement of the worker's standard of requirements. It increases the population's need for association'. Based in science and modern technologies, capitalism has resulted in the weakening, and in some cases, demolition, of the worn-out traditions of patriarchal life and of pre-capitalist prejudices and irrational ideas. Large-scale machine-based capitalist production has resulted in the employment of women and has thus weakened 'personal dependence and patriarchalism in relationships', including of women on men. Large-scale industry and uneven development have caused mobility of common people inside countries and across countries, which in turn allows inter-mingling of people.

Capitalism has produced a general universalization of human interaction, both socially and spatially. It destroys the age-old isolation and seclusion of systems of economy (and, consequently, the narrowness of intellectual and political life). It links all countries of the world and all sub-national regions of a country (at least the developed ones) into a single economic whole as they exchange their products within the world market. Countries and regions are thus increasingly integrated, a process helped by improvements in the means of communication across countries. In fact, imperialism, globally integrated socialization of production under capitalism at a high level of technologically developed stage represents – creates opportunities for – the transition to socialism.

Under capitalism, humanity's history is increasingly world history, not just materially but also culturally. The intellectual creations of individual nations become common property of the multi-national global humanity and take the form of such things as world literature, world science, world political economy, etc. By promoting universalization in the sense just discussed, the capitalist system not only creates conditions for socialist *struggle* but also becomes an objective step towards socialist society which can only exist as *world socialism*. Further, capitalism is a progressive social form because it brings into being its grave digger – the world working class – the greatest anti-capitalist subjective factor. Capitalism simplifies class structure by increasingly splitting the society into two great classes (big capital and the proletariat).[15] So it brings into being a class (the proletariat) which can emancipate itself and in the process emancipate all other oppressed classes and which can politically lead the non-proletarian suffering masses in its revolution against capitalism. This is why the proletarians are a special class (Llorente, 2013).

Recognition of capitalism's progressiveness relative to pre-capitalist systems means that in societies with pre-capitalist relations the latter have to be destroyed. However, this can only happen under the leadership of the proletariat because for political reasons capitalists can enter into agreements with reactionary pre-capitalist relations.

6.2 *Dark Sides of Capitalism and Fettering of Productive Forces*

Recognition of capitalism's progressive nature does not mean that this progressive nature is evenly present in time- and space. Marxist political economy explores the *dialectical* relation between productive forces and production relations. Social relations of production do *fetter* the development of productive forces. This is true about capitalism as it was true about previous class societies.

For us to better understand this insightful thesis of Marx, we have to go beyond Marx's schematic remarks as well as beyond some of its modern-day interpretations. Social relations of capitalist production fetter the development

15 Of course, that does not mean that the proletariat is a homogenous class. The proletarians are divided along lines of gender, age, race and nationality, etc. (which means that the proletarians experiencing special oppression may be over-exploited). They are also divided on the basis of income, education, skill level, 'social capital', location (rural vs urban), economic sector, exposure to adverse physical/natural conditions in the workplace, and so on. They are also divided in terms of their class consciousness. Many simply accept trade unionism rather than the agenda of the abolition of capitalism. Large sections of the proletariat are vulnerable to being bribed by the ruling class. In *Manifesto*, Marx says: the conditions of life of lumpenproletariat, 'that passively rotting mass', the lowest sediment of the reserve army, prepare it 'for the part of a bribed tool of reactionary intrigue'. Lenin says that a section of the working class in imperialist nations is bribed into supporting imperialism. Thus some (e.g. labour aristocracy) may be subjected to 'under-exploitation' to a degree, while others (workers in the less developed world) may be subjected to 'over-exploitation'.

of productive powers of nature by failing to improve it: that is, by failing to bequeath the natural conditions of production 'in an *improved* condition to succeeding generations' (Marx, 1894: 567; italics added). Social relations of capitalist production also fetter the productive powers of direct producers (workers who sell their labour power, and petty producers who sell products of their labour) not only by fettering the development of means of production (this happens, for example, during crises) but also by failing to meet the need of direct producers for means of subsistence without which they cannot possess and use their productive abilities. In capitalism workers are treated to some extent as means of production (as coal); workers are also treated as those who must be fed and housed well in order for them to continue to produce value and surplus value. This points to the fact that workers' needs under capitalism are not seen as needs that exist irrespective of whether they produce for capitalists. This fact is inherent to the logic of capitalism production and can only be transcended under communism where people contribute to according to their abilities and their needs, which vary from one person to another, are met.

The concept of fettering indeed draws attention to a vision of socialist society. Fettering is relative not only when the actual output of a society is less than it is thought to be, because of the costs for planet and people. It is also relative because the net output is less than what it would be under socialist relations where nature and labour, the two co-producers of wealth, will not be sapped the way they are now. And, nature and labour will not be sapped because common people will have control over production which they lack now. A socially just and ecologically sustainable development of productive forces in the collective interest of common people will be possible. Labour and nature will not be under the law of value which measures society's wealth in terms of socially necessary abstract labour time as the source of value and surplus value, and not in terms of whether wealth meets people's needs. So there will be no need for relations between things to replace the relations between producers. The slight reformulation of the concept of productive forces proposed chapter 5 sees workers as productive human beings with social-ecological needs which must be met for their productive powers to be maintained and developed. So, workers are not just class actors in pursuit of class justice. They are also ecological actors in pursuit of sustainable development.

Capitalist relations fetter the development of productive forces in the same process in which these relations also develop these forces. The mechanisms of fettering include: private ownership and control over means of production; monopolization; tendency towards the organic composition of capital to rise faster than the rate of exploitation; mutilation of the worker in the labour process; lack of control over production and distribution on the part of direct producers; non-satisfaction of direct producers' needs without which their productive abilities cannot exist; incessant pursuit of profit at the cost of the planet and people, and so on.[16] Imperialism as the highest stage of capitalism also fetters the development of productive forces, especially, in the Global South: surplus transfer from the imperialized nations fetters their productive forces; wars prompted by imperialism – wars over minerals, strategic location, markets, etc. – destroy a massive amount of resources, the resources that could have been used to, say, fight climate change and to build physical infrastructure or to provide healthcare and education, all of which would develop/improve productive powers of people. Imperialism also fetters the development of productive forces in the imperialist countries:

> [T]he deepest economic foundation of imperialism is monopoly. … [L]ike all monopoly, it inevitably engenders a tendency of stagnation and decay. Since monopoly prices are established, even temporarily, the motive cause of technical and, consequently, of all other progress disappears to a certain extent and, further, the economic possibility arises of deliberately retarding technical progress. (Lenin, 1916a)

Imperialism may also fetter the development of productive forces in the imperialist countries by converting many big businesses into coupon clippers: if big monopoly capitalists can make a lot of profit merely through the payment of interests and dividends, etc. from the less developed world, this may adversely affect the pressure for systemic technological change in the imperialist countries.

We must note that a major problem with Marx's and Lenin's political economy is that it says little about how capitalism at the national scale in the South is itself a barrier to the development of productive forces. For example, given the massive presence of a reserve army of labour in part created by class differentiation of petty producers that he has so eloquently explained, capitalists can resort to the formal subsumption of labour, a mode of accumulation based on longer working days rather than switch to real subsumption of labour which is associated with economic development based on technological changes, and this is especially the case in rural and semi-rural areas. Marx and Lenin often assume that once there are commodity relations and wage

16 On Lenin's elaboration of the development and limits of capitalism, including the contradictions of monopoly capital, see Buzgalin (2020). On the development of monopolies and their fettering of productive forces (see Mandel, 1999, and Baran and Sweezy, 1966).

labour, capitalism will automatically become developed capitalism based on systemic technical changes.

It is futile to expect capitalism to develop productive forces including abilities of common people anymore. Capitalism is in terminal decline.[17] The crisis of livelihood in a massively unequal world, climate change and threat of endless wars mainly caused by imperialism mean that capitalism is beyond its shelf-life – it cannot but fetter the development of productive forces more than it develops these forces. Some of the productive forces it creates it destroys them through periodic crisis, climate crisis and endless destructive wars.

Some of the discussion in current political economy, including on the relations between productive forces and relations, has veered towards anti-production and towards 'degrowth type' claims in the context of the climate change. One scholar has recently said: 'a genuinely progressive change in social relations requires a prior transformation in the nature of the productive forces, including a reduction in their scale, speed of operation, and complexity. As the environmental crisis worsens, people may be more willing to accept lower levels of production and consumption in exchange for a fairer society, as well as a slower, more precious, and more sustainable quality of life. Marx's theory of fettering may support this new sensibility, but only if its productivist assumptions are cast aside and a more nuanced version of the concept is embraced' (Bowring, 2011: 153). Prabhat Patnaik, a Marxist from India says: 'The historical obsolescence of capitalism, no matter what the case might have been with earlier modes of production, has to be assessed not with reference to its capacity to develop the productive forces, but with reference to the desire for human freedom and the awareness on the part of society that freedom is unachievable under this system'. This implies that socialism cannot be justified, at least partly, on the ground that it will unfetter the development of productive forces. The editor of a new translation of *Capital* volume 1 has also said that Marx's advocacy for greater development of productive forces in socialism cannot be accepted given the current ecological disasters.

These anti-production views conflate production with its social form, with capitalist form of production. Productive forces can grow in a manner that is ecologically and bodily healthy if the social relations of profit-motive and the private control over the means of production and their use are removed. But production for the sake production – increase in production at the cost of the planet and the people – will not be allowed in socialism. In fact, increase in

17 'When the reproduction of capital becomes a barrier to the further development of the productive powers of social labour, capitalism loses the last remnants of its claim to a progressive historical role' (Clarke, 1990–1991: 465).

production at the expense of the planet and the direct producers constitutes a case of fettering productive forces and not their development.

Many scholars say that in advanced capitalist countries, a large number of people are not emotionally happy and that Marxism mistakenly shares with bourgeois thinking a commitment to the need for greater level of economic development. This sort of anti-development view conflates development with its capitalist form of production. Marxist political economy would respond by saying that: economic development (i.e. the development of the forces of production expressed in rising labour productivity and increasing availability of a variety of things that people need to meet their needs) is necessary for emotional happiness but the relations of production under which capitalist economic development occurs make people less happy than they otherwise would be. The development of productive forces in socialism will contribute to happiness to a greater extent than in capitalism because a) the *level* and *pace* of economic development will be greater with the fetters of capitalist relations being removed (consequent to the overthrow of capitalism), and b) productive forces now will occur under the new relations of production which will have two qualities. One is that these will be the relations of solidarity, cooperation and non-alienation that are conducive to greater happiness. Another is that these relations of production will make possible conscious, mindful planning of the use of resources relative to people's material and emotional (including secular-spiritual) needs, something that is not possible in capitalist anarchy.

There are reasons why capitalism is inferior to socialism, from the standpoint of fettering of productive forces by production relations. Capitalism may develop productive powers better than socialism but if socialism makes better use of existing powers, then socialism may be preferable (Cohen, 2000). Social change can happen because of the gap between what could be achieved now and what is being achieved rather than because of the gap between how fast capacity is improving and how fast it could be improved (Cohen, 2000: 330). Instead of GNP, or some such measure of aggregate output, if we use standard of living (which is a composite index of income and health, educational etc. status and happiness levels) that a set of productive forces is utilized to produce, socialism is enduringly superior because it offers a better way of life, says Cohen. But as argued in chapter 5, the non-enhancement of the standard of living is itself indicative of fettering of productive powers of labour by capitalist relations. And, in reality, socialism may develop productive forces more rapidly, because the capitalist relations of production that fetter the development of productive forces in pre-socialist societies will cease to exist.[18]

18 There is no basis for the argument that 'state property (which "belongs to everyone and to no one") is the socialist fetter; it is contrary to the requirement of adequate incentives, the

Contrary to those who argue that socialist relations of the former USSR fettered productive forces and resulted in the transition to capitalism, the following must be said: the 1917 revolution created a condition for a massive development of productive forces in a technologically backward and peasant-dominated society and that if the socialist transition was not successful it was because the relations of capitalist law of value at the global scale along with the power of the imperialist states and the attendant arms race, acted as a fetter on the development of productive forces in that society and that the isolation of the transitional society from the advanced centers of the world economy led to bureaucratization of postrevolution social relations of production which did fetter the development of productive forces.

> The continuing privations of the masses in the USSR, the omnipotence of the privileged caste, which has lifted itself above the nation and its misery, finally, the rampant club-law of the bureaucrats are not consequences of the socialist method of economy but of the isolation and backwardness of the USSR caught in the ring of capitalist encirclement. (Trotsky, 1939)

The direct intervention of the masses would have been 'able to sweep away the reactionary obstructions and lay the foundations of a new regime'. 'Abolition of private ownership in the means of production is the first prerequisite to planned economy, i.e., the introduction of reason into the sphere of human relations, first on a national and eventually on a world scale. Once it begins, the socialist revolution will spread from country to country, with immeasurably greater force than fascism spreads today. By the example and with the aid of the advanced nations, the backward nations will also be carried away into the main stream of socialism. The thoroughly rotted customs toll-gates will fall.' (Trotsky, 1939). This did not happen because of the capitalist relations of production in developed, imperialist societies.

Fettering of productive forces by production relations does not guarantee the replacement of existing relations with new ones, contrary to what Marx (or others) might have thought.

> to save society, it is not necessary either to check the development of technique, to shut down factories, to award premiums to farmers for sabotaging agriculture, to turn a third of the workers into paupers, or to call upon maniacs to be dictators. Not one of these measures, which are a shocking mockery of the interests of society, are necessary. (Trotsky, 1939)

---

disposition for innovation and risk-taking and the necessity for personal responsibility on the part of decisionmakers.' (Lebowitz, 1991: 358).

What is necessary is to end the 'The bourgeois mode of production [which] is the last antagonistic form of the social process of production', as Marx (1859) says in his famous Preface. Or, as Trotsky says:

> What is indispensable and urgent is to separate the means of production from their present parasitic owners and to organise society in accordance with a rational plan. Then it would at once be possible really to cure society of its ills. All those able to work would find a job. The work-day would gradually decrease. The wants of all members of society would secure increasing satisfaction. The words "property," "crisis," "exploitation," would drop out of circulation. Mankind would at last cross the threshold into true humanity. (Trotsky, 1939)

Organized class struggle is necessary for ending capitalism, to 'separate the means of production from their present parasitic owners and to organise society in accordance with a rational plan' (ibid.). Mere fettering of productive forces will not end capitalism, irrespective of whatever Marx might have thought in his famous 1859 sketch of political economy. Economic contradictions between forces and relations of production do not automatically lead to revolution nor can the latter happen without those contradictions.

When there is an ongoing unresolved economic crisis because of fettering, the ruling class cannot live – cannot exist – in the way it has. It fails to appropriate surplus value at the usual rate (with the rate of profit falling, the mass of profit tends to fall). On the other hand, given the economic crisis, the exploited masses continue to suffer, and a point comes when they feel they cannot continue to live their miserable life any more. A crisis of profit for the ruling class and a crisis of livelihood for the masses come to coexist. Yet, economic crisis on its own because of fettering of productive forces will not result in the revolution against capitalist class relation, while it is true that it is relative use fettering, more than relative development fettering, that is more conductive to revolutionary change.[19] Class struggle has to be combined with economic crisis to produce revolution, as we will see below.

If capitalism is not overthrown, it is not because it promotes productive forces either in the narrow traditional sense or in the broad sense understood here (that is, capitalism saps the productive powers of labour and stops

19 As we have seen, 'since the discrepancy between capacity and use is more perceptible than, and is, therefore, a more potent stimulant of unrest, protest, and change than, the shortfall in rate of development implied by Relative Development Fettering' (Cohen, 2000: 331).

improvements in nature). Consider the inference (noted earlier) drawn by Cohen (2000) that capitalism 'persists because and as long as it is optimal for further development of productive power' (p. 358). Capitalism can continue even if it does not optimally develop productive forces of people and nature. Capitalism may persist because of various obstacles to people's struggle, including the fact that the very process of capitalist production reproduces workers who view the necessity of capital as self-evident (Bowring, 2011: 149–150) because of the treacherous role played by the leaders of many large unions.

Capitalism's adverse impacts are not confined to the economic realm. There are profound, all-round, inherent social contradictions in the political and cultural spheres (e.g. the fact that while capitalism promotes scientific attitude it also makes use of irrational beliefs and lies). In developed countries such as those in Europe, capital fears the growth and increasing strength of the proletariat, as both Marx and Lenin say. So, it supports everything backward, moribund and medieval and can go to any length of brutality and crime to uphold the dying capitalism. This tendency to fear the proletariat and therefore to turn to reaction also in evidence in less developed nations.

Other adverse cultural impacts of capitalism include the fact that it has, more or less, reduced the nexus between people to naked self-interest and cash payment and has weakened solidarity and reciprocity among people that were rooted in a society where the commodity form of wealth was not dominant. Capitalism has reduced personal worth into how much one earns (exchange value), as Marx and Engels say in the *Manifesto*. The capitalist relations have impacted the family too, which used to be a part of extra-economic realm, one that is beyond the considerations of cash nexus. The family is increasingly stripped off its sentimental veil and has been reduced to a mere money relation. By fetishizing the cash nexus, the capitalist system has produced an impoverished view of human beings: if one fails to make money by investing money, one is not (much of) an individual, while if one has money, one can do many things that one's individuality does not allow one to.[20] By

20 'The extent of the power of money is the extent of my power. Money's properties are my – the possessor's – properties and essential powers. Thus, what I am and am capable of is by no means determined by my individuality. ...

I, according to my individual characteristics, am lame, but money furnishes me with twenty-four feet. Therefore I am not lame.

I am bad, dishonest, unscrupulous, stupid; but money is honoured, and hence its possessor. Money is the supreme good, therefore its possessor is good. Money, besides, saves me the trouble of being dishonest: I am therefore presumed honest. I am brainless, but money is the real brain of all things and how then should its possessor be brainless? ...

producing adverse cultural impacts, capitalism is driving people towards a conception of society where the cash nexus and self interest do not trump the greater values of humanity, the values of love and solidarity. If capitalism is promoting unceasing commodification in everyday life, then people's demand must be for de-commodification and therefore reduction in the importance of the cash nexus.

Marx's and Lenin's analysis of the cultural impacts of capitalism, including emotional impacts, can be expanded but it is not necessary to advocate for a shift *from* political economy to a cultural economy or to an 'emotional economy' approach. Capitalism *is* producing emotional impacts (people are becoming anxious about, and angry with, their living and working conditions) and recent literature discusses this.[21] But what is under-emphasized is that emotions have a *class* aspect. This is evident from, for example, Lenin's work, especially in his political writings.[22] The anger/hatred of the exploiting class and that of the exploited class are *different*. As an example of ruling class emotions, consider this: 'During the lifetime of great revolutionaries, the oppressing classes constantly hounded them, received their theories with … the most furious hatred' (Lenin, 1949: 7). 'Marx earned the honour of incurring the hatred of these disreputable persons [leaders of the labour aristocracy] by openly branding them as traitors' (1920b: 42). The capitalist class people, 'in their hatred for socialism', try to advocate for mere trade union struggle, the struggle for small concessions only, in order to prevent workers from fighting for socialism (Lenin, 1902b: 21). Lenin talks about the anger of the exploited people in the following way. 'The unprecedented horrors and miseries of the protracted war are making the people's position unbearable and increasing their anger.' (Lenin, 1949: 4). He talks about the 'noble and working class hatred for the bourgeois "class politicians"', … a hatred understood and shared, however, not only by proletarians but by all working people …' (Lenin, 1920b: 80). 'In

---

Do not I, who thanks to money am capable of all that the human heart longs for, possess all human capacities? Does not my money, therefore, transform all my incapacities into their contrary?' (Marx, 1844; for a recent commentary on the power of money, see Das, 2020b).

21 Emotions such as pride, patriotism, fear, helplessness and alienation (the feeling of isolation from the community, including those experienced by the lumpen proletariat without any experience of regular wage work) are used by politicians of bourgeois reaction (see Ahmad, 2013). Capitalism makes use of affective aspects of labour power to exploit labour (Hardt and Negri, 2004). Capitalism commodifies romance and personal happiness, shaping emotional life according to the market logic (Illouz, 2018; see Das, 2023e). On the emotional aspects of capitalism, see also Konings (2015).

22 These include: *The State and Revolution*, *What is to be done?*, and *Leftwing communism: an infantile disorder*.

a representative of the oppressed and exploited masses, this hatred is truly the "beginning of all wisdom", the basis of any socialist and communist movement and of its success' (Lenin, 1920b: 80). Lenin directly points to the usefulness of the anger of the exploited class as a part of its class consciousness: there is a need to 'criticise the bourgeoisie, arouse hatred of the bourgeoisie among the masses, and foster class-consciousness and the ability to unite their forces' (Lenin, 1920b: 290). As Thompson (1963) noted, emotions like anger, solidarity, and resentment are central to the dynamics of class struggle in Marxist theory. But there is hardly any need for a *shift* from political economy, a shift indicated by, for example, the analytical Marxist, Elster (2018).

7 Political Economy of the Capitalist State

The bourgeoisie is not just in control of the economic and cultural conditions of society. It also controls politics and the state. The capitalist class has geographically 'agglomerated population, centralised the means of production, and has concentrated property in a few hands' (p. 17). The necessary consequence of this economic process of centralization is 'political centralisation'. As *Manifesto* famously claims: 'The executive of the modern state is but a committee for managing the common affairs of the whole bourgeoisie'. Implicit in the above claim is the idea that the state, over the long run, looks after the common affairs of the class of capitalists (at the expense of those of the masses).[23] Also implicit is the idea that to meet the common affairs, the state may need a degree of independence vis a vis individual competing capitalists, including capitalists of different regions and sectors.[24]

7.1 *Commodity, Value and Property Relations and the State*

State power – both in terms of what the state does and what it does not – is very much implicit in Marx's analysis of the commodity character of capitalism. The state sustains property, commodity and value relations in various ways. Firstly, the state, the sphere of extra-economic coercion, makes sure that commodity exchange can freely happen, that is, that one parts with what truly

23 Consider how the state dealt with the 2008 economic crisis (it basically bailed out the capitalist class) as opposed to how the state dealt with the Covid crisis that was allowed by the state to kill millions.

24 These ideas about the state, including the state as an 'agent' of the capitalist class, are defended in Das (2022b), where the state and the capitalist class are conceptualized as two arms of the body of capitalist class relationship.

belongs to one, that there is therefore no cheating or extra-economic coercion in the sphere of economic exchange, and that commodity exchange happens on the basis of the principle of 'the equivalent for the equivalent'. The state also affects the ways in which commodity exchange happens (e.g. investment in science which affects value; contribution to wages falling below the value of labour power, through the provision of de-commodified services). Secondly, it tends to take steps to stop the violation of the law of commodity exchange. Thirdly, in certain cases, it itself enforces unequal exchange (or it tolerates or encourages unequal exchange on the part of commodity producers), when it is necessary in the immediate interest of capitalist class as a whole, or in the interest of a hegemonic fraction of that class, or when the long-term interest of capitalist society is at stake. Colonialism/imperialism is an expression of this tendency.

Partly given that capital does not need the state's extra-economic force to make people go to work, the capitalist state, with its relative autonomy, is able to protect and promote a degree of freedom and equality: according to the state, all commodity owners are equal and that workers are free to work for whoever they wish to. Whether the owner of labour power or of any other commodity, everyone is a commodity owner and seller. In addition, all are regarded as equal before the law irrespective of what commodity – or how much of it – each owns. It is precisely by means of this neutrality of the state towards all commodity owners that it secures legitimacy and it secures 'the foundations of capitalist relations of domination and exploitation' (Heinrich, 2004: 205).

Yet one cannot fetishize equality and freedom in the sphere of capitalist exchange that the state protects. But this is exactly what most of the public and most of the scholars do: prompted by the surface appearances of free exchange, they fetishize the idea that there is freedom and equality and that there is respect for private property (private property is sacrosanct), even if millions of workers experience unfreedom in the labour market and even if millions of small-scale producers lose their property through commodity exchange every year in major capitalist countries.

The equality and freedom that the capitalist state 'protects' are the *capitalist* form of equality and freedom within the sphere of exchange relations. The freedom to buy and sell is the freedom of large-scale businesses to a) buy labour power from its owners (the working class), b) to buy commodities (e.g. raw materials) from small-scale producers, and c) to sell commodities to small-scale producers and wage workers (e.g. means of production to the former, and means of subsistence to both), in a way that affects these classes adversely. The state protects this specific economic freedom, the freedom of capitalists that exists at the expense of the masses. Such equality and freedom are transformed into their opposites, i.e. inequality and unfreedom, within the sphere of property relations and production relations.[25] This is because: a) workers are not free not to work for the capitalist class as a whole, a fact which the state as the state of the capitalist class *as a whole* absolutely cannot do anything about, b) workers lack control over production and over the fruits of their labour, a fact that makes possible the appropriation of unpaid labour from sellers-cum-owners of commodity labour power. The state ensures conditions that produce substantial inequality between capital and labour. The state justifies unfreedom and inequality through violence and through cheap concessions, and not just through what Heinrich says, i.e. the fact that the state treats its citizens, including workers, 'as free and equal owners of private property' (Heinrich, 2004: 204).

The idea of the separation of the state from the economic sphere means that individual capitalists generally do not need to exercise extra-economic coercion against other capitalists or against their workers in economic transactions. This approach sees the relation of capitalism to the state from the standpoint of individual capitalists rather than that of a class. But the capitalist class as a whole, by virtue of their control over property, does exercise political, cultural, and juridical functions in the lives of the masses in the sense that these functions are collectively performed by the collective capitalist, the state.

The property question is absolutely crucial to the state question. And that is because: '[t]he question of property ... has always been the vital question for a particular class' (Marx, 1847). Historically speaking: prior to the 19th century, 'when the point at issue was the abolition of feudal property relations, the question of property was the vital question for the bourgeois class', which was the new ruling class. 'In the 19th century [and today], when it is a matter of abolishing bourgeois property relations, the question of property is a vital question for the working class (ibid.), the class that is going to be the new ruling class, temporarily in the first stage of communism, in order to finish task of the abolition of capitalism.

The state plays an immense role in the reproduction of capitalism, and yet the state in capitalism is not the main cause of people's economic and other problems or indeed of the class relations as such. Marx (1847) says, once again: the bourgeoisie is politically, that is, by its state power, 'maintaining injustice in property relations', but it is not *creating* it. The 'injustice in property relations' which is determined by the modern division of labour, the modern form of exchange, competition, concentration, etc., by no means arises from

25 In fact, and as mentioned earlier, *even in* exchange relations, there are inequality and unfreedom.

the political rule of the bourgeois class, but vice versa, the political rule of the bourgeois class arises from these modern relations of production which bourgeois economists proclaim to be necessary and eternal laws.

The ideas about the relation between the state and capitalist property that are presented in this book go against several prevailing scholars. According to the post-modernist Marxists such as Resnick and Wolff (2016), property ownership is neither necessary nor sufficient for the wielding of state power. In their view, the nature of class society and nature of the state are a matter of politics and ideology, and not the social nature of the economic system.

Like post-modernist Marxists mentioned above, Block (2019), the social-democratic scholar, advocates for 'the Polanyian view of socialism' which 'is not tied to property, but rather to the ability of the citizenry, through democratic means, to exercise sovereignty over the market' (p. 1173). He rejects Marxism's view that without ending private ownership of the means of production, reforms won today would be reversed tomorrow. From the Analytical Marxism camp, Wright is also sceptical of revolutions against capitalist property relations. Echoing the post-modernist view, he says that 'Anticapitalist revolutions attempt to eliminate the distinctively capitalist form of exploitation', by putting the means of production in the hands of the state (nationalization), but nationalization would not necessarily affect non-capitalistic exploitation that is, exploitation based on unequal ownership of such assets as skills/credentials, and nationalization may in fact increase bureaucratic control over people's lives (Wright, 1989: 20). All these views call into question Marx's (1887: 540) call in *Capital* volume 1 for expropriation of the capitalist property-owners, i.e. 'the expropriation of a few usurpers by the mass of the people'.

If the state just existed and impacted all classes equally, then people could fight against class exploitation and significantly and durably reduce the problems caused by capitalist class relation. The capitalist class relation is social power. If the political power is really 'the most concentrated strength of the ruling class' and serves the economic interests of the capitalist class and big landowners and protects their property rights, then what must be on the agenda is the seizure of political power through revolution against the state, and not a never-ending pursuit of economic and political reforms that are aimed at the democratization and humanization of the state. The nature of state power is political, and political power is important. Indeed, why do socialists fight for the political dictatorship of the proletariat if political power is economically not important? (Engels, in Marx and Engels, 1975: 402). If people could solve their fundamental problems within the framework of capitalist property relations that the state defends, why would Marx, once again, give a clarion call for expropriating the property of the expropriators (i.e. capitalists)?

Why did Marx not think that the state could eliminate the problems created by capitalist production and exchange based on capitalist private property? The answer lies in the class-character of the state, the state seen from the standpoint of class relation as such rather than any particular form of class relation such as capitalism. As indicated already, a major practical implication of the class theory of the state in *Capital* Volume 1 is that as long as class relations exist, the state, the main task of which is the political subjugation of the masses, will exist, so the overthrow of class relations, including property relations, and the overthrow of the existing state are a necessary condition for a classless and stateless society.

The reason why it is not enough to prioritize class and class struggle in the analysis of economy and society must be taken as the reason why it is not enough to prioritize class and class struggle in the analysis of the state too. Mere (economic) class struggle (i.e. the trade union–type struggle) will not solve the problems of the masses until they control state power. That means that the capitalist state must be partly seen as an obstacle to that project. A proper Marxist state theory does not merely relate the state to class struggle; it must point to the inherent lack of the control of the masses over the state, and to state's fundamental character as a coercive organization to maintain the class order by oppressing the masses. Therefore, a proper Marxist state theory must point to the inevitable and unavoidable need for the conquest of state power and establishment of a new transitional state, as Lenin, following Marx, had emphasized.

As we have seen, the capitalist state not only protects capitalist property rights. It also protects the actual mechanisms through these relations work – i.e. commodity relations under the law of value. There is a major political implication of the relation between the state and the law of value in the context of the struggle for socialism. Two aspects of the law of value are worth noting here. One is that commodity exchange presupposes a complex division of labour: different countries (just as different enterprises in a country) produce different commodities, at varying level of development of productive forces. Another is that the value of commodities changes as the development of productive forces – productiveness of labour – changes. In relation to both, the role of the state in protecting a country against the law of value is limited.

Let's start with the uneven productiveness of labour. The state can help a given enterprise under its jurisdiction to close the gap between its own value and the social value (or the gap between the value of all commodities produced in a country and the value of all these commodities produced globally) (Das, 2013b). In fact, the extent to which a state can protect its economy against the law of value is a major contributory factor to the economic development of that country (e.g. China), under the limits of global capitalism. By investing in science and technology and through other measures the state can create a situation where the value of commodities produced by capital under its jurisdiction is reduced below the global average and enhance competitiveness. States's ability to do this in unequal: some states can do this to a greater extent than other states. This creates geopolitical tension among them. Presiding over declining and stagnating economies, imperialist states accuse of the Chinese (or other similar states in the South) of distorting market relations through their interventions on behalf of their own producers.

There is, however, a limit to the extent to which the state can protect the enterprises (e.g. small-scale producers) that produce above the social value. The nation-state's own economic health, to the extent that it operates under capitalism, depends on the total social wealth produced under its jurisdiction. A given country needs resources to pay for the commodities it needs, so it must itself commodities produce competitively to be able to sell them. The state must therefore ensure that this happens. It must maintain commodity relations (the law of value). It can regulate the law of value operating in terms of how it affects the country under its jurisdiction but cannot eliminate it because a given state as well as the economy under its jurisdiction are parts of a bigger whole (the world-economy). That is why, 'Marxism takes its point of departure from world economy', but it sees the world economy 'not as a sum of national parts but as a mighty and independent reality which has been created by the international division of labour and the world market, and which in our epoch imperiously dominates the national markets' (Trotsky, 1931a). The capitalist world economy subjugates its component parts (e.g. national economies and their states). As commodities are circulated at a global scale, an introduction of a machine in one country can affect the value of commodities in another country: the value of commodities is affected by society-wide labour productivity. No country can remain competitive if its labour productivity per hour does not rise to the global average. 'The strength and stability of regimes are determined in the long run by the relative productivity of their labor' (Trotsky, 1991: 41).

If a socialist revolution occurs in a country surrounded by capitalist countries, there are two ways in which the latter can influence the new state, as discussed earlier. One is military threat. Another is the global law of value supported by the guardians of law of exchange (nation-states) and the guardians of the guardians (imperialist states). The importance of the military threat should not be over-emphasized at the expense of the law of value. There are two processes involved. Firstly, 'by the rapid improvement of all instruments of production, by the immensely facilitated means of communication' the capitalist class draws all the countries, including the less developed ones into one world market. Secondly, cheaper commodities produced in advanced countries break into the markets of LDCs and break their protected economies.

In the context of the post-1917 Russia, this is what Trotsky said, in his *Third international after Lenin*, critiquing those who believed in the idea and practice of socialism in one country, that it is possible for the state to construct socialism in a single isolated country:

> To the extent that productivity of labor and the productivity of a social system as a whole are measured on the market by the correlation of prices, it is not so much military intervention [by the state of an advanced country] as the intervention of cheaper capitalist commodities that constitutes perhaps the greatest immediate menace to [the new state of a post-revolution society]. (Trotsky, 1996: 71–72)

To the extent that greater level of productiveness affects the value of commodities and enhances the competitiveness of a country, it is important to remember that an advanced country may enjoy greater productiveness, which acts as a threat:

> [A] Ford tractor is just as dangerous as a Creusot gun, with the sole difference that while the gun can function only from time to time, the tractor brings its pressure to bear upon us constantly. Besides, the tractor knows that a gun [i.e. coercive powers of the state] stands behind it, as a last resort. (ibid.)

Then there is the second aspect of the value: international division of labour. A given country, whether it is more or less developed, is affected by the division of labour at the international scale. In capitalism, there is an 'incompatibility between the present productive forces and the national boundaries' (Trotsky, 1996: 78), which means that productive forces are being developed at a global scale, while the political system of capitalism is still more or less dominated by nation-states. This implies that even if a country is more developed and the value of its commodities is lower than that in other countries, that country and therefore its state are no less dependent on other countries than the LDCs and their states. Every state, developed or not, must depend on imports and exports. This means that:

> highly developed productive forces are by no means a lesser obstacle to the construction of socialism in one country than low productive forces, although for the reverse reason, namely, that while the latter are

> insufficient to serve as the basis, it is the basis which will prove inadequate for the former. (ibid.: 83)

This means that on the whole the modern productive forces are incompatible with national boundaries', that is, the boundaries controlled by particular nation-states (ibid.). If, thanks to the global law of value, the construction of socialism by a state in an isolated country is difficult, the same law of value also limits the extent to which the capitalist state can take steps to improve the conditions of the majority under its jurisdiction in a significant and durable manner.

The dominant aim of capitalist production is not the production of things to directly meet the needs of people. Its dominant aim is the production of use-values that have value in exchange. Thus, capitalism is indifferent to whether a commodity is smelly or flavourful. It is even indifferent to whether a commodity is harmful to the body (if it is, say, cancerous) or to nature (increased toxicity in water or air). Whichever product can be sold more profitably, not necessarily what people need for a healthy life, will be produced and sold. The state, which claims to represent the general interests of society, fails to make sure that there are enough of the things that people need (e.g. food and shelter, protective equipment during a deadly pandemic) to meet their needs. The fact that the dominant aim of capitalist production is not to directly meet the needs of people but to incessantly pursue exchange value (money), i.e. the fact that use-values are *never treated* as the immediate aim of the capitalist who only aims at the restless never-ending process of *profit-making* imposes 'constraint' on what the state can do for common people, those who do the work of production. The state can do little even if toxic and useless commodities are produced that are not useful to the vast majority of the people. Yet, some Marxists advocate for the idea that capitalism can be made to depend less and less on profitable production and that it can be organized in such a way that use-values will be produced. David Harvey (2019), for example, says:

> a socialist program, or an anti-capitalist program, of the sort that I would want is one about trying to manage this capitalist system in such a way that we stop it being too monstrous to survive at the same time as we organize the capitalist system so that it becomes less and less dependent upon profitability and becomes more and more organized so that it delivers the use values to the whole of the world's population.

This view amounts to a most fundamental distortion of the very core of Marxist view of capitalism as Marx laid out in *Capital* volume 1. This view completely contradicts Marx's value theory and its relation to the state.

7.2 *Capitalist Production and the State*

On the basis of commodity circulation and creation of capitalist property from pre-capitalist or non-capitalist (small-scale owners') property, fresh wealth (capitalist value) is ultimately produced inside the hidden abode of production, and it is here that the state plays an important role. Following the completion of the sale and purchase of commodities, including labour power, and on the basis of capitalist property rights, all of which the state supports, the process of capitalist production (labour process) begins. The workplace (the space of labour process or the hidden abode of production) is a space of certain rights of the exploiting class. These rights are defended by the state. Therefore, the sphere of production, including the workplace, reveals important attributes of the state. The logic of capitalist social relations and production produce an imperative for the state to act.

The state is connected to the successive phases of the capital circuit (MC (MP + LP)–P–C′–M′): purchase of means of production and the labour power, commodity production in value form, and realization. There are several theoretical implications of the relation between the capital circuit and the state.

Firstly, it is by virtue of the class character of the capitalist state that the state has the power to aid capital, and there is an imperative that it must aid capital, in the various phases of the capital circuit. Yet, by virtue of the same class character of the capitalist state that the state lacks the power to take over the capital circuit, including the sphere of production, in the interest of the common people. Given the complex division of labour in society and within the workplace, capital engages in complex planning process but it resists the planning process at the level of society by the state:

> The same bourgeois mind which praises division of labour in the workshop, lifelong annexation of the labourer to a partial operation, and his complete subjection to capital, as being an organisation of labour that increases its productiveness – that same bourgeois mind denounces with equal vigour every conscious attempt to socially control and regulate the process of production, as an inroad upon such sacred things as the rights of property, freedom and unrestricted play for the bent of the individual capitalist.[26] (Marx, 1887: 246–247)

The state cannot and will not overcome such resistance of capital to society-wide planning.

26 Marx adds: 'It is very characteristic that the enthusiastic apologists of the factory system have nothing more damning to urge against a general organisation of the labour of society, than that it would turn all society into one immense factory'. (ibid.)

Secondly, in my view, if the state supports capitalist accumulation, it is not fundamentally because it depends on capitalists and on capitalist economy for its survival (that it needs taxes and loans, and so on). This view is only implicit in *Capital* volume 1. The fact that the state needs taxes and loans – i.e. its so-called economic 'dependence' on capitalists and capitalists-controlled economy – is a concrete expression of the fact that it is inherently a class institution. This means that in the capitalist form of class society, the state is fundamentally a *capitalist* institution. So it must not only support capitalist property rights but also seek to promote the expansion of wealth in its capitalist form. The capitalist class relation cannot continue to exist without capitalists having capitalist property rights and right to exploit direct producers defended by the state (especially, its coercive powers against the masses). Given class relations, there is a need for the state (special public power). In this sense class relations are prior to – a conceptual presupposition for – the state. *Once* the state exists, it needs taxes and loans in a society. So it is the classness of society which explains the classness of the state that is behind state's so-called reliance on private accumulation. Consider this: the state does have all the power in the world to dispossess capitalists, a tiny minority, take over their property and be self-reliant and serve the vast majority (bottom 80–90%). Or, indeed, the state has the coercive power to take the property from a tiny minority and give it to the vast majority and help them use it collectively in order to meet their needs through society-wide planning of the use of means of production, and the majority can set aside some resources for the management of their common affairs (i.e. to do things that are necessary for the society as a whole). If the capitalist state does not do this, and therefore, if it is reliant on capitalists financially, it is because the state is, above all, a class – capitalist – institution. The state is the capitalist state *not* because it relies on the capitalist class. The state *relies* on the capitalist class *because* it is the capitalist state. The state power is necessarily a form of class power. That is, the relation between the two forms of power is an internal one and not an external one. Theory of class relations, including of capitalist social economy, and theory of the state, an important arena of 'extra-economic' sphere, intersect with theory of capitalist economy (Das, 2017b: chapter 5).

Thirdly, the relation of the state to the capital circuit sheds light on the idea of state capitalism.[27] People use the term 'state capitalism' without making clear just what they mean by that. State railroads are state capitalism. Industries receiving state subsidies are said to represent state capitalism. Post-colonial

27 See Sperber (2019) for a critical survey of 120 years of reflections on state capitalism and read back through the prism of class-state relations. See also Alami (2021).

state-led capitalist development is often called state capitalism. The former Soviet economy, according to some, was state-capitalist (Cliff, 1955). Indeed, 'the entire nationalized and plan-directed Soviet economy is supposedly also state capitalism [no matter that it was "the result of a revolution"]' (Trotsky, 1979: 340). Thus, the capitalist state can acquire attributes of 'state-capitalists', with state-managers effectively acting like capitalists.[28] One has to adequately distinguish between state capitalism and state-ism, from the standpoint of property relations or class relations. Once again:

> State capitalism means the substitution of state property for private property, and for that very reason remains partial in character. State-ism … means state intervention on the basis of private property, and with the goal of preserving it. Whatever be the programs of the government, stateism inevitably leads to a transfer of the damages of the decaying system from strong shoulders to weak. (Trotsky, 1991: 209)

Fourthly, the state plays an immense role in the reproduction of capitalism, and yet the state in capitalism is not the main cause of people's economic and other problems or indeed of the class relations as such. Marx (1847) says: [I]f the bourgeoisie is politically, that is, by its state power, 'maintaining injustice in property relations', it is not *creating* it. The 'injustice in property relations' which is determined by the modern division of labour, the modern form of exchange, competition, concentration, etc., by no means arises from the political rule of the bourgeois class, but vice versa, the political rule of the bourgeois class arises from these modern relations of production which bourgeois economists proclaim to be necessary and eternal laws.

Engels presented two views (Marxist and anarchist). Theoretically speaking, the anarchist view (e.g. Bakunin) is that 'it is the *state* which has created capital, that the capitalist has his capital *only by favour of the state*', while in the Marxist view, 'state power is nothing more than the organisation with which the ruling classes, landlords and capitalists have provided themselves in order to protect their social prerogatives' (in Marx and Engels, 1975: 257).

As often is the case, these contrasting *theoretical* views are translated into contrasting *political* differences. Consider the political differences between Marxism and anarchism. They are united in that they hope to see a society without class and the state. However, anarchists do not 'regard capital, and therefore the class contradiction between capitalists and wage earners … as

28 This is to be distinguished from the nationalization of industries following anti-capitalist revolutions in the early parts of the 20th century.

the main evil to be abolished' in Marx and Engels, 1975: 257. They say that 'the state is the chief evil', so 'it is above all the state which must be done away with and then capitalism will go to hell of itself' (ibid.). Marxists think differently. Engels speaks for Marxists when he says:

> We, on the contrary say: do away with capital, the appropriation of the whole means of production in the hands of the few, and the [post-capitalist] state will fall away of itself. The difference is an essential one. Without a previous social revolution the abolition of the state is nonsense; the abolition of capital is in itself the social revolution and involves a change in the whole method of production. (ibid.: 257–258)[29]

Of course, the abolition of capitalism is not possible without abolishing *the capitalist form of the state*, which is the greatest violent defender of capitalism.

Finally, to some extent, the capitalist state intervention can have a progressive character, even if not always intentionally. For example, state regulation tends to hasten concentration and centralization of capital, and therefore, the rise of large-scale enterprises. Large-scale production is a pre-condition for socialism where people work together using means of production on a large scale which is 'consciously regulated by them in accordance with a settled plan' (p. 52). The large-scale enterprises that capitalism has created with the support of the state, because of their large-scale character, can only be used in common, so they make it possible for the massive development of productive forces beyond the limits set by capitalist social relations, and thus increase the availability of leisure time.

7.3 *The Working Class, Labour Circuit, and the State*

The state is related to labour in many ways. It 'helps' them in part as a response to the working-class agency, as its relation to the labour circuit shows define. As we have seen, through its legislations and policies, the state seeks to force the capitalist class to make the conditions of workers a little tolerable by such processes as reduction of the length of the working day; it has tried to put a floor below which wages are not to fall. The state allows, or helps, people to freely sell their labour power and small-scale producers to freely sell products of their labour. It contributes to the reproduction of segments of the reserve army through unemployment insurance and similar anti-poverty measures. There have been legislations concerning health and safety at work. The working class

29 For further discussion, see Das (2022b: 164–165).

has also received benefits in the form of subsidized health and education. The state can positively affect the value of labour power itself.

There are definite driving forces behind the state's pro-worker measures. There is an objective pressure on the state, coming from the general and long-term interests of capital-as-a-whole, to intervene on behalf of the masses, although this objective pressure is 'subjectively' mediated by the struggle of the masses. The long-term interests of the capitalist class (or of its hegemonic fraction) (and of the capitalist state) may coincide with workers own interest in better working and living conditions, and this partly drives state functions in favour of the working class.

Capitalists' 'own most important interests dictate' that 'all *legally* removable hindrances to the free development of the working class' (e.g. the crippling of the quality of labour power due to overwork) be removed. Partly for this reason, Marx (1887: 7) says, he gives 'so large a space in this volume to the history, the details, and the results of English factory legislation'. And this is why it is important to re-examine Marx's discussion of the workplace legislation and to reflect on what the state does for the workers' welfare. *Capital* volume 1 reveals the economic laws of motion of capitalism. It also sheds light on the power of the working class struggle and on the conditions for, and the barriers to, the development of the working class struggle.

One implication of the class character of the state is that apart from the state having to meet the fundamental needs of the capitalist class, it must also respond to the struggle of the masses for concessions mainly to gain and reproduce their consent to it.[30] There are limits to how much concession the state can give to workers under capitalism, the limits that exist because of the capitalist control over property and production, nature of capitalist accumulation and its crisis-proneness, and the capitalist state's bureaucratic functioning and its anti-worker politics.

The state itself represents class struggle from above. It is in the form of the state's anti-worker economic policies and the suppression of strikes against these policies. The state is the biggest and most trusted trade union of the capitalist class that counters the trade unions and other organizations of workers. As the political arm of the capitalist class, the state supremely signifies class struggle from above by suppressing any significant potential or actual threat from workers to commodity relations, relations of property, and profit-making in capitalist production.

30 The state rules on behalf of the exploiting class by means of coercion, consent, concessions, each of which has a cost.

Marx begins *Capital 1* with the idea of 'directly associated labour' (p. 50) and with the conception of 'production by freely associated [people]' (p. 52).[31] If Marx thought that the state could improve conditions of common people significantly and permanently, he would not do this. What the capitalist class does to the most vulnerable among workers – male and female children – sums up the nature of capitalism and of the conditions of the working class as a whole. If the state has failed to protect the children from the juggernaut of capitalism, it cannot be expected to do much for the working class as a whole.

The capitalist state is a contradiction-ridden *personification* of illusory *common* interests, and it supports the personification of the two basic classes of capital society. The capitalist 'is only capital personified'. As the conscious representative of the capital circuit or the movement in which money is advanced to make more money, the possessor of money *becomes* a capitalist, says Marx. Similarly, and from the standpoint of capital, the worker is nothing more than personified labour-time. These two forms of personification of class interests – capital's and labour's – are contradictory: for example, capital wants people to work longer while labour wants to work shorter hours. That contradiction is represented in the heart of the state, which is partly represented in state legislations to improve working conditions of workers, while these legislations make numerous concessions to capital (as discussed in the next chapter). In spite of these contradictions and in spite of the fact that the state is fundamentally the state for, and of, the capitalist class, it is often perceived as representing – as being the personification of – common interests of society, and such perception helps to justify blatantly anti-people (anti-worker) actions of the state, including state violence. Given that the state is fundamentally a class institution, and given that its main aim is to support capitalist class interests, violence by the state against common people does not and must not have any legitimacy whatsoever. The state cannot be allowed to inflict violence on common people in the name of maintaining order because that order is basically another name for the domination of the ruling class over the common people.

While the state is basically a class institution and under capitalism, it is fundamentally a capitalist institution, at a concrete level, in terms of its day-to-day action in a specific time and place, its capitalist character can vary a little as it is mediated/affected by the struggle of the people (workers and petty producers)

31 'The life-process of society, which is based on the process of material production, does not strip off its mystical veil [i.e. the fetishism of the commodity] until it is treated as production by freely associated [people], and is consciously regulated by them in accordance with a settled plan' (ibid.).

in their own interests which are in higher standard of living and better health and physical environment. The opposite view is not true: it is wrong to think that the state belongs to everyone equally, to all the people under its jurisdiction, but that *how* pro-people it is – i.e. to what extent it acts in the interests of everyone – is affected/mediated by the influence of the capitalist class on its functioning. Also it is not true that the state is equidistant from capital and people (wage workers and petty producers), that it is autonomous of capital on the one hand and labour (or common people) on the other.

The state gives concessions improving the health and education of the workers. What this means is that to the extent that capitalism, in its own interest, creates an educated workforce, such a workforce is also being trained to manage the affairs of society on their own without the interference of capitalists or bureaucratic state actors. Capitalism not only develops the material conditions for socialism (e.g. large-scale production, technical improvements, and so one), that are partly spurred on by the pro-worker action by the state. It also matures various contradictions which are economic, which are expressed in the form of periodic crises, prompting state action. These contradictions are also political: contradictions between (a) the image that the state is for all and (b) the reality of its structurally inscribed inherent 'biases' in favour of the propertied classes. Given these contradictions, a new force is created that can, under proper conditions, overthrow the state along with the capitalist property relation that it defends, and begin to create a new society by utilizing the conditions already maturing under capitalism:

> By maturing the material conditions, and the combination on a social scale of the processes of production, it [pro-worker state intervention] matures the contradictions and antagonisms of the capitalist form of production, and thereby provides, along with the elements for the formation of a new society, the forces for exploding the old one. (Marx, 1887: 329)

8 Political Economy of the Conditions of Workers and Petty Producers

Marxist political economy points to fundamental relations of exploitation and inequality in capitalism that are maintained by the state. These relations, the cause of people's suffering, are the relations of: exploitation of workers by capitalists; exploitation of petty producers by capitalists, landlords, merchants and money-lenders; exploitation of poorer countries by imperialist countries; exploitation of women by men; and rural-urban inequality. And the state is not able to do much to significantly and durably mitigate people's sufferings, so its *failure* contributes to people's suffering.

There is no such thing as exploitation in general: it is precisely the exploitation of a specific class, the wage-labour class, that forms the basis of the whole system of class relations today. It is the exploitation of wage-labour, whether the wage is below the value of labour power or not, that leads to the main division of society into irreconcilably opposed classes and that leads to class struggle, covert or overt. Only from the point of view of *this* class antagonism can all other manifestations of exploitation be consistently gauged.

The working class is subjected to secondary or derivative exploitation that happens in the spheres outside of production – by shopkeepers/merchants, financial capitalists, etc.[32] It is subjected to primary exploitation – 'exploitation proper' – i.e. appropriation of surplus value in the sphere of production. Capitalists resort to various mechanisms to extract more labour from the working class every hour/day. One mechanism is to hire workers for above normal – very long – working days. Another is to extract through mechanization and rationalization. The fact that capitalists organise and rationalise labour within the factory to increase exploitation of the workers (Lenin, 1914a) has political implication: the rational organization of social labour under capitalism 'is preparing the time when the proletariat will take over all social production and appoint its own workers' committees for the purpose of properly distributing and rationalising all social labour' (ibid.).[33] As well, large-scale capitalist production, machinery, railways, telephone, etc. provide thousands of opportunities to cut production time enormously (ibid.).

Apart from being economically exploited, workers at work are subjected to the despotic power of the capitalists. And, apart from being exploited in the sphere of economy, workers are subjected to subjugation in the political (extra-economic) sphere. Workers are slaves not only of the bourgeois class but also of the bourgeois State. When workers go on a strike, the full force of the state in the form of the police, courts, etc. faces them.

Workers' life is one of insecurity, or precarity, in terms of employment and wages. Workers live only so long as they find work for a wage, and they find work that only so long as their labour increases capitalist profit. Wages are

32 In recent political economy literature, some of the processes of secondary exploitation are wrongly included under the problematic concept of 'accumulation by dispossession', which is often seen as accumulation that is not *capitalist* accumulation proper.

33 'Capitalism is thus creating a condition where "workers" committees, assisted by the workers' unions, will be able to apply these principles of rational distribution of social labour when the latter is freed from its enslavement by capital' (ibid.).

low – just enough for the maintenance of the working bodies, if at all. Not just that. Wages fluctuate enormously because of growing competition among the bourgeois masters and the resulting economic crises. The precarity that Marx's and Lenin's political economy draws attention to continues to define the life of the proletariat, signifying the lack of 'stable work and steady incomes' (Kasmir, 2018). Precarity includes a combination of low wages and insecure and involuntary part-time employment. It is the condition of the global reserve army (Jonna and Foster, 2016). Precarity exists in rich and poor countries (Benanav, 2015; Choonara, 2019; Nees, 2017; Pradella, 2015; Tencer, 2018).[34]

While capitalism is exploitative, some groups of workers such as women and children are subjected to above-average exploitation. This happens both in the petty production sector and in large-scale industry. The sphere of petty production (in agriculture) faces stiff competition from the capitalist sector. Yet, the continued existence of petty production is made possible because of self-exploitation, because of a *larger* amount of work being squeezed out of the worker in the petty production sector than is squeezed out of the worker in large-scale production. This tendency towards above-average exploitation by competing capitalists has adverse implications for the especially oppressed groups such as women and for children in the petty production sector.

The formation of a reserve army of the unemployed is characteristic of capitalism in general. Apart from the expropriation of the small scale producers, the introduction of machines expands the reserve army of labour. A reserve

34 Corporations and employers are reducing their pool of permanent workers in an effort to cut labour cost thus creating a situation where precariously employed workers are responsible for the workload of a permanent job, yet they do not enjoy the advantages of permanent employment (e.g. higher wages; secure employment; normal working hours, pensions and other benefits, etc.).

A precarious workforce allows companies 'to boost stock prices and to pay back their enormous debts to the banks and Wall Street' (Goldstein, 2017). Arguably, even if a part of the workforce is precarious, that itself puts pressure on those who are not precariously employed.

Precarious employment means that workers have limited rights (i.e. to be part of a union) or job protection, which puts them in a vulnerable position of being easily replaceable. Many of them, in spite of their higher level of education and skills, work for lower wages per hour, and for longer hours in a week than workers with more secure tenure. They also work in multiple and multi-local workplaces, and this can potentially impede workplace-based trade union organization, although it does not entirely exclude the possibility of economic struggle. While the phenomenon of precarity that Marx (see chapter 25 of *Capital* Volume 1) and Lenin shed light on has received some attention in recent political economy, some scholars (mistakenly) say that precarious people constitute a new class (whose interests are opposed to those with stable employment) (for a critique, see Choonara, 2020; Palmer, 2013; Wright, 2016; Munck, 2016).

army is a necessary requirement for, and a necessary product of, capitalism and yet its specific mechanisms and effects could be different in different sectors. The reserve army of labour is a lever of increasing exploitation as it puts a downward pressure on wages of the currently employed. The introduction of technical change, via increased employment of women and children, can increase the rate of exploitation of the working class as a whole.

Because of primary exploitation in its absolute and relative forms, and derivative exploitation, and market relations (of competition, centralization, class differentiation, etc.), capitalist development results in absolute and relative impoverishment (the phenomenon where people's needs remain unmet), worsening health conditions of workers (and petty producers) and in rising inequality, especially between large-scale business owners and common people.

A fundamental reason for the poor conditions of workers is unemployment/under-employment which is rife. On top of this, wages are generally low relative to the value of labour power, and they are low relative to the cost of living steadily rising (which means that real wages decrease). Wages do not rise, or when they do, they increase much more slowly than the necessary family expenditure. If due to an increase in total investment, real wages do rise, as soon as there is a dent in the 'expected' rate of profit because of reduction in unpaid labour appropriated by capital, wages stop rising or wages fall. To increase profit, the pace of work is intensified or workers are made to work long days, and workplace safety rules, even if ordained by the state, are compromised by capital, so workers suffer from injury. But wages are not increased as a compensation for the injury to the working bodies.

Low wages, and petty producers not being able to earn an adequate remuneration for their work due to stiff competition from, or exploitative relations with, the capitalist sector (including traders, MNCs buying agro-raw materials), explain low income of common people, and their worsening diet, which has adverse health impacts. Capital throws the whole of its crushing weight upon the ruined small producers and the proletariat, constantly threatening to force these people down to starvation level and to death from starvation (Lenin).

Only a small part of the value created by the working class and only a small part of the fruit of the labour of the petty producer go to them while the capitalist class pockets a large proportion of the net social product. The inequality between capital and labour is expressed in the form of workers' impoverishment caused by capitalist technological change, economic crisis, etc. As mentioned already, workers become impoverished *absolutely*. They also experience impoverishment in its relative form: i.e., the diminution of their *share* in the national income.[35] Economic inequality is seen from the standpoint of class relations, which are the major reason for the inequality in the distribution of income and inequality in the level of consumption between the capitalists and the direct producers. Such differences coexist with gender oppression. Once again:

> There cannot be, nor is there nor will there ever be "equality" between the oppressed and the oppressors, between the exploited and the exploiters. There cannot be, nor is there nor will there ever be real "freedom" as long as there is no freedom for women from the privileges which the law grants to men, as long as there is no freedom for the workers from the yoke of capital, and no freedom for the toiling peasants from the yoke of the capitalists, landlords and merchants. (Lenin, 1919c)[36]

In capitalism, the conditions of the proletariat may be better than petty producers'; as well, petty production represents a massive wastage of resources. However, these facts do not mean that Marxist political economy would advocate for dispossessing the peasantry of the land. On the contrary, Marxist political economy would advocate for abolishing all restrictions on the small-scale producers' right to freely dispose of their land and to migrate from where they live and work, or indeed for the petty producers to get a remunerative price for the products that are the fruits of their labour. In fact, petty producers are subject to class differentiation, extra-economic dispossession, secondary exploitation, and some of them may be subjected to primary exploitation, and therefore, the cause of their suffering is capitalism, which is also the cause of suffering of the proletariat. This means that there is a solid political economic basis for workers-peasant alliance (Das, 2023f).

Capitalism is thus a deeply unequal society in terms of class relations (i.e. production relations) and attendant unequal relations of distribution, exchange and consumption. In contrast, socialism, based on the abolition capitalist private property, is a deeply egalitarian society: firstly, no one monopolizes

35 Impoverishment can be seen in terms of what Marx (and Luxemburg) call relative wage: wage of workers (value of labour power) relative to how much the capitalist class earns (surplus value) (see Guerrero, 1999: 14). Impoverishment is experienced in the less developed world as well as in the developed world (see Pradella, 2015 on workers' impoverishment in Europe). Certain groups of workers (and petty producers) (e.g. women and racialized peoples) experience impoverishment to a greater degree than others.

36 See Pateman (2021) on Lenin's insightful views on women's oppression in capitalism, and on the necessary relation between women's emancipation and socialism.

control over means of production, so no one has the right to appropriate surplus labour from another, so there is no question of inequality in production relations. Lenin's class-based political economy leads him to conclude that 'the abolition of classes as the socialist agenda means placing *all* citizens on an *equal* footing with regard to the *means of production* belonging to society as a whole. It means giving all citizens *equal* opportunities of working on the publicly-owned means of production. There will not be inequality of the type that is seen in capitalism – i.e. the inequality in income and consumption caused by the fact that people do not have access to education and healthcare and are denied productive employment with a living wage, although there will be *some* inequality, initially at least, partly because some people may work harder or more than others, in part because of the differences in natural abilities, and so on. Marxist political economy considers it absurd to expect *equality* of natural abilities in socialist society. In brief, when it speaks of equality it always means *social* equality, equality of social status, and not by any means equality of individuals in terms of physical and mental quality.

9 Political Economy as a Guide to People's Struggle against Capitalism

9.1 *Capitalism Impedes and Promote People's Struggle*

Marxist political economy sees the proletariat is not just a suffering class but also as a fighting class. In fact, as soon as it came into being it locked horns with capitalism. Workers do engage in struggle against the state and capital, for the improvement in their conditions (although within narrow limits set by wage-slavery that characterizes capitalism). Petty producers, another suffering class, also fights for the improvements in its conditions.

Capitalism creates conditions for, and impedes, workers' struggle. Capital pushes people to engage in class struggle by subjecting them to 'accumulation of misery, agony of toil slavery, ignorance, [and] mental degradation'. And, by proletarianizing large masses of (rural) petty producers, developing means of transportation and communication, geographically concentrating workers in cities, increasing mobility across regions and countries, increasing their level of education, capital creates also conditions for class struggle against it.

At the same time, capital also makes people' struggle against it difficult. As large-scale machine-based production expands, the number of destitute and unemployed/under-employed people increases which makes it harder to fight for a decent standard of living. In order to divide the masses, capital pits one group of workers against another (e.g. migrants of one national or other cultural identity against those with another). The bourgeoisie also makes use of state's coercive forces (e.g. police) against workers involved in resistance. It also bribes, or otherwise influences, workers' leaders, directly or through bourgeois political parties, to discipline rank-and-file workers. Using some of their super-profit obtained from poor countries, imperialist capitalists bribe the labour leaders and the upper stratum of the labour aristocracy, as Lenin says. And such a process supports imperialist exploitation – and super-exploitation – of the workers of the less developed nations and thus creates an obstacle to workers' unity across countries. Because of all these reasons, when wages rise, wages do not rise much, *even if* workers struggle is hard. Also, workers do not always succeed in resisting capital.

9.2 *Why Need for Fight for Reforms?*

Marxist political economy recognises the struggle for reforms, i.e., for measures that improve the conditions of the working people without destroying the power of the capitalist class. The struggle for economic and political reforms is important, not only because some concessions (e.g. state-funded education; minimum wage policy) may be obtained which can counter the despotism of capital in the workplace and improve the desperate conditions of the masses temporarily. An improvement in the conditions of the masses might also facilitate further struggle: it is easier for literate and healthier people who live in cities and in villages well connected with modern means of communication and who enjoy shorter working hours and democratic rights, to struggle for self-emancipation, than for the illiterate, hungry, and ill people living in areas without any means of communication or culture or democratic rights or without any resources for their struggle (e.g. strike fund). Also, the very practice of fighting for economic and political concessions can lead the masses to discover the limits to what the state can actually do to help the masses, and therefore the real class-political nature of the state, which falsely represents itself as the state of, and for, everyone, i.e. both capital and labour.

Marx indeed says that if Marxism denies the importance of such struggles, then 'what is certain is that I myself am not a Marxist' (Marx and Guesde, 1880). Althusser (2001: 54) notes: 'Marx ... proves irrefutably that the working class cannot hope to gain from the modern growth of productivity before it has overthrown capitalism and seized State power in a socialist revolution'. But Marx also 'proves that from here to the revolutionary seizure of power which opens the road to socialism, the working class can have no other objective, and hence no other resource, than to struggle *against* the effects of exploitation produced by the growth of productivity, in order to *limit* these effects (struggle *against* speed-up, *against* arbitrary productivity bonuses, *against* overtime, *against* redundancies, *against* 'automation unemployment')' (ibid.).

Workers' successful struggle for concessions has implications for the establishment of socialist society. First of all, as we have seen, pro-workers policies have unintentionally contributed to large scale production which is a precondition for socialism. Secondly, workers' successful struggle for concessions points to a possibility of a society beyond capitalism:

> Though the Factory Act, that first and meagre concession wrung from capital, is limited to combining elementary education with work in the factory, there can be no doubt that when the working-class comes into power, as inevitably it must, technical instruction, both theoretical and practical, will take its proper place in the working-class schools. There is also no doubt that such revolutionary ferments, the final result of which is the abolition of the old division of labour, are diametrically opposed to the capitalistic form of production, and to the economic status of the labourer corresponding to that form. (Marx, 1887: 319)

We have seen that the masses get little without a fight. It is also the case that to obtain some concessions, their organizations (e.g. trade unions) have to often support – or they have to make sure they do not undermine conditions for – national- and regional-level capitalist accumulation. The fact that capitalist investment in many sectors can move across state's territorial jurisdictions at national and sub-national scales – a movement that *can be stopped* but will *not be* stopped by the nation-states working together – imposes a limit on the extent to which the state can grant workers significant concessions. All these facts together have specific political implications. One is that trade union struggle is not *un-important* in spite of these facts:

> [I]n spite of the progressive degeneration of trade unions …, the work within the trade unions not only does not lose any of its importance but remains as before and becomes in a certain sense even more important work than ever for every revolutionary party. The matter at issue is essentially the struggle for influence over the working class [including communist caucuses within trade unions]. (Trotsky, 1940)

Therefore,

> Every organization, every party, every faction which permits itself an ultimatistic position in relation to the trade union, i.e., in essence turns its back upon the working class, merely because of displeasure with its organizations, every such organization is destined to perish. And it must be said it deserves to perish.

9.3 *Need to Overthrow Capitalism*

But the struggle for concessions only is a limited form of struggle, informed as it is by a trade union or spontaneous consciousness, a consciousness of the surface reality (especially, exchange relations including in the labour market), a consciousness that does not yet see irreconcilable incompatibility between the interests of capital and labour. All in all, the state and the capitalist economic system cannot meet the needs of the people. There are limits to the improvements that the bourgeoisie can bring in the lives of the people it exploits (proletarians and other groups) – these limits exist, as we have seen, because as soon as an increase in wages adversely impacts profit rate, the increase in wages will be stopped, and these limits increasingly exist because productive forces are being fettered by production relations, and so on. So there is a need for overthrowing the bourgeois rule. With increasing development of productive forces, common people are becoming impoverished and pauperized, and 'pauperism develops more rapidly than population and wealth' (Marx and Engels, 1848: 20). This means that 'the bourgeoisie is unfit any longer to be the ruling class in society' as it 'is incompetent to assure an existence to its slave within his slavery' (ibid.). The political aim of the proletarian movement therefore must be, as Marx, Engels, Lenin, Luxemburg, and Trotsky have said, 'the conquest of power by the proletariat for the purpose of expropriating the bourgeoisie' (Trotsky, 1938a).[37]

The capitalist system is vulnerable to collapse when several processes combine: a) current class relations (unequal social relations of production) fetter further development of productive forces thus producing a) an economic crisis, or a crisis of profitability, causing b) a crisis of livelihood of the masses, with the economic crisis and the consequent livelihood crisis prompting a c) governmental crisis, as the political parties of the ruling class get confused about how to rescue the system; and 2) an intense class struggle against the

---

37 This genuine Marxist approach is different from many contemporary Marxists. For example, in *Envisioning Real Utopias*, Erik Wright says that capitalism's productive capabilities open opportunities for reform which incrementally will lead to systemic change: that is, social reforms within capitalism such as welfare programs or cooperative enterprises could demonstrate alternative ways of organizing society, gradually leading toward socialist principles (Wright, 2010; for a critique of political gradualism and its underlying theory, see Das, 2017b: 111–174).

Similarly, Panitch says that the pressure from below will democratize the capitalist state to such an extent that it will not be the *capitalist* state – in other words: small changes will cause a big leap: 'what will ultimately be needed, as both the old and new Marxist theories of imperialism tell us, is the development of socialist political parties capable of bringing about a radical restructuring of states on all continents so as to really make them substantively democratic in ways that capitalist states can never be.' (Panitch, 2014: 27).

system in response to such crises and in response to the attempt of the capitalist class and the state to resolve the crisis through heightened exploitation of workers, violence, and similar other methods (e.g. war, etc.). The economic crisis on its own caused by the fettering of productive forces by social relations will not result in the socialist revolution. Nor will class struggle on its own without there being an economic crisis result in the revolution against capitalist class relation.[38] The ruling class can indeed survive the crisis of the development of productive forces unless the masses refuse to bear the consequences of such crisis. Marx's hope was that the scandal of capitalist fettering of productive forces 'would not be tolerated indefinitely, so eventually the means of production would be taken into public ownership, the profit motive eliminated, and the process of production organised according to a rational assessment of capabilities and needs.' (Bowring, 2011: 144).

Political economy of capitalist society points to the idea of a world socialist society that is technologically advanced, popular-democratic and culturally modern and that meets the material and cultural needs of all the people of the world, irrespective of their gender, race, nationality, in a manner that is socially equitable, ecologically sustainable, emotionally compassionate, and bodily healthy. The ultimate aim of the labour movement is not and cannot be to continue to fight merely for better conditions under which people can sell their labour power, but to abolish the conditions for such sale, that is, to abolish wage labour itself and capitalist social relations of production, and to establish a socialist society. This cannot be done without overthrowing the capitalist state that defends the slavery of wage labour:

> The political movement of the working class has as its object, of course, the conquest of political power for the working class, and for this it is naturally necessary that a previous organisation of the working class, itself arising from their economic struggles, should have been developed up to a certain point. (Marx, 1871b)
>
> Where the working class is not yet far enough advanced in its organisation to undertake a decisive campaign against the collective power, i.e., the political power of the ruling classes, it must at any rate be trained

38 Revolution happens only when there is a crisis (contradiction between class relations and productive forces): 'Given this general prosperity, wherein the productive forces of bourgeois society are developing as luxuriantly as it is possible for them to do within bourgeois relationships, a real revolution is out of the question. Such a revolution is possible only in periods when both of these factors – the modern forces of production and the bourgeois forms of production – come into opposition with each other' (Marx, 1850: 71).

> for this by continual agitation against and a hostile attitude towards the policy of the ruling classes. (ibid.)

It would indeed be mistaken to ignore/under-stress 'the organisation of the working class as a class through the medium of trade unions' even if unions fight for concessions only, because through the unions the proletariat 'fights its daily battles with capital, in which it trains itself' (Engels in Marx and Engels, 1975: 275).

But workers cannot fight only for economic concessions. If there are limits to the state's concessions, there are limits to the struggles that are only for concessions from the state that help produce unreason trust in the state. As we have seen, through economic concessions the state 'hopes to win the confidence [i.e. consent] of the working masses' cheaply (Lenin, 1901). 'For this very reason', communists '*must not* under any circumstances or in any way whatever create grounds for the belief (or the misunderstanding) that we attach greater value to economic reforms, or that we regard them as being particularly important, etc.' (ibid.).

The working class must be conscious of the following fact: if the increased access to use-values via a rise in wages from employers can, at best, means that the length and weight of the golden chain the wage worker has already forged for himself, allow of a relaxation of the tension of it' (p. 434) so increased public wage in the form of government benefits can only have a similar effect as long as the working class has no direct control over the means of production and over the very purpose of production of wealth (satisfaction of human needs versus profit for a few) and over how the state works. Such direct democratic control cannot occur without the masses creating their own transitional state, after replacing the current state. The fusion of economic and political struggle should neither be shaped by mere spontaneity, by the desire to obtain more concessions. It has to be based on *class* consciousness, which, in its fully developed form, is the idea that capitalist interests and masses' interest are fundamentally incompatible, and that this incompatibility cannot be abolished until the capitalist state is overthrown. Their conditions cannot be improved durably and significantly under capitalist property relations by their economic struggle only. The proletariat can meet its needs only under communism.

According to Marxist political economy, capitalism has some essential/fundamental features (wage slavery, competition, exploitation, imperialism, etc.). It also has derivative features or symptoms (e.g. excessively difficult economic conditions; capital's attacks on democratic rights), or it coexists with pre-capitalist relations which impede its fuller development. Such a view of capitalism points to the need for 1) a fight for land by peasants, including those who are oppressed by pre-capitalist landlords, and 2) a fight for liberty and for economic concessions (e.g. progressive taxation, increased remuneration, etc.) by workers and petty producers', a fight that must be a part of, and linked to, 3) a fight for socialism, or against wage-slavery itself.[39] Given that class exploitation coexists with national exploitation, there is a need for anti-capitalist struggle to be anti-imperialism struggle too to ensure that that currently oppressed nations' exercise their right to self-determination, both economically (vis a vis economic annexation) and politically. The anti-capitalism struggle must be anti-imperialism, and the anti-imperialism struggle must be, ultimately, anti-capitalism.

The fight for reforms – including reforms of the system of abuses in the workplace – is not automatically reform*ism*. Reformism is that which *restricts* the aims and struggles of the working class to the winning of reforms. We may recall that 'Reformism is bourgeois deception' – and bourgeois politics – of the workers, a deception that makes workers forget that 'despite individual improvements', they will always remain wage-slaves of capital (Lenin, 1913a). Marxist political economy of capitalism makes people aware of the need for the fight for significant and durable reforms under capitalism, of the obstacles to such fight, and of the limits to the reforms that the state will concede.

Marxist political economy also points to the need for making transitional demands in order to raise the level of struggle beyond the struggle for reform. Transitional demands are of a different type than the usual trade union (or partial) demand such as a rise in money wages which the system *can* accommodate to a certain extent. The essence of transitional demands 'is contained in the fact that ever more openly and decisively they will be directed against the very bases of the bourgeois regime' (ibid.). Transitional demands are those that stem 'from today's conditions and from today's consciousness of wide layers of the working class and unalterably leading to one final conclusion: the conquest of power by the proletariat' (ibid.). Transitional demands include housing for all, indexed wages ('an automatic rise in wages in relation to the increase in price of consumer goods'), and the right to employment, including

39 The less developed world has a specificity: in many parts of the South, property-owners appropriate surplus in ways that are not exactly capitalist. In this context, the land question – agrarian revolution – is very important. In some parts of the South, given that the bourgeoisie is linked to the feudal type classes and given that it is scared that any struggle against non-capitalist exploiters might spill over to be an anti-capitalist struggle, the bourgeoisie will not support any struggle to eliminate the feudal remnants, so the land question and any pre-capitalist sources of oppression can be eliminated only by a proletarian government that comes on the back of the communist revolution.

on public works (Trotsky, 1938a). Transitional demands must now include sustainable development too, including just transition (Das, 2018a).

The need for transitional demands is to be connected to a need for solidarity across the social-cultural divides within the working class. Racial and other divisions undermine workers' unity; the state, including the bourgeois parties, promotes such division and non-class identities. So the fight against racial oppression and the efforts to create racial unity must be parts of people's struggle against capital, including that which demands concessions. Marx (1887: 195) was aware of the matter: 'In the United States of North America, every independent movement of the workers was paralysed so long as slavery disfigured a part of the Republic. Labour cannot emancipate itself in the white skin where in the black it is branded' (ibid.). Besides, there is a need for solidarity between currently employed workers and unemployed workers in cities, and between all of them and small-scale producers.

It is true that in mobilizing workers for reforms, trade unions often lose their independence vis-à-vis the capitalist state, especially during the imperialist stage. But:

> Does this mean that in the epoch of imperialism independent trade unions are generally impossible? It would be fundamentally incorrect to pose the question this way. Impossible are the independent or semi-independent reformist trade unions. Wholly possible are revolutionary trade unions which not only are not stockholders of imperialist policy but which set as their task the direct overthrow of the rule of capitalism. (Trotsky, 1940)[40]

Trade unions (and other organizations of the masses such as factory committees) must remain independent of the state (and of bourgeois parties) to play a revolutionary role. For this to happen, they need to employ democratic slogans (e.g. right to unionize) and combine them with the transitional demands as well as minimum economic demands (e.g. a rise in wages):

40 [T]he trade unions in the present epoch cannot simply be the organs of [liberal-capitalist] democracy as they were in the epoch of free capitalism and they cannot any longer remain politically neutral, that is, limit themselves to serving the daily needs of the working class. They cannot any longer be anarchistic, i.e. ignore the decisive influence of the state on the life of peoples and classes. They can no longer be reformist, because the objective conditions leave no room for any serious and lasting reforms. The trade unions of our time can either serve as secondary instruments of imperialist capitalism for the subordination and disciplining of workers and for obstructing the revolution, or, on the contrary, the trade unions can become the instruments of the revolutionary movement of the proletariat. (Trotsky, 1940)

> In the epoch of imperialist decay the trade unions can be really independent only to the extent that they are conscious of being, in action, the organs of proletarian revolution. In this sense, the program of transitional demands ... in its fundamental features is the program for the activity of the trade unions [and not just for that of the communist political movement].

While there is a need to overthrow the dictatorship of the bourgeoisie which exploits proletarian and non-proletarian masses (i.e. the lower middle class, the small manufacturer, the shopkeeper, the artisan, the peasant, etc.), the non-proletarian masses cannot be truly revolutionary.[41] They only fight against capitalists to save themselves from extinction *as* fractions of the middle class and in order to reproduce capitalism in a modified form, i.e. a capitalism without landlords, usurers, greedy merchants, authoritarian officers/politicians, etc. Lenin's political economy of class differentiation leads him to conclude not only that petty production is not viable under capitalist commodity production, but also that the petty producers (e.g. peasantry) cannot play a leading role in the socialist fight against capitalism because of their *proprietary* class status, even if they can valiantly fight against non-capitalist exploiters and oppressors. So, as Lenin says, the petty producers must adopt the attitude not of a small proprietor (an attitude that overlaps with that of the bourgeoisie) but standpoint of the revolutionary proletarian which must lead the non-proletarian masses.

Only an independent organisation of wage-workers which conducts a consistent class struggle can wrest the peasantry from the influence of the bourgeoisie and explain to them the absolute hopelessness of the small producers' position in capitalist society. Of course, there are capitalists and their parties that are more democratic, or more favourable towards petty producers than other capitalists or capitalist parties, so the proletariat in its pursuit of state power must not ally itself with any faction of the bourgeoisie, even in the name of fighting the lesser evil.

Marxist political economy has explained the true position of the proletariat, the primary exploitation of which is the axis on which the system revolves. The proletariat is the only potentially revolutionary class. This is the class that

41 A large part of thinking within 'Marxism' seeks to autonomize consideration of politics and political strategy from political economy, and one consequence of this has been the neglect of the unique role of the proletariat in socialist revolution and attendant over-emphasis on the revolutionary quality of non-proletarian masses. This sort of thinking is inspired by, among others, Fanonism and Third Worldism.

produces the wealth in its capitalist form, without which there is no capitalism nor the capitalist class, which is why only the proletariat, when class conscious and adequately organized, can stop the production of that wealth. The proletarians have no property, they have 'nothing of their own to secure and to fortify', so their objective mission is to 'destroy all previous securities for, and insurances of, individual property' (Marx and Engels, 1848: 20). Their ability to work is the only thing they have but this cannot be put to work unless it is combined with the means of production which they lack. The proletariat cannot become the masters of the productive forces in a future society, except by abolishing their own previous mode of appropriation (i.e. their wage-slavery), and thereby also every other previous mode of appropriation. Given its role in the social economy, the strength of the proletariat in the process of history is immeasurably greater than its share of the total population. Besides, the proletariat has also numbers on its side. It is the majority of the global population. To recall Marx's point: 'All previous historical movements were movements of minorities, or in the interest of minorities. The proletarian movement is the self-conscious, independent movement of the immense majority, in the interest of the immense majority'. For all these reasons the proletariat is the main agent to fight for that society. There can be no substitute for the proletariat in the socialist struggle against capitalism. *This* is a major implication of the political economy of Marx and Lenin.

Bibliography

Ahmad, A. 2013. Communalisms: changing forms and fortunes. *The Marxist*, vol. XXIX, No. 2. https://mulpress.mcmaster.ca/globallabour/article/view/2583/2595.

Alami, I. 2021. State Theory in the Age of State Capitalism 3.0?, *Science & Society*, 85(2), 162–170.

Althusser, L. 1970. Philosophy as a Revolutionary Weapon. *New Left Review*. 1/64.

Amin, S. 2018. The Communist Manifesto, 170 Years Later., *Monthly Review*, 70(5), 1–14.

Baran, P. and Sweezy, P. 1966. *Monopoly Capital: An essay on the American economic and social order*. New York: Monthly Review Press.

Barrow, C. 1993. *Critical Theories of the State: Marxist, Neo-Marxist, Post-Marxist*. Madison: The University of Wisconsin Press.

Barrow, C. 2000. The Marx Problem in Marxian State Theory. *Science and Society*, 64(1), 87–118.

Barrow, C. 2002. The Miliband-Poulantzas Debate: An Intellectual History., In S. Aronowitz and P. Bratsis (eds.) *Paradigm Lost: State Theory Reconsidered*, 3–52. Minneapolis: University of Minnesota Press.

Benanav, A. 2015. Precarity rising, *Viewpoint magazine*, https://www.viewpointmag.com/2015/06/15/precarity-rising/.

Berberoglu, B. 2022. Capitalism and Imperialism in the Twentieth and Early Twenty-First Century: A Critical Analysis of Conventional and Marxist Theories of Imperialism. *International Critical Thought*, *12*(1), 55–80. https://doi.org/10.1080/21598282.2022.2035794.

Bidet, J. 2009. *Exploring Marx's Capital: Philosophical, Economic and Political Dimensions*. Chicago: Haymarket.

Black, G. 2022. Critical resources, imperialism and the war against Russia. *World Socialist Website*. https://www.wsws.org/en/articles/2022/05/28/mine-m28.html.

Blackledge, P. 2006. *Reflections on the Marxist Theory of History*. Manchester: Manchester University Press.

Boeri, T. 2012. Setting the Minimum Wage. *Labour Economics*, 19(3), 281–290.

Bowring, F. 2011. Marx's concept of fettering: A critical review. *Critique*, 39(1), 137–153. https://doi.org/10.1080/03017605.2011.537457.

Brass, T. 1994. Some observations on unfree labour, capitalist restructuring, and deproletarianization. *International Review of Social History*, 39(2), 255–275.

Brass, T. 2011. *Labour Regime Change in the Twenty-First Century: Unfreedom, Capitalism and Primitive Accumulation*. Leiden: Brill.

Brass, T. 2022. Twisted Trajectories, Curious Chronologies: Revisiting the Unfree Labour Debate. *Critical Sociology*, 48(1), 7–19. https://doi.org/10.1177/08969205211017969.

Brenner, R. 1977. The Origins of Capitalist Development: A Critique of Neo-Smithian Marxism. *New Left Review*, 104, 25–92.

Brenner, R. 1986. The social basis of economic development. In J. Roemer (Ed.), *Analytical Marxism* (pp. 23–53). Cambridge: Cambridge University Press.

Brewer, T. 1990. *Marxist Theories of Imperialism:A Critical Survey*: London: Routledge.

Burawoy, M. 2000. Marxism after Communism. *Theory and Society*, 29(2), 151–174. http://www.jstor.org/stable/3108567.

Burkett, P., and Foster, J. 2017. *Marx and the Earth: An Anti-Critique*. Chicago: Haymarket.

Burns, T. 2024. Marx's Capital and the concept of super-exploitation. *Capital & Class*, Vol. 48(3) 335–355.

Buzgalin, A. 2020. Creating the Impossible: Lenin's Legacy. *International critical thought*, Volume 10:4, 519–534.

Byres, T.J. 2006. Differentiation of the Peasantry Under Feudalism and the Transition to Capitalism: In Defence of Rodney Hilton. *Journal of Agrarian Change*, Vol. 6:1, 17–68.

Callinicos, A. 1988. *Making History: Agency, Structure, and Change in Social Theory*. Ithaca, NY: Cornell University Press.

Callinicos, A. 2001. Periodizing Capitalism and Analyzing Imperialism: Classical Marxism and Capitalist Evolution. In: Albritton, R., Itoh, M., Westra, R., Zuege, A. (eds.) *Phases of Capitalist Development*. Palgrave Macmillan, London. https://doi.org/10.1057/9781403900081_14.

Callinicos, A. 2006. G.A. Cohen and the critique of political economy. *Science & Society*, 70(2), 252–274.

Callinicos, A. 2009. *Imperialism and Global Political Economy*. Oxford: Polity Press.

Capitalism: In Defence of Rodney Hilton. *Journal of Agrarian Change*, 6(1), 17–68.

Capitalist money. 2024. The Marxist Moment: Why is everyone talking about Marxism in 2024? https://capitalistmoney.com/the-marxist-moment-why-is-everyone-talking-about-marxism-in-2024/.

Carchedi, G., & Roberts, R. 2018. *A world in crisis*. Leiden: Brill.

Carchedi, G., & Roberts, M. 2021. The Economics of Modern Imperialism. *Historical Materialism*.

Carver, T. and Farr, J. 2015. *The Cambridge Companion to the Communist Manifesto*. Cambridge: Cambridge University Press.

Chattopadhyay, P. 1991. Economic Content of Socialism in Lenin: Is It the Same as in Marx? *Economic and Political Weekly*, 26(4), 2–5,7–8. https://www.jstor.org/stable/4397239.

Choonara, J. 2019. *Insecurity, Precarious Work and Labor Markets: Challenging the Orthodoxy*. London: Palgrave Macmillan.

Choonara, J. 2020. The Precarious Concept of Precarity. *Review of Radical Political Economics*, 52(3), 427–446.

Clarke, S. 1990–1991. The Marxist Theory of Overaccumulation and Crisis, *Science & Society*, Winter, 1990/1991, Vol. 54, No. 4: 442–467.

Clarke, S. 1991. *The State Debate*. London: McMillan.

Cleaver, H. 2019. *Thirty-Three Lessons on Capital: Reading Marx Politically*. London: Pluto Press.

Cliff, T. 1955. *State Capitalism in Russia*. Retrieved from https://www.marxists.org/archive/cliff/works/1955/statecap/intro.htm.

Cohen, G. 2000. *Karl Marx's Theory of History: A Defence* (*Expanded Edition*). Princeton, NJ: Princeton University Press.

Cousins, B. 2022. Social differentiation of the peasantry (Marxist). *The Journal of Peasant Studies*, 49(7), 1387–1398. https://doi.org/10.1080/03066150.2022.2125805.

Dahlgreen, W. 2016. British People Keener on Socialism Than Capitalism. *YouGov*. https://yougov.co.uk/topics/politics/articles-reports/2016/02/23/british-people-view-socialism-more-favourably-capi.

Dao, M.C., Das, M., Koczan, Z., and Lian, W. 2017. Drivers of Declining Labor Share of Income. *IMF Blog*. Retrieved from https://blogs.imf.org/2017/04/12/drivers-of-declining-labor-share-of-income/.

Das, R. 1999. Politicism and Idealism in State Theory. *Science & Society*, 63(11), 97–104.

Das, R. 2012. Forms of subsumption of labour under capital, class struggle and uneven development. *Review of Radical Political Economics*, 44(2), 178–200.

Das, R. 2013a. Capitalism and Regime Change in the (Globalizing) World of Labour. *Journal of Contemporary Asia*, 43(4), 709–723.

Das, R. 2013b. Agrarian Crisis as the Crisis of Small Property Ownership in Globalizing Capitalism, *Monthly Review Online*. https://mronline.org/2013/10/01/das011013-html/.

Das, R. 2014. *A Contribution to the Critique of Contemporary Capitalism: Theoretical and International Perspectives*. New York: Nova Science Publishers.

Das, R. 2017a. David Harvey's Theory of Uneven Geographical Development: A Marxist Critique. *Capital and Class*, 41(3), 511–36.

Das, R. 2017b. *Marxist Class Theory for a Skeptical World*. Leiden/Boston: Brill.

Das, R. 2017c. David Harvey's Theory of Accumulation by Dispossession: A Marxist Critique. *World Review of Political Economy*, 8(4), 590–616.

Das, R. 2018a. A Marxist Perspective on Sustainability: Brief Reflections on Ecological Sustainability and Social Inequality, *Links: International Journal of Socialist Renewal*. https://links.org.au/marxist-perspective-sustainability-brief-reflections-ecological-sustainability-and-social.

Das, R. 2018b. Fascistic Politics in India, the Left, and Lenin's Theory of Temporary Compromise. *Sanhati*. https://sanhati.com/excerpted/18677/.

Das, R. 2018c. Anti-materialism, Capitalism, and Violence against the Human Body: Some Preliminary Comments. *Monthly Review Online*. https://mronline.org/2018

/04/20/anti-materialism-capitalism-and-violence-against-the-human-body-some-preliminary-comments/.

Das, R. 2019. Politics of Marx as Non-sectarian Revolutionary Class Politics: An Interpretation in the Context of the 20th and 21st Centuries, *Class, Race and Corporate Power*, 7(1), DOI: 10.25148/CRCP.7.1.008319. Available at: https://digitalcommons.fiu.edu/classracecorporatepower/vol7/iss1/8.

Das, R. 2020a. *Critical Reflections on Economics and Politics in India: A Class Theory Perspective* Leiden/Boston: Brill. 658 pages.

Das, R. 2020b. The social power of money and the neoliberal capitalist model of development', *Links: International Journal of Socialist Renewal.*

Das, R. 2022a. On The Communist Manifesto: Ideas for the Newly Radicalizing Public. *World Review of Political Economy*, 13(2), 209–244. DOI: 10.13169/worlrevipoliecon.13.2.0209.

Das, R. 2022b. *Marx's Capital, Capitalism, and Limits to the State: Theoretical Considerations*. London: Taylor & Francis.

Das, R. 2022c. Social Oppression, Class Relation, and Capitalist Accumulation. In *Marx Matters*, edited by D. Fasenfest. Leiden/Boston: Brill.

Das, R. 2022d. What is Marxist Geography Today, or what is Left of Marxist Geography? *Human Geography*, 15(1), 33–44.

Das, R. 2023a. Marxism and Revisionism in the World Today. *Capital & Class*, 47(3), 383–406.

Das, R. 2023b. Why is Identity Politics not Conducive to Achieving Sustained Social Justice?. *Dialectical Anthropology*, 47, 19–31.

Das, R. 2023c. Capital, Capitalism and Health. *Critical Sociology*, 49(3), 395–414.

Das, R. 2023d. How to think and write theoretically and critically about society. Links: *International Journal of Socialist Renewal.*

Das, R. 2023e. *Contradictions of Capitalist Society and Culture: Dialectics of Love and Lying*. Leiden/Boston: Brill.

Das, R. 2023f. On the worker-peasant alliance in India (and other countries of the Global South). *Links: International Journal of Socialist Renewal.* https://links.org.au/worker-peasant-alliance-india-and-other-countries-global-south.

Das, R. 2024a. Marx's Grundrisse: Introduction to political economy and historical materialism. *World Review of Political Economy* (forthcoming).

Das, R. 2024b. On Marx's Theory of Fettering of Productive Forces by Social Relations of Production. *Critique: Journal of socialist theory.*

Das, R. 2024c. Capitalism, Climate Change and Workers' Health: Notes on a Research Agenda. *Links: International Journal of Socialist Renewal*. https://links.org.au/capitalism-climate-change-and-workers-health-notes-research-agenda.

Das, R. 2024d. The centrality of Marx to the global periphery. In T. Brass and R. Das (eds.). Interrogating the Future: *Essays in Honour of David Fasenfest*, Leiden/Boston: Brill.

Das, R. 2024e. A Theoretical Enquiry into Social and Spatial Inequalities: An Urban-regional political economy perspective. *World Review of Political Economy*. (forthcoming).

Das, R. 2024f. Questioning Poverty, Questions for Poverty Analysis: Towards a Basic Theoretical Framework. *World Marxist Review*, 2(2), 103–126. https://doi.org/10.62834/yewzr905.

Das, R. 2025. Theses on Lenin's Political Economy after Marx. *World Marxist Review*. Vol 4.

Das, R., Gough, J., & Eisenschitz, A. 2023. *The Challenges of the New Social Democracy: Social Capital and Civic Association or Class Struggle*? Leiden/Boston: Brill.

Dooley, D., Prause, J., and Ham-Rowbottom, K. 2000. "Underemployment and Depression: Longitudinal Relationships." *Journal of Health and Social Behavior*, 41(4), 421–436.

Eagleton, T. 2011. *Why Was Marx Right?* New Haven: Yale University Press.

Elliott, L. 2021. Progressive Economic Policies Are Back on the Agenda – Time for Starmer to Catch Up. *The Guardian*. Retrieved from https://www.theguardian.com/commentisfree/2021/may/20/progressive-economic-policies-starmer-catch-up-state-intervention.

Ellner, S. 2017. Implications of Marxist State Theory and How They Play Out in Venezuela. *Historical Materialism*, 25(2), 29–62.

Elster, J. 2018. From Marx to Emotions. *Tidsskrift for samfunnsforskning*, Volume 59, Issue 2.

Engels, F. 1872. *Letter from Engels to Theodore Cuno*. https://www.marxists.org/archive/marx/works/1872/letters/72_01_24.htm.

Engels, F. 1878. *Herr Eugen Dühring's Revolution in Science*. https://www.marxists.org/archive/marx/works/download/pdf/anti_duhring.pdf.

Engels, F. 1884. Origins of the Family, Private Property, and the State. IX. Barbarism and Civilization. *Marxists.org*. Retrieved from https://www.marxists.org/archive/marx/works/1884/origin-family/ch09.htm.

Fine, B. 1991. Production. In T. Bottomore (Ed.), *A Dictionary of Marxist Thought* (pp. 487–488). Cambridge, MA: Blackwell.

Fine, B. 2006. Debating the 'New' Imperialism. *Historical Materialism*, 14(4), 133–156.

Foster, J. 2019. Late imperialism. *Monthly Review*. https://monthlyreview.org/2019/07/01/late-imperialism/.

Goldstein, J. 2017. *Millions of workers in the US face a life of part-time, precarious employment*. https://www.wsws.org/en/articles/2017/11/16/jobs-n16.html.

Grossman, H. 1929. *Law of the Accumulation and Breakdown*. https://www.marxists.org/archive/grossman/1929/breakdown/index.htm.

Gustavo, D. 2021. New Poll Shows Growing Majority of Youths in the United States Now Hold a Negative View of Capitalism. Retrieved from: https://www.wsws.org/en/articles/2021/07/16/143e-j16.html.

Hahnel, R. 2002. Amartya Sen: Late Twentieth Century's Greatest Political Economist?, In D. Dowd (ed.), *Understanding Capitalism: Critical Analysis from Karl Marx to Amartya Sen*, London: Pluto Press.

Hall, S. 2021. *Selected Writings on Marxism*. Durham: Duke University Press.

Harding, N. 1977. *Lenin's Political Thought*. London: Macmillan.

Hardt, M., & Negri, A. 2004. *Multitude: War and Democracy in the Age of Empire*. New York: Penguin.

Harman, C. 1991. The State and Capitalism Today., *Marxists.org*. Retrieved from https://www.marxists.org/archive/harman/1991/xx/statcap.htm.

Harriss-White, B. 2022. Petty commodity production. *The Journal of Peasant Studies*, 50(1), 295–314. https://doi.org/10.1080/03066150.2022.2138354.

Harvey, D. 1978. The urban process under capitalism: a framework for analysis. *International Journal of Urban and Regional Research*. Vol. 2:1–3, 101–131.

Harvey, D. 2003. *New Imperialism*. Oxford. Oxford University Press.

Harvey, D. 2006. *Spaces of Global Capitalism: Towards a Theory of Uneven Geographical Development*. London: Verso.

Harvey, D. 2007. Neoliberalism as Creative Destruction. *The Annals of the American Academy of Political and Social Science*, 610, 22–44.

Harvey, D. 2008. Introduction to the Communist Manifesto. In *The Communist Manifesto*, edited by D. Harvey. London: Pluto Press.

Harvey, D. 2010. *A Companion to Marx's Capita*l. London: Pluto.

Harvey, D. 2012. *Spaces of Capital*. London: Routledge.

Harvey, D. 2014. *Seventeen contradictions and the end of capitalism*. London: Profile Books.

Harvey, D. 2023. *A Companion to Marx's Grundrisse*. London: Verso.

Heinrich, M. 2004. *An Introduction to the Three Volumes of Karl Marx's Capita*l. New York: Monthly Review Press.

Higginbottom, A. 2023. *Superexploitation and the Imperialist Drive of Capitalism: How Marini's 'Dialectics of Dependency' Goes Beyond Marx's 'Capital'*. Monthly Review Press, 74(11).

High, S., & Lewis, D. 2007. *Corporate Wasteland: The Landscape and Memory of Deindustrialization*. Ithaca: Cornell University Press.

Holloway, J., and Picciotto, S. 1978. *State and Capital: A Marxist Debate*. London: Arnold.

Holt, J. 2014. *The Social Thought of Karl Marx*. Los Angeles: Sage.

Howard, M. and King, J. 1988. Lenin's Political Economy, 1905–1914: The Prussian and American Paths to the Development of Capitalism in Russia. *Historical Reflections*, 15(3), 497–521.

Illouz, E. (ed.) 2018. *Emotions as Commodities: Capitalism, Consumption, and Authenticity*. London: Routledge.

ILO. n.d. Details of Indicators for Labour Exploitation. *International Labour Organization.* Retrieved from https://www.ilo.org/wcmsp5/groups/public/ed_norm/declaration/documents/publication/wcms_105035.pdf.

ILO. 2017. 40 Million in Modern Slavery and 152 Million in Child Labour Around the World. *International Labour Organization.* Retrieved from https://www.ilo.org/global/about-the-ilo/newsroom/news/WCMS_574717/lang-en/index.htm.

ILO. 2018. New ILO Figures Show 164 Million People Are Migrant Workers. *International Labour Organization.* Retrieved from https://www.ilo.org/global/about-the-ilo/newsroom/news/WCMS_652106/lang-en/index.htm.

Jeffries, S. 2012. "Why Marxism is on the Rise Again." *The Guardian.* Retrieved from https://www.theguardian.com/world/2012/jul/04/the-return-of-marxism.

Jeong, S. 2011. Lenin's Economics: A Marxian Critique. In *Revitalizing Marxist Theory for Today's Capitalism*, edited by Zarembka, P. and Desai, R., Vol. 27, 223–254. Emerald Group Publishing Limited. https://doi.org/10.1108/S0161-7230(2011)0000027010.

John, M. 2020. Capitalism Seen Doing 'More Harm Than Good' in *Global Survey.* Retrieved from https://www.reuters.com/article/us-davos-meeting-trust-idUSKBN1ZJ0CW.

Jones, J. 2021. Socialism, Capitalism Ratings in U.S. Unchanged. *Gallup.* Retrieved from https://news.gallup.com/poll/357755/socialism-capitalism-ratings-unchanged.aspx.

Jonna, J., & Foster, J. 2016. Marx's Theory of Working-Class Precariousness: Its Relevance Today. *Monthly Review.*

Kasmir, S. 2018. *Precarity. Cambridge Encyclopedia of Anthropology.* https://www.anthroencyclopedia.com/entry/precarity.

Katz, C., & Fidler, R. 2018. Revisiting the Theory of Super-Exploitation. *Links.* https://links.org.au/revisiting-theory-super-exploitation.

Kiely, R. *Capitalist expansion and the imperialism–globalization debate: Contemporary Marxist explanations.* Journal of International Relations and Development, 8, 27–57. https://doi.org/10.1057/palgrave.jird.1800043.

King, S. 2014. Lenin's theory of imperialism: a defence of its relevance in the 21st century. *Marxist Left Review.* https://marxistleftreview.org/articles/001/.

Konings, M. 2015. *The Emotional Logic of Capitalism: What Progressives Have Missed.* Stanford, CA: Stanford University Press.

Krishnan, K. 2017. India: Why Are Suzuki Automobile Workers in Jail? *Links: International Journal of Socialist Renewal.* Retrieved from http://links.org.au/india-why-are-suzuki-automobile-workers-in-jail.

Küttler, W. 2023. Lenin's Marxism. In *Historical-Critical Dictionary of Marxism*, 505–531. https://doi.org/10.1163/9789004679023_025.

Lasslett, K. 2015. The State at the Heart of Capitalism: Marxist Theory and Foucault's *Lectures on Governmentality. Critical Sociology*, 41(4–5), 641–658.

Latimer, A. 2021. Super-Exploitation, the Race to the Bottom, and the Missing International. In: Ness, I., & Cope, Z. (eds.) *The Palgrave Encyclopedia of Imperialism and Anti-Imperialism.* Palgrave Macmillan, Cham. https://doi.org/10.1007/978-3-030-29901-9_273.

Lebowitz, M. 1991. The Socialist Fetter: A Cautionary Tale, in Ralph Miliband and Leo Panitch, eds., *Socialist Register 1991, Communist Regimes: The Aftermath.* London: Merlin Press.

Lebowitz, M. 1992. Beyond Capital?. In: *Beyond Capital.* Palgrave Macmillan, London. https://doi.org/10.1007/978-1-349-21831-8_7.

Lebowitz, M. 2009. "Situating the Capitalist State." In *Following Marx: Method, Critique and Crisis.* Chicago: Haymarket.

Lenin, V. 1893. *On the so-called market question.* https://www.marxists.org/archive/lenin/works/1893/market/07.htm.

Lenin, V. 1898. Book Review: *A. Bogdanov. A Short Course of Economic Science.* https://www.marxists.org/archive/lenin/works/1898/feb/bogdanov.htm.

Lenin, V. 1899a. The Development of Capitalism in Russia. *Marxists.org.* Retrieved from https://www.marxists.org/archive/lenin/works/1899/devel/index.htm#Chapter2.

Lenin, V. 1899b. *Review of Hobson's Imperialism.* https://www.marxists.org/archive/lenin/works/1899/apr/hobson.htm.

Lenin, V. 1899c. Our Programme. In *Articles for Rabochaya Gazeta.* https://www.marxists.org/archive/lenin/works/1899/articles/arg20p.htm.

Lenin, V. 1901. *What Is to Be Done? Burning Questions of Our Movement.* Marxists.org. Retrieved from https://www.marxists.org/archive/lenin/works/1901/witbd/iii.htm.

Lenin, V. 1901. *What Is to Be Done?* https://www.marxists.org/archive/lenin/works/1901/witbd/i.htm Is it separate from the above?.

Lenin, V. 1902a. *Vulgar Socialism and Narodism as Resurrected by the Socialist-Revolutionaries.* https://www.marxists.org/archive/lenin/works/1902/nov/01.htm.

Lenin, V. 1902b. *What is to be done?* https://www.marxists.org/archive/lenin/works/download/what-itd.pdf.

Lenin, V. 1904. *Plan for a Propaganda Talk on Crises.* https://www.marxists.org/archive/lenin/works/1904/oct/00.htm.

Lenin, V. 1908. "Marxism and Revisionism." *Marxists.org.* Retrieved from https://www.marxists.org/archive/lenin/works/1908/apr/03.htm.

Lenin, V. 1911. *Plan for a Lecture in a Course on "Fundamentals of Political Economy": Lecture IV.* https://www.marxists.org/archive/lenin/works/1911/jan/27.htm.

Lenin, V. 1912a. *Impoverishment in Capitalist Society.* https://www.marxists.org/archive/lenin/works/1912/nov/30.htm.

Lenin, V. 1912b. *Capitalism and Popular Consumption.* https://www.marxists.org/archive/lenin/works/1912/jul/20.htm.

Lenin, V. 1912c. *Workers' Earnings and Capitalist Profits in Russia.* https://www.marxists.org/archive/lenin/works/1912/aug/08b.htm.

Lenin, V. 1912d. *Concentration of Production in Russia.* https://www.marxists.org/archive/lenin/works/1912/aug/12c.htm.

Lenin, V. 1913a. *Marxism and Reformism.* https://www.marxists.org/archive/lenin/works/1913/sep/12b.htm.

Lenin, V. 1913b. *Backward Europe and Advanced Asia.* https://www.marxists.org/archive/lenin/works/1913/may/18.htm.

Lenin, V. 1913c. *The Three Sources and Three Component Parts of Marxism.* https://www.marxists.org/archive/lenin/works/1913/mar/x01.htm.

Lenin, V. 1913d. *Armaments and Capitalism.* https://www.marxists.org/archive/lenin/works/1913/may/21b.htm.

Lenin, V. 1913e. *The Growth of Capitalist Wealth.* https://www.marxists.org/archive/lenin/works/1913/jun/09b.htm.

Lenin, V. 1913f. *A 'Fashionable' Branch of Industry.* https://www.marxists.org/archive/lenin/works/1913/jul/21.htm.

Lenin, V. 1913g. *The Peasantry and the Working Class.* https://www.marxists.org/archive/lenin/works/1913/jun/11.htm.

Lenin, V. 1913h. *Capitalism and Female Labour.* https://www.marxists.org/archive/lenin/works/1913/apr/27.htm.

Lenin, V. 1913i. *Petty Production in Agriculture.* https://www.marxists.org/archive/lenin/works/1913/jul/18b.htm.

Lenin, V. 1913j. *Child Labour in Peasant Farming.* https://www.marxists.org/archive/lenin/works/1913/jun/12.htm.

Lenin, V. 1913k. *Capitalism and Workers' Immigration.* https://www.marxists.org/archive/lenin/works/1913/oct/29.htm.

Lenin, V. 1913l. *The Three Sources and Three Component Parts of Marxism.* https://www.marxists.org/archive/lenin/works/1913/mar/x01.htm.

Lenin, V. 1914. The Right of Nations to Self-Determination. *Marxists.org.* Retrieved from https://www.marxists.org/archive/lenin/works/1914/self-det/ch05.htm.

Lenin, V. 1914a. *The Taylor System – Man's Enslavement by the Machine.* https://www.marxists.org/archive/lenin/works/1914/mar/13.htm.

Lenin, V. 1914b. *Forms of the Working-Class Movement.* https://www.marxists.org/archive/lenin/works/1914/apr/04.htm.

Lenin, V. 1914c. *A Liberal Professor on Equality.* https://www.marxists.org/archive/lenin/works/1914/mar/11.htm.

Lenin, V. 1914d. *Four Thousand Rubles a Year and a Six-Hour Day.* https://www.marxists.org/archive/lenin/works/1914/jan/01.htm.

Lenin, V. 1914e. *Marx's Economic Doctrine.* https://www.marxists.org/archive/lenin/works/1914/granat/ch03.htm.

Lenin, V. 1915a. *Socialism and war.* https://www.marxists.org/archive/lenin/works/1915/s-w/ch01.htm.

Lenin, V. 1915b. *On the Question of Dialectics*. https://www.marxists.org/archive/lenin/works/1915/misc/x02.htm.

Lenin, V. 1915c. *Socialism and War*. https://www.marxists.org/archive/lenin/works/1915/s-w/ch01.htm.

Lenin, V. 1916a. *Imperialism, the Highest Stage of Capitalism: A Popular Outline*. https://www.marxists.org/archive/lenin/works/1916/imp-hsc/imperialism.pdf.

Lenin, V. 1916b. "A Caricature of Marxism and Imperialist Economism." https://www.marxists.org/archive/lenin/works/1916/carimarx/3.htm.

Lenin, V. 1916c. "Imperialism and the Split in Socialism." https://www.marxists.org/archive/lenin/works/1916/oct/x01.htm.

Lenin, V. 1917a. "War and Revolution." https://www.marxists.org/archive/lenin/works/1917/may/14.htm.

Lenin, V. 1917b. "The Capitalists Must Be Exposed." https://www.marxists.org/archive/lenin/works/1917/may/27b.htm.

Lenin, V. 1917c. "The Tasks of the Proletariat in Our Revolution." https://www.marxists.org/archive/lenin/works/1917/tasks/ch09.htm.

Lenin, V. 1917d. "New Data on the Laws Governing the Development of Capitalism in Agriculture: Part One – Capitalism and Agriculture in the United States of America." https://www.marxists.org/archive/lenin/works/1915/newdev/index.htm.

Lenin, V. 1918. "Extraordinary Seventh Congress of the R.C.P.(B.)." https://www.marxists.org/archive/lenin/works/1918/7thcong/01.htm.

Lenin, V. 1919a. "The State: A Lecture Delivered at the Sverdlov University." https://www.marxists.org/archive/lenin/works/1919/jul/11.htm.

Lenin, V. 1919b. "Answers to an American Journalist's Questions." https://www.marxists.org/archive/lenin/works/1919/jul/20.htm.

Lenin, V. 1919c. "Soviet Power and the Status of Women." https://www.marxists.org/archive/lenin/works/1919/nov/06.htm.

Lenin, V. 1919d. *To an American journalist's questions*. https://www.marxists.org/archive/lenin/works/1919/jul/20.htm.

Lenin, V. 1920a. "Interview with Lincoln Eyre, Correspondent of the American Newspaper The World." https://www.marxists.org/archive/lenin/works/1920/feb/20b.htm.

Lenin, V. 1920b. *Leftwing communism: an infantile disorder* in his *Collected works*, vol. 31. Moscow: Progress Publishers.

Lenin, V. 1949. *The State and Revolution*. Moscow: Progress.

Lewis, N., and Malone, J. 1996. *Introduction to Lenin's Imperialism: The Highest Stage of Capitalism*. London: Pluto Press.

Llorente, R. 2013. Marx's Concept of "Universal Class": A Rehabilitation. *Science & Society*, 77(4), 536–560.

Mandel, E. 1969. Marxist Theory of the State. *Marxists.org*. Retrieved from www.marxists.org/archive/mandel/1969/xx/state.htm.

Mandel, E. 1999. *Late Capitalism*. London: Verso.

Maniatis, T. 2014. Does the State Benefit Labor? A Cross-Country Comparison of the Net Social Wage. *Review of Radical Political Economics*, 46(1), 15–34.

Mao Tse-Tung. 1933. How to Differentiate the Classes in the Rural Areas. *Marxists.org*. Retrieved from https://www.marxists.org/reference/archive/mao/selected-works/volume-1/mswv1_8.htm.

Marini, R. 2022. *The Dialectics of Dependency. Trans. and Introduction by Amanda Latimer*. Monthly Review Press, New York.

Marx, K. 1844. "Critical Notes on the Article: 'The King of Prussia and Social Reform. By a Prussian.'" *Marxists.org*. Retrieved from www.marxists.org/archive/marx/works/1844/08/07.htm.

Marx, K. 1844. *Economic and Philosophical Manuscripts*. Moscow: Progress Publishers.

Marx, K. 1847. *Poverty of philosophy*. https://www.marxists.org/archive/marx/works/download/pdf/Poverty-Philosophy.pdf.

Marx, K. 1850. *Class struggles in France*. https://www.marxists.org/archive/marx/works/download/pdf/Class_Struggles_in_France.pdf.

Marx, K. 1857. *Letter to Engels*. https://marxists.architexturez.net/archive/marx/works/1857/letters/57_09_25.htm.

Marx, K. 1859. *A Contribution to the Critique of Political Economy: Preface*. https://www.marxists.org/archive/marx/works/1859/critique-pol-economy/preface.htm.

Marx, K. 1868. *The German Ideology*. https://www.marxists.org/archive.

Marx, K. 1880. "A Workers' Inquiry." *Marxists.org*. Retrieved from www.marxists.org/archive/marx/works/1880/04/20.htm.

Marx, K. 1881. *Letter to Vera Zasulich*. https://www.marxists.org/history/etol/newspape/ni/vol08/no10/marx-zas.htm.

Marx, K. 1887. *Capital, Volume I*. https://www.marxists.org/archive/marx/works/download/pdf/Capital-Volume-I.pdf.

Marx, K. 1894. *Capital, Volume III*. https://www.marxists.org/archive/marx/works/download/pdf/Capital-Volume-III.pdf.

Marx, K. 1973. *The Grundrisse: Foundations of the Critique of Political Economy (Rough Draft)*. https://www.marxists.org/archive/marx/works/download/pdf/grundrisse.pdf.

Marx, K., and Engels, F. 1848. *The Communist Manifesto*. Retrieved from: https://www.marxists.org/archive/marx/works/download/pdf/Manifesto.pdf.

Mavroudeas, S. and Papadatos, D. 2018. "Is the Financialization Hypothesis a Theoretical Blind Alley?" *World Review of Political Economy*, 9(4), 451–476. https://doi.org/10.13169/worlrevipoliecon.9.4.0451.

Mcdonough, T. 1995. Lenin, Imperialism, and the Stages of Capitalist Development. *Science & Society*, 59(3), 339–367.

McLellan, D. 2003. *Karl Marx: Selected Writings*. Oxford: Oxford University Press.

McNally, D. 2019. Thoughts on Marxism and the State. *Historical Materialism*. Retrieved from www.historicalmaterialism.org/blog/thoughts-marxism-and-state.

Meckstroth, T. 2000. Marx and the Logic of Social Theory: The Capitalist State. *Science & Society*, 64(1), 55–86.

Melnik, D. 2021. Lenin as a Development Economist: A Study in Application of Marx's Theory in Russia, *Russian Journal of Economics*, 7(1), 34–49. https://rujec.org/article/57963/.

Milios, J. 1999. Preindustrial Capitalist Forms: Lenin's Contribution to a Marxist Theory of Economic Development, *Rethinking Marxism*, 11(4), 38–56. https://doi.org/10.1080/08935699908685607.

Munck, R. 2013. The Precariat: A View from the South. *Third World Quarterly*, 34(5), 747–762. https://doi.org/10.1080/01436597.2013.800751.

Nees, V. 2017. *Millions of European Workers in Precarious Employment*. https://www.wsws.org/en/articles/2017/09/26/prec-s26.html.

Niemuth, N. 2017. Majority of Young Americans Prefer Socialism or Communism to Capitalism, *World Socialist Web Site*. Retrieved from www.wsws.org/en/articles/2017/11/07/soci-n07.html.

O'Kane, C. 2014. State Violence, State Control: Marxist State Theory and the Critique of Political Economy, *Viewpoint Magazine*. Retrieved from www.viewpointmag.com/2014/10/29/state-violence-state-control-marxist-state-theory-and-the-critique-of-political-economy.

O'Kane, C. 2020. Capital, the State, and Economic Policy: Bringing Open Marxist Critical Political Economy Back into Contemporary Heterodox Economics, *Review of Radical Political Economics*, 52(4), 684–692.

O'Kane, C. 2021. Critical Theory and the Critique of Capitalism: An Immanent Critique of Nancy Fraser's 'Systematic' 'Crisis Critique' of Capitalism as an 'Institutionalized Social Order.' *Science & Society*, 85(2), 207–235.

Ollman, B. 1976. *Alienation: Marx's Conception of Man in Capitalist Society*. 2nd ed.

Ollman, B. 1982. Theses on the State. *Monthly Review*, 34(7), 41–6.

Ollman, B. 2003. *Dance of the Dialectic: Steps in Marx's Method*. Urbana: University of Illinois Press.

Osorio, J., & Reyes, C. 2024. *Labour Super-Exploitation, Unequal Exchange and Capital Reproduction: Writings on Marxist Dependency Theory*. ibidem Verlag, Hannover, Stuttgart.

Palmer, B. 2013. Reconsiderations of Class: Precariousness as Proletarianization. *Socialist Register 2014: Registering Class*. London: Merlin.

Panitch, L. 2014. Rethinking Marxism and Imperialism for the Twenty-first Century. *New Labor Forum*, 23(2), 22–28.

Panitch, L., and Leys, C. 1998. The Communist Manifesto Now. *Socialist Register* 1998. London: Merlin Press.

Pateman, J. 2021. V.I. Lenin on the 'Woman Question. *Science & Society*, 85(3).

Pateman, J. 2022. The Centrality of Africa in Lenin's Theory of Imperialism. *Review of African Political Economy*, 49(172), 287–302. https://doi.org/10.1080/03056244.2022.2026765.

Patnaik, P. 2014. Lenin, Imperialism, and the First World War. *Social Scientist*, 42(7/8), 29–46.

Patnaik, P. 2015. Defining the Concept of Commodity Production. *Studies in People's History*, 2(1), 117–125.

Patnaik, P., & Patnaik, U. 2016. *A Theory of Imperialism*. New York: Columbia University Press.

Patnaik, U. 1986. The Agrarian Question and Development of Capitalism in India, *Economic and Political Weekly*, 21(18), 781–793. http://www.jstor.org/stable/4375629.

Pfeffer, J. 2018. "How Your Workplace is Killing You." *BBC*. Retrieved from www.bbc.com/worklife/article/20180502-how-your-workplace-is-killing-you.

Plender, J. 2008. The Return of the State: How Government is Back at the Heart of Economic Life. *Financial Times*, August 21.

Poulantzas, N. 2008. *The Poulantzas Reader: Marxism, Law, and the State*. Edited by J. Martin. London: Verso.

Pradella, L. 2013. Imperialism and Capitalist Development in Marx's Capital. *Historical Materialism*, 21(2), 117–147. https://doi.org/10.1163/1569206X-12341300.

Pradella, L. 2015. Beyond Impoverishment: Western Europe in the World Economy. In: Pradella, L., & Marois, T. (Eds.) *Polarizing Development: Alternatives to Neoliberalism and the Crisis*. Pluto Press. https://doi.org/10.2307/j.ctt183gzzt.

Pröbsting, M. 2015. Migration and Super-exploitation: Marxist Theory and the Role of Migration in the Present Period of Capitalist Decay. *Critique*, 43(3–4), 329–346. https://doi.org/10.1080/03017605.2015.1099846.

Pushpendra. 2001. Liberalization and Agrarian Reforms: Some Recent Controversies. In B.K. Sinha & Pushpendra (Eds.), *Land Reforms in India*: Vol. 5. Delhi: Sage Publishers.

Randall, K. 2018. Fifty-One Million US Households Cannot Afford 'Survival Budget'. *World Socialist Web Site*. Retrieved from: https://www.wsws.org/en/articles/2018/05/26/ceos-m26.html.

Roberts, M. 2010. Overproduction and Capitalist Crisis. The Next Recession. https://thenextrecession.wordpress.com/2010/01/29/overproduction-and-capitalist-crisis/.

Roberts, M. 2016a. *The Long depression: Marxism and the global crisis of capitalism*. Chicago: Haymarket.

Roberts, M. 2016b. Imperialism and Super-exploitation.

Roberts, M. 2019. Productivity, investment and profitability.

Roberts, M. 2022. *Russia under Putin. Brave new Europe*. https://braveneweurope.com/michael-roberts-russia-under-putin.

Roberts, M. 2024. *Further thoughts on the economics of imperialism.* The Next Recession. https://thenextrecession.wordpress.com/2024/04/23/further-thoughts-on-the-economics-of-imperialism/.

Robinson, W. 2007. Beyond the Theory of Imperialism: Global Capitalism and the Transnational State. *Societies Without Borders* Vol. 2, 5–26.

Saad-Filho, A. 2019. *Value and Crisis.* Leiden: Brill.

Saad-Filho, A. 2020. From COVID-19 to the End of Neoliberalism. *Critical Sociology,* 46(4–5), 477–485.

Sakellaropoulos, S., & Sotiris, P. 2015. From Territorial to Nonterritorial Capitalist Imperialism: Lenin and the Possibility of a Marxist Theory of Imperialism. *Rethinking Marxism,* 27(1), 85–106. https://doi.org/10.1080/08935696.2014.980676.

Sayer, A. 1992. *Method in Social Science.* London: Routledge.

Science & Society. 2021. "Marxist State Theory Today: A Symposium." *Science & Society,* 85(2), 162–206.

Sen, A. 1999. *Development as Freedom.* Delhi: Oxford University Press.

Smith, M. 2019. *Invisible Leviathan: Marx's Law of Value in the Twilight of Capitalism.* Leiden: Brill.

Smith, M., Wright, E., Levine, A., & Sober, E. 1992. *Reconstructing Marxism.* London: Verso.

Smith, J. 2016. *Imperialism in the Twenty-First Century: Globalization, Super-Exploitation, and Capitalism's Final Crisis.* New York: Monthly Review Press.

Smith, J. 2018. Exploitation and Super-Exploitation. *MR Online.* https://mronline.org/2018/04/14/exploitation-and-super-exploitation/.

SuttonThompson, M. 2021. Thirty-Five Percent of Canadians Oppose Capitalism. *Fightback.* Retrieved from: https://marxist.ca/article/thirty-five-per-cent-of-canadians-oppose-capitalism.

Timpanaro, S. 1985. *On materialism.* London: Verso.

Trotsky, L. 1931a. *The Permanent Revolution.* Marxists.org. Retrieved from www.marxists.org/archive/trotsky/1931/tpr/prge.htm. Is it correct to make it 1931a? Is something missing here?.

Trotsky, L. 1939. Marx in Our Time. https://www.marxists.org/archive/trotsky/1939/04/marxism.htm.

Trotsky, L. 1991 [1937]. *The Revolution Betrayed: What is the Soviet Union and Where is it Going?* Detroit: Labor Publications, Inc.

Trotsky, L. 2008. *The History of the Russian Revolution.* Chicago: Haymarket.

Trotsky, L. 1997. Labor, the State, and Class Struggle. *Monthly Review,* 49(3), 1–14.

Trotsky, L. 1998. The Communist Manifesto After 150 Years. *Monthly Review,* 50(1), 14–35.

Trotsky, L. 2005. *Empire of Capital.* London: Verso.

Trotsky, L. 2012. *The Ellen Meiksins Wood Reader*. Edited by L. Patriquin. Leiden and Boston: Brill.

White, J. 2017. "What the Maruti Suzuki Workers Were Fighting For." *World Socialist Web Site*. Retrieved from www.wsws.org/en/articles/2017/04/12/mswu-a12.html.

Wood, E.M. 1996. *Democracy Against Capitalism*. Cambridge: Cambridge University Press.

World Bank. n.d. Expense (% of GDP) – European Union. *World Bank*. Retrieved from https://data.worldbank.org/indicator/GC.XPN.TOTL.GD.ZS?locations=EU.

Wright, E. 1978. *Class, Crisis and the State*. London: New Left Books.

Wright, E. 1985. *Classes*. London: Verso.

Wright, E. 1989. *The Debate on Classes*. London: Verso.

Wright, E. 1995. The class analysis of poverty. Int J Health Serv. 1995;25(1), 85–100. doi: 10.2190/WYRM-630N-8M6V-7851.

Wright, E. 2015. *Understanding Class*. London/New York: Verso.

Zarembka, P. 2003. Lenin as Economist of Production: A Ricardian Step Backwards, *Science & Society*, 67(3), 276–302.

Index

www.ingramcontent.com/pod-product-compliance
Lightning Source LLC
Chambersburg PA
CBHW071248230926
51849CB00001B/268
9789004730397